BEAU MONDE ON EMPIRE'S EDGE

State and Stage in Soviet Ukraine

T0374756

In *Beau Monde on Empire's Edge*, Mayhill C. Fowler tells the story of the rise and fall of a group of men who created culture both Soviet and Ukrainian. This collective biography showcases new aspects of the politics of cultural production in the Soviet Union by focusing on theatre and on the multi-ethnic borderlands. Unlike their contemporaries in Moscow or Leningrad, these artists from the regions have been all but forgotten despite the quality of their art. *Beau Monde on Empire's Edge* restores the periphery to the centre of Soviet culture. Sources in Russian, Ukrainian, Polish, and Yiddish highlight the important multi-ethnic context and the challenges inherent in constructing Ukrainian culture in a place of Ukrainians, Russians, Poles, and Jews. *Beau Monde on Empire's Edge* traces the growing overlap between the arts and the state in the early Soviet years and explains the intertwining of politics and culture in the region today.

MAYHILL C. FOWLER is an associate professor of history at Stetson University.

MAYHILL C. FOWLER

BEAU MONDE ON EMPIRE'S EDGE

State and Stage in Soviet Ukraine

UNIVERSITY OF TORONTO PRESS
Toronto Buffalo London

Reprinted in paperback 2023

ISBN 978-1-4875-0153-2 (cloth)   ISBN 978-1-4875-1344-3 (EPUB)
ISBN 978-1-4875-5352-4 (paper)   ISBN 978-1-4875-1343-6 (PDF)

Library and Archives Canada Cataloguing in Publication

Title: Beau monde on empire's edge: state and stage in Soviet Ukraine/
    Mayhill C. Fowler.
Names: Fowler, Mayhill Courtney, 1974– author.
Description: Paperback reprint. Originally published 2017. | Includes
    bibliographical references and index.
Identifiers: Canadiana 20230147798 | ISBN 9781487553524 (softcover)
Subjects: LCSH: Theater and state – Ukraine – History – 20th century. |
    LCSH: Dramatists – Biography.
Classification: LCC PN2859.U47 F69 2023 | DDC 792.0947709/04 – dc23

Cover design: John Beadle
Cover image: Berezil' company meeting in Odesa with Mykola Kulish.
Kurbas is in the second row from the back, first on the right; Kulish is sitting
next to him in the embroidered shirt. (Photo courtesy of Shevchenko archive
and museum, Kharkiv)

We wish to acknowledge the land on which the University of Toronto Press
operates. This land is the traditional territory of the Wendat, the Anishnaabeg,
the Haudenosaunee, the Métis, and the Mississaugas of the Credit First
Nation.

Publication of this book was made possible, in part, by a grant from the First
Book Subvention Program of the Association for Slavic, East European, and
Eurasian Studies.

University of Toronto Press acknowledges the financial support of the
Government of Canada, the Canada Council for the Arts, and the Ontario Arts
Council, an agency of the Government of Ontario, for its publishing activities.

Canada Council   Conseil des Arts
for the Arts   du Canada

ONTARIO ARTS COUNCIL
CONSEIL DES ARTS DE L'ONTARIO
an Ontario government agency
un organisme du gouvernement de l'Ontario

Funded by the   Financé par le
Government   gouvernement
of Canada   du Canada

Canadä

The purpose of poetry is to remind us
how difficult it is to remain just one person,
for our house is open, there are no keys in the doors,
and invisible guests come in and out at will.
What I'm saying here is not, I agree, poetry,
as poems should be written rarely and reluctantly,
under unbearable duress and only with the hope
that good spirits, not evil ones, choose us for their instrument.
                              – from Czesław Miłosz, Ars Poetica?*

Contents

Illustrations

Foreword

This is a book about a period of great transformation, the years of revolution, war, and early socialism in twentieth-century Ukraine. This book was also written during another period of great transformation – I first went to Ukraine in 2006, just a few years after the Orange Revolution, and I write this foreword in 2023 with Russia's full-scale war in Ukraine already in its second year. I would write this book differently, knowing what I know now. But I stand by its arguments and its importance, as Russia attempts to erase Ukrainian culture and as public discourse throughout the West misses the specificity and the significance of art in Ukraine.

I wrote this book with the intention that it be read not by scholars of Ukraine but rather by scholars of Soviet culture. Yet the book's arguments about the intertwining of art and politics have not yet been seriously engaged with by scholars of Soviet culture, and my efforts to decolonize this world remain ongoing. This decolonization is so urgent because many scholars in the West persist in seeing Moscow as the most important (and the only!) artistic centre. What they then miss is, as I call it, the geography of revolutionary culture, and how centre and periphery radically shifted during the Soviet period. Ignoring Ukraine – or rather, imagining it as producing only copies of art produced in Moscow – misses the cultural explosion that happened in Soviet Ukraine, and more broadly, the way that it functioned as a driving force in the Soviet Union (and, as we see, in the post-Soviet world today). Ukraine matters.[1]

My goal was to expand the Russia-dominated view of Soviet culture by showing how artists in Ukraine made great art totally unlike that in Moscow. And yet at the same time, my goal was to bring the imperial and Soviet context to these figures in Ukraine. Contextualizing does not mean "rehabilitating" the Russian Empire or Soviet Union: not at all. It simply means that we need to draw those contexts into explanations of how they made the art that they did where they did. The artists featured in this book faced a huge challenge: How does one make art that is Soviet, but also somehow Ukrainian? What *was* Soviet Ukrainian culture? I argue that this category was a real one, that it was constructed, and that there was internal dissent about its content and form. To engage with that dissent – with how provocative and harsh Kurbas could sound in meetings of the Arts Workers Union, for example – does not lessen cultural brilliance in Soviet Ukraine; it simply means that the task of creating Soviet culture was a challenge here. To remove this task from its larger context diminishes its difficulty, and Kurbas and his milieu's success in their creation. In few other places was there such a creative outpouring as there was in Soviet Ukraine: because of the diversity of the region (a region I call the Russian imperial southwest), because of the productivity resulting from artists from one tradition encountering artists from another, because the experience of war shaped artists here more than elsewhere, because it was here that people who were not pre-war intelligentsia suddenly had the chance to tell their stories. All of these reasons made this region, Soviet Ukraine, unique within the Soviet Union and Eastern Europe, demanding that it be analysed in its larger context.

Because most of these geniuses I wrote about ended up murdered by the state in the 1930s, today the emphasis is on Soviet vs. Ukrainian, but in their time these Ukrainian cultural figures were deeply involved in the Soviet state. That is the tragedy. These social justice warriors, these believers in the power of art, became disillusioned and crushed by that same state they had helped to build. No one saw the 1930s coming in the 1920s. Many of these artists truly believed that theatre could change the world for the better – and why not? Their lives in the Russian Empire were often poor and shoddy and lacked prospect. Class mattered to them; making the world better mattered to them. Ignoring how these artists built and engaged in this Soviet infrastructure flattens them. Kurbas's goal was to create art that was as innovative as the best in Europe and he and his friends succeeded in doing so. They were brilliant, and they deserve to be known beyond Ukraine and Ukrainianists.[2]

This book also takes the multi-ethnic context of Soviet Ukrainian culture seriously. One of Ukraine's distinguishing features as a Soviet state was its multi-ethnicity. The Polish language theatre in Kyiv was the only one in the entire Union; its story is important. The study of Yiddish theatre tends to centre around Solomon Mikhoels, but the heartland of this theatre was here in Soviet Ukraine, as this book explains. Jews, Poles, Russians, and Ukrainians: they all made up Soviet Ukrainian culture. There is a larger argument here about the benefits of diversity. In many books, and certainly in public discourse, it often seems that it is the single unified nation that inspires creativity; but in fact, creativity comes from difference, not from homogeneity.

So this is not a book exclusively about Berezil', or about Kurbas.[3] This book is an argument about more than the theatre: it is about the intertwining of artists and officials, and about the constructed-ness of Soviet Ukrainian culture. This is a book about nationality policy and its challenges, and about a generation of men who literally built an entire cultural infrastructure from scratch in an attempt to transform how people saw the world. Their goals were breathtaking.

Despite this book being about more than the theatre, it has been sidelined because people perceive it to be "just" about theatre. In both Ukraine and in the West there is a divide between theatre (history or studies) and "real" history. Why do people dismiss theatre so? Theatre – as we see in this book – reflects society and the state, and this book is about officials as much as it is about artists. The archival trove of this book is not memoirs and personal collections, but rather the state archives, where theatre was discussed at the highest levels.

My own work has shifted since I wrote this book. While in keeping with my training his book largely focuses on pre-1939 Ukraine, that area of Ukraine that was part of the Russian Empire, in more recent years, I have become interested in the Galician region and the roles played by the itinerant Ukrainian language theatre and Polish theatre in shaping artists such as Hanna Babiivna and Sofia Fedortseva, as well as Kurbas. I have also become much more interested in the women of Berezil', who are largely missing from this book; don't worry, my next book puts them front and centre.[4]

Since the publication of this book, scholars such as Olena Palko and Bohdan Tokarskyi have taken up some of these questions of the Soviet Ukrainian state.[5] Virlana Tkacz and Tetiana Rudenko created several exhibits on Kurbas; one at Kyiv's Mystetskyi Arsenal featured *Allo na khvyli 477!*. I was able to be there for a performance of Iulii Meitus's score. It was not at all what I imagined – it was … big and jazzy and Busby Berkeley Hollywood musical-ish. It was lavish music that filled the cavernous space of Arsenal, the way it must have filled the theatre back in 1929. The photographs of the show convinced me that it must have been even more bizarre than I had imagined. Yes, Vyshnia really was in a *vyshniak* jar. Yes, actresses were dressed as ducks. Yes, there was a dragon!? What boldness! As I sat listening, I reflected that this book does indeed capture some of that outpouring of creativity, and yet it also falls short. We can never fully capture the past. Adeeb Khalid, writing on the Muslim intellectuals creating early Soviet Uzbek culture, says that they are "dimly visible," suggesting that we need to respect the long expanse of time separating author and subject.[6]

And yet the stories of our subjects resonate with our own. Were I to write this book now, I would add a different epilogue. Kurbas and his colleagues created the Berezil' after the war. After the violence, after survival, after trauma, they made art. That fact – the *after*-ness of Berezil' – sits with me differently now since the onset of Russia's full-scale war. Theatre was booming in Ukraine before February 2022, with new institutions (the Ukrainian Cultural Fund and the Ukrainian Institute) and a new generation making brilliant work across the country. May they continue to make art during war, and may they make a new Berezil' for our times after victory has been won.

Thank you to the University of Toronto Press for their support of scholarly work on the arts in Ukraine by publishing a paperback version when the hardback has not yet sold out. The driving force behind this paperback is actually Sofia Dyak at the Center for Urban History in Lviv, who believed in this book enough to encourage me to push for a more accessible paperback in English, as well as a version in Ukrainian.[7] If you read Ukrainian, check out Iaroslava Strikha's brilliant translation coming out soon from Rodovid' Press. But let me leave the last word for the theatre-makers. In metro stations, in shelters, in theatres lacking heat, with the threat of missiles, with audiences who have lost homes, cities, and, of course, loved ones, artists persist in making theatre in Ukraine. They are also fighting for their country with weapons on the frontlines and demonstrating the power of Ukrainian culture abroad. This book may be about art as a part of empire, but it is also about art as resisting empire. I believe the artists featured in this book stand behind these brave artists of today.

1 March 2023

Acknowledgments

It takes a village to write a book. I thank everyone whose intellectual guidance, challenge, and support made this endeavour possible. First of all, this book has benefited from the financial support of many institutions: the Graduate School and Department of History at Princeton University, the American Council of Learned Societies dissertation write-up fellowship, the Mihaychuk fellowship at the Harvard Ukrainian Research Institute, the Petro Jacyk Foundation, and, finally, the Dean of the College of Arts and Sciences as well as the Brown Center for Faculty Innovation and Excellence at Stetson University. My thanks as well to the First Book Subvention Program of the Association for Slavic, East European, and Eurasian Studies, which greatly assisted in bringing this manuscript to publication.

My deepest gratitude to Stephen Kotkin at Princeton, who not only took on a graduate student with a passing knowledge of Russian history, but also encouraged me to find my own voice. His support has been unflagging, even when I have not deserved it. The other members of my dissertation committee also profoundly shaped my thinking: Ekaterina Pravilova encouraged me to follow the money, Jan T. Gross held a transformative seminar on totalitarianism, and Serhy Yekelchyk continues to inspire me to make the cultural history of Ukraine comparative, theoretical, and a good read. Robert Darnton taught me cultural history, and Harold James asked me a question in Florence about why manuscripts don't burn that set me thinking.

While writing my first paper in graduate school on Kurbas and the Berezil', I was fortunate to meet Virlana Tkacz, who gave me a long list of contacts for my first summer in Ukraine. She also connected me with Irena Makaryk, whose incisive and generous commentary on my work continues to be much appreciated. Through a contribution to their majestic edited volume on Kyiv and modernism, I met Myroslava Mudrak. I learned my first word in Ukrainian (*mystetstvo*, art) from Myroslava's book on *Nova Generatsiia*, and she has been a wonderful mentor to me. The beautiful exhibit she organized in 2015 at the Ukrainian Museum in New York City inspired me to finish this project.

In Ukraine, Iryna Chuzhynova and Nadia Sokolenko offered an entrée into the world of theatre, and I cannot thank them enough for that trip to Kharkiv in 2009, for inviting me to a conference in 2013 on Kurbas, and for taking better photographs than I did. Endless conversations about art and history with Orysia Kulick and Larissa Babii and friendship with Natalia and Joseph Sywenkyi, Natalia Olesnicky, and Lua Pottier made my time in Ukraine emotionally possible. I thank all my housemates, Andrei Shlyakhter, Heather Coleman, Faith Hillis, Jared McBride, and Emily Baran. This book, like so many others, benefited from the dacha vegetables and Kyiv guidance of Anton Antonovich Strutinskii, may he rest in peace. Thanks to Matthew Pauly, Victoria Smolkina, and Zbigniew Wojnowski for being Kyiv research buddies.

Thank you to the archivists at collections across Ukraine and Russia – in particular the ladies at the Instytut Iudaiky and the theatre museum at the Lavra who put up with me for a year and chatted with me and did not laugh at my Ukrainian. Special thanks to Tetiana Rudenko, who opened the collections to me and made many of the photos in this book possible. Thank you to Anastasia Ivashchenko, whose great-grandmother was an actress in Kurbas' company, and who introduced me to her mother, who let me read her grandmother's papers. I hope to tell Hanna Babiivna's story someday.

Back at Princeton, the *kruzhok* of Elidor Mehilli, Jeff Hardy, Pey-Yi Chu, Piotr Kosicki, Anne O'Donnell, Franziska Exeler, and Kyrill Kunakovich challenged my work to be more about the Soviet and less about Ukraine. Christienna Fryar always reminds me there are other empires than the Soviet.

Thank you to Sofia Dyak and the Centre for Urban History of East Central Europe in L'viv. Thanks to Tarik Cyril Amar, who has always supported my work, and who, with Sofia, manoeuvred a postdoctoral fellowship for me in L'viv. It was that semester that allowed me to rethink the dissertation. L'viv is now a second home, thanks to Sofia. From crashing on the couch at Bohomol'tsia 6 to closing down the Ibis hotel bar in Warsaw, our transnational friendship makes me excited about continuing to research Ukraine.

At Harvard, Oleh Kotsyuba and Nadia Kravets welcomed me with endless ideas and zest for Ukrainian studies. Serhy Plokhy inspired me to globalize Ukrainian history, and George Grabowicz finally made me understand why people care about Shevchenko.

I was so lucky to get the Petro Jacyk Postdoctoral Fellowship at the University of Toronto. At Toronto, thank you to Peter and Susan Solomon, Tracy McDonald, Alison Smith, Susan Grant, Seth Bernstein, and Lynne Viola's Russianist *kruzhok*. In Canada I also met the inestimable Dominique Arel at the Danyliw Seminar in 2012. The comments at the seminar and the now several years of conversations, colloquia, and critique with Dominique and with Anna Colin Lebedev and Ioulia Shukan have made my work sharper, with a *soupçon* of French sociology. Thank you to Francois-Xavier Nérard, Sophie Lambroschini, Anna Muller, Alissa Klots, and all the participants of the Summer School of the Social Sciences in Ukraine, perhaps the most intellectually generous group of scholars I have yet encountered.

This is a project that needed languages: thank you to Yuri Shevchuk for teaching me Ukrainian, Anna Vershchik, Sunny Yudkoff, and Anna Shternshis for Yiddish, and Charles Townsend and Piotr Kająk for Polish.

At Stetson, I have been welcomed by my colleagues in the Department of History and the Program in Russian, East European and Eurasian Studies (SPREES). Thank you especially to my chairs, Eric Kurlander and Emily Mieras, model classroom professors and scholars both who consistently encouraged me to finish this book and somehow made it possible. Thank you to my SPREES colleagues – Michael Denner, Gene Huskey, Katya Kudryavtseva, Jelena Petrovic, Daniil Zavlunov, and fellow-traveller Rob Watson – for making the hamlet of DeLand, Florida, a buzzing centre for the study of the most interesting region in the world. Thank you to everyone who gathers at Casa Amelia and makes this town a home.

It's clear, by now, that many people shaped this project and made it possible. But with a full-time teaching job this book seemed impossible to complete. I am deeply grateful to Orysia Kulick and Iryna Vushko for reading chapters and making me excited again about my own work. I owe a huge debt to Tracy McDonald, who helped me believe that this was a book and not a torn-apart dissertation. She introduced me to Richard Ratzlaff and fielded many breakdowns in the final stretch. Much of the final version of this book was written at Trilogy Coffee, so thank you to Clay and Michelle Cass.

Thank you to everyone who has invited me to present various incarnations of various chapters – Gennady Estraikh at the Fisher Forum at the University of Illinois Urbana-Champaign, Serhy Yekelchyk at ASEEES, Michael David-Fox at Georgetown, Tarik Cyril Amar at

Columbia, Robert Pyrah in both L'viv and Cracow, Francesca Silano and the graduate students in the Slavic Graduate Conference at the University of Toronto.

My deepest thanks to Richard Ratzlaff of University of Toronto Press for his gracious support. I could not believe it when he expressed an interest in this project, and I am so grateful for his mild sense of humour, his patience, and his good eye. Thank you, as well, to the two anonymous reviewers who immensely improved this text.

This project was over a decade in the making and bits of it can be found in other places as I wandered around trying to secure employment and refine my ideas. Thank you to the editors of *Kritika: Explorations in Russian and Eurasian History*, *Ab Imperio*, and the Ukrainian Museum in New York City for permission to reproduce parts of these articles in this book:

"Mikhail Bulgakov, Mykola Kulish, and Soviet Theater: How Internal
  Transnationalism Remade Center and Periphery," *Kritika: Explorations in Russian and Eurasian History*, vol. 16, no. 2 (Spring 2015): 263–90.
"Yiddish Theater in Soviet Ukraine: A Re-Evaluation of Jewish-Slavic
  Relations in the Arts," *Ab Imperio* 2011/3 (December 2011): 167–88.
"Berezil: Theater as Institution in Soviet Ukraine," in Myroslava Mudrak and
  Tetiana Rudenko, eds., *Staging the Ukrainian Theatrical Avant-Garde of the 1920s and 1920s* (New York: Ukrainian Museum, 2015).

Finally, on a personal note, thank you to my sister, Caroline O. Fowler, who is a great friend, colleague, and roommate, and thank you to my cat. Thank you to my parents, who read me Shakespeare and took me to the Oregon Shakespeare Festival in 1978 and instilled in me an abiding love of theatre. This book began as a dissertation about Les' Kurbas and Mykola Kulish and the productions they created. Fresh from my own acting career, their unquestioning belief in the ability of theatre to change the world took my breath away. I was disillusioned by theatre; they held their illusions about the theatre, even as they were disillusioned by the state. May their lives and their work continue to inspire other artists and scholars.

This book, in a way, is the unintended consequence of an acting career. I dedicate it to theatre people, the music-makers and dreamers of dreams, who believe in the importance of telling stories in live performance and the sustaining power of imagination.

Note to the Reader on Transliteration

Transliteration is a challenge for any scholar delving into this part of the world. I have attempted to negotiate simplicity for readers, accuracy for scholars, and the politics of the moment. Cities in this book are written as they are commonly known today: *Kyiv*, *Odesa*, and *Kharkiv*. If I use a different name, I put today's name in parentheses. As this book was entering production de-communization laws in Ukraine changed some city names. Specifically, Dnipropetrovs'k became Dnipro, so I have inserted that change at the final stretch. I am not making a political statement with my city names; the complication only reflects the very real circumstances under which people in the region still live.

In general I have used the Library of Congress and YIVO systems of transliteration. I have left the names of several figures, such as Stanislavsky and Meyerhold, as they are commonly known (i.e., not Stanislavskii and Meierkhol'd). The original version of this text included soft signs only in the scholarly apparatus. On the advice of one of my readers, I have added soft signs (an apostrophe after a palatalized consonant) throughout the body of the text, so the reader will always see *Les' Kurbas*, for example. I will have missed a few – *mea culpa*. As I painstakingly added the soft signs, I realized that their addition does – to anyone who knows a Slavic language, and perhaps even to those who do not – convey the sound of the language, and the difference between Ukrainian and Russian.

All the figures in this book lived in multiple languages, as reflected by the archival documents. An official might speak in both Russian and Ukrainian in one meeting, or even one single speech. People might be ethnically Ukrainian but the only document in which they appear in the archives is a secret police interrogation in Russian. This is a story of Soviet Ukraine and Soviet Ukrainians, and so I have opted for the Ukrainian spelling of Balyts'kyi, Zatons'kyi, Kosior. They may more frequently be found as Balitskii, Zatonskii and Kossior, but they appear as both in the archives. Some figures, David Volskii and Aron Dymarskii, for example, I only ever found in Russian and to transliterate their names into Ukrainian felt like too much authorial privilege.

Abbreviations

Archival Abbreviations

DAKhO	Derzhavnyi arkhiv Kharkivs'koi oblasti, Kharkiv
DMTMKU	Derzhavnyi muzei teatral'noho, muzychnoho ta kinomystetstva Ukrainy
DAKO	Derzhavnyi arkhiv Kyivs'koi oblasti, Kyiv
DALO	Derzhavnyi arkhiv L'vivs'koi oblasti, L'viv
GARF	Gosudarstvennyi arkhiv Rossiiskoi Federatsii, Moscow
RGALI	Rossiiskii gosudarstvennyi arkhiv literatury i iskusstva, Moscow
RGASPI	Rossiiskii gosudarstvennyi arkhiv sotsial'no-politicheskoi istorii, Moscow
SBU	Haluzevyi derzhavnyi arkhiv Sluzhba bezpeky Ukrainy, Kyiv
SBU Kharkiv	Kharkiv Haluzevyi derzhavnyi arkhiv Sluzhba bezpeky Ukrainy, Kharkiv branch
"Shevchenko"	Kharkivs'kyi derzhavnyi akademichnyi dramatychnyi teatr im. T. H. Shevchenka, arkhiv-muzei
TsDAHOU	Tsentral'nyi derzhavnyi arkhiv hromads'kykh ob'ednan' Ukrainy, Kyiv
TsDAMLM	Tsentral'nyi derzhavnyi arkhiv-muzei literatury i mystetstva, Kyiv
TsDAVOU	Tsentral'nyi derzhavnyi arkhiv vyshchykh orhaniv vlady Ukrainy, Kyiv
TsDIA	Tsentral'nyi derzhavnyi istorichnyi arkhiv, Kyiv
TsDKFFA	Tsentral'nyi derzhavnyi kinofotofonoarkhiv Ukrainy im. H. S. Pshenychnoho, Kyiv

Abbreviations for Archival Holdings

f. *fond*, a large holding of archival material
op. *opys'* (Russian *opis*), a subsection of a fond
s. *sprava* (Russian d. *delo*), individual file
ark. *arkusha* (or l. *list*), page number

BEAU MONDE ON EMPIRE'S EDGE

State and Stage in Soviet Ukraine

Introduction: The Beau Monde on the Borderlands

A Phone Call

On 18 April 1930, Joseph Stalin called Mikhail Bulgakov at home to discuss the latter's career dissatisfaction. As a result of the conversation, Stalin inserted himself in the contretemps between the writer and the Moscow Art Theatre management and ensured Bulgakov future employment. Stalin loved Bulgakov's 1926 play *Days of the Turbins*, a civil war melodrama about a family of Kyiv White Guardists and hardly a Soviet propaganda piece. The dictator saw the production fifteen times and even defended Bulgakov's play in 1929 to an angry delegation of Soviet Ukrainian writers petitioning to shut down the production. The legendary phone call is not simply an anecdote for a kitchen table, however, but rather central to understanding Soviet culture.[1]

The phone call speaks to a connection between the artist and the dictator, and to the unique connection between the arts and the state in the Soviet Union. This was a place where dictators called writers at home and personally involved themselves in the aesthetics of their work. Moreover, Stalin's phone call to Bulgakov lies on an enormous network of personal and professional relationships between artists and officials that covered all of the Soviet Union. The intertwining of artists and the Soviet state has been shrouded in oft-recounted legends, such as the famous phone call to Bulgakov, and mythic heroes and villains: the noble artist (like Bulgakov), the oppressive dictator (like Stalin and his cronies), the mediocre artists denouncing their fellows, the philistine officials who failed to recognize great art, the audiences who, filling the seats of theatres from Moscow to Vladivostok, made the Soviet Union a place where art mattered, where it was so important that artists received the highest accolades, as well as prison sentences and bullets in the head.

This is not, however, a story about Bulgakov. This is not a story about Stalin. This is not, actually, a story about literature. Of course, Bulgakov, Stalin, and literature all play a part, but this is a story about that 1929 delegation of Soviet Ukrainian writers who so despised *Days of the Turbins*. Bulgakov, they seem to have felt, misrepresented them with his White Guard melodrama. After all, Bulgakov was a Kyiv native from a wealthy intelligentsia family who now had a smart life in Moscow and worked at the most famous theatre in the Soviet Union. Hardly had he struggled, as had all members of the delegation, to win Soviet authority in the borderlands during the crucible of the Civil War, nor was Bulgakov a part of the building of something entirely new: culture both Soviet and Ukrainian, in an entirely new place called Soviet Ukraine. This book tells their story.

The Story: The Theatre

This is a story about the theatre, a popular form of entertainment in imperial Russia transformed and challenged by technological changes in the twentieth century. In an age of mass culture, somehow audiences across the Soviet Union attended the theatre. In the West, theatre artists struggled with the place of the stage during the overwhelming surge of innovation in film and radio; in the Soviet Union, by contrast, theatre held onto a privileged place. Theatre is sensorial – the sound of language and the taste of words, the smell of musty costumes and stage makeup, the glow of dust in the stage lights, the soft whirr as the curtain rises while the audience settles in their seats, the rush of adrenalin as the actor takes the stage. Theatre is a way of life for its practitioners, a life made up of jokes on rehearsal breaks, nerves battled with superstitions, drinks at the restaurant after the show trading war stories. Above all, theatre is play. To play well on stage demands spontaneity, improvisation, and creativity. To play well in the audience demands a willingness to experience emotion or the unexpected. In other words, planning and control, with which we associate the Soviet project, are inimical to good play. The world of the theatre then allows an examination of the paradoxes of Soviet artistic culture: theatre was by its nature not a mass medium, yet it was created for the Soviet masses. Theatre was a place of spontaneity and play, in a planned and controlled dictatorship. Theatre represented the world, and simultaneously tried to change it.

Theatre is not literature. The world of the stage highlights Soviet cultural production and reception in ways different from literature, visual art, film, or music. Of course, artists, their managers, and their audiences faced similar challenges across these media, but theatre offers two important contours to the conundrum of art and dictatorship.[2] Theatre was mass culture in the nineteenth century. Players travelled along the muddy roads and byways of the Russian empire to entertain audiences of all classes and confessions in taverns, theatres, and town halls. It was in the theatre that Soviet officials, artists, and audiences recalibrated what was culture for the masses, and what was culture for the elites, what was entertainment, and what was education. But moreover, theatre involves multiple agents in multiple spaces. Soviet theatre unfolded in the liminal spaces: the backstage, the dressing rooms, the foyer, the buffet, the offices of theatre management, the special boxes designated for officialdom. Managing, consuming, and creating theatre involved a large cast of characters with competing personal and professional agendas. Theatre, then, offers a productive window on the changing dynamics between artists and the state. Artists may have performed on the stage, officials may have watched from the loge, but artists and officials circulated in the same milieu, the beau monde.

The Cast of Characters: The Beau Monde on the Borderlands

This is a collective biography about a group of men who made theatre that was Soviet and Ukrainian. They were all deeply connected with the 1929 group of Soviet Ukrainian writers who met with Stalin and were devastated by Bulgakov's *Days of the Turbins*. Unlike their contemporaries in Soviet Moscow or Leningrad, these men were not pre-revolutionary elites, intellectuals, or artists. They may have had interest in the arts or worked in theatres far from the metropolis as a youth, but under the conditions of empire they could not achieve their dreams. Rather, these men worked their way up through the ranks of the Red Army or the Communist Party. They gained positions in the new Party-state from 1922 in Soviet Ukraine; they were not elites, but they became elites. They were friends and enemies and belonged to one social milieu in early Soviet Kharkiv.

Here are the players:

Les' Kurbas (1887–1937): ascetic visionary from a small town perched on a hill in Galicia. His first theatrical experience was directing local Jewish youth in Verdi's *Aida*. An intellectual with a university education from Habsburg Vienna and Lemberg (today's L'viv), he brought a German expressionist bent to his interpretation of theatre in Ukrainian. Although he had read about the Moscow Art Theatre, his formative years were spent outside the Russian company's sphere of influence. Kurbas, whose career started in an itinerant troupe in Habsburg Galicia, chose to stay in the Soviet Union in the 1920s to make modern and experimental theatre in the Ukrainian language. This he did. He was artistic director of the most celebrated theatre in Soviet Ukraine, the Berezil'. Kurbas has been the subject of much scholarship in Ukraine, but rarely contextualized in a wider narrative of Soviet culture, or as part of a multicultural world.[3]

Mykola Kulish (1892–1937): poor kid from the steppes of Kherson, liberated by the era of revolution and civil war to pursue a career in the arts. A Red Army veteran, a tireless activist for socialism, a prolific playwright delving into the stories of his peers, a true believer in the power of revolution, Kulish, like so many in the Soviet period, was ultimately deeply disillusioned.[4]

Kurbas and Kulish created a series of legendary theatrical productions at the Berezil' Theatre in Kharkiv. They were arrested in 1933 and 1934, respectively, and shot in Soviet Karelia on the same day, 3 November 1937.

Ostap Vyshnia (1889–1956): class clown. From Poltava region, Pavlo Hubenko trained as a medic in Russian imperial Kyiv. Hubenko-Vyshnia's medical skills, and the whim of fate, saved his life when he was originally on the same list marked for death as Kurbas and Kulish. A writer of comic feuilletons, sketches, and theatrical adaptations, he survived ten years in the camps of the gulag archipelago. His funeral in 1956 sparked mass demonstrations of support on the streets of Kyiv from the many Soviet Ukrainians who loved his writing. He is still one of the most popular Ukrainian comic writers of the twentieth century, yet unknown outside Ukraine or outside Ukrainianist circles.[5]

Andrii Khvylia (1898–1937): apparatchik who wanted to be a writer, but became a manager of artists instead. He wrangled top awards for his Soviet Ukrainian artists in Moscow, he pushed for a comprehensive and cohesive artistic program in Soviet Ukraine, and he negotiated between multiple Party and artistic cliques both at home and in the Kremlin. He believed in Soviet Ukrainian culture and in socialism, and was murdered just like the artists whose careers he made and destroyed. Khvylia's multiple reports on Kulish and Kurbas provide one of the primary sources of information on the backstage corridors of cultural authority in the early Soviet Union.[6]

These men knew each other, socialized together, worked together, and created art together. Their names may not mean much to the layperson, or even the expert in Soviet culture. This is but a trick of fate, a consequence of the centralization of culture in Moscow. The work of Vyshnia, Kulish, and Kurbas (all managed and challenged by Khvylia) was extraordinary. Although these artists were (relatively) well known in their day, they have fallen by the wayside of scholarship on Soviet culture writ large. Their homologues in Moscow, however, have not. Selected artists much more celebrated today who moved from the borderlands to Moscow suggest "pairs" with these Soviet Ukrainians, which highlights the spatial contours of the emerging Soviet theatrical landscape.

Few may know Les' Kurbas, but many know Solomon Mikhoels (1890–1948): law student from Dvinsk who ended up one as of the greatest actors of his generation. He worked almost entirely in Yiddish, and his murder in 1948 heralded the end of Yiddish culture in the Soviet Union. Both Mikhoels and Kurbas – who knew and admired each other – created theatre in non-Russian languages, both died at the hands of the state, but their careers unfolded differently in the centre and in the regions.

Few know Mykola Kulish, but many know Mikhail Bulgakov (1891–1940): Kyiv doctor, creator of the brilliant cult novel *Master and Margarita*, never published in his lifetime, as well as Stalin's favourite play, of course, *Days of the Turbins*. Bulgakov was haunted by his phone call with the Great Leader, but he died in his bed at home in 1940. Both Bulgakov and Kulish created plays about revolution and civil war, but their visions differed radically.

Few know Ostap Vyshnia, but many know Il'f-Petrov: the dynamic duo of Il'ia Il'f (1897–1937) and Evgenii Petrov (1903–1942), *Odessity*, Odesa natives, who moved north to Moscow in 1923 and who wove tales of the ultimate urban con man, the Golden Calf, and the circus. Il'f died of tuberculosis in 1937, but Petrov kept writing, albeit with less success, until his untimely death during the Second World War. These comic writers were all Soviet celebrities; yet while Ostap Vyshnia was serving time in the gulag, Il'f-Petrov's sketches were performed at the Kremlin. Both created Soviet popular culture, but the content and reception of that culture reflected different audiences.

Andrii Khvylia managed the Soviet Ukrainians directly, but a Bolshevik known on an all-Union level contributed to the development of the arts in Soviet Ukraine: secret police chief Vsevolod Balyts'kyi (1892–1937). He was a golden-boy apparatchik in Soviet Ukraine and in Moscow, and he personally signed the arrest orders of several key artists in the Soviet Ukraine, including Ostap Vyshnia. Yet he, too, died in the "meat grinder."[7]

Other names appear throughout the story of the beau monde on the borderlands: Soviet Ukrainian actor Iosyp Hirniak (1895–1989), from Galicia like Kurbas and keeper of his legacy in the postwar West; Soviet Ukrainian writer Iurii Smolych (1900–1976), keeper of the beau monde's legacy in postwar Soviet Ukraine; Ivan Mykytenko (1897–1937), former medical student-turned-playwright who never broke the rules and whom later generations of Ukrainian intelligentsia have never forgiven; loyal Communist activist Mykola Khvyl'ovyi (1893–1933), whose 1933 suicide rocked the world of Soviet Ukrainian artists and officials. From the ranks of the celebrated Soviet-level artists this story includes actress Faina Ranevskaia (1896–1984); theatre director Aleksandr Tairov (1885–1950); Stalin's right hand Lazar Kaganovich (1893–1991); and, of course, the primary arts patron of the pre-war period, Joseph Stalin (1878–1953) himself. This group of people knew each other, or at least knew of each other. Some performed together, or toured together, or socialized together. Yet they are rarely, if ever, placed in the same story.

How did one group of artists come to dominate scholarship on Soviet culture and one group of artists come to interest only specialists? The rise of figures from the centre and fall of figures from the periphery reveals the transformation in the region's cultural topography. By "cultural topography" I refer to the shift in artistic centres, as artists, officials, and publics re-ascribed significance and authority to various places, remaking the relationship between centre and periphery. The central characters in this story grew up in the Russian empire and came from a place with multiple cultural centres; yet during the Soviet 1920s and 1930s theatrical culture centralized in Moscow. Moscow only became the theatrical centre; it was not the only theatrical centre before the late 1920s.

And what of the provinces? The borderland regions were not peripheral to the creation of Russian imperial culture, and they were not peripheral to the early cultural production and reception of the Soviet Union. After all, most Soviet artists came from the imperial borderlands. Yet one of the features of Soviet culture was that Moscow came to be perceived, by audiences, by officials, and by artists themselves, as a centre; the provinces, in turn, came to be perceived as peripheral. Perception became reality; the cultural production of the Soviet period may have been ultimately more extraordinary in Moscow than in Kyiv, but this productivity resulted from a radical shift in cultural topography. The story of the beau monde on the borderlands restores the position of the periphery as central to early Soviet cultural production and reception. An exclusive focus on Moscow has obscured the stories in the provinces, and these stories are essential for a more nuanced understanding of how Soviet culture developed across the Soviet Union.

The Scene: The Russian Imperial Southwest

This is the story of a place. The lives of these men unfolded in a specific region far from the centre, which I call the Russian Imperial Southwest. This is a region that, because of (or despite) demographics and imperial policies, proved extraordinarily culturally productive. The contours of this cultural space, as with all cultural spaces, were not firm; rather, the shape of the region can be imagined as circumscribed by the interactions between Jews and Slavs in the multi-ethnic imperial borderlands of the Habsburg empire, the Polish-Lithuanian Commonwealth, and the Russian empire. Essentially, this region comprised the lands extending from both banks of the Dnipro – or Dniepr – River and the southern regions of the former Pale of Settlement, where Jews were legally allowed to live and to work in the Russian empire. The imperial terms for this region are hardly neutral: this territory was administratively the "southwestern region," or *iugo-zapadnyi krai*. It included right-bank Ukraine, that is, the area to the west of the Dnipro that would be "right" if one were facing from the Muscovite north, as indeed it was Muscovy and Poland that had divided the region in the seventeenth century. This cultural sphere would also include *Malorossia*, or Little Russia, which was the former Cossack Hetmanate known as left-bank Ukraine, and *Novorossia*, or New Russia, comprising the lands along the Black Sea coast. Right-bank, left-bank, Little Russia, New Russia: by using the term "southwest," I am not reifying the imperial gaze. Rather, this region, ruled by the tsarist state, included a diverse population living and working on the edge of empire. The Russian empire's policies did shape this population's culture, and in turn, this population itself shaped imperial culture. The presence of multiple groups, particularly Jews and Slavs, contributed not only to the modern pogrom but also to an extraordinary musical-theatrical culture of entertainment. The young people who grew up in this culture moved north to make Soviet culture in Moscow; the region then became Soviet, and a cultural periphery. This is the story of the unmaking of the Russian Imperial Southwest and the making of the Soviet cultural periphery.[8]

Why this region? While one could look at the periphery anywhere in the Russian empire and uncover a story of cultural transformation, this region proves particularly rich. A truly staggering number of Soviet cultural elites came from the Russian Imperial Southwest to Moscow and made Soviet culture. Liliana Riga, examining the quantity of Bolsheviks hailing from the imperial borderlands, argues that it was precisely this outsider quality that made the Bolshevik political ethos ethnically universal. The Bolsheviks in the centre promoted ethnic universalism precisely because they were themselves ethnic minorities. Riga's argument may hold for cultural elites as well. Certainly Soviet culture deserves to be inscribed in Soviet space.[9]

The experiences of so many cultural elites in the Russian Imperial Southwest may have shaped their aesthetic output once they came to Moscow and may have contributed to the peculiar supra-ethnic quality of much Soviet art. Placing Soviet culture in Soviet space shows the enormous achievement in creating all-Union Soviet culture: the 1934 film classic *The Circus*, Soviet jokes (even under Stalin), and the songs of jazzman Leonid Utesov enjoyed from the 1920s to the 1960s and today, were all understood across eleven time zones. Soviet culture united Soviets. But the very reach of Soviet culture also reveals the lacunae. What of local cultures? What of local circuses, local political jokes, and local jazz? The southwestern provinces offered precisely such a breadbasket of local cultures, yet lost that cultural tapestry under the centralization of Moscow. The enormous universalism of Soviet culture stuns as much as does the lack of modern and urban local cultures.

I build here on recent work on transnationalism that has challenged the autarchy of the Soviet arts. Katerina Clark has internationalized Soviet culture with her notion of "cosmopolitan patriots," working out how famous Soviet artists could have remained loyal to the Union while still circulating in the West. The border between the West and the East in her account was both permeable (i.e., the leftist project flourished on both sides) and fixed (i.e., Soviets were Soviets, even in the West). Michael David-Fox explores the opposite trajectory, analysing not Soviets abroad, but foreigners in the Soviet Union. Through studying how the Soviet bureaucracy managed foreign cultural figures ("fellow-travellers") in the Soviet Union, he brings transnational studies to Soviet culture. I take the importance of transnational exchange, but I focus here on internal transnationalism, as opposed to a Soviet-non-Soviet circulation between the USSR and Europe.[10]

The Soviet Union had many regions, and their dynamics with Moscow contributed to creating Soviet culture. In other words, circulation between the former Russian Imperial Southwest and newly Soviet Moscow – between the south and the north – proved consequential for Soviet cultural production and reception. Theatre artists, officials managing the arts, and productions themselves travelled from one region to another; the mobility of the theatrical network inside the Soviet Union must have proved as significant for shaping its culture as exchanges with the West. If there were different regions in the Soviet Union, then surely the relationship between them is as important as the relationship between the Soviet Union writ large and the West. Taking transnational methodologies to cultural production incorporates centre and periphery, Moscow and the regions, in one story; transnationalism, as a concept, requires taking the variety of cultures inside the Soviet Union seriously. The path to Soviet socialism, quite simply, was different in different places. What would happen when the Russian Imperial Southwest became Soviet Ukraine?[11]

De-provincializing Ukraine[12]

This is a story about Ukraine, a land pulled between Europe and Russia, Vienna and St. Petersburg, Berlin and Moscow, Catholicism and Orthodoxy, the heartland of Cossacks, Hassidism, and Ashkenaz culture. Formerly the borderlands of the Polish Lithuanian Commonwealth, this was a place that Poles, Jews, Ukrainians, and Russians (among others) called home. Multiple cultures created overlapping cultural layers: Polish, Jewish, Ukrainian, Russian, Orthodox, Catholic; this multiplicity could prove extraordinarily violent, but also extraordinarily culturally productive.[13]

Imperial Russian and Soviet culture has become understood as exclusively Russian culture, and specifically as the artistic output of Moscow and Leningrad. The Soviet artists most studied are those who lived in the state-subsidized and centrally located apartments in the capital cities, who performed at the state-supported theatres, and who were known by the Politburo. But the Russian empire and the Soviet Union were much larger, more diverse, and quite simply different from the capital cities. In the Russian empire Moscow and St. Petersburg concentrated money and talent and therefore became two important cities for the arts, but they ultimately constituted only two of many cities that became meccas for the arts, such as Kyiv, Tbilisi, and Vil'nius. In the Soviet Union, by contrast, Moscow became the one and only cultural centre. These spatial dynamics of imperial and Soviet culture may not be visible from an exclusive focus on the centre. But they reveal themselves with a focus on the periphery.

Soviet Ukraine and Its Culture(s)

This book does not assume Ukrainian culture as an objective category, but rather traces the construction of "Soviet Ukrainian" culture as a result of a struggle between competing groups in Soviet Ukraine, and between Soviet Ukraine and Moscow. This focus on cultural construction suggests a new interpretation of Soviet nationality policy. Generally, scholars have focused on the following chronology for Soviet nationality policy: first came *korenizatsiia*, indigenization, a series of policies drafted in 1923 promoting the "affirmative action" of non-Russian minorities, and promoting the arts and culture of the titular nationality of each Soviet republic and autonomous region. Non-Russian culture flourished under korenizatsiia, which provoked its oppression by an increasingly Russifying Stalinist state. There is truth in this interpretation. The policies coming out of the imperial court in St. Petersburg did restrict non-Russian minorities. Printing was not allowed in Ukrainian; theatre was not allowed in Yiddish; the Polish language was only allowed in Congress Poland, and then only when approved. It is not hard to conclude that the government's sudden permission to create culture in these non-Russian languages led to artistic explosion. It did, indeed.[14]

But then what happened to that cultural explosion? Was Soviet Ukrainian culture a product, a side effect, or an unintended consequence of Soviet nationality policy? The story of the beau monde on the borderlands highlights the challenges of korenizatsiia, which were twofold for artists and officials: first, the policies reinforced ethnic separation, and second, they reified ethnic cultures. In other words, it was not clear what constituted "Ukrainian" culture, let alone "Soviet Ukrainian" culture, and how that culture in form or content might differ from Jewish, from Russian, or from Polish cultures. In a place with multiple ethnicities and confessions, the organization and hierarchization of ethnicities demanded by korenizatsiia challenged cultural production and reception.

In other regional fields of study, it has been long ago accepted that culture is constructed. No one would argue that a primordial "French" culture teleologically emerged over the centuries; rather, Eugen Weber has argued that "peasants became Frenchmen." Linda Colley has shown how the idea of "Britons" emerged at a certain historical conjuncture for certain historical reasons. The very notions of national cultures have not been considered objective categories, but rather analytic problems.[15]

Yet few scholars have focused on the multi-ethnic and constructed quality of Soviet culture itself. The constituent cultures of the Soviet Union have appeared as concrete and unquestioned categories, as if there were a fixed and determined Ukrainian or Georgian or Uzbek culture. This cannot surely be the case, and indeed, for the Soviet Ukrainian beau monde the task of creating culture that was both Soviet and national posed a massive challenge. I build here on work by Serhy Yekelchyk, who restores agency to indigenous elites in the creation of their Soviet Ukrainian culture, and Adeeb Khalid, who shows how local actors made use of the Soviet socialist project. Indeed, the monumental upheaval caused by revolution and civil war offered young people an opportunity to redefine the form and content of their art.[16]

Literary scholars have mapped out the terrain of artistic culture. But the backstage world of artists and officials – the beau monde – incorporates not only the text, but also the live performance in its greater context. Exploring how embedded artists actually were within the state raises the question of how their theatrical culture was both Ukrainian and Soviet. The beau monde created Ukrainian culture in a Soviet context, and that Soviet layer was not imposed from above, but – as Khalid shows for Central Asia – was part of the mentality of the young elites making early Soviet culture. I take Soviet Ukrainian not as an oxymoron but as a real category that requires unpacking.[17]

Artists and the State

Ultimately, this is a story about the arts and the state. In Eastern Europe the arts are considered to have an importance that they do not have in Western Europe. As Yevgeny Yevtushenko aptly observed, "The poet in Russia – is more than a poet."[18] Rather than figuring out to what degree this may or may not be true, my interest is in the nature of the relationship between artists and the state, how it evolved, and its consequences.

The story of the beau monde on the borderlands offers new contours to the relationship between the arts and the state in the Soviet Union. These artists were not pre-war intelligentsia, except Kurbas, and he worked in the Habsburg empire, not in the world of the tsars. Kurbas did not even go to Moscow until 1927. A smaller milieu in a smaller city highlights the webs of personal and professional connections between artists and officials; in Kharkiv artists may have socialized more and worked more closely with officials simply because there was a smaller number of elites, and because most elites were veterans of the Red Army or working their way up through the Party. Soviet Ukraine also shows a distinct break with the Russian empire in the question of funding and managing the arts: Russian imperial officialdom was far less invested and interested in artists and the arts than Soviet officialdom, and this shift is perhaps most apparent in the borderlands.

In the Russian empire lack of political avenues for expression meant that written literature acquired a relevance unknown in Western Europe. The comparatively low literacy levels meant that it was a small group of officials able to put quill to paper to write at all, and the tsar himself knew them all personally. This importance ascribed the arts, even beyond literature, continued into the Soviet period, with an important addition. Artists themselves brought the state even further into the arts, for the purposes of financial support, guaranteeing audiences, and enacting their artistic agendas. More importantly, although the arts flourished in the late imperial period, artists were still not protected from the dark side of the arts market: actors, dependent on the whim of fickle audiences and philistine patrons for survival, could be stranded by entrepreneurs and left destitute in a remote village. In the early Soviet period, artists took care to make the state accountable to its artists. Kulish, Vyshnia, and Kurbas all depended on state institutions, and all worked with state institutions, to make art. No one, of course, foresaw the consequences – that artists and their imaginations would then be accountable to the state.[19]

The importance ascribed the arts went hand-in-hand with increased authority for artists. In the imperial period, artists did not belong to high society. High society frequented the imperial state theatres to see and be seen, but theatre artists only frequented society salons (and occasionally bedrooms) as entertainment, not as social equals. Early Soviet artists, by drawing the state into the arts, and by joining the state themselves to enact artistic agendas, managed to raise the social position of the artist. Artists became some of the most privileged members of Soviet society. They enjoyed the best apartments in the city centre, the best vacations in Crimea and even abroad, their memoirs were published and sold widely across the Soviet Union, and their performances on stage and screen were beloved by millions of Soviet subjects.

On the one hand, this embrace between artists and officialdom led to extraordinary artistic output during the Soviet Union: Bulgakov's prose, the humour of Il'f-Petrov, the legendary theatrical performances of Mikhoels, to give just a few examples of the output of artists discussed and debated today. The Soviet state supported all of these artists, whose memoirs tell not only of financial support for costumes, sets, and props, but also of the time and energy allocated to the arts: hours spent in rehearsal perfecting a monologue or a duet, the number of state-supported training programs, and the respect accorded those spending their lives in the performing arts.

There is another side, however, to the intimate intertwining of state and arts. The state facilitated funding and a stable lifestyle for artists, to be sure. But the state also demanded fulfilling the plan. Can creativity happen on schedule? If the arts are supported by the state, can artists fulfil the function of speaking not for the state, but for the general audience? Leszek Kołakowski argued that the creative output of Communism declined as the system aged. The "cultural formation of communism," in his terms, ultimately strangled artistic innovation. For Czeslaw Miłosz, artists' minds could become "captive" under the total state monopoly of the Communists. Miklos Haraszti, describing the phenomenon of the toll taken on artists by total state, wrote that artists existed in a "velvet prison." Theatre was funded, but at what cost? When the audience became circumscribed inside the Soviet state, did art fundamentally transform?[20]

This toll taken on artists, combined with the paradox of often-extraordinary artistic output, has created the myth of the noble Soviet artist. Like all clichés, this myth is based in truth. As archival documents clearly demonstrate, officialdom forced artists to denounce their fellows, sent artists to the gulag, and shot artists in prison basements. What other state has murdered so many of its finest talents? But the relationship between artists and officialdom was multidimensional. The state spent an enormous amount of time, money, paper, and bullets on artists, and the relationship between the arts and the state was one of the peculiarities of the Soviet Union. The space between the worlds of people working in the state and those working in the arts dissolved in the early Soviet years, consolidating into the categories of official artists and arts officials in the Stalinist 1930s.

This world of artists and officials, then, is the *beau monde* of the book's title. The concept refers to elites, artists, officials, hangers-on, friends, enemies, and the loose circles of *milieux* crossing the world of the arts and the world of officialdom. William Weber, in his work on concert life in eighteenth- and nineteenth-century Britain, describes the beau monde as "elites, together with professionals and artisans who worked for them," creating "a tightly knit network of institutions and personal relationships." In the Soviet case, it might not be clear who were the elites (artists or Party officials) and who were the professionals working for them (professional artists, or professional officials). The beau monde is the world that emerges between the lines in memoirs: secret police officials dating actresses, the billiard hall and the late-night drinking parties, the scramble for apartment living ... a world of artists socializing with officialdom.[21]

Weber sources the rise of London's beau monde to a post-Restoration decline in absolutist power and consequent shift from court to city culture. Rather than a product of a rising democracy, however, the Soviet beau monde emerged together with a rising authoritarianism. I track the emergence of the Soviet beau monde in two stages. The first is the *literary fair*, the name of a journal produced during Soviet Ukraine's artistic Golden Age, but later used in a memoir to summon up the people, places, and sociability behind the journal and the entire world of the 1920s. The literary fair offers a model of an early Soviet beau monde composed of artists and officials together taking on the task of building Soviet culture. Marked by a certain sociability and sensibility, the literary fair also produced the best cultural objects of the early Soviet period. The literary fair then collapsed into *official artists* and *arts officials*, still a beau monde, but one with a different sociability and sensibility and fully absorbed into the Soviet Party-state.

The concept of the beau monde might be jarring; after all, the term conjures up artists sipping wine in Parisian cafes, debating over coffee in London coffee shops, or enjoying elegant concerts on landed estates, and not performing in the Kremlin's Hall of Columns or editing a Communist Party newspaper. Yet this dissonance is precisely the point: there was no Montmartre, London coffee shop, or salon where dandies talked art in the Soviet Union. Rather, art was discussed in the state apparatus, in state-owned apartments, or in the editorial boards of state-owned newspapers, among other locations frequented by state officials as much as by artists.

This beau monde became the engine of cultural production and reception in the Soviet Union. This is, on the one hand, a local story focused on the Kremlin and exemplified by artists who worked closely with

Stalin. However, the Soviet beau monde existed throughout the Soviet Union, in Soviet Ukraine, in Soviet Georgia, and in Soviet Belarus, for example. But – perhaps most interestingly – there was a beau monde that was supra-republic, an all-Union beau monde. This was the beau monde of Soviet Ukrainian filmmaker Oleksandr Dovzhenko and Soviet Ukrainain playwright Oleksandr Korniichuk, for example. These official artists moved between the Kremlin and the periphery, negotiating the cultural topography of the Soviet Union, using the periphery against the centre and the centre against the periphery. In this way, they were able to accumulate cultural and political capital in the cultural infrastructure of the Soviet Union.[22]

The beau monde, in fact, allows for a different chronology and sociology of the arts under Stalin. The early Soviet cultural explosion emerged as much from the structures of the Russian empire and the demographic changes of the Civil War as from early Soviet decrees. More than aesthetic change, which might have happened in any case just as it did in Europe or the United States, the structural change of the arts and artists absorbing into officialdom was not imposed by Stalin, but rather resulted from a transformed relationship between artists, officials, and the larger public during the years of civil war and early building of socialism. The beau monde, too, included officials, loyal Communist artists, and people who defy classification as part of the Party-state or part of the arts. Kulish and Vyshnia, for example, were central figures in the arts, but also central figures in publishing, unions, and management. Fundamentally, then, the beau monde allows for artists and officials circulating in the same milieu and challenges the binary of artist-state.[23]

There has, since the collapse, been an obsession with the relationship between artists and the state. Essentially, these works put "artist" and "authority" in opposition, whereas artists had authority through a relationship with the state, and the state acquired authority through sponsorship of culture. The beau monde as a concept, then, hopes to show how the relationship between art and authority worked in practice, aside from any assumed guilt or innocence, complicity or dissent. Socialist realism may not have been "caused" by the Soviet state as much as it emerged from a relationship between artists and authority founded in the Russian imperial theatre network, forged in the era of war and revolution, and transformed by the early Soviet experience.[24]

The Arts and the State in the Soviet Regions

Focusing on the periphery and not the centre allows for a fresh examination of Soviet entertainment and demands new categories for cultural analysis. The world of the Russian Imperial Southwest centred less on letters and more on performance. Live performance was, it should be noted, *entertainment*. The intelligentsia in the Russian empire always – naturally – condescended towards art that entertained, as opposed to edified or educated. Yet, as scholars of popular culture have shown, audiences crave entertainment, for better or for worse, and what entertains them illuminates social values and meanings. Live theatrical performance was, in fact, the popular culture of the nineteenth century. Lawrence Levine's separation of highbrow and lowbrow cultures happened later in the Russian empire than in America, and in the Soviet period these categories collided. On the one hand, artists and officials strove to make low culture more respectable by creating state-sponsored vaudeville houses; on the other hand, artists and officials strove to make high culture more accessible by controlling ticket prices, overseeing repertory and casting, and bringing in audiences. High, low, popular, mass: categories classifying art were open for re-evaluation.[25]

This ambivalent relationship towards entertainment would challenge early Soviet cultural elites, especially in the provinces. After all, this was a place where audiences loved their weepy diva actresses in predictable melodramas that taxed the emotions and not the mind. Audiences missed these entertainments when they were gone, replaced in large part by experimental theatrical productions. And what of entertainment? Entertainment would be both relegated and promoted to the all-Union level (*The Circus* and the jazz hit); non-Russian culture would enjoy high culture, such as that available at the opera and academic theatres, and ethnographic kitsch, such as dances and folk songs in embroidered blouses. Non-Russian culture would lose the local entertainments of the urban and modern street.

The Story Unfolds

This book opens with an argument for the Russian Imperial Southwest as a cultural region. I detail the theatrical network in the Russian empire, which shows the artistic richness of the southwest provinces. Features of the network, such as the position of the artist in society, the failure of state protection in the commercial marketplace, and the multi-ethnic imperial fabric, shaped the desires, possibilities, and limitations for artists and officials in the early Soviet period. Much scholarship has illuminated theatre in the Russian empire.[26] Work has focused largely on the cultural achievements of the capitals, especially the Moscow Art Theatre, and the provinces have received less attention. Yet the provinces were central to theatrical production in the Russian empire, and the lived experience of theatre in the southwest borderlands created the necessity for structural change in the Soviet period.[27]

Chapters 2 through 4 use the artistic pairs mentioned earlier to detail the processes and consequences of *officialization*, the state taking over the theatre, and *provincialization*, theatre in the provinces becoming peripheral. Chapter 2 focuses on Mikhail Bulgakov and Mykola Kulish, both playwrights from the southwestern provinces who experienced revolution and civil war and lived to write plays about it. Both plays succeeded because of the emergence of networks of artists and officials facilitating cultural production and reception in the early Soviet period. Bulgakov enjoyed a network of theatrical and literary colleagues, as well as the support of Stalin himself. Kulish became a key figure in Kharkiv's *literary fair*, the term I use for the early beau monde of Soviet Ukraine. The literary fair was a physical space, an edited journal, and a loose association of friends and enemies making culture both Soviet and Ukrainian. Both Bulgakov and Kulish benefited from these networks facilitating their artistic creation, but their case studies show how the making of Soviet culture unfolded differently in Moscow and in the provinces. Moreover, the textual interplay between Bulgakov's and Kulish's work on the years of revolution and civil war highlights the importance of internal transnationalism in Soviet culture and suggests why culture unfolded differently in different places.

In the early 1920s there were multiple literary fairs creating multiple milieus of artists and officials throughout the Soviet Union. The main figures in this story are Soviet Ukrainians, but the concept of the literary fair could travel well beyond Soviet Ukraine. The Georgian Blue Horn poets described by Harsha Ram offer one example. The Blue Horns coalesced in the modernist cabarets of late imperial Tbilisi. Declaiming verse from the treetops in the early Soviet years, the Blue Horns joined with the Bolshevik Revolution in Georgia and slowly became part of officialdom. Denunciation, arrest, and death awaited the Blue Horns in the 1930s. One poet, Galaktion Tabidze, survived, only to go insane and throw himself from a hospital window in 1959.[28]

The Yiddish culturalists described by, among others, Kenneth Moss and Jeffrey Veidlinger, offer another example of an early beau monde. Educated in the late empire, these Jewish artists created new theatre, prose, and poetry in a Soviet Yiddish idiom. Solomon Mikhoels' Moscow Yiddish Theatre might serve as their most famous cultural product, for example. Soviet Yiddish culture managed to survive the decimation of the Jewish population during the Second World War, but Mikhoels' murder in 1948 heralded the end of culture in Yiddish. Denunciations, arrest, and death came to the Yiddishists culminating in the so-called Night of the Murdered Poets on 12 August 1952, when the secret police shot leading Jewish cultural figures in the basement of Moscow's Lubianka Prison.[29]

Within the artistic lifetime of Kurbas, Bulgakov, Mikhoels, and Tabidze artists came to acquire so much importance that the Party-state invested untold resources in simultaneously supporting and oppressing them. These artists then become examples, each interesting and tragic in its own way, of a deeper structural interlocking of artists and officialdom. Quite simply, as the literary fair (and the Blue Horns or the Yiddishists) shows, culture happened under the aegis of the state. Rather than focusing on the aesthetic achievements of the 1920s (and there were extraordinary achievements), this chapter explains how those achievements were possible by a dissolving between the boundaries of artists and officials.

Chapter 3 turns to the knot of Soviet entertainment. Il'f-Petrov was one of the most celebrated author-duos of their time, and they wrote for not the elite Moscow Art Theatre but the mass-oriented Moscow Music Hall. The culture that they created came from the inspiration of the Russian Imperial Southwest, and their hometown of Odesa, but theirs was an all-Union culture meant for a supra-ethnic Soviet audience. By contrast, Il'f-Petrov's Soviet Ukrainian equivalent, Ostap Vyshnia, wrote comedy for an audience both Soviet and Ukrainian. His humour reflected rural culture, not city culture: Vyshnia's narrative voice represented a village hick, not an urban con man. Vyshnia (or rather, a puppet of Vyshnia) starred in 1929's *Hello from Radiowave 477!* the first-ever Ukrainian-language variety show, at the Berezil' Theatre, by this time the premier theatre in Soviet Ukraine. This production underscores the difficulty of making local and popular culture in the Soviet Union. The policies of *korenizatsiia*, although they encouraged the literary fair's cultural production, may have had a negative consequence through forcefully separating ethnic cultures and preventing hybridity. *Hello*, for example, was decisively not a product of korenizatsiia.[30]

The focus on popular culture challenges the standard timeline of Soviet culture, which identifies the 1920s as an era of experimentation followed by a more conformist 1930s. This story does not use the term NEP, or New Economic Policy. For these men on the borderlands the NEP was a troublesome era, when their goal of state monopoly and control and support of the arts was not yet achieved. In fact, great artistic achievements in popular Soviet culture came in the 1930s, not the 1920s, and were facilitated by the cultural matrix proposed here: official artist, arts official, and official audience.

While work informed by the so-called linguistic turn and post-colonial theory has (importantly) provided for a more varied picture of an audience, very little documentation remains to flesh out exactly how spectators reacted to, interpreted, or experienced the theatre. Theory can offer only a partial answer to what meaning live performance had for those in the audience. Kurbas, like most artists, was well aware of the problem posed by the audience. He explained to his company in 1924 that they as artists needed to conjure up "certain associations, like a metaphor in a poem" in the minds of the spectators. The challenge was, simply, figuring out what theatrical images would conjure up which associations through which metaphors. What the audience brings with them to the theatre shapes the meaning of the performance, and with the new audience members, new patrons, and new artists, the meaning of theatre was up for contestation in the early Soviet period.[31]

Chapter 4 turns to the category of the official artist. Solomon Mikhoels, born Shlomo Vovsi, is perhaps the most famous non-Russian artist who created theatre in a non-Russian language. His GOSET, the Moscow State Yiddish Theatre, was one of the most important theatrical institutions, proving that Soviet culture could not only include Yiddish but also foster non-Russian arts. Until, of course, Mikhoels was murdered in 1948. By contrast, Kurbas lived a different trajectory in the borderlands. Creating art in Ukrainian (i.e., also a non-Russian language) Kurbas experienced the cultural topography of the Soviet Union differently. Creating excellent art in a non-Russian language like Mihkoels, he faced the challenge of creating that art not in Moscow (in the centre), but in Kharkiv (in the periphery). Art in the so-called peripheral regions could never compete with that produced in Moscow (regardless of its artistic merits), and Kurbas rejected the staid melodramas and ethnic kitsch promoted by apparatchiks like Andrii Khvylia.

Kurbas' 1930 production of Ivan Mykytenko's *Dyktatura* shows how radically Kurbas' vision of Soviet Ukrainian culture differed from that emerging in Soviet Ukraine, and how his idea of the function of an

artist differed from that emerging in the Soviet Union. It was Khvylia's vision that won out, and the literary fair turned against Kurbas,
who was exiled and arrested. Soviet Ukraine offers a particularly fruitful lens on the emergence of the official artist because Kurbas and
his milieu all started without such authority, which provides a sharp
contrast with Moscow, where the new political Bolshevik elite had to
cope with many non-Communist, non-revolutionary intelligentsia artists from the imperial era. Kurbas, Vyshnia, and Kulish, by contrast, all
came from small towns on the borderlands of the Austro-Hungarian
and Russian empires. War and revolution brought them to Kharkiv,
where they formed a class of new elites building culture in Soviet
Ukraine.

It is Khvylia himself who takes up chapter 5. Here I propose the category of the Soviet arts official. Exploring the world of officials whose
signatures and denunciations were responsible for the death of artists,
chapter 5 looks in detail at the logistics of managing an entire arts system. This chapter details the arts officials, from Khvylia and his circle
to Balyts'kyi, to the great arts patron of them all, Stalin, sitting in the
Kremlin dispensing apartments and privileges to the best artists from
the Union, especially those in Moscow. This chapter explores the world
of those managing the arts. What does a state monopoly on the arts
mean in practice? The chapter also argues that managing multi-ethnic
culture in the Soviet context raised a host of challenges that Soviet
nationality policy failed to solve. The case of the State Polish Theatre –
the only such one in the USSR – and the State Yiddish Theatres in Soviet
Ukraine show the complications for non-Ukrainian-language theatres
in the region. Governmental involvement in culture may be nothing
new, but this chapter seeks to articulate the contours of what made this
governmental involvement particularly Soviet.[32]

Sheila Fitzpatrick has written on patronage networks in the Soviet
context and identified the categories of patron, client, and broker to discuss Soviet how Soviet artists operated in the context of Soviet bureaucracy. Kiril Tomoff has illustrated this with an examination of patronage
in the (primarily post-war) music world that existed through unofficial
networks. The only way musicians could survive was through writing letters, currying favour, or making a well-placed telephone call
to a political elite, who could facilitate material comfort, professional
advancement, and in a few cases, life. While this chapter builds on this
sociological understanding of the Soviet arts world, I prefer to use the
category of "arts official" rather than "patron." Khvylia, for example,

was not just a patron; his actual job was managing the arts. The peculiarity of the Soviet system was not patronage or its widespread nature, but rather that Khvylia's job existed in the first place. A legion of officials managed the arts, and it is their role in shaping the arts that this chapter illuminates.[33]

Chapter 6 sets out the new Soviet theatrical network. Transformed from the Russian imperial theatre network, the Soviet cultural infrastructure included two new – and central – locations: the gulag and the Kremlin. Les' Kurbas and his colleagues made theatre in the camps of the gulag archipelago. The patronage extended to artists by camp officialdom, the role of artists in the camps, and the Soviet practices of surveillance and denunciation all speak — tragically — to the importance of the gulag as an artistic site in the Soviet Union. This chapter follows the members of the literary fair in the gulag, Kurbas and Kulish in one camp, Hirniak and Vyshnia in another. That the Soviet state murdered Kurbas and Kulish in November 1937 is a tragedy, and one with consequences for the development of theatrical culture in the republic; it is a tragedy, sadly, not restricted to Ukrainians, but typical of the Soviet period. The tragedy lies not only in the state violence, but also in the failure of the monumental task these artists set before themselves. They aimed to change the theatre, and from theatre the world – and nothing less. Their lives were cut short in the Soviet north.

Yet the beau monde continued. Hirniak and Vyshnia survived, for example: Hirniak rejected the Soviet Union, remained in Nazi-occupied Ukraine, and emigrated to the West; Vyshnia remained in the Soviet Union and embraced the mantle of the most celebrated Soviet Ukrainian writer. Kurbas' theatre continued, as well. One of the best theatres in the entire Soviet Union, the company was entrenched as a regional theatre on the periphery by the late 1930s. By the late 1930s, with the arrest and murder of the majority of the literary fair, new figures emerged. Here the story of hack playwright Oleksandr Korniichuk shows the great success possible for official artists. Fully absorbed into the state, an official as much as artist, and working the dynamic relationship between the centre and periphery, Korniichuk offers a prime example of official Soviet Ukrainian culture as he was able to make a relationship with the most important spot on the Soviet theatrical network: the Kremlin. The Kremlin was the centre of entertainment in the Soviet Union and the best and brightest stars graced its spaces of performance. Yet the literary fair and the former southwestern borderlands were largely not a part of this story.

But my story does not end in the Kremlin. Rather, it ends in the afterlife of the literary fair. These legendary figures, and the art they created – Kurbas' productions at the Berezil' Theatre still studied, Kulish's plays still performed, and Vyshnia's humorous feuilletons still published – have created a rich legacy. No longer do people have to refrain from speaking of these artists, no longer are their lives blank spots … yet the world in which they lived and worked has faded. The context to their work, the choices they made, and the limitations and possibilities shaping their careers, is increasingly lost. This book hopes to restore the context of the literary fair.

In 1927 Les' Kurbas lamented the lack of change in the relationship between the arts and the state in the Soviet Union:

> There really was no October in the theatre. What was new, what came into the theatre after the October revolution, was ephemeral and did not contain elements of anything permanent, of the epochal restructuring brought by the political October. The social and political themes were only temporary and were the natural response of artists who had been sleeping, who took the interests of a long-suffering class for their own … but the forms and principles in terms of their formal evolution remained the same … with corrections from the proletariat. It's the same in the West – without revolution.[34]

But that was 1927. "October" did eventually come to the theatre and marked an "epochal restructuring." Certainly not in 1917, and not one day in the 1920s, but by the end of the decade, the arts were absorbed into the state. Theatrical content may have seemed the "same in the West," but the deeper structures were radically different. Moreover, Kurbas' own world, one artistically fruitful in its own right, was slowly transforming into a periphery. The concepts elaborated in this book, such as the Russian Imperial Southwest, cultural topography, internal transnationalism, the official artist and the arts official, and the beau monde all aim to re-narrate the story of Soviet culture: a culture not divided into artists and officials, but with artists and officials intertwined; one not separated into separate ethnic stories, but one that explains that ethnic separation and its consequences; and one that pulls back to a larger perspective to reveal the transformation of the artistic space of the Russian empire into that of the Soviet Union. That fundamental restructuring unfolded through officialization and, in Soviet Ukraine, provincialization, and created the Soviet Ukrainian beau monde. The culturally rich Russian Imperial Southwest would become the Soviet cultural periphery.

1 The Russian Imperial Southwest: Theatre in the Age of Modernism and Pogroms

Part I: Rothschild's Fiddle

Anton Chekhov's 1894 short story "Rothschild's Fiddle" takes place in a small town "worse than the country." The anti-hero of the story, Iakov Ivanov, is a coffin-maker and committed anti-Semite, who nevertheless plays the fiddle so well that the local Jewish orchestra often invites him to join them. His anti-Semitism manifests itself particularly strongly towards the orchestra's flute player, a "thin red-bearded Jew ... carrying the name of the rich man Rothschild," who suffers under Iakov Ivanov's blows. After a typically Chekhovian epiphany of the ephemerality of life, however, Iakov Ivanov plays for Rothschild a mournful tune, bequeaths him the fiddle, and dies. The story ends with the Jew playing the Christian's violin:

> And now in town everyone's asking: where did Rothschild get such a nice violin? Did he buy it or steal it, or, maybe, did he get it from a pawnshop? He has long ago stopped playing the flute and now plays only the violin. Out from his bow flow the same mournful sounds like before from the flute, but when he tries to repeat what Iakov played when sitting on the porch, something so melancholy and mournful springs from him that all the listeners cry, and he himself at the end screws up his eyes in pain and says, "Vakh!" And everyone in town is so taken with this new song that the merchants and government bureaucrats invite Rothschild over nonstop and make him play it ten times at least.[1]

The world of Rothschild's fiddle is that of the Russian Imperial Southwest: the Jewish and non-Jewish cultural milieux interweaving, the

productivity of cultural exchange, such as Iakov playing with the Jewish orchestra, or Rothschild playing on Iakov's violin, and the everyday
quality of such an artistic environment. Entertainment, multiplicity,
the quotidian: the story weaves anti-Semitism, violence, and music all
together, and results in a tear-jerker that entertains the local population.

The great state-supported theatre, ballet, and opera troupes may have
graced the imperial capitals of Moscow and St. Petersburg; a musical-
theatrical culture of entertainment thrived in the southwestern provinces of the Russian empire. Whether in Odesa, Ekaterinoslav, or Kyiv,
or in the small towns "worse than the country," the local population
in their theatres, taverns, or streets experienced an artistic culture that
rarely reached the capitals. Mikhail Bulgakov, a Kyiv native who grad-
uated from medical school in 1916, later described pre-revolutionary
Kyiv as legendary: "In a word, a beautiful city, a happy city. The mother
of all Russian cities." Kyiv may indeed have been the capital of Kyivan
Rus', but it was also, long ago, the far eastern holdout of the Polish-
Lithuanian Commonwealth, and also *Yehupetz*, the fictional urban
centre of Sholem Aleichem's world of Jewish peddlers, milkmen, and
wayward daughters. Chekhov himself grew up in the Pale of Settlement. Jewish orchestras and the creative and destructive interaction
between Jews and Slavs formed an integral part of his childhood.[2]

The culture of the Russian Imperial Southwest was not exclusively
Russian, but reflected the multi-ethnicity of the region's population. A
Jewish actor reminisces about the beautiful songs sung by local Ukrainian girls; a Russian *estrada*, or variety theatre, artist began his career in
an amateur Jewish club; a Russian writer growing up in Kyiv notes a
Polish grandmother on one side, a Cossack one on the other. The region
comprised multiple confessions, ethnicities, and cultural layers: Polish, Jewish, Ukrainian, and Russian (not to mention German, Turkish,
Armenian, and Bulgarian, among others). The region may have been the
heartland of national projects – Ukrainian, Jewish, and indeed Russian –
but it was also, and necessarily, a place of everyday cultural entwining,
such as that depicted in Chekhov's story. Here was the place where
Yiddish culture, Polish culture, Ukrainian culture, and Russian culture
developed; but they developed in concert with each other to create a
regional culture. The desire for national culture, perhaps, resulted from
the multiplicity encountered in everyday life.[3]

The Russian Imperial Southwest was never an official entity with
borders neatly traced by cartographers and analysed by politicians.
Artistic culture does not respect political borders, but state policies

and economic realities do shape the contours of artistic possibilities, and that was true in these imperial borderlands. From Kyiv, the former borderland city of the great Polish Commonwealth, to cosmopolitan Odesa, to Ekaterinoslav, now Dnipro, to all the *shtetlech* and *mistechka* in between, this region proved extraordinarily fertile ground for culture in both the Russian empire and the Soviet Union. The southwest provinces of the Russian empire may have been provinces, but they were hardly peripheral to the cultural production of the empire. A confluence of factors, political, social, religious, and legal, allowed for the creation of a distinctive culture.

Demographics: Russians, Ukrainians, Poles, Jews

A peculiarly potent combination of Russians, Ukrainians, Poles, and Jews inhabited these borderland regions by the late nineteeth century. Importantly, all of these groups enjoyed a developed musical and theatrical performing arts culture; artistic culture for all groups aimed to entertain as well as to enlighten or to contribute to nation building. Ivan Kotliarevs'kyi's 1819 operetta *Natalka from Poltava* and Hryhorii Kvitka-Osnovianenko's 1836 *Matchmaking at Honcharivka* were hugely popular among the Ukrainian-speaking population of the southwest provinces. One particular family, the Tobileyvich clan, and their *Teatr koryfeiv*, the Theatre of Luminaries, first professionalized Ukrainian-language theatre and entertained wide swathes of the population in the Russian Imperial Southwest and beyond, from tsarist St. Petersburg to Habsburg Galicia. Personal connections linked them to the Ukrainian intelligentsia in Kyiv and their project of a politically autonomous Ukraine. The Ukrainian-language entertainments were not nationalist in their aim or content, but were promoted by a national imaginary in the imperial context.[4]

Poles enjoyed a Polish-language theatre in the urban centres of the lands of the former Polish-Lithuanian Commonwealth. In Habsburg Cracow the art nouveau Young Poland (*Młoda polska)* flourished with the symbolist theatrical experiments of poet playwright Stanislaw Wyspiański. It was the intentional and aggressive anti-Polish policies of Russification that transformed the language of Kyiv's theatrical scene from Polish to Russian. Still, even as late as the early twentieth century, Polish writer Jarosław Iwaszkiewicz remembers a Polish-language artistic culture in what is today Central Ukraine. Polish-language clubs in Kyiv promoted tours of the best Polish-language theatre companies from the Habsburg empire, for example. And on the eve of the First World War, the centre of Polish-language theatrical experimentation was in Russian-ruled Warsaw.[5]

Jewish culture, too, constituted an integral part of the Russian Imperial Southwest. The Russian empire's seizure of Poland during the Partitions brought a sizeable Jewish population into Russian territory and confined them to the so-called Pale of Settlement through a series of policies restricting Jewish subjects' possibilities for living and working to the western regions of the empire. In the lands of the Pale of Settlement – also the home of Belarusians, Poles, Lithuanians, Ukrainians, and Russians, among others, of course – Jews, too, encountered modernity. Vil'nius (or Polish Wilno, or Yiddish Vilne), in the northwest, with its Jewish enlighteners centred around the celebrated Gaon of Vilna, promoted an educated Jewish intellectualism. In the southwest, however, Hassidism emerged. The Baal Shem Tov, or the Besht, or the Rabbi Yisroel ben Eliezer, proclaimed that any Jewish person could find closeness to God through exalted prayer, and a culture of music and song resonated throughout the small towns where *tzaddikim*, Hassidic holy men, ruled with their courts, followers, and numerous Jewish faithful making pilgrimages to their graves long after their deaths. The relationship between Hassidism and other cultures is still more speculative than sure, but the sounds of clapping and dancing, the melodies of the songs, and the religious transformations in the Jewish community may have influenced other ethnic groups as much as they influenced the faithful circled around their holy leader.[6]

Yiddish theatre may have begun with the Haskalah in the German princely states, as Jewish Enlightenment authors attempted to bring Yiddish-language culture into European modernity, but it gained steam in Hassidic Eastern Europe, in the eastern provinces of the Polish Lithuanian Commonwealth. Joel Berkowitz notes that the Hassid tzaddiks used an expressive performance style when telling their stories; in addition, Hassidism, as a movement, also inspired many dramas criticizing the Hassids, often perceived as non-modern, non-European, and holding Jewish culture hostage to the traditional and conservative past. Yet it was indeed in the heartland of Hassidism that Yiddish theatre thrived.[7]

Finally, of course, ethnic Russians themselves contributed to the regional culture of the southwest provinces with the variety of theatre performed on the imperial theatre network. In other words, the Russian

Imperial Southwest was a place where various groups of people lay claim to the culture of the region, a place that various groups of people not only called their own, but also considered central to their people's history.

Urban Space

Cities in the Russian Imperial Southwest, such as Odesa and Kyiv, have received scholarly treatment.[8] But these cities were connected and formed a larger region. Catherine the Great invested in the southern provinces in the eighteenth century, because of a desire for warm-water ports on the Black Sea. This state investment in urban development and the need to entertain urban workers led to the creation of a cultural infrastructure. Several important urban centres, such as Kyiv, Ekaterinoslav (today's Dnipro, formerly Dnipropetrovs'k), Khar'kov (today's Kharkiv), and Yuzovka (today's Donets'k) formed part of a belt of industrial development – and therefore, places of urban entertainment – across the southwest provinces of the Russian empire. This presence of urban industry distinguishes this region from, for example, the western regions that would later become Belarus, where Minsk and Smolensk could hardly have been called booming factory towns.[9]

Odesa alone has inspired much work in literary history. The Odesa School of writers – Isaak Babel', Valentin Kataev, Iurii Olesha, and Eduard Bagritskii – was termed the "southwest school" by Viktor Shklovskii in an influential 1933 pamphlet. Recent scholarship in literature has taken inspiration from Shklovskii's notion. Anne Dwyer argues that "Shklovskii maps the canon of Russian literature as a history of borderland encounters," and Rebecca Stanton refers to the "self-invention" of Odesa modernism. Shklovskii was right, in fact, to note both that a significant group of young artists came from this particular crucible, and that the city itself must have shaped their aesthetic output.[10]

But Odesa, in fact, belongs to a greater cultural phenomenon of the entire region. Multi-ethnic interactions in the small towns and cities throughout the southwestern provinces inspired and shaped the many artists featured in this book, such as Iurii Smolych, Mykola Kulish, and Ostap Vyshnia. Ukrainian-language culture naturally played a smaller role in Odesa proper; ethnic Ukrainians constituted only about 10 per cent of the city's pre-revolutionary population. Yet Odesa's artistic landscape forms part of a larger question: why was this entire region, including Odesa but beyond Odesa, so fertile, in not only Russian and Jewish but also in Ukrainian cultures?[11]

Live Entertainment

The Russian Imperial Southwest was also the heartland of imperial entertainment. For the cultural elites of Soviet Ukraine in this book, local entertainments formed a part of their childhood. Most grew up in the Russian empire, a few grew up in Habsburg Galicia, but all grew up in the smaller towns and cities far from the imperial capitals of St. Petersburg, Vienna, or Moscow. Iurii Smolych, future official literary figure, remembers the railway theatre in Zhmerynka, where he finished school. Mykola Kulish, born to a peasant family in the village of Chaplynka, was lucky enough to attend school in the larger town of Oleshky. Humorist writer Ostap Vyshnia, born Pavlo Hubenko in Hrun', attended primary school in Zin'kiv. Future apparatchik Andrii Khvylia grew up in a peasant family in Rengach in Bessarabia. Zhmerynka, Chaplynka, Oleshky, Hrun', Zin'kiv, Rengach ... hardly a list of metropolitan capitals known well to the average reader. The cities close to these towns might ring more bells – Vinnytsia, Kherson, Poltava, Chernivtsi – but the point remains that the movers and shakers in Soviet Ukrainian culture were not from Moscow, St. Petersburg, or even Kyiv. They were from the multi-ethnic small towns and cities in the imperial borderlands.[12]

The world of the small towns and villages, most known today differently in the Russian, Ukrainian, Polish, or Yiddish languages, shaped the early experiences of the artists and officials in this book. None of them attended a performance in one of the grand imperial palaces in St. Petersburg or witnessed one of the more wildly experimental shows in Moscow. Certainly, future theatre critic Aleksandr Deich remembers Konstantin Stanislavsky's 1907 tour of the Moscow Art Theatre to Kyiv, but the entertainment that this future first Soviet generation was more likely to have seen was that of itinerant theatre, performances that mixed music with theatrical spectacle, and touring troupes that shifted their casts and repertory with each season. It is these young people's experience with the Russian imperial theatre network that would shape their expectations and desires for the theatrical culture that they would create in the early Soviet period. What was their experience of theatrical entertainment?[13]

This world of provincial theatre remains opaque. Most of what scholars know of theatre comes from St. Petersburg and Moscow and the
grand imperial houses, or the celebrated and much-studied theatres
such as the World of Art (*Mir iskusstva*), the Moscow Art Theatre, or
Diaghilev's Ballets Russes, which travelled west in the late imperial
and early Soviet years and became famous with Western audiences.
These are but a small part of the extensive imperial theatre network,
however. Richard Stites enlarged the field of the history of the arts in
the Russian empire with his work on serfdom and the arts based on an
exhaustive reading of memoirs of former serf artists.[14] Indeed, refocus-
ing an examination of theatre in the Russian empire from the capital
cities to the provinces reveals that the richness of imperial theatre lay
in the extensiveness of the network itself. It is this theatre network, particularly in the southwest provinces, that would explode with artistic
experimentation in the era of revolution and civil war and prove foun-
dational for the elites shaping cultural production and reception in the
brave new world of Soviet socialism.

Part II: The Russian Imperial Theatre Network

The Russian Imperial Southwest constituted part of the Russian imperial theatre network, an expansive web of theatres, audiences, officials,
and entrepreneurs spreading various kinds of live performance across
the vast expanse of the Romanov-ruled Russian empire.[15] Professional
theatre in the Russian empire began comparatively late, in 1756. There
were, of course, live performances long before throughout the lands
that eventually gathered under Muscovy, such as the *skomorokhy*, the
jesters, immortalized in the frescoes of Kyiv's eleventh-century Sofia
Cathedral. The city was a cultural capital on the eastern edges of the
Polish-Lithuanian Commonwealth. Here the Kyiv-Mohyla Academy,
founded by Petro Mohyla in 1632, had seminary students creating
vertep, puppet shows performed on two levels depicting sacred themes
in the upper level, and secular themes below. During the wars of the
seventeenth century, as Paulina Lewin has shown, roaming bands of
seminary students seeking money performed popular religious drama
throughout the lands of the Commonwealth. At the same time, the Jewish Purimspielers, enjoying the holiday's respite from the traditional
Jewish ban on images, covered the same territory of the Commonwealth, albeit performing for a different audience. Yet it seems that it
was, similarly, Jewish yeshiva students performing the Esther drama;

different confessions, to be sure, but similar traditions of students performing dramas at religious holidays and drawing a large audience for entertainment.[16]

Ukrainian churchmen eventually brought their tradition of Jesuit school drama to Moscow, where they created the Latin-Greek-Slavonic Academy. It was the tradition of Jesuit school drama that inspired Yaroslavl' merchant Fedor Volkov to start a theatre company, and it was with this company that Elizabeth Petrovna founded an imperial Russian theatre troupe. Theatre, then, came to Russia via Ukrainian churchmen from the Polish-Lithuanian Commonwealth.[17]

From 1756, then, the network of theatres subsidized by the Russian imperial state expanded. Just as it created laws and administrative institutions, the state created culture by decree. Catherine II formed the Directorate of Imperial Theatres in 1766 to manage and regulate the theatres in St. Petersburg. Ranked officials, generally with military backgrounds and a penchant for the arts, staffed the Directorate, hired and fired artists, and regulated repertory, according to the various decrees, which were issued by the Ministry of Internal Affairs (from 1811). In 1826 under Nicholas I, the Directorate was moved under the aegis of the new Chancellery of the Ministry of the Imperial Court, *Kantseliariia ministerstva imperatorskogo dvora*, further reflecting the theatre's connection with the heart of the imperial state.[18] State-supported culture entertained audiences in neoclassical theatre buildings, most of which survive to this day: the Bol'shoi and Malyi in Moscow, and the Mikhailovskii, Mariinskii, and Aleksandrinskii in St. Petersburg. Built in the nineteenth century, these elegant palaces of high culture offered opera, theatre, and ballet, all see-and-be-seen opportunities for high society in the imperial capitals. They were the homes of illustrious stars such as Maria Savina, Vera Komissarzhevskaia, and Vladimir Davydov, and supported schools for talented students who would fill the ranks of the imperial companies and all the troupes beyond, covering the expanse of the empire. The officials of the Directorate managed these five theatres from their central offices, located in St. Petersburg's aptly named Theatre Street, in long mustard-coloured neoclassical buildings that also housed the celebrated training school for dancers still active today.[19]

Over 150 years later, the Russian imperial theatre had mushroomed from this small state-supported enterprise to a robust network of state and commercial stages. The state-subsidized imperial houses in the capital cities of Moscow and St. Petersburg competed with private enterprises of all kinds. Most artists, of course, never stepped on the boards of the palatial imperial stages; most audiences never sat even in those balcony loges. Rather, artists and impresarios travelled along railways and muddy roads to rent theatres, taverns, or clubs from entrepreneurs, make deals with local officials, and entertain audiences from Zhmerynka to Odesa, from Moscow to Riga, Tbilisi, and beyond. In Yiddish, Polish, Ukrainian, Georgian, and, of course, Russian, subjects of all ranks (*soslovie*) created and enjoyed theatre, from the taverns in the provinces to the grand nineteenth-century palaces of St. Petersburg. At the turn of the century the imperial theatre network exploded with new artistic experiments: the Moscow Art Theatre, Meyerhold, and the World of Art movement in the imperial capitals, as well as modernist efflorescences in many of the imperial languages.

Managing the Imperial Theatre Network

The imperial theatre network was part of a highly centralized authoritarian state. State regulation, just as much as state subsidies for the grand imperial houses, shaped the cultural output of the Russian empire, including the theatrical entertainments that audiences in the provinces would have seen. Theatre throughout Europe operated with licensing, which meant that entrepreneurs had to secure permission from state authorities in order to present professional theatre. Russia was no exception. From 1804 until 1882, the Directorate held a virtual monopoly on theatres in the capitals of Moscow and St. Petersburg; any entrepreneur wanting to put on a production for paying audiences in the capitals needed a license – granted solely by the Directorate – to do so. Even after the repeal of the imperial theatre monopoly in 1882, the state still controlled public performances through preliminary censorship of production.[20]

The tsarist state may have only financially supported a handful of theatres in the capitals, but it subjected all public performances throughout the empire to the regulations of censorship, which evolved from unofficial policies in the late eighteenth century to, by the early twentieth century, a highly developed tier of codes: for publication, for theatrical performances, for theatrical performances in non-Russian languages, and for theatrical performances for the masses. From 1828 until the reforms of the 1860s, the infamous Third Section, Nicholas I's secret police operating under the Ministry of Internal Affairs, managed censorship of print and performance. Censors wrote précis of playscripts and forwarded them to the minister of internal affairs himself, who was required to personally sign off on each one. To complicate matters further, each production of a play required its own approval from the Third Section, so even if a play had been officially approved for performance in one theatre, a different theatre would still have to obtain permission to perform the same play.[21]

The reforms of the 1860s shifted responsibility for censorship to a team of officials in the newly created Main Administration for Affairs of the Press (*Glavnoe upravlenie po delam pechati*), also under the aegis of the Ministry of Internal Affairs. Unlike the situation under the pre-1865 policies, a play approved in St. Petersburg could now be performed anywhere throughout the empire, and each censor had the authority to permit, permit with changes, or ban a text for printing or performance. The abolishing of the Directorate's Imperial Theatre Monopoly in March 1882 complicated regulation, however, because of the sudden increase in the number of theatrical enterprises in the capitals all requiring oversight and regulation. Russia now joined Vienna, Paris, London, and Berlin in enjoying a mix of commercial and state-sponsored stages. Wealthy merchant entrepreneurs such as Fedor Korsh, Savva Mamontov, and Aleksei Suvorin dropped thousands of rubles into theatrical enterprises that competed with the imperial stages and greatly increased the opportunities for artists and audiences. The imperial stages remained competitive with the new private enterprises, however, and their stable salaries, pensions, and elite status guaranteed that they would remain a dream, albeit one rarely fulfilled, for artists throughout the empire.[22]

The growth of People's Theatres, charity projects of intelligentsia members that actively tried to make theatre mass culture, or rather, to bring culture to the masses, drove Minister of the Interior Dmitrii Tolstoi to issue an additional set of circulars adding yet another level of censorship. After all, after the assassination of Tsar Aleksandr II in March 1881, mass culture could be seen as tantamount to inciting revolutionary terrorism. As of 1888, all "popular" theatres had to submit to a more stringent level of censorship. Tolstoi defined "popular" by ticket price: the lower the price, the higher the censorship. Artists shaped their product to work with, or work around, the censorship regulations. For example, Konstantin Stanislavsky and Vladimir Nemirovich-Danchenko imagined their future theatre company as a theatre that was *obshchedostupnyi*, accessible-to-all, with low prices but but offering experimental productions. Conversations with the Moscow Police

Chief, however, convinced Nemirovich that they would have to choose between pursuing their artistic goals and their desire to reach a larger audience. If they wanted to be accessible to a popular audience with low ticket prices, they would have to submit to the 1888 regulations that would make their artistic dreams impossible. So they raised ticket prices, pursued art, and created a world famous theatrical phenomenon, the Moscow Art Theatre.[23]

After the 1867 *Ausgleich*, or Compromise, when Franz Joseph I established the dual monarchy of Austria-Hungary, Vienna centralized censorship policy throughout the Habsburg lands, but decentralized censorship practice by delegating it to local officials. The Polish-administered Galician Diet (Sejm), for example, had to follow Vienna's censorship laws, but could regulate culture on its own. The officials generally seem to have followed the centre's policies, which marks a difference from the Russian empire. By the end of the nineteenth century Russia had a censorship stricter than the Habsburgs in policy, but more decentralized in practice. It was up to the offices of local governors general to enforce the centre's policies: they could both interpret imperial policy as they saw fit and alter imperial policy as required to maintain order in the empire. Rarely did the centre intervene in the matters of local censorship, and local practice often differed from imperial policy, whether by intention or not.[24]

The challenge of putting policy into practice in Russia lay in *malo-liudstvo*, the lack of officials in the state apparatus. Habsburg Vienna had enough police officials to attend most performances and verify the implementation of censorship policy. St. Petersburg, quite simply, lacked such personnel. In 1915 St. Petersburg had only four censors, for example, hardly enough to attend every performance, considering there were three imperial stages, fourteen private commercial theatres, and seventeen pleasure gardens in the city (according to statistics of 1901), all offering a full roster of performances. Never mind the many performances in theatres, gardens, taverns, and clubs taking place all across the empire outside the capital: officials could not keep up with local cultural production. Another challenge for censorship in the Russian empire was the multilinguistic quality of the scripts requiring regulation. The decentralization of the Habsburg empire meant that local officials handled the play scripts in the local non-German languages. In other words, Polish officials handled scripts in Polish; no German-speaking censor in Vienna had to assess Polish-language plays for performance in Galicia. In the Romanov empire, by contrast, a small number of officials in St. Petersburg were tasked with managing the entire cultural output of the empire in its numerous languages – and these men may not have been fully comfortable reading Yiddish or Ukrainian, to take two examples. The regulations issued by the Main Administration for Affairs of the Press may have been strict, but the Administration's capacity to enforce them lay in a small handful of officials. The decentralization and the maloliudstvo created a culture of officials and artists manoeuvring around censorship policy.[25] Censorship statistics from the centre, then, may suggest a monolithic and oppressive policy; but far from the centre, practice often did not reflect policy.

Part III: The Russian Imperial Southwest on the Imperial Theatre Network

The imperial state shaped the theatre network through management and regulation, yet it was the challenges posed by imperial populations that drove the state's agenda. Specifically, the tsarist state was concerned about the Jewish, Polish, and Ukrainian populations. With the Partitions of Poland in the late eighteenth century the Russian empire acquired both Jewish and Polish populations, the non-Russian minorities living in the Russian Imperial Southwest. The Polish population rebelled repeatedly – in 1794, 1830, and 1863 – and caused the imperial state much anxiety. Ted Weeks argues that the Russification policies on the western borderlands were in fact largely directed against the Poles rather than the Lithuanians or Ukrainians; the concern of officials like Petr Valuev, for example, architect of the 1863 Valuev Circular forbidding Ukrainian-language printing, lay in the Ukrainian population's potential for succumbing to the Polish Catholics. The presence of these potentially rebellious non-Russian populations forced the state to create a series of regulations managing their cultural production and reception. Yet under autocracy's sharp control, paradoxically, non-Russian-language theatre developed in ways that it did not in other multi-ethnic empires, such as Habsburg Austria-Hungary.[26]

Because of the Imperial Theatre Directorate's control over licensing in the capitals until 1883, there was incentive for entrepreneurs to develop theatres in the provinces outside Moscow and St. Petersburg. In addition, the presence of war meant that suddenly there were captive audiences of military personnel in the borderlands eager for entertainment. It was the potential for profit on the borderlands that drove the cultural production of the Russian Imperial Southwest. During the Crimean War, for example, itinerant theatrical companies toured the region extensively, thanks to the spread of garrison towns filled with soldiers with salaries to burn. For the locals of Bobrynets', a town in Kherson province with no library, no access to railway lines, and no newspapers, the arrival of the famous troupe of Ludvik Mlotkovskii constituted a watershed event. The owner of the local tavern built a small room to serve as a theatre, and the troupe entertained the entire town for weeks. In the audience was a young Marko Kropyvnyts'kyi (1840–1910), who would become central to the founding of professional Ukrainian-language theatre in the empire.[27]

The Russo-Turkish War continued to transform the theatrical landscape. In 1877 Tobileyvich brothers Mykola and Panas volunteered for war, attended officer training school, and seem to have distinguished themselves in the Russian imperial army, Mykola even meriting the prestigious Cross of St. George. Mykola performed in amateur soldier performances in Bendery with a Russian officer's wife, Maria Khlystova, née Adasovs'ka. The two starred in Ukrainian-language performances for the troops; while the 1876 Ems Decree forbid professional performances in Ukrainian, these performances were only amateur military entertainment and, as such, were permitted. During the Russo-Turkish War, the town of Iaşi (in today's Romania) transformed into a garrison town filled with Russian-Jewish conscripts and entrepreneurs. Avrom Goldfadn seized the opportunity to stage a few Yiddish-language shows in a cafe, and thus began professional Yiddish-language theatre in the Russian empire.[28]

Yiddish-language theatre developed in Russia not from state support but from lack of state capacity to enact its own policy. The tsarist state banned theatre performances in Yiddish in 1883, but recent scholarship has shown that the ban did not erase, only hampered, the Yiddish-language troupes. Many companies simply called themselves "German-Jewish" and switched to a more Germanized Yiddish dialect (daytshmerish) should a tsarist official enter during a performance. John Klier argues that the ban resulted from the lack of officials capable of enforcing it (once again, maloliudstvo): both the Press Administration's lack of capacity for coping with the hundreds of Yiddish scripts pouring in to St. Petersburg for approval and the police's lack of personnel for monitoring potential unrest at the performances. But Yiddish theatre continued, and, as Klier notes, many provincial authorities assumed the ban had been lifted. In 1905 Konstantin Maksimovich, the Governor

General of Warsaw, and, in 1906, Vladimir Sukhomlinov, the Governor General of Kyiv, wrote to the Department of Police in St. Petersburg to inquire whether the ban was still in force. Presumably the presence of Yiddish theatre in the regions under their authority led them to assume that imperial policy had changed and the ban had been lifted. Seamstress-turned-actress Ester-Rokhl Kaminska, in fact, traversed the Russian imperial borderlands throughout the 1890s performing Yiddish-language theatre. She was able to found a new Yiddish-language European-oriented *Literarishe trupe*, Literary Troupe, in 1907 in Warsaw, after the official repeal of the ban, precisely because she already had the authority, audience, and experience for her enterprise to successfully turn a profit. Her troupe was so renowned that they toured St. Petersburg in 1908. Desire for profit and the realities of bureaucracy could trump imperial regulation.[29]

Polish-language theatre, to offer a final example, developed differently in the Austrian and Russian partitions. Polish culture enjoyed enviable autonomy under the Polish-run Galician Diet in the Habsburg empire. Russia, by contrast, managed Polish-language theatre with far more state regulation, because the state was concerned about the potentially rebellious population in Crown Poland. Yet that concern led to greater allocation of state resources of money and officials, and therefore, paradoxically, more state support. As Zbigniew Raszewski shows, the Russian imperial management of the official Polish-language theatres in Warsaw manifested itself in active support of Polish-language theatre, which the state perceived as the most effective way of managing a potentially rebellious Polish population.[30] By the 1880s, a team of Russian officials, including the Chief Police Officer of Warsaw, managed the WTR, *Warszawskie Teatry Rządowe*, Warsaw State Theatres, a behemoth organization that comprised 800 employees managing and performing opera, dance, and drama in Polish fully subsidized by the tsarist government. One piquant anecdote told of a Russian official who so loved the Variety Theatre (*Teatr Rozmaitości*) in Warsaw that he even wanted his daughter to go on the Polish stage. By the 1910s Warsaw (in the anti-Polish Russian empire) had, for some, surpassed Cracow and Lemberg (in Polish-run Austrian Galicia) as the most innovative Polish-language theatrical centre. Arnold Szyfman (1882–1967), a subject of Austria-Hungary, chose to found his experimental *Teatr polski*, Polish Theatre, in 1913 not in his native Cracow, but in Warsaw. The Russian imperial state's control of the theatre ensured support for Polish-language culture.[31]

The development of theatre in non-Russian languages does not mean that the Russian empire was not a centralized authoritarian state oppressive towards the arts. The goal of state management, however, was control. This marks a major difference with Soviet-era censorship, which included an ideological component and was therefore involved in creating Soviet culture – the empire was not concerned with creating culture, but with suppressing anything that could endanger the state. How those decrees were (not) enforced created a platform for non-Russian language theatre to develop.

The Imperial Theatre Network in Action: The Theatre of Luminaries

The case of Ukrainian-language theatre in the Russian Imperial South-west offers an example of the way in which state regulation and local needs created a unique cultural product. Impresario Grigorii Ashka-renko ran a Russian-language troupe in southern Russia and by mid-1881 in Kremenchuk, he was in a terrible state. His shows were not pulling in any audience and his profits were down. In fact, he had started to pay out of his own pocket in order to keep his company afloat. As if things were not bad enough, the actor playing the First Lover role had just run off with a cash advance in his pocket, which left Ashkarenko without a full complement of artists. Nor could Ash-karenko hope to attract another young actor to his company this late in the season. One of Ashkarenko's actors was Marko Kropyvnyts'kyi – the child from Bobrynets' who had fallen in love with the itinerant theatre during the Crimean War. Kropyvnyts'kyi had left his job as a clerk in the local administration to work full-time in provincial Russian-language theatre in 1871. Visiting Kropyvnyts'kyi was Mykola Tobi-levych, a decorated soldier on leave and the younger brother of his best friend, Ivan Tobilevych.[32]

Kropyvnyts'kyi and Tobilevych solved Ashkarenko's dilemma. Kropyvnyts'kyi knew that Mykola had performed extensively in amateur theatre in the military and offered him up to Ashkarenko as a potential First Lover. Mykola Tobilevych replied that he could do Ukrainian-language plays, such as Ivan Kotliarevs'kyi's operetta *Natalka from Poltava*, which he had performed in the army garrison at Bendery. Kropyvnyts'kyi and Tobilevych convinced Ashkarenko to put on a few performances of this classic repertory. He would get a new First Lover and get out of debt, given the largely Ukrainian-speaking area and pop-ularity of *Natalka from Poltava*. It sounded like a great plan.[33]

The only catch was that the 1876 Ems Decree unequivocally prohibited the use of Ukrainian in "all stage performances, lyrics to music, and public readings (as they presently have the character of Ukrainophile manifestations)." This decree ended Ukrainian-language education, most printing, and whatever Ukrainian-language theatre had existed in the Russian empire.[34] No professional troupes had performed in Ukrainian since 1876, but some amateur theatre had continued in Ukrainian, such as the performances at the garrison in which Tobilevych had participated. Kropyvnyts'kyi, Tobilevych, and Ashkarenko decided to send a letter to Mikhail Loris-Melikov, the minister of internal affairs in St. Petersburg, begging for permission to stage a few Ukrainian-language shows. The two Ukrainians urged Ashkarenko to write the request, since his gentry rank gave his complaint about imminent bankruptcy more weight. Ashkarenko sent the letter, and they waited.

The narrative of the genesis of professional Ukrainian-language theatre appears with virtually no variation in multiple accounts. The story ends happily: the two friends and the beleaguered impresario outwitted the minister of internal affairs, who gave permission to do a few Ukrainian-language shows and thus unwittingly opened the door to professional Ukrainian-language theatre in Russia. As predicted, the ticket sales from performances of the crowd-pleaser *Natalka from Poltava* saved Ashkarenko's season. This success convinced Kropyvnyts'kyi to start his own troupe based on a Ukrainian-language repertoire. Joining him was Mykola Tobilevych, who left the army and took the stage name Sadovs'kyi, soon followed by the youngest Tobilevych brother, Panas, who also left a military career and took the stage name Saksahans'kyi. Sadovs'kyi wrote to Maria Khlystova, that same Russian-speaking officer's wife with whom he had performed in the Bendery garrison, and invited her to join the company, which she did in 1882 – leaving her husband and taking the stage name Zan'kovets'ka. The oldest Tobilevych, and Kropyvnyts'kyi's friend, Ivan, was fired from his job as a clerk in the police administration in Elizavetgrad in 1883, so he joined the company and took the name Karpenko-Karyi. In the unstable market of imperial theatre the artists created the *Teatr koryfeiv*, the Theatre of Luminaries, which seized the opportunities offered by the Russian imperial theatre network to professionalize and popularize Ukrainian-language theatre in the 1880s and 1890s: Ivan, the phlegmatic clerk-turned-playwright; Mykola, the dashing officer and leading man; Panas, the youngest brother and class clown; Marko, their temperamental friend; and, lastly, Maria Zan'kovets'ka, Mykola's sometime girlfriend, a star of melodrama both in theatre and in life.[35]

Figure 1.1. Theatre of Luminaries: Maria Zan'kovets'ka in the role of Motria Kochubei in Ivan Karpenko-Karyi's *Мазепа* (TsDKFFA 2-121776)

Not surprisingly, the legend glosses over some of the details that add far more contingency to the story. After the assassination of Tsar Aleksandr II in March 1881, Loris-Melikov resigned from the government. Mikhail Chertkov, Governor General of Right-Bank Ukraine, and Aleksandr Dondukov-Korsakov, Governor General of Kharkiv, complained to Loris-Melikov's successor, Aleksei Ignatev, about the angry response among the populations in their regions to the Ems' ban on performances in Ukrainian. Local concerns pushed against the imperial decree. It was Ignat'ev who first authorized Ukrainian-language performances, presumably with the aim of quelling any potential discontent in the post-1881 atmosphere. Dmitrii Tolstoi, appointed minister of internal affairs in June, codified the amendments to Ems in a circular in October. Tolstoi, in fact, made the Ems Decree considerably stricter for Ukrainian-language theatre in terms of content – but he did allow for certain kinds of Ukrainian-language shows when performed together with Russian-language plays. Professional Ukrainian-language theatre emerged from a confluence of luck and wiliness (Ashkarenko and Sadovs'kyi), official desire to quell rebellion (the governors general), and state intervention in culture (Tolstoi). The result of these factors was the development of professional theatre in Ukrainian in the Russian empire.[36]

This case offers just one example of how impresarios worked with officials to keep the Russian imperial theatre network in motion. The motivating factor for both was, in fact, the audience, a source of rebellion or profit. Officialdom's desire to contain rebellion and managers' desire to secure profit shaped the practice of making theatre. Impresarios had to negotiate with state officials, for example, to get their repertory approved. Upon arrival in a city, the impresario, or his representative, had to visit the local chancellery office of the Governor General (or local police, in small towns) with a St. Petersburg-censor-approved copy of each play proposed for performance. The St. Petersburg censor's seal served as proof of permission, as well as the *Pravitel'stvennyi vestnik*, the Imperial Herald, a news leaflet that came out periodically listing all plays approved for performance. The local administrator would then sign – or not – the posters advertising the performances.

Memoirs boast, unsurprisingly, of how managers manoeuvred around state officials. In 1884 Tolstoi sent out a circular stating that not only must Ukrainian troupes perform Russian-language plays to accompany the Ukrainian-language plays, but also that the length of the Russian plays must equal that of the Ukrainian ones. But what did this mean in practice? Did five short vaudevilles equal five acts of a Ukrainian-language play? Odesa Governor General Christof Roop, whose wife "hardly left the theatre" whenever one of the Tobilevych troupes was in town, decided that, in fact, one short vaudeville in Russian would suffice for a long evening of Ukrainian-language theatre. Presumably, Roop did not want to incite his Ukrainian population and (one presumes) enjoyed the free tickets – and Tobilevych could not afford to bore his audience.[37]

In 1886 St. Petersburg theatrical entrepreneur Vera Lin'skaia-Nemetti, who used to perform with Marko Kropyvnyts'kyi in provincial Russian-language theatre back in the 1870s, persuaded Piter Gresser, the mayor of St. Petersburg, to allow her to bring the "Little Russians" to the capital to perform. The performances proved a huge hit in society; Sadovs'kyi recalls that ladies would have them over for tea and boast to their friends, "I'm having the Little Russians over today." Tsar Aleksandr III commanded them to perform in January 1887 at the Mariinskii Theatre, which marked the first time a provincial troupe had graced the stage of St. Petersburg's venerable opera house. The troupe also performed for charity events sponsored by court nobility. The troupe won their success in the imperial capital among tsarist and high society precisely when Kyiv's Governor General, Aleksandr Drentel'n, had forbidden any and all Ukrainian-language theatre in the provinces under his bailiwick.[38] In other words, Ukrainian-language theatre was forbidden but performed for the tsar.

Audiences, too, contributed to the success of the Theatre of Luminaries through their support of the repertory. The tsarist policies created challenging conditions for Ukrainian-language theatre: productions in Ukrainian could not present anything other than village life, and authors could not translate contemporary Russian or classic European plays into Ukrainian. Yet this state regulation actually created a boon for the theatre of the stars, and their repertory, created essentially *ex nihilo*, responded to their local audiences' contemporary needs. When Catherine the Great incorporated the lands of the southwest provinces into the Russian empire, she expanded the practice of serfdom into this area. Many poor nobles from the Polish or Cossack gentry became serfs, through inability to adequately prove noble status. Many of the estates in the region had large quantities of serfs. Evdokiia Tobilevych, whose father of Cossack descent found himself enserfed in the late eighteenth century, offers an example of a serf with musical and theatrical talents she managed to develop despite her life in unfree bondage, by seeing local provincial theatre

in Kherson province whenever the Ludvik Mlotkovskii troupe performed. She would learn all of the shows by heart, then teach the estate
serfs the productions so that her owners could enjoy performances at
home. She remained illiterate, but a local estate clerk, Karpo Tobileyvich, from impoverished gentry himself, bought her freedom and married her. Just as she had taught her fellow serfs, so she passed down to
her children the repertory she had learned. From this oral heritage her
children Panas Saksahans'kyi, Mykola Sadovs'kyi and Ivan Karpenko-
Karyi together created professional Ukrainian-language theatre in the
Russian Imperial Southwest in the late nineteenth century.[39]

The plays of the Ukrainian-language repertoire, shaped by tsarist
regulation, tell the stories of the failure of the 1860s reforms to alter
village hierarchies. These melodramas depict doomed love affairs, the
plot of which went generally as follows: the son of a former landlord
falls in love with the daughter of a former serf, the son then abandons
the often-pregnant daughter (despite his best liberal intentions), the
village then scorns the daughter, and she dies – either by poison, as in
Staryts'kyi's *It Was Not Destined!* or as in Kropyvnyts'kyi's *By the Time
the Sun Rises, Dew Will Devour Your Eyes*, by a broken heart. Occasionally, as in Kropyvnyts'kyi's *A Parasite, or Even a Spider* and *Give the Heart
to Freedom and It Will Lead You into Slavery*, the villain is the village elder,
or the wealthy former serf, who wants the pretty heroine for himself
and will use whatever means necessary to get her. Karpenko-Karyi's
play (based on Taras Shevchenko's poem) *The Hireling*, portrays a poor
and helpless Ukrainian orphan caught between an older villager and
her abusive Jewish masters. Karpenko-Karyi's *Ill-Fated* depicts the rural
life of former serfs, oppressed not by landlords but by their wealthier
village neighbours.[40]

Melodrama was extraordinarily popular throughout nineteenth-
century Europe, and serfdom provided a perfect vehicle for the genre
in the Russian empire. The quantity of Ukrainian-language plays
dealing with serfdom's legacy shows not only how successfully these
playwrights were able to manoeuvre within imperial regulations, but
also that the popularity of the Ukrainian-language troupes may have
resulted from the timeliness of their repertoire. Audiences responded to
these plays, presumably, because of the popularity of melodrama and
also because the themes of the persistence of village hierarchies and the
difficulties of emancipation resonated with audiences who themselves
were experiencing the transition from a serf to a non-serf society.[41] For
those writers attempting to create a new Ukrainian-language culture in

the early Soviet period, this repertory – and the audiences who loved it – constituted one of the primary obstacles.

The story of the emergence of professional Ukrainian-language performance in the Russian empire highlights the interplay of artists, officials, and audiences making theatre. While the state regulated theatre, management was decentralized. It was up to local officials – from censors in St. Petersburg to local Governors General – to enact the policies. The large demand for theatre offered opportunities for interpreting tsarist policies as officials saw fit: to fulfil the demand, to make a few rubles along the way, and to control potentially rebellious populations. The archives of the chancellery of Kyiv's Governor General contain hundreds of petitions to perform "Russian-Little Russian" plays. As in the cases of the Polish and Yiddish-language theatre, audiences wanted to see Ukrainian-language shows, and the officials in the chancellery office managed to provide them. Local needs came before the needs of the centre, and the memoirs of these early Ukrainian-language artists reveal artists who managed within the structures of the empire to create a successful and profitable business on the Russian imperial theatre network.[42]

Paradoxically, the Russian imperial state's management of theatre created a growth of professional Ukrainian-language theatre that never occurred in Austria-Hungary. While Russia was limiting Ukrainian-language theatre with the 1863 Valuev Circular and the 1876 Ems Decree, the mid-nineteenth-century Habsburg empire witnessed a state-sponsored "ethnicization" in the arts: the Hungarian Theatre in 1840, the Croatian Theatre in 1860, Serbian in 1861, Ruthenian in 1864, Slovenian in 1867, and Czech in 1881. Some of these theatres began as amateur literary drama societies, but some, like the Ruthenian *Rus'ka Besida,* emerged as professional troupes in non-imperial languages. These national theatres were promoted by local populations and allowed by the Viennese state. German-language theatre, as Alice Freifeld shows, actually lost popular support throughout the nineteenth century as intellectuals hoped to popularize non-imperial languages and develop non-German language cultures. This spread of national theatres happened in an imperial context in Austria-Hungary; in the east that process would happen in a Soviet context, driven by local populations, to be sure, but with far more top-down state intervention.[43]

The *Rus'ka Besida,* or Rusian Conversation, founded in 1864, remained the only professional Ukrainian-language theatre in Galicia, while in Russia the number of Ukrainian-language troupes multiplied throughout the late imperial period. The Besida even received a subsidy from the Galician Diet and, while they were not permitted a permanent theatrical home, they could perform the repertory that they wished. Or rather, they were limited in the same way all theatre was limited, based on Vienna's policies enforced by the Polish officials. The Besida, as memoirs of Galician actors show, drew an audience, but never reached the phenomenon of the Theatre of Luminaries in Russia. Hugo Lane shows how the Ukrainian intelligentsia never supported the development of culture to the degree that either the Czechs or Poles did in Austria-Hungary, or the Ukrainians in Russia. The Besida's central problem, then, lay in its lack of audience. The troupe had more autonomy from the state than the Ukrainian artists in Russia, but less success with an audience. The decentralized authoritarianism combined with eager audiences allowed the theatre to flourish in a way that it did not under seemingly more lenient management in Galicia.[44] In fact, small-town Galician youth Les' Kurbas joined the Besida, because his parents had been part of the company, but he found it not dynamic enough for his talents. During the First World War he left Galicia for good, and joined the Ukrainian-language theatre in Russia. He called Russian imperial Kyiv a "theatrical mecca."

Jewish Musicians and the Ukrainian Stage

The regulations of the Russian empire not only shaped the development of individual non-Russian-language cultures but also contributed to their often unconscious entwining. The Russian Imperial Southwest was the heartland of the Pale of Settlement, but certain cities such as Kyiv still required that Jews acquire a special *pravozhitel'stvo*, or permission to live, in order to take up residence. One path to the coveted pravozhilel'stvo was through professional music. The archives contain countless petitions to the Governor's General's office requesting permission for Jewish artists to live in town for the duration of the season, and their pro forma nature suggests that such requests were, more often than not, granted. The entrepreneur Semen Novikov, who owned Kyiv's Bergonnier Theatre as well as several café-chantants, wrote repeated permission requests for two Jews here, five Jews there, thirty Jews there, for work "as artists and chorus members" or "musicians" during the season. The owner of the Hotel Continental also wrote, asking for two musicians who would play in the hotel to entertain guests and diners at the restaurant. Isaak Duvan-Tortsov, the manager of the Solovtsov Theatre, also requested permissions for thirty Jews to play in his theatre orchestra. One Jewish entrepreneur, Moisei Genfer, wrote for permission for himself and his company to present "Jewish-German" (i.e., Yiddish) operettas in Kyiv.[45]

Legal regulations shaped encounters in the cultural sphere between artists of different ethnic groups. Most theatres, including Ukrainian-language troupes such as those of Mykola Sadovs'kyi's, presented plays with music, and most musicians were Jewish. Saksahans'kyi wrote in his memoirs about the hassle of constantly writing the petitions – but he does not say that their musicians were ever forbidden from playing. Actor Ivan Mar'ianenko recalls that the orchestras were the "Achilles heel" of itinerant troupes because they had to pay off the local police in every town to ensure a trouble-free tour if their itinerary departed beyond the bounds of the Pale of Settlement. Jewish musicians travelled and performed with the Ukrainian actors, and local police turned a profit from the practice.[46]

Scholars of *klezmer* music note that often Ukrainians studied with Jewish musicians, and that Jews imitated the sound of the Ukrainian hurdy-gurdy in their music. These cultural exchanges created an Eastern European "aural environment." Soviet ethnomusicologist Moshe Beregovskii told a revealing story about recording a musician he assumed was an authentic *klezmer*, only to find out that the fellow was, in fact, a Pole playing Jewish tunes in Kyiv courtyards. Unlike Austria-Hungary, whose strictly enforced guild system made it difficult for musicians to travel outside their local district, Russia had no such guild system limiting musicians' mobility. Jewish musicians could play anywhere – and they did. "Belf's Romanian Orchestra" originated in Russian Podolia – far from Romania, and with no Romanians involved at all. The artists were Jews who recorded in Warsaw and Kyiv, but their records gained renown with Jews throughout Russia.[47]

The participation of Jewish musicians in Ukrainian theatre offers one example of the overlapping cultures of the Russian Imperial Southwest. Such hybridity sprinkles itself through memoirs. Jewish actor Dmitri Zhabotinskii's childhood in Cherkassy shows the richness of the multiple cultures of the region. His earliest memories were of lying in bed and hearing non-Jewish girls singing "beautiful Ukrainian songs." His encounters with the performing arts included studying with a local cantor, performing in the choir of a Russian-language theatre, attending Yiddish-language performances of the entrepreneur Moisei Genfer, the circus, and a certain Barech the Klezmer. Within this

Russian-Yiddish-Ukrainian "aural" environment, he started his acting career in Russian-language theatre, and then moved to Russian *kupletn*, rhymed couplets, but done "in a Jewish style," whatever that may have meant. Zhabotinskii's memoirs unconsciously reflect this fluidity of cultures – Ukrainian songs, Jewish music, Russian and Yiddish theatre.[48]

Leonid Utesov, a.k.a Weisbein, describes the Odesa streets of his childhood, when three competing violinists would play on one street competing for the ear of the listener. They were from orchestras run by an Italian, a Romanian, and a fellow named Chernets'kii. Utesov famously claimed that New Orleans improvisatory jazz started in Odesa. Utseov himself ran away with the circus in 1912, much to the chagrin of his father, who recounted a cautionary tale of the one time that he himself had tried to leave the Pale of Settlement and dreamed that Pushkin's Bronze Horseman was chasing him around St. Petersburg. That Utesov's father was concerned about his son leaving the Pale suggests that this was not a "Jewish" circus but rather composed of a motley crew of artists of multiple ethnicities gathered from the region. In 1912 Utesov joined a variety theatre in Kremenchuk run by an impresario named Shtigler that toured with artists from Moscow together with artists from the Pale based in Odesa – in other words, this was a Russian and Jewish (and Ukrainian? or even Romanian?) troupe created to make a profit for its owner. Utesov's tales of backstage antics – including an unreliable cocaine-snorting prompter – may seem realms away from the high culture world of St. Petersburg. However, in this world they represent the kind of theatrical experience – provincial theatre, multi-ethnic cast, for profit – that young people in the Russian provinces, such as the major figures in this book, would have seen.[49]

This everyday cultural entwining is an important feature of the Russian Imperial Southwest. Jews and Slavs lived next to each other and so would have performed in and enjoyed the same theatre troupes. In Chekhov's "Rothschild's Fiddle," therefore, it was not surprising that a non-Jew should play in a Jewish orchestra. Ethnomusicologist Beregovskii pointed to the everyday factors that may have contributed to this overlap between music identified as "Ukrainian" and "Jewish": Ukrainian women often served in Jewish homes. Jews, therefore, would hear Ukrainian lullabies and everyday songs and, in turn, Ukrainian women would have taken Jewish melodies back to their own families.[50]

Zhabotinskii described the biography of the ultimate cultural hybrid: Semen Semdor, a.k.a Semen Doroshenko, a.k.a Shimon Goldshtein. Born in a shtetl in the southwest provinces to a shoemaker, Shimon

Goldshtein fell in love with travelling Ukrainian-language players and ran off with the troupe. First tasked with carrying props, later playing small roles, he finally worked his way up to becoming Semen Doroshenko, leading Ukrainian actor. His "rebellious nature, a wanderer" took him from place to place searching for new forms in art, and he finally landed in Kyiv. As Semen Semdor he was one of the first members in Kurbas' Young Theatre, then switched over to the Yiddish Theatre and founded *Onheyb*, Beginning, a studio that drew much of the young Jewish talent right after the revolution. When the group folded, he returned to the Ukrainian-language theatre, and then back again to the Yiddish-language theatre, until he died of sunstroke in Crimea in 1925.[51]

This is not to suggest that the world of the Russian empire encouraged nothing but peaceful cultural exchange. It does, however, suggest a contact zone between Jews and non-Jews in the theatre, from which cultural hybridity ensued both violence and art. Theatre could be a site of everyday interaction between Jews and Slavs, a place for exchange of all kinds, both creative and destructive.[52]

The southwestern borderlands of the Russian empire, then, belonged to a regional cultural sphere. Scholar Natalia Kuziakina describes late imperial Kyiv:

> In the movement of the multi-linguistic artistic trends in the Kyiv of those years, where you heard the melody of Ukrainian speech, and the softening of the Russian speech with Ukrainianisms, and the certainty of the Jewish intonation, and the fluid rustling of Polish, there was a connection that was important, if invisible to the eye. The culture of the city consisted in a complicated interweaving of these multi-national layers.[53]

This invisible connection, then, marked the theatrical landscape of the Russian Imperial Southwest.

Part IV: The Imperial Theatre Network at Empire's End

By the late nineteenth century, the imperial theatre network was highly developed. Circuses, variety theatres, and higher-quality theatrical productions traversed the southwestern borderlands. Advances in technology were slowly changing the theatrical experience for audiences and for artists. Until the mid-nineteenth century theatres used kerosene lamps and candles, which meant that the house was just as illuminated as the stage. Theatres began using gaslight in the 1860s, so that techni-cal personnel could manipulate stage lighting and create artistic effects. By the turn of the century, finally, theatres were slowly equipped with electric light. This demanded changes in scenery because set decora-tions, costumes, and backdrops appeared completely different. Electric stage lighting ushered in the era of the set designer; modernist painters began to work in the theatre because their creations would be finally visible to the audience. The spread of railroads facilitated the use of elaborate sets and props that could take full advantage of electric the-atre lighting. Previously, transportation limited the quantity of props, wigs, costumes, and sets that companies could carry with them, and troupes depended upon the stock supplied by local theatre owners; in any case, audiences could not even see details in sets, props, or cos-tumes. Once troupes could travel more frequently by railway than by carriage, however, the game changed.[54]

Train travel facilitated tours: Stanislavsky's Moscow Art Theatre, Meyerhold's troupe, and Max Reinhardt's troupe all toured from the imperial capitals of Moscow, St. Petersburg, and Vienna, respectively, across the rail network of European Russia. Young theatre lovers like future writer Iurii Smolych or future critic Aleksandr Deich would have seen not only the smaller troupes like Utesov's based in Kremen-chuk but also the more celebrated tours of Meyerhold, Stanislavsky, and Reinhardt, arriving with their huge theatre companies by train. In turn, rail travel enabled tours inside the Russian empire as well, as well. Troupes like Avram Fishzon's based in Odesa could travel all the way to Dvinsk, near Riga, where they impressed a young Shlomo Vovsi, whose stage name became Solomon Mikhoels; Esther Rokhl Kaminska could travel from Warsaw to St. Petersburg to Odesa and impress young Jew-ish youth across the Russian empire with her Literary Troupe.

But the Russian imperial theatre network carried its own series of risks. Provincial theatre was always a gamble for artists and officials.

The Ukrainian-language troupes of the Theatre of Luminaries were constantly fighting with each other, and all over money. Live theatre offered no safety net for artists during the Russian empire. Anyone with start-up capital and a little luck could call himself an impresario and take the risk of running a theatre company for profit. Impresarios negotiated directly with theatre owners or with freelance entrepreneurs working as middlemen in order to secure several weeks or months in a particular performance space. Theatre owners supplied most chorus costumes, sets, and technical personnel for a fixed per performance fee. Impresarios, then, hired a troupe of artists and travelled with them along railways and roads from rented space to rented space hoping to turn a profit.[55]

The world of provincial theatre could be brutal. For impresarios, the loss of a star actor, the whim of local officials, or a recalcitrant audience failing to line up at the box office could mean bankruptcy. In turn, impresarios could leave actors stranded in a small town, with no wages and no way back home. Once in the theatre, an artist had to string together enough work to survive. This often meant moving every six months, first for the summer season that began after Lent, and then for the winter season that began in the fall. One actor noted in his memoirs that he worked in seventy-two cities in the Russian empire. Another actor listed in chronological order the various cities he had worked in from 1905 to 1917: Elizavetgrad, Arkhangel'sk, Minsk, Melitopol', Vitebsk, Smolensk, Kaluga, Poltava, Ekaterinoslav, Vil'nius, Ufa, Saratov, Ufa, Odesa, Novorossiysk, Iaroslavl', Moscow, Nizhnii Novgorod, Ekaterinoslav, Yuzovka, Astrakhan. This list is not unusual: twenty-one cities in twelve years – and moreover, all for the same three impresarios, all of whom were cobbling together troupes in different cities. These stories of extraordinary mobility are far more common than stories of actors working exclusively in St. Petersburg or Moscow for their entire career.[56]

Artists were at the mercy of entrepreneurs and destitution was always a possibility. Troupes could either operate as private enterprises, with the impresario controlling all decisions and distributing fixed salaries determined in advance, or *na paiakh*, on shares, where each member of the troupe was a partner in the enterprise and received a certain percentage of the profit based on status in the troupe – assuming there was a profit. Chorus members wore costumes provided by theatre owners, but more established artists owned their own costumes and wigs, which were considered precious property. In fact, early Soviet artists often wrote to the local state organs with requests to keep their expensive costumes and wigs, because they needed them to perform their job properly. If hired by an impresario, an artist would not receive payment until performances began, and if an actor objected to his salary, he could always leave the troupe. Many actors were illiterate, and had to pay someone to read the script out loud so that they could memorize their lines. At the same time, however, many actors (even if illiterate) knew several languages and could switch easily from Polish to Ukrainian to Russian depending on repertory and theatre location. One of the most important figures in Imperial theatre was the prompter, sitting in a box at the front of the stage, because every show received only two or three rehearsals and actors depended on assistance with lines throughout the performance.[57]

Actors worked their way up the theatre network hoping to land in one of the better enterprises in the major cities that could guarantee salary, reputation, and even a pension. This included Korsh's in Moscow, Nezlobin's in Riga, or Solovtsov's in Kyiv, later the Moscow Art Theatre, maybe, perhaps, the imperial stages. Even if an actor reached the coveted goal of a salary and pension and celebrity at an imperial theatre, he/she would never completely belong to elite society. Actress Maria Savina's story offers a cautionary tale. Talent and smarts brought her from a peasant background to earning a salary of 1,200 rubles a year as a star at St. Petersburg's Aleksandrinskii Theatre, all without any professional acting training. She was feted by high society, but as soon as she married a member of that society, Nikita Vsevolozhskii, it shunned her. Never would the higher ranks accept artists to their inner circle. Savina continued performing, however, and working to improve conditions for artists in the empire. The 1894 Russian Theatrical Society founded by Savina hoped to provide some measure of security for artists, and their all-empire conferences in 1897 and 1901 drew artists from all around the empire. By 1902 the Society had 4,444 members. Later statistics claim there were 6,000 actors in the Russian empire working in 224 theatrical enterprises; my assumption is that this number is low. Many actors may not have registered with the authorities, or may have slipped through the cracks.[58]

Features of the imperial theatre network, such as the low position of the artist in society, the failure of state protection in the commercial marketplace, and the multi-ethnic imperial fabric, shaped the desires, possibilities, and limitations for artists and officials in the early Soviet period. Hardships of the theatrical work under the tsars translated into artists' agendas in the early Soviet state; artists shaping Soviet theatre wanted both respect and social opportunity for actors, as well as state protection against commercially minded entrepreneurs and potentially fickle audiences.

Theatre reflects many paradoxes: non-Russian language theatre was rarely subsidized and often oppressed, yet flourished in a way it did not in the nationalized theatrical culture of Austria-Hungary. The Russian state created a strict censorship regime, yet its inability to enact those policies in practice created great opportunities for artists and impresarios. Legal restrictions circumscribed certain regions of the empire, such as the Pale of Settlement or Congress Poland, yet the network produced an extraordinary mobility as artists and impresarios, working with officials and audiences, traversed the empire.

In the early twentieth century changes in regulation opened the door to artistic experimentation. After the revolution of 1905, Tsar Nicholas II relinquished some of the state's hold on controlling repertory. Preliminary censorship of theatre continued, but the tsar abolished the Ems Decree, so that Ukrainian-language theatre could finally claim a permanent performance space. In 1907 Sadovs'kyi made a deal with Isaak Duvan-Tortsov, manager of the theatre at the intelligentsia-run Literacy Society, whereby he rented the space for part of the season. Sadovs'kyi engineered the first permanent, professional Ukrainian-language theatre company not only in the Russian empire but in the world. Sadovs'kyi translated European hits and performed new modernist Ukrainian writers such as Lesia Ukrainka and Volodymyr Vynnychneko. A major triumph, to be sure – but Sadovs'kyi's theatre opened a pandora's box. If Ukrainian-language theatre were not restricted to song-and-dance melodramas, what should it be? What of their audience, so attached to the old favourites? What distinguished the Ukrainian-language stage from the Russian, Jewish, and Polish stages if they were all performing European classics and modernist experimental plays?[59]

This question over Ukrainian-language theatre was but one manifestation of a general sense of searching and discontent among young artists in the late imperial period. In Ukrainian-language theatre, the enemy was *pobutovy*, everyday theatre like the Theater of Luminaries' melodramas. In Yiddish-language theatre, it was *shund*, low-quality theatre that only entertained. In Russian language theatre, it was *khaltura*, trashy popular entertainment for the masses. Young people across Europe wanted to transform and renovate the theatre. Pobutovyi, shund, and khaltura had in common an element of naturalism, presenting theatre like life. So all along the Russian imperial theatre network young artists wanted to turn away from realism and naturalism, and towards theatricality. Aesthetic explosions rippled across the Empire, and the First World War only catalyzed this artistic experimentation as armies moved and empires collapsed.

The summer of 1916 saw the Brusilov Offensive on the Eastern Front, the battles of the Somme and Verdun on the Western Front, but in Russian imperial Kyiv life continued, and theatrical life especially, making

Kyiv a desired destination for artists struggling in the occupied border-lands. Civil war Kyiv became in 1918 and 1919 a refuge for those fleeing both from and towards the Bolsheviks, such that everyone who was anyone spent some time in Kyiv during the years of war and revolution. Through the vicissitudes of political change – the Ukrainian Rada, the 1918 Bolshevik occupation, the German Hetmanate, Petliura's Direc-tory, and the 1919 Bolshevik occupation – young artists in Ukrainian, Polish, Yiddish, and Russian attempted to transform the theatre. In the provinces the mobility created by the war and revolution, paradoxi-cally, allowed for a cultural flourishing.[60]

On Prorizna Street

Les' Kurbas offers one example of this demographic change and cul-tural flourishing. Kurbas avoided conscription into the Habsburg army and started a Ukrainian-language theatre in Ternopil', which ran into increasingly hard times as armies of the Eastern front crisscrossed Gali-cia. So he accepted the invitation extended by Mykola Sadovs'kyi, artis-tic director of the only permanent and stationary Ukrainian-language company, to join his company in Russian Kyiv. It was the war that made such a decision possible: first of all, Sadovs'kyi had lost company mem-bers to the Russian tsarist army and was desperate to replace the ranks of his company; moreover, Kurbas might never have accepted the invi-tation and left the Habsburg empire had it not been for the war.[61]

Through his work at Sadovs'kyi's, he met a group of young gradu-ates of Kyiv's Lysenko Drama Academy. These amateur artists wanted to transform Ukrainian-language theatre but lacked a leader. With them, Kurbas created the much-studied Young Theatre, *Molodyi Teatr*, and created experimental productions in Ukrainian.[62]

But the Young Theatre was only one of several experimental groups in wartime Kyiv benefiting from the demographic changes brought by the war. These aesthetic explosions may have happened along ethnic lines, but they were fundamentally interwoven. In one block of Pro-rizna Street, for example, three innovative theatre groups rehearsed and performed: Kurbas' Young Theatre, the Polish studio of Stanisława Wysocka, and the drama studio of the Kultur-Lige.[63]

The centrality of Warsaw to Polish theatrical culture meant that with the outbreak of the First World War, many Polish artists who were sub-jects of Austria-Hungary found themselves on "enemy" (i.e., Russian) territory and had to go to the Russian interior. Polish-language artists from Cracow, Lemberg, and Warsaw all met in Kyiv and the result was artistically fruitful. One of the centres of Polish culture was the studio of Stanisława Wysocka (née Dzięgielewska, 1878–1941), who performed in Austrian Cracow and studied in Moscow and was now living in Russian Kyiv.[64] Wysocka, for example, took from her youth in Cracow innovative lighting effects by manipulating projectors to illuminate the actors' bodies unevenly, keeping parts of their bodies intentionally in shadow. Later this chiaroscuro technique was criticized in Warsaw as coming from the Russian East, but, in fact, this idea travelled from Austrian Cracow into the Russian empire, then back westwards from civil war Kyiv to Polish Warsaw, all via Wysocka and the mobility created by the war.[65]

The collapse of the Pale of Settlement transformed the artistic world of the Russian Imperial Southwest as much as the creation of an independent Poland in 1918. For a brief suspended moment, after the revolution and the collapse of the Pale, Kyiv was the centre of a Yiddish cultural renaissance. As in Ukrainian, Russian, and Polish, in Yiddish, too, young artists longed to renovate their theatre. Warsaw's Esther Rokhl Kaminska and her husband Avrom Kaminsky were pioneers in this movement, and when they fled German-occupied Warsaw for Kyiv, their performances impressed Jewish youth wherever they appeared.[66] The new freedoms accorded the Jewish community gave these ideas institutional structure in the form of the drama division of the Kultur-Lige, a Jewish enlightenment organization founded in 1918. The Kultur-Lige has inspired much scholarship in the narrative of Jewish cultural development, but the institution was also deeply connected with similar trends in Ukrainian, Polish, and Russian theatrical art.[67]

Each ethnicity's theatre was not separated from the others on Prorizna. Wysocka taught at the Kultur-Lige, Semen Semdor-Doroshenko worked with Kurbas' Young Theater and with the Kultur-Lige. Helping Kurbas out with choreography was Polish-speaking St. Petersburg-trained dancer, Bronisława Nijinska, who also ran a studio for dancers. These artists pushed the aesthetic boundaries of theatre in the same physical space. Prorizna Street, then, constituted a microcosm of the cultural productivity of the borderlands, and suggests the consequences of war-induced mobility and the future of artists searching for new solutions to aesthetic crises. Artists and officials in Soviet Ukraine, in the early Soviet years, would continue to struggle with the tension between the imperial and the national in artistic development.

The culture of the Russian Imperial Southwest collapsed with the Russian empire during the years of war and revolution. Many former imperial subjects emigrated to Europe or to the United States. Many left the region during the war, searching for opportunities or simply to survive. This cultural sphere, where Jews and Slavs had made a musical-theatrical culture of entertainment, dissolved. As war turned to revolutions, Kyiv transformed: no longer a haven from war and politics, the city became the epicentre of conflict between Ukrainian nationalists, Soviets, Russian monarchists, and partisans of various affiliations. While the mobility of the era of war and revolutions had enabled creative production, it eventually drove it into the ground. Bulgakov, writing about Kyiv, notes that those who survived the wartime years remember eighteen revolutions, but he could "precisely report that there were fourteen, and I personally lived through ten of them."[68]

On 24 January 1920, an engineer, a certain Morgulev, reported on the material condition of theatres to the board of the Sub-department of the Arts of the local Kyiv branch of the People's Commissariat of Enlightenment. He described how water damage had destroyed the wooden infrastructure of the theatre, and how the theatre where Kurbas' artists were currently performing was located next to a hotel whose plumbing was leaking through the theatre roof all the way down into the foyer. Theatre was nearly impossible in these conditions. Gone were the local officials who loved theatre and knew they were miles from St. Petersburg. Gone was the infrastructure of the network, the sprawling web of officials, artists, and audiences, the lone censors sitting in St. Petersburg. Gone were many of the artists who had traversed the network, gone were many of the audience members and many of the tsarist officials. Gone was the funding, and gone were the theatrical spaces, and many of the inspired artists and eager audiences providing the structure for theatrical production and consumption in the Russian empire.[69]

Artists, if they stayed in the region, had to look for new sources of financial support. In June 1920, Kurbas left Kyiv accompanied by a group of actors to seek safety and food in the countryside. His troupe, named the Kyidramte, for Kyiv Dramatic Theatre, ended up right in the middle of the fighting between the Poles and Red Army General Iona Iakir's 405th Regiment of the 45th Volyhnian Rifle Division of the 12th Army. But the Red Army became an unexpected patron for Kurbas' troupe. New possibilities opened the door to new relationships between artists, officials, and audiences.[70]

The revolution in theatre would happen over the next decade as artists joined with officials to fundamentally transform the place of the stage in the emerging Soviet space. The cultural mobility created by war and revolution had fuelled the experimental artistic explosion of the late imperial era; but the war's consequences imploded the imperial theatre network and catalyzed change across the empire. Artists' experiences in Russia inspired a desire for national culture and for state investment. The world of Rothschild's fiddle, the world of the Russian Imperial Southwest, would soon become Soviet.

2 The Literary Fair: Mikhail Bulgakov and Mykola Kulish

It was in general a joyful and reckless time ... the era of *Literary Fair*.
– Iurii Smolych, *A Tale of Unrest*[1]

Part I: Moscow, 1920s: The Imperial Southwest in the Soviet North

Mikhail Bulgakov writes in "Notes off the Cuff" that there were only three writers in Soviet Moscow in 1920, including him. The troika worked every day at Lito, the Literature Department of the Central Political Enlightenment Committee, and wrote nothing with nothing. Lito had no paper and no ink, and the three writers, as a consequence, produced no literature. Although exaggerating for emphasis in a feuilleton, Bulgakov was not far wrong. The world of Soviet writers housed in centrally located apartment buildings, allocated vacations in Crimea, and decorated with titles and financial prizes was still a decade off, and young artists like Bulgakov struggled in the big city living hand to mouth.[2]

But Bulgakov's "salad days" anecdote is also disingenuous. From the very beginning of Soviet authority, officialdom took a vested interest in supporting and managing culture. In turn, artists took a vested interest in drawing the state into their own agendas. This made practical sense. After all, the state took culture seriously because Communism was a project not only economic and political, but also cultural: creating an entirely new culture for an entirely new society. The arts were therefore not a luxury, but rather a central component of the Soviet project. Consequently the state created, managed, and financially supported newspapers, journals, and arts institutions, all of which offered jobs for artists. Writing for a paper, or working on the editorial board of a journal, or performing in a newly formed "state" theatre provided artists with a salary, however meagre. Bulgakov's Lito was one such place. And after all, this was one of the goals of most artists emerging from the Russian empire. Growing up in a state that had failed to protect artists, artists naturally desired state support for themselves and for their artistic agendas. Sharing common goals of building a new culture, artists and officials contributed to creating a structural connection between the world of the arts and the world of the state. This Soviet cultural infrastructure began to emerge during the Civil War.

Moscow offered a host of possibilities for young artists at that time. As the Whites, Reds, Poles, and anarchists of various flavours fought over the former imperial borderlands, Moscow enjoyed a position removed from the fray. There may not have been adequate ink or paper in civil war Moscow – at least according to Bulgakov – but there was a possibility of a home, a job, and an opportunity to participate in the revolutionary task of building a new culture for a new state. Many young people from the Russian Imperial Southwest went north to Moscow seeking new horizons, or at least relative safety and security. Personal and professional connections made back home would often continue in Moscow or Leningrad, shaping social networks in the big city as former provincials rose to fame and fortune.

For Jewish subjects of the Russian empire, the collapse of the Pale of Settlement meant the legal right to move to Moscow or Petrograd. No longer did the Pale restrict Jews to the southwestern provinces; they were permitted to move north, and many did. The violent pogroms of the Civil War, moreover, compelled many Jews to leave home, whether they wanted to or not. For example, future filmmaker Aleksei Kapler's early theatrical misadventures took place in Kyiv with two other future cinema artists, Sergei Iutkevich and Grigorii Kozintsev. Il'ia Ehrenburg, perhaps because he was dating Kozintsev's sister Liuba, allocated funds from the Soviet Ukrainian Commissariat of Enlightenment during the short-lived 1919 Bolshevik occupation of the city to fund the young artists. But their avant-garde experimentation did not last long; Kapler remembers a friend killed by Petliura's troops on the city streets, and the family soon left Kyiv and relocated to Moscow.[3]

Indeed, the ravages of civil war made life difficult for everyone. Future jazzman Leonid Utesov remembers that "there was nothing in Odesa, not even water." But more than the prosaic necessities of survival, many young people felt that opportunity called from the new Soviet centre.

The quantity of future Soviet elites from the Russian Imperial Southwest who moved north to Moscow or Petrograd —or beyond— in the early 1920s is staggering. Few of these figures will play a role in this book, but the list – overwhelming as it is – reveals this density of connections coming from this particular place in the former empire. Let me map out this list of connections: Kapler, Kozintsev, and Iutkevich ended up working in Leningrad, where Kozintsev and Iutkevich, together with *Odessit* Leonid Trauberg and Kyivan Grigorii Kryzhyts'kii, founded FEKS, the Factory of the Eccentric Actor. Kapler starred in Kozintsev's 1926 film of Gogol's *The Overcoat*. In 1923, Isaak Babel' complained in a letter that Odesa was becoming a province and moved north to Moscow; also leaving Odesa were Il'ia Il'f and Evgenii Petrov, who were not yet Il'f-Petrov and had not yet conjured up the ultimate Soviet urban con man, Ostap Bender. Preceding them was Petrov's brother, writer Valentin Kataev, who quickly made a name for himself in Moscow and paved the way for his *Odessit* compatriots. Konstantin Paustovskii's sweeping memoir *Story of a Life* details his childhood and youth in the southwestern provinces and ends with his move north to Moscow after much wandering in the Civil War. Journalist Mikhail Kol'tsov (a.k.a. Fridliand) moved north from Kyiv after creating a name for himself both by dating theatre diva Vera Iureneva and by writing copy for the local Soviet newspaper. His brother, cartoonist Boris Efimov, joined him. Young actress Natalia Rozenel', née Sats, also moved north to Moscow; her second husband was former Kyiv theatre critic, now Bolshevik Commissar of Enlightenment, Anatolii Lunacharskii. In Kyiv the poet Osip Mandel'shtam met the artist Nadezhda Khazina, who studied at the painter Aleksandra Ekster's studio with artists and set designers Isaak Rabinovich and Aleksandr Tyshler. Jewish culturalists Peretz Markish, Dovid Bergel'son, Leyb Kvitko, and Der Nister (Pinchas Kaganovich) lingered in Kyiv, but ended up writing Yiddish modernism in Moscow, Warsaw, Berlin — and even back in Ukraine. And of course, after surviving much of the Civil War in Kyiv and wending his way through Odesa, Crimea, and the Caucasus, Mikhail Bulgakov came north to Moscow with the beginnings of a novel called *The White Guard*, detailing his experiences during the Civil War in his hometown of Kyiv. It would eventually become *Days of the Turbins*.[4]

The above list of cultural elites is staggering, and hardly complete. Whether fleeing pogroms, chasing new opportunities, or simply following the zeitgeist of the age to join the new movers and shakers in Moscow, the demographic shift from south to north proved one of the most significant factors in the creation of Soviet culture. Leningrad, to be sure, also offered opportunities for young artists, such as Kapler,

Kozintsev, and Iutkevich. Shlomo Vovsi, a young law student from Dvinsk studying at the university in Petrograd/Leningrad, fell in with the actors of Aleksei Granovskii's Jewish Chamber Theatre and soon left the law for the stage, after taking a new name, Solomon Mikhoels. Kharkiv's Isaak Dunaevskii and Odesa's Leonid Utesov first worked in jazz at the Leningrad Music Hall. But the next step, and what they all considered career advancement, was moving to Moscow.[5]

These young artists ended up in the new Soviet capital, often sharing living spaces and helping each other to secure a paying job. Bulgakov moved to Moscow from the Caucasus in September 1921 and started to scrape together freelance writing, including at Lito. After two years, in 1923, he began to write for *The Whistle* (Gudok), a comic literary journal coming out of the Railway Workers' Union whose pages trained an entire generation of writers, most of whom eventually became household names in the Soviet Union. Petrov's brother Kataev, for example, began working there in 1922 upon his arrival; he presumably helped secure his younger brother a staff position several years later. Bulgakov held himself aloof from the *Whistle* crowd; he saw the feuilletons as a means of funding his far grander artistic ambitions. His sister, however, dated Kataev, much to Bulgakov's displeasure. For these young artists the state was an opportunity: the jobs created by the state not only confirmed the importance of artistic culture in the new society, they also offered them a way to pursue their careers. The cultural products they created, such as Bulgakov's *Turbins*, became classics loved by audiences and readers and studied by several generations of scholars.[6]

Bulgakov drew from his own experience for *Turbins*, the story of a charming Russian intelligentsia family living in central Kyiv beset by the Bolsheviks, the Germans, and the Ukrainian nationalists during the Civil War. The Turbins' world had vanished; their loss mirrored Bulgakov's own. It seems that there was a stage production of an early version in Vladikavkaz in 1921, but it was his publication of *The White Guard* in the journal *Rossiia* in 1924 that sparked his friends' encouragement to theatricalize the story for the stage. A mere five years after arriving in Moscow, Bulgakov saw his play *Days of the Turbins* performed by the best actors at the Moscow Art Theatre, one of the best theatres in the entire Soviet Union.[7]

Part II: Mykola Kulish: The New Soviet Southwest

But Bulgakov's is not the only story of the 1920s. The milieu of *The Whistle*, the Moscow Art Theatre, and the apartments of central Moscow certainly proved a crucible for Soviet culture, but hardly the only one. After all, much of the region of the former southwest provinces became Soviet Ukraine, where artists and officials created an entirely new culture for this entirely new place. The creation of Soviet culture in Soviet Ukraine offers a parallel narrative, a story of cultural construction connected with that unfolding in Moscow, but diverging from it as well.

The creation of Soviet culture in Soviet Ukraine differs in two major ways from the creation of Soviet culture in Moscow. First of all, many of the artists in Soviet Ukraine were also officials. As such, they invested as much in the creation of a new state as in the creation of a new culture. The milieu of *The Whistle* certainly enjoyed their state-supported positions and were – to greater or lesser degrees – invested in the Communist project. But they (generally) did not fight in the Red Army and came to Moscow hoping for an artistic career. And Moscow was home, of course, to scores of pre-revolutionary artists, such as the artistic personnel of the Moscow Art Theatre where Bulgakov's *Turbins* would debut, attempting to make the transition to the new era. Soviet Ukraine, however, offered a place of opportunity for those who did not belong to the intelligentsia before the Civil War, but who rather climbed their way up through the military and party apparatus to garner the status to be able to write professionally. Far more common in Kharkiv's early beau monde than in Moscow's was a distinguished Red Army career, perhaps even underground party work during the Civil War, and close connection with those who became political elites in Soviet Ukraine.

Second, many of the artists in Soviet Ukraine were ethnically Ukrainian. For them, Soviet Ukrainian culture should be in the Ukrainian language and include a somehow "Ukrainian" content. Of course, articulating the precise form and content of that "Ukrainian" culture would turn out to be a complex and contested process. While artists in Moscow were building culture that was Soviet, artists in Soviet Ukraine were building culture that was both Soviet and Ukrainian. In this way, Soviet Ukraine was shaped by the introduction of *korenizatsiia*, indigenization, a series of policies pronounced in 1923 promoting ethnic cadres and the culture of each ethno-national unit in the Soviet Union. The idea was to promote Bolshevism in all the languages of the Union, and to promote ethnic cadres who had – perhaps – suffered under the tsarist yoke. In Soviet Ukraine these policies made up *ukrainizatsiia*, Ukrainization, and the implementation of these policies occurred simultaneously with expansion and experimentation in the arts.

Kulish and his fellows were the men of Ukrainization; the necessity of promoting Ukrainian-language cadres and culture made their careers and constituted the heart of their agenda. But Ukrainization posed a challenge for building that culture: how should artists articulate what was Soviet, what was Ukrainian, and what was Soviet Ukrainian? What did those categories mean to artists, to officials, and to audiences? For the political and cultural elites like Kulish making culture in the former Imperial Southwest in the 1920s the answer was clear: modern, urban, and excellent. But combining those qualities perceived as Soviet with qualitatively "Ukrainian" characteristics – previously understood as traditional and rural, oriented on the village – proved vexing. For a short time, these elites succeeded and created a series of cultural products that were modern, that were urban, that were excellent, and that were in Ukrainian. These men of Ukrainization were similar to Bulgakov and the *Whistle* milieu in their messianic élan of creating revolutionary art, a new Soviet art for a new socialist world. Yet they were also inspired by the equally messianic élan of building a new Ukraine, and a new Soviet Ukrainian art. This was the world of the literary fair.

The Literary Fair

Out of the crucible of war there emerged a new group of cultural elites coalescing in 1920s Kharkiv. Born at the end of the imperial age in the small towns and villages of the borderlands, these men acquired cultural authority during the Civil War and came together by the mid-1920s creating an early Soviet beau monde. They were former Red Army soldiers, idealistic Party members, or former artistic intelligentsia enjoying Red Army patronage, and they all shared the goal of creating culture both Soviet and Ukrainian. Soviet Ukrainian writer Iurii Smolych called these men, who constituted the milieu of his youth, the *literary fair*, in honour of a journal they sponsored, wrote, and read. The journal may not have lasted long – a mere twelve issues from 1928 to 1929 – but in Smolych's memoirs the term *literary fair* takes on wider significance. It conjures up for him not only the journal itself, but also the people and places behind the journal dominating the newspapers, journals, theatres, cafes, and police denunciations: in short, the entire world of 1920s Kharkiv. Smolych's colleagues, all the major talents of Kharkiv's Golden Age, wrote *Literary Fair* collectively, so each issue had a different editor. In its pages the editors advertised other journals and theatre productions, all the while referencing the cafes, clubs, and Party-state institutions where culture was created – and doing it all with a sense of wit and irony. Smolych's equation of *Literary Fair* with the era is apt: the literary fair was a journal, a place, a network of relationships, a mode of creating, in short, a catch-phrase for the world of the first generation of cultural elites leading the creation of Soviet Ukrainian culture. The literary fair was the first generation of a Soviet beau monde.[8]

From Red Army to Cultural Apparat

The imperial theatre network collapsed under the strain of the Civil War. Impresarios and theatre managers either emigrated, or could not come up with the money to sponsor troupes, or could not find performance space in cities overrun with violence and disease. The Red Army picked up the pieces and organized culture along front lines. Political divisions of the Red Army sponsored theatre troupes; in addition, many local Revolutionary Committees, Party Committees, and local branches of the Commissariat of Enlightenment sponsored various performance ensembles to entertain the local population and the troops. This was the case, for example, with Red Army general Iona Iakir's sponsorship of Les' Kurbas' troupe, travelling outside Kyiv in 1919 searching for food and safety. In Iurii Smolych's Zhmerynka, for another example, one of the new Soviet authority's first decrees was the mobilization of all local actors to form three troupes, one in Russian, one in Ukrainian, and one focusing on song and dance performances. These troupes may have been agitprop in intent, but their consequences went much further. Smolych, an artistically inclined small-town youth, for example, joined the "Red Army Theatre-Studio under the Military Commissariat of Zhmerynka District" and that association led him to professional theatre work, then to literary work in Kharkiv, and eventually elite status as a Soviet Ukrainian writer. Theatre sponsored by the Red Army, for Smolych as for many others, proved an entrée to both the world of art and the apparat.[9]

Smolych himself never served in the Imperial Army or the Red Army because he was too young. But military service often served as the gateway to positions in the cultural organs in Soviet Ukraine. Bulgakov may have worked only as a doctor, but most elites in early Soviet Ukraine were deeply involved in the Civil War, serving in the military and/or the Party organs. Future writer Oles' Skrypal' took the *nom de guerre* "Dosvitnyi," meaning "pre-dawn," referring perhaps to his contributions to the dawn of a new socialist age. He and his wife Mariia were early converts to Bolshevism and worked in the Communist underground in Poland attempting to foment revolution. They did not get far; as Dosvitnyi later told the story, a Polish Communist betrayed them and they spent eight months in a Polish prison and returned to Kyiv only in 1920. The couple worked on an agitprop train for several years that spread Bolshevik culture on the frontlines during Red Army battles against anarchist leader Nestor Makhno. From the Makhno period, Dosvitnyi preserved a defused grenade that would later come to play a pivotal role in his life: first an anecdotal object in his home enjoyed by his children, and then the "proof" of anti-Soviet plotting confiscated by the secret police during his arrest in 1933. But arrest was years away. Many members of the literary fair shared the common experience of battling at the dawn of socialism to build a new world on the frontlines of the Civil War.[10]

Mykola Kulish

Another such member of the literary fair was writer and activist Mykola Kulish. Kulish came from nowhere, but always had literary aspirations. He was born to a rural peasant family in 1892 in Kherson province. A poor village child desperate to acquire an education in order to pursue bigger and better dreams, he managed to move to Oleshky, a small town, but one bigger than a village, to attend school. He and his best friend, Ivan Shevchenko (whose literary pseudonym was *Dniprovs'kyi*, that is, of the Dnipro River, flowing southwards and cutting Ukraine in half), created a series of amateur journals using European *noms-de-plume*. Ivan was *Jean* (i.e., the French version of Ivan), or *Henrikh Kudriaha*, while Mykola was *Klaus* (i.e., Niklaus, the German version of Mykola) or *August Khaliava* (a word meaning "freebie," perhaps referring to the price of their amateur gazettes or "bootlegger," perhaps suggesting a touch of danger to small-town literary life). They used these playful nicknames throughout their correspondence until 1934, when Dniprovs'kyi died of tuberculosis and Kulish was arrested. His wife claimed that Kulish always wanted to have a literary career; how likely would that career have been possible for a poor kid from the middle of nowhere in the Russian empire?[11]

The war opened up possibilities, however. Kulish joined the tsarist army in 1914, sustained injuries on the Smolensk front, and by 1917 he had attained the rank of lieutenant. Following the February Revolution he served on his division's soldiers' committee. The tsarist army led to Party work back in Oleshky. He even survived a jail sentence during the German Hetmanate and was evacuated from Oleshky with the other local Party members. In 1919 Kulish officially joined the Communist Party. He also joined the Red Army and fought against Denikin, against Petliura, and against Wrangel' until the bitter end of the Civil War in 1922.[12]

From the imperial army to the Party and Red Army via soldiers' committees: Kulish was not the only one, certainly, to follow such a path, but his biography shows how powerful that path could be. A peasant child lucky to attend school with literary dreams, Kulish fought his way up the ranks to attain opportunities he would never have had in the empire. Kulish appears to have been a loyal and trusted Party and Red Army member, given his assignments and ranks. He was even given the task in late 1919, for example, to connect with underground Party organizations in the Oleshky area during the fight against Denikin.[13] He continued his work in the both the Party and the early Soviet state committees back in Oleshky. He also, it should be noted, edited the local paper. He must have been doing a good job, because he was soon promoted. In 1923 he became a member of the Collegium of the Odesa Regional Commissariat of Enlightenment, where he took up a position of authority: school inspector. He now tried to pursue his dreams of the fulfilling the Soviet project and a literary career with equal passion.[14]

Kulish's job as a school inspector made it difficult for him to pursue his writing: "Early in the morning I get up, hurriedly eat breakfast and go to work in the city. Trams, offices, commissions, receiving hours, circulars, operational plans, kids, smoke, fumes – and all the same up until the evening. In the evening, already after sunset, I return home. Well, of course, my mood is as if I'd boiled the whole day in a cauldron." He often wrote to Olimpiia Korneeva-Maslovaia, a young teacher with whom Kulish had started an affair, with his impressions from his business trips: "Dirt and shadows, and I am again at the window in a train car ... Hello emptiness of the steppe ... There is talk of markets, the smell of leather, talk of horses and nails, and covering my eyes with my hands, I think of you." Still, Kulish managed to find the time to write a play, *97*, which told the story of a zealous and heroic Communist, Musii Kopystka, taking charge during a famine. Kulish's childhood friend Dniprovs'kyi (a.k.a. Zhan), already established in literary circles in Kharkiv, read the play, liked it, and managed to get it staged.[15]

Because he wanted to write, Kulish hungered for information about the literary and theatrical world in Kharkiv. He wrote Dniprovs'kyi that he "was eager to know what's happening in the literary circles, at least in Kharkiv, who's fighting with whom, who's taking whose bread, who's on the bottom, who's on Olympus. As they say – the back-stage, what's happening in the wings." He wanted to understand the "meaning" that people were ascribing to literature: "About the role of literature before the revolution I know, but now – I can't figure it out. I'm only guessing that the revolution pushed it from the sticks to the threshold, to an 'important' place. Literature, art now lives as a ser-vant and not the mistress. Is that right?" Kulish revealed his percep-tivity; certainly, it seemed that literature had taken up an important place, managed and promoted, as it was, by CP(b)U Central Committee members, and discussed at Soviet Ukrainian Politburo meetings, but in that important world of officialdom, literature was only a servant. His query suggests that he could not figure out what was happening "backstage" from Odesa.[16]

Kulish was far from blind to the difficult nature of the task of building Communism in Soviet Ukraine. In 1924 he wrote Dniprovs'kyi, "The green path is creeping behind me, and on it lie my blue and red dreams all beaten and scattered. By now you can't go back and get rid of it. My life (and maybe yours too my friend) is already being covered by evening shadows. It's getting darker, devil take it." He was particularly dismayed when he ran afoul of rising apparatchik Andrii Khvylia, who ordered him relocated from the big city of Odesa to the comparative rural depths of Elizavetgrad, now renamed Zinovievs'k, and dubbed by Kulish "Eldabesht." He complained to Dniprovs'kyi that Khvylia had removed him from the Odesa apparat precisely "in order that some of his people stay in Odesa." Indeed, Khyvlia was building up his own circle – and that network did not include Kulish. Despite all, Kulish was a believer. He wrote to his mistress, "I love revolution and struggle. I love the Party – because only in its path is the start of a new life ... I often say to myself: these are my personal sufferings in comparison with the sufferings of those who cannot even write about their sufferings." Kul-ish was worried about his fate during an Odesa regional Party purge, but wrote Dniprovs'kyi in relief that "everyone was convinced" that he was "a good Party man." To remain in the Party and the struggle, then, was crucial to Kulish – despite his "dreams all beaten and scattered."[17]

Kulish's letters reflect his desire to observe every moment of the extraordinary time in which he was living; he pursued his job, his mistress, and his literary passions with equal energy. He also seems to have believed in a special place for Soviet Ukraine in emerging Soviet culture. He wrote his friend that he should focus on humour: "Ukraine should give out the best Mark Twains in the world. And Mark Twains will never die out. Laughter, a smile through tears – this is rain for parched earth." Ukraine, then, could provide the "best Mark Twains" – better than Moscow? than Europe? – and yet still be part of larger Soviet culture.[18]

Kulish visited Kharkiv several times, and his letters suggest his desire to stay there permanently: "And the horses in Kharkiv are good, and the people, and everything, my brother, is good."[19] Finally, the republic-level Central Committee of the CP(b)U transferred Kulish to Kharkiv because he was "needed ... as a red writer." The Red Army had opened up for Kulish not only a world of ideas, then, but also a world of opportunity: posts in Party and state committees that he executed well, and literary connections to pursue his artistic dreams.[20] Yet Kulish wrote his mistress soon after his arrival, disappointed:

> I thought I'd find friends here, advisors, but I've looked around – there aren't any. Details, politicking, envy, competition, gossip, stiltedness, falseness and old age, old age all dressed up in an official's uniform – that's the literary field. There are certain wonderful workers, but they wisely hide their creativity and thinking in the sink.[21]

Still, Kulish dove into artistic and official life in the capital of the Soviet Ukrainian republic. He eventually pursued a staggering number of positions: he served on the Higher Repertory Committee, the board of the Literary Club, multiple writers' organizations, multiple educational organizations, and several literary journals. In fact, the journal *Literary Fair* made a joke on how involved Kulish was in local and republic-level institutions. Explaining why Kulish only wrote on Sundays while taking a bath, the editors lamented Kulish's overinvolvement:

> The thing is, our esteemed creator devotes Monday to the Repertory Committee (he's a member of the Presidium of the Repertory Committee), but Tuesday is perforce given to the Ukrainian Society of Playwrights and Composers (he's the head of the Society), Wednesday is devoted to the Committee For School Aid (he's a member of the "Committee for School Aid"), but Thursday perforce to the Literary Club (he's a member of the Presidium of the Literary Club), Friday he devotes to the Housing Cooperative (he is, if we are not mistaken, President), but perforce Saturday to "Red Path" (he is, if we are not mistaken, a member of the Editorial Board).[22]

For Kulish, the revolution was all. He wanted to capture his experience in writing: "1914-1922 (the war and revolution) will not leave me until I pour it out on paper in words that are alive and in clumps of truth." Indeed, the revolution, the Civil War, and the challenges both tragic and comic in building early Soviet culture would provide the inspiration for all of his plays.[23]

The World of Kharkiv

Iurii Smolych claims responsibility and credit for transferring Kulish from "Eldabesht" to Kharkiv. This may not be entirely correct, but Smolych's patron certainly must have been involved. The centre of most cultural activity in the new republic from 1920 to 1925, in fact, was Vasyl' Ellan-Blakytnyi's office in Kharkiv. Born Vasyl' Ellans'kyi, he published as a poet in the late Civil War under the name Vasyl' Ellan, and worked in the Party-state apparat as Vasyl' Blakytnyi. Blakytnyi, or "blue" in Ukrainian, could have carried a variety of resonances for the activist: the blue of the Ukrainian flag, or the world of dreams, or the idealism of a new Ukrainian state in a post-revolutionary and post-imperial world. Blakytnyi, like the images suggested by his political nom-de-plume, was an idealist, a socialist, a Ukrainian, and a poet. He was one of the leading *Borot'bisty*, essentially Left Socialist Revolutionaries who took their name from their party journal, *The Struggle* (Borot'ba), edited by Ellan-Blakytnyi. In fact, most of the cultural elites in the new Soviet Ukrainian republic were Borot'bisty. Borot'bist, importantly, did not signify anti-Soviet (after all, they were socialists, even if more Socialist Revolutionaries than Bolsheviks), but rather Soviet and Ukrainian, which was not a dichotomy at the time. Together with Oleksandr Shums'kyi, Blakytnyi led the joining of the Borot'bisty to the Bolsheviks in March 1920 at the Fourth Conference of the CP(b)U, the Communist Party (Bolsheviks) of Ukraine.[24]

In early Soviet Kharkiv, Shums'kyi and Blakytnyi were central figures in the Party and the state apparat. Both served on the CP(b)U's Central Committee, and Shums'kyi ran the Soviet Ukrainian People's Commissariat of Enlightenment and edited the journal *Red Path* (Chervonyi Shliakh). Blakytnyi served on the All-Ukrainian Central Executive Committee, edited the Committee's newspaper, *News* (Visti), and could be found almost any time of day or night in his long and narrow office on the second floor of Eleven Sums'ka Street. Blakytnyi took the artistic élan of the wartime years and combined it with the organizational energy of the early Soviet state. By providing jobs to Red Army veterans and identifying talented young people interested in building a new culture, he and Shums'kyi essentially created the literary fair.[25]

Perhaps Shums'kyi's most celebrated protégé was Mykola Khvyl'ovyi.

Mykola Khvyl'ovyi: The Agitator

Khvyl'ovyi was born Fitil'ev in a village near Sumy to a teacher's family. His pseudonym might have come from the verb *khvyliuvaty*, to agitate: Khvyl'ovyi was truly an agitator. Like Kulish, he had basic education, but no university, and like Kulish, he was drafted into the Imperial Army. After serving in the "Volhynian swamps," Bukovina, Romania, Galicia, and Poland, he joined the Red Army and fought in the Civil War. Like Kulish, he distinguished himself in military service and rose through the ranks. Khvyl'ovyi joined the Communist Party in 1919, like Kulish. He was demobilized in 1922 and published his first work in Kharkiv, eventually becoming a major literary figure and editing *Red Path*. In 1924 he wrote an autobiography in which he claimed that he was intellectually committed, but questioned his own commitment: "I am struggling with this question – whether I have the right to carry a party card, am I ballast for the Party? ... in me there is a romantic, a dreamer – there's always an inner struggle." He concluded by saying he was, maybe, more of a *communard* than a Communist.[26]

The Agitator was, however, a committed communard, even if not a self-identified Communist in this one moment. And he was deeply committed to building Soviet society. In 1928 he wrote a friend in defence of a short story that had been fodder for classifying him as anti-Soviet: "I am disappointed that even you thought that this was a sign of me leaving the Communist Party. Not only am I am not going to give up my party ticket, but I'll even go to Stalin himself if someone tries to do it for me."[27] He argued in 1926 that the best path for Soviet Ukraine culturally was Europe, because Moscow had fallen: "Moscow has powerful traditions that profoundly create petty bourgeoisie [*meshchanstvo*]. Moscow as Moscow (and even Russia without Siberia), in essence, did not see the October Revolution and its heroic struggle." Moscow, therefore, and by extension Russian culture, could offer no help for Soviet Ukraine; rather, they should turn towards Europe. Khvyl'ovyi's scandalous pamphlets made their way to the Kremlin, but Shums'kyi reminded the Soviet Ukrainian Politburo that Khvyl'ovyi, "was taken from the factory into the Army, where he spent the whole Civil War ... he arrived half-literate in the city in 1922 and in the space of three years he has achieved a high level of culture and development. This is a talented writer and person."[28]

Blakytnyi's Protégés

Blakytnyi, like Shums'kyi, patronized and connected artistic youth who might not have had the most pristine political records. Blakytnyi started a group in 1923 called *HART* (Tempering), designed to serve as an umbrella organization for creating Soviet culture throughout Soviet Ukraine with branches in Kharkiv, Kyiv, and Odesa, and supporting all kinds of cultural production. Most of the literary fair started their Soviet Ukrainian artistic careers in HART. Blakytnyi's childhood friend, poet Pavlo Tychyna, who was neither in the Party nor in the army but used his symbolist poetry to support socialism, involved himself in the organization.[29]

Blakytnyi, however, even recruited cultural figures from non-Soviet spheres. He used his connections, for example, to release writer Pavlo Hubenko (who had been with the non-Bolshevik UNR, Symon Petliura's Ukrainian People's Republic, in Kamianets'-Podil's'kyi) from secret police imprisonment in 1921. Blakytnyi then gave Hubenko a job as a Ukrainian translator for *News*; writers like him were needed in the age of Ukrainization because so few cultural elites actually knew the intricacies of the written Ukrainian language. Soon Hubenko discovered his talents as a humorist writer, renamed himself *Ostap Vyshnia* (i.e., Ostap Cherry), and quickly became the most widely read writer in Soviet Ukraine. Hubenko-Vyshnia later wrote that he was one of many who *perepetliurylysia*, who "went through a Petliura phase," during the Civil War. When in 1925 the Ukrainian Politburo objected to a feuilleton of Vyshnia's, they chastised Blakytnyi for publishing it and trusted Blakytnyi to remove the offensive piece. From managing writers, to reporting data on books, to journal organization, the Central Committee of the CP(b)U and the Ukrainian Commissariat turned to Blakytnyi, the Soviet Ukrainian Party-state's point person for all matters cultural.[30]

Iurii Smolych was another one of Blakytnyi's early protégées. Smolych, who started his artistic career in the troupes sponsored by the Red Army in Zhmerynka, joined a non-military theatre and came with that company to Kharkiv in 1923. Blakytnyi then hired Smolych to run the theatre division of HART aimed at uniting amateur drama groups throughout urban and village areas. The position brought Smolych to

HART and gave him – a youngster who had started acting only a few years earlier – an incredible amount of authority in the early Soviet cultural field. Smolych describes Blakytnyi as his literary mentor, his Party sponsor, and, in short, the most influential figure in his personal, intellectual, and artistic development. Through Blakytnyi Smolych received a promotion: Inspector of Theatres in the People's Commissariat of Enlightenment's Arts Department. Like Kulish, Smolych had risen in an extraordinarily short period of time to a position of authority in this new Soviet Ukrainian state.[31]

Politicking and Gossip

Nor was Kulish wrong about the "politicking, envy, competition, gossip" characterizing early Soviet Kharkiv. Perhaps such are the ingredients of any artistic milieu, especially one with high stakes in revolutionary times. Kharkiv was full of men like Kulish: talented and ambitious former lower-class imperial subjects who had risen through the ranks and now wanted success for themselves and to change the world. Kulish was also typical in his involvement in both cultural and political activities. Indeed, the cultural and the political were inextricable from the very beginnings of the early Soviet Ukrainian state.

The manoeuvring on the literary field was inseparable from the Soviet Ukrainian Politburo. One brief example shows the way that artistic and official worlds overlapped: Kruchynin, the deputy head of the Arts Department of the Commissariat of Enlightenment, wrote the Central Committee a memo describing literary groups in Soviet Ukraine. This would be unremarkable, except that the memo was deeply biased. This was because Kruchynin led the VUSPP, the All-Ukrainian Union of Proletarian Writers, one of the major literary groups, and one directly opposed to Blakytnyi's HART. Kruchynin noted in detail that although HART, which had eighty-five members filling three divisions in Kharkiv, Kyiv, and Odesa, had promoted famous writers Tychyna and Khvyl'ovyi, "it has not paid enough attention to national minorities or to the working masses." VUSPP in contrast, argued Kruchynin, had more members in more branches (160 members over six branches), boasted a Jewish section and a Russian section (as opposed to the exclusively Ukrainian HART), and was more connected with the proletariat, at least as Kruchynin saw it. Culture was indistinguishable from officialdom: Kruchynin headed VUSPP, but his boss was Mykola Khrystovyi, who was committed to Blakytnyi's HART. In one office managing culture were representatives from cultural opponents. The internecine literary battles intertwined with political tensions as the world of letters connected to the Commissariat of Enlightenment, which connected to the Soviet Ukrainian Politburo.[32]

Stalin's right hand, Lazar Kaganovich, was General Secretary of the Soviet Ukrainian Politburo from 1925 to 1928; his protégé, Veniamin "Fusia" Furer, ran one of the major newspapers and socialized with Mykola Khvyl'ovyi. Khvyl'ovyi, however, was a protégé of Shums'kyi, who was opposed to Kaganovich. The Soviet Ukrainian Politburo officially declared that they rejected any one literary group's claim to represent Soviet Ukrainian art and stated that "not even HART could claim singular representation of the Party in this sphere of artistic literature and on a monopoly of carrying through the Party line in this sphere." Still, the Politburo supported HART "because any activity against HART is nationalist, harmful to the Party" and – perhaps most importantly – the most "vital and talented forces in contemporary Ukrainian literature and poetry" were members of HART.[33] Note that questions of culture necessitated discussion at the highest level of the Soviet Ukrainian Politburo – and why not? Blakytnyi, Shums'kyi, and Kaganovich all understood that they were indeed creating a culture as much as an economy and a political structure. The enormity of this task demanded a huge organizational capacity, which leading Bolsheviks managed to fill with aspiring artists like Smolych and with Red Army veterans like Kulish.

The task before this first generation creating Soviet Ukrainian culture both energized these early elites and fractured their ranks. Khvyl'ovyi drew many new cultural elites towards himself and away from Blakytnyi in search of quality over mass, at least as he saw it. Smolych argues in his memoirs that anti-Khvyl'ovism emerged not from the Party but from Blakytnyi himself. The stakes were so high precisely because the task was so great: creating Soviet Ukrainian culture, and deciding what the arts' relationship to the people would be. Smolych remembers one tense meeting in Blakytnyi's office where Khvyl'ovyi cut Blakytnyi to the quick: "The apparatchik Vasyl' Blakytnyi has strangled the poet Vasyl' Ellan." Blakytnyi, describes Smolych, put his head in his hands and replied, "Cain." The literary fair could be brutal.[34]

Perhaps the most influential and provocative journal was that formed by Khvyl'ovyi shortly after Blakytnyi's death in 1925: *VAPLITE*, the Free Association of Proletarian Literature, which promoted excellence as opposed to massism. Its members wanted the journal to serve as a platform creating modern, urban culture, both Soviet and Ukrainian, as the editorial board understood those two categories. Briefly, if Blakytnyi wanted, through HART, to spread Ukrainian-language culture to the masses, Khvyl'ovyi wanted to create high Ukrainian-language culture that might have little to do with the masses: "For proletarian creative literature there is no doubt that the Soviet *intelligent* Zerov, who is armed with the higher mathematics of art, is–hyperbolically speaking – a million times more useful than a hundred *prosvita*-types who understand art as well as a pig does orange-growing." For Khvyl'ovyi Soviet Ukrainian culture was not simply "a few red phrases" with Ukrainian endings, but a culture somehow both simultaneously all its own, and yet belonging to the larger Soviet whole. The tragedy would be returning to *prosvita*, to the Russian imperial-era educational and cultural organizations that sponsored a folkish Ukrainian culture of village dances, songs, and verses by nineteenth-century poet Taras Shevchenko. The way to avoid this tragedy, argued Khvyl'ovyi provocatively, was Europe. As a believer in the socialist project, Khvyl'ovyi did not mean that Soviet Ukraine should turn to bourgeois capitalism. But he did mean that the centuries of European culture, as he understood it, offered an alternative path for artists and officials making culture in Soviet Ukraine. As opposed to resigning themselves to being secondary to Moscow, they could take advantage of Soviet Ukraine's past and turn to Europe for cultural inspiration.[35]

The men in Khvyl'ovyi's VAPLITE, and they were indeed all men, formed the core of cultural elites in Kharkiv. It was these men who would go on to create *Literary Fair*, and dominate the cultural world of 1920s Kharkiv. They did so, however, not individually, but collectively, through journals, debates, and late-night socializing. As organized by Blakytnyi, Soviet culture happened in these milieus. Everyone who was anyone in Soviet Ukraine was in Kharkiv; cultural production and consumption centred on that beau monde of insiders. In other words, what emerged in Kharkiv, through Blakytnyi, Shums'kyi, Khvyl'ovyi, Vyshnia, Kulish, and others, was not just a renaissance in Ukrainian letters, but a milieu creating that renaissance.[36]

Vasyl' Ellan-Blakytnyi died in 1925, but his organizational efforts left a structural legacy in Soviet Ukrainian culture. The Blakytnyi Literary House (Literaturnyi budynok imeni Blakytn'oho) was founded in 1925 as a writers' club at number 4 Kaplunivs'ka Street in the centre of Kharkiv near all central political and cultural institutions. The Literary Club quickly became a locus of elite sociability. Rather than

Blakytnyi's office, now the Literary Club hosted debates, fights both verbal and physical, and parties in its rooms, including the billiard hall in its basement. Khvyl'ovyi became the central figure shaping Soviet culture in Ukraine with VAPLITE, and several officials took over Blakytnyi's role of Party-state patron: two such were editor Veniamin "Fusia" Furer, close to Kaganovich, and editor Borys "Boba" Lifshyts', who had headed the Kyiv affiliate of HART. Blakytnyi may have taken the first steps in creating a new cultural milieu from the chaos of the Civil War, but the movers and shakers of Ukrainian Soviet culture wove together a dense network of people and places reorganizing urban space in Kharkiv, and contributing to reorganizing the cultural topography of the former Imperial Southwest.[37]

Despite his initial misgivings, Kulish did quickly link up with simpatico cultural elites in Kharkiv. Antonina Kulish described the group that gathered frequently around their kitchen table: her husband; Ostap Vyshnia, who kept his hands in his pockets and complained of rheumatism until Kulish poured him a vodka; Pavlo Tychyna, the lone vegetarian for whom Antonina's mother made onion-filled dumplings; and Mykola Khvyl'ovyi, who "smoked non-stop and could never sit peacefully in one place." These men felt "full responsibility for the future of the new art," and believed that it was up to them to make culture for Soviet Ukraine.[38]

One other figure would be crucial for Kulish's life and work, and for the literary fair: theatre director Les' Kurbas. As the literary fair was coalescing in Kharkiv, Kurbas was building a theatrical empire based in Kyiv based around his Artistic Organization Berezil' (Mystets'ke ob'iednannia Berezil', or MOB), founded in 1922. This organization mushroomed to include over 300 members (artistic and technical), six workshops including outposts in Bila Tserkva and Boryspil', a directors' laboratory, a museum, and a published journal. Kurbas not only directed productions but also taught his acting company, mentored and supervised the young directors, micro-managed design and managerial decisions, secured funds from almost every city and regional (oblast') Party or state institution, took over Kyiv's former Solovtsov Theatre (renamed the Lenin Theatre) and received an official title of People's Artist of the Republic – and all by 1925. When the Party-state finally transferred the Berezil' to Kharkiv in 1926 and the Kyiv regional Commissariat of Enlightenment was preparing to honour the theatre company publicly, it compiled a list of the organizations that would take part: the Regional Party Committee, the Regional Executive

Committee, the City Council, the regional branch of the Arts Workers' Union, and the 45th Division of the Red Army. The Berezil' was not simply a theatre, but a city institution.[39]

Despite their subsidies and success, Kurbas was not satisfied. Soviet Kharkiv, not Kyiv, was now the cultural centre of Soviet Ukraine. Kyiv was merely "a province," as Kurbas told his actors. Kurbas wanted to make a great theatre, and he could not do that in the provinces. He wanted a theatre that was a "social institution that's needed," where the "need lives in the spectator ... like a restaurant, or office, or something else: I go to such and such a theatre because I have to go there, because I often go there." "We don't have that kind of theatre right now," he concluded, "we are not yet that theatre, but the historic task of this moment is to found that theatre." Indeed, the Berezil' Theatre would soon become an important centre in the personal and professional networks in Kharkiv, the locus of early Soviet creativity and exchange: the literary fair.[40]

Figure 2.1. Meeting of Kurbas' Director's Lab, Kyiv 1924. Kurbas is sitting fifth from left (TsDKFFA 0-149777)

Part III: The Literary Fair: Artists and Officials

By the mid-1920s the literary fair had emerged as a milieu of those artists, officials, and artist-officials shaping culture in Soviet Ukraine. The boundaries between artists and officials were dissolving – with writers working for the state, state officials editing newspapers, and personal and professional links tying the world of letters together with the theatre, the Party-state, and the police. Rather than artist or official, the more meaningful division seems to have been between those in the literary fair and those outside it as artists and officials circulated in the small world of early Soviet Kharkiv.

Literary Fair was a journal started by Khvyl'ovyi, each issue of which was supervised by a different editor-member of the milieu of cultural elites. More than a journal, however, the literary fair was a world of artists and officials circulating in the centre of Kharkiv publishing, writing, performing, socializing, drinking, as they made culture that was Soviet and that was Ukrainian. As exemplified by the journal, they created collectively – together, not as individuals. Like a market, they negotiated, exchanged, bought, and sold culture. Like a fair, they exuded energy and the messianic élan of building socialist culture. It was, as Smolych describes, a great deal of fun: "In general that was a happy and reckless time." The 1920s were the "years of the stormy growth of the literary boheme, the intoxicating time of literary *kozakuvannia*, the era of *Literary Fair*." Smolych's memoirs trace the geography of the literary fair, which took place in Kharkiv's Latin Quarter. Just like the *quartier latin* in Paris, the publishing heart of Kharkiv took place in a dense network of streets, institutions, and people in the city centre:

> On the sidewalks of these three blocks you could always meet with a writer or editorial worker: here were exchanged literary news and editorial sensations. Here you could "sell" and "buy" verse, poems, stories, plays and novels. And here, having stopped in to the publishing house or the editors' office, you could catch hold of an advance and immediately "exchange" it – in Café Pok, at Parfishka's restaurant at the billiard hall, or in the restaurant "Business club" on the corner of Rymarska Street.[41]

Iarmarok, or "fair," also means "market," of course, and the literary fair constituted the early Soviet cultural market, the source of patronage and barometer of supply and demand in non-capitalist Soviet culture. This exchange occurred among worlds often thought of as separate: the arts, the Party-state, and the police.[42]

!.Галло! Галло! Усім! Усім! Усім! Говорить Ярмарком „Літературного Ярмарку" на хвилі 500.000 метрів із міста Харкова, столиці Української Соціялістичної Радянської Республіки. Читайте, шановні товариші, чергову 135 книгу нашого позагрупового альманаху!

Figure 2.2. *Literary Fair* frontispiece (author's collection)

The Literary Fair and the Party-State

Theatre Square marked the cultural heart of Kharkiv. The former nineteenth-century villa housing the publishers *Soviet Village* (Radians'ke selo) headed by Fusia Furer – patron and Kaganovich client – stood on one side of Theatre Square. The newspaper *The Proletarian* (Proletar') occupied two floors in another nineteenth-century villa housing the state's central news organ, *News* (Visti), on the other side of the square. Boba Lifshyts', the editor, kept his door open and ran a game of chess all day; the loser had to write a column for the next day's issue. In the *News* building one could find editorial offices and, in the basement, a billiard hall and restaurant run by a celebrated billiard player, Parfishka. The literary fair wrote for the newspapers and writers socialized with Boba and Fusia in their editorial offices, over billiards, and in Café Pok, which stood near Theatre Square behind Kurbas' Berezil' Theatre. Artist Anatol' Petryts'kyi painted portraits of the literary fair, about 150 of the cultural and political elite of Kharkiv – from Party-state officials like Oleksandr Shums'kyi and Fusia Furer, to writers and artists like Kurbas and Smolych. The portraits hung in an exhibit in the Writers' Club and were published in a book by the State Publishing Agency DVU headed, of course, by a fellow member of the literary fair. Petryts'kyi's portrait of futurist provocateur Mykhail Semenko placed the poet at a cafe sitting across from an anonymous blond in a swirl of tobacco smoke. Indeed it was a café – Café Pok, according to Smolych – that served as the "office" for Semenko and his literary journal, *New Generation*.[43]

Between the two newspaper buildings on Theatre Square stood the Berezil', a music box-shaped nineteenth-century theatre, where Les Kurbas ruled the theatrical landscape.

Kurbas and Kulish had never met before 1926, but once Kurbas moved to Kharkiv, the two became not only friends but also colleagues; their best work would be together. Kulish started to write exclusively for the Berezil' and the theatre's most talked-about Kharkiv productions, *The People's Malakhii*, *Myna Mazailo*, and *Maklena Grasa*, were all Kulish-Kurbas collaborations. Kurbas now had a theatre that was indeed a "social institution" – people may have hated or loved the Berezil', but it was always the talk of the town. Fusia Furer and Boba Lifshyts' were avid supporters of the Berezil', and would defend the widely condemned 1927 Kurbas production of Kulish's *The People's Malakhii*. Furer would write the Repertory Commission a passionate

Figure 2.3. Berezil' theatre, 2006 (author's collection)

defence of the play, liaise with the Politburo over theatre reviews in his paper, and eventually head the Berezil''s own Artistic-Political Council (Khudpolitrad).[44]

Khvyl'ovyi's journal *Literary Fair* included witty interludes, *intermediia*. The editors claimed that the sketches "were written in the corridors of the Berezil'," or in Café Pok, or even in the elevator of a hotel "assisted by a Ukrainian ballerina." Indeed, the Berezil' offered not only a place of presenting and seeing theatre but also a space of sociability. The literary fair wrote, acted in, directed, discussed, reviewed, or simply saw every Berezil' production, so the theatre became a touchstone in the world of elites in Kharkiv. Smolych notes that all the critics, whose journals or papers enjoyed permanent seats in the theatres would gather at intermission to discuss the production and decide what they would write in their reviews; criticism, as Smolych describes it, was a collective effort. One *Literary Fair* issue featured literary sketches on automobiles. Apparently, during a premiere at the

Berezil', Boba Lifshyts' had urged the editor of that particular issue to encourage writers to create comic sketches inspired by the theme of the automobile. Thanks to a conversation in the theatre, the desired automobile sketches appeared in the journal. From the far side of Theatre Square extended Artem Street, home of the Commissariat of Enlightenment, the state institution running the arts headed by Blakytnyi's colleague and fellow patron, Shums'kyi. Here Smolych worked, and here arts officials organized cadres, their salaries and contracts, and their repertory across a network of theatres. The journal, the theatre, the editors, the writers, and the actors were all part of the same milieu.[45]

Kaganovich, First Secretary of the Central Committee of the CP(b)U, was close to Stalin, removed from the former-Borot'bist group of Shums'kyi and Blakytnyi, and had his own people. Yet he still actively concerned himself with literature and received reports on the literary scene, including from personal informers. His protégé, Fusia Furer, who ran the newspaper *Soviet Village*, was a major patron of the arts. Actor Iosyp Hirniak, however, writing his memoirs in emigration claimed that Furer was a stooge who reported on all artistic activity, and all personal activity of artists, to Kaganovich. Yet Furer vigorously defended Hirniak's theatre, the Berezil', at the Higher Repertory Commission and the Soviet Ukrainian Politburo. Writer Arkadii Liubchenko claimed that Raisa Azarkh, Party member and arts patron, also personally informed on her clients to Kaganovich. Yet Liubchenko also admits that Azarkh helped arranged Khvyl'ovyi's trip abroad in 1927, and that Khvyl'ovyi knew Azarkh was informing on him and used that to his advantage. Kaganovich's milieu and the literary fair overlapped; who was using whom?[46]

The Party-state also furnished artists with housing, which in the 1920s meant subsidized rooms in hotels. The leading lights of the Berezil' rented rooms in a dormitory on the Zhatkinskii alley near the river. Smolych called it the *Villa Zhatkina*, named after its former aristocratic inhabitant. The villa had enjoyed a pre-revolutionary incarnation as a cabaret offering rooms where customers could become more intimately acquainted with the performers after the show. In this former theatre-brothel Kurbas lived with his mother, Vanda Ianovych (Yanovych), a former actress from Galicia who never learned Russian, and his wife, Valentyna Chystiakova, an ethnic Russian who learned Ukrainian when she fell in love with Kurbas in civil war Kyiv. Down the hall lived the Petryts'kyi couple and lead Berezil' actress Natalia Uzhvii, married to poet and Café Pok-denizen Mykhail' Semenko.[47]

Such personal connections bound the literary fair together. Several actresses married writers. Actress Varvara Masliuchenko married Ostap Vyshnia. Vyshnia wrote for *News* and his brother Vasyl' Chechniavs'kyi wrote for *Red Pepper*, a humour journal published under the auspices of Lifshyts' *The Proletarian*. Caricatures in *Red Pepper* in the late 1920s once offended certain Politburo members and the Politburo removed Lifshyts' as head of the *Pepper*. Not only did the Politburo read *Red Pepper*, then, they also understood its cultural value and when a caricature might have negative political consequences.[48]

The network of connections comprising the literary fair structured sociability in the early Soviet world. The literary fair organized the urban space of Kharkiv, marking the important centres, such as the Writers' Club, or the Berezil' Theatre, or Café Pok, and creating a network of elites who knew each other and worked together in the important institutions, such as the newspapers, the Commissariat of Enlightenment, and the Party. But the literary fair itself became an institution; it was through the sociability of the literary fair, such as drinking at Café Pok, playing billiards in the basement of *News*, or chatting in the corridors backstage at the Berezil', that the Soviet cultural infrastructure emerged.

The Literary Fair and the Police

The State Political Administration (GPU, forerunner to the NKVD and KGB), from its headquarters a few blocks from Theatre Square, was thoroughly briefed on the world of the literary fair through its own network of informers. Sources sporting nicknames like "Marxist," "Engineer," and "Literary Man" reported to the GPU, whose officers then summarized the information in order to "illuminate" certain circles. "Donbas Man," for example, informed that editor Boba Lifshyts' drank in a hotel until 2 a.m. with various literary figures. He further claimed that another writer claimed that Khvyl'ovyi was looking for protection and found it at *The Proletarian*, where Lifshyts' had recently hosted a banquet for artists Khvyl'ovyi, Petryts'kyi, Smolych, and others. Sources reported not only on extracurricular activities but also briefed the GPU officers on the content of the literary world. Screenplay Writer summarized the first issue of *Literary Fair*, and Donbas Man and Marxist denounced the second issue, which contained a satire on literary disputes entitled "The Green Mare." Marxist noted that it was written by Ivan (a.k.a. Israel) Kulyk, which shows Marxist's proximity to the fair because Kulyk never listed his name as the author of the piece. The literary fair and police circles moved in tandem, since the GPU tracked the moves of the cultural elite. Moreover, many of those giving information to the GPU were themselves part of the literary fair, and so were contributing to the dance with the information they were able to give, whether truthful or not, whether forced or not. GPU reports demand circumspect reading – violent force, jealousy, desperation, or flights of imagination may have produced these illuminations. However, their existence, whether from a writer's mind, a jealous informer's tip, or a GPU agent's suspicions, speaks to an obsession with literary and cultural elites and illuminates the world of interwar Kharkiv very well.[49]

The GPU, however, was actively involved in culture not only to suppress but also to create a Soviet artistic culture. The Second Section in the new Poland, just across the border from Soviet Ukraine, was also heavily involved in artistic censorship, but Polish agents censored texts in order to protect the interests of the state, not to create a new "Polish" culture. Soviet GPU officials, by contrast, served on various repertory committees approving each theatre's season and actively participated in the process of culling and solidifying repertory. GPU officers sorted through hundreds of comedy sketches and dance routines, as well as the more dramatic full-length plays, in order to determine suitability for performance. Officers often voiced aesthetic or personal opinions about the quality of the material with the officials and artists also serving on repertory committees and seem to have considered themselves integral in creating Soviet Ukrainian culture. The GPU structurally overlapped, then, both overtly (on repertory commissions working with literary fair members) and covertly (in the denunciations between informers and officers) with the cultural elites. Rather than the GPU as an agent of (exclusive) oppression operating against the artists, the GPU emerges from the documents as intimately connected with the literary fair, and as such, proactively involved in shaping culture.[50]

As well as a partner (albeit a strange one) in creating culture, the police constituted an everyday fact of life for the literary fair. Antonina Kulish wrote that Dniprovs'kyi once drunkenly and tearfully confessed to Kulish, his best friend from childhood, that he was informing on him to the GPU. He promised Kulish, however, that he never gave anything compromising to his police handlers. Given that Khvyl'ovyi had a file, which attests to a surprising number of acquaintances informing on him, Kulish must have had a file, and must have had informants in his personal and professional circles. There is no reason to doubt Antonina

Kulish's memory of Dniprovs'kyi's tears; there is equally no reason, however, to doubt the genuineness of the friendship between Kulish and Dniprovs'kyi, or doubt Dniprovs'kyi's sincerity when, in his letters, he calls Kulish "dear Klaus, the only friend of my soul." Such, in short, were the times. The GPU was part of the literary fair, and one characteristic of the literary fair was that its members informed to or were informed on at the GPU.[51]

The Literary Fair and Play

What was the literary fair at its essence? It was connections between officialdom and artists that enabled Soviet culture to emerge. These were connections of friendship, romance, work, and surveillance that created a network enabling and shaping culture. Soviet culture existed in a collective – these early Soviets lived together, drank together, created together, wrote together, and ruled together. The literary fair reveals the fluidity between the Party committee, the editorial office, the billiard hall, the apartment, and the theatre. The literary fair overflows with anecdotes, from the serious (Blakytnyi and Khvyl'ovyi's tense exchange) to the absurd (the endless denunciations of who drank too much with whom). These little stories perhaps best reveal the nature of the literary fair – to access the literary fair required knowing its secrets, its urban myths, its legends. Kulish was correct when he wrote Dniprovs'kyi that he needed to know "as they say – the backstage, what's happening in the wings" in order to understand the literary world of Kharkiv.

But these anecdotes also suggest the world of play intrinsic to the literary fair. The literary fair was, in fact, a *fair*, "joyful and reckless," as Smolych would later write. Play, as Johann Huizinga explains, is crucial for creativity so it is no wonder that the literary fair at its height created a renaissance in art. Huizinga himself connected fascism and Communism with "false play," and that may have later been true. The avowedly communist literary fair, however, exhibited precisely the intertwining of order and fun, of poetry and statecraft, described by Huizinga, yet one creating a cultural formation of Communism.[52]

The Literary Fair: Soviet Ukrainians

The literary fair was, it should be added, Ukrainian. These men of Ukrainization were Soviet, but figuring out how to be Soviet in a

Ukrainian key. They took on responsibility for making Soviet Ukraine. Khvyl'ovyi stated the problem:

"Will we consider our national art subservient (in this case it serves the proletariat) and eternally dependent, eternally reserved, in relation to those global arts that have attained their highest development? Or, leaving behind this subservient role, will we find it necessary to raise our artistic level to a level of worldwide masterpieces?" The task was as extraordinary as making "masterpieces" and forever "leaving behind a subservient role."[53] Khvyl'ovyi, with his polemical pamphlets, believed that it was possible to be Soviet and Ukrainian, and together with the literary fair was arguing for a certain interpretation of Ukrainian: Ukrainian as European, cultured, urban, modern, indeed, Soviet.

In the creative output of the literary fair one can find characters, themes, or images that emerge from a multi-ethnic landscape, such as the translations from Yiddish to Ukrainian of Jewish modernist Der Nister's prose, or the self-conscious satire on Ukrainization in Ostap Vyshnia's short stories. Neither were the institutional boundaries between ethno-national theatres always fixed. Director Favst Lopatyns'kyi, for example, worked in the Yiddish and Ukrainian-language theatres, as did actor Shimon Goldshtein-Semen Doroshenko. Set designers and composers worked for Yiddish, Ukrainian, and Russian theatres.[54]

Indeed, at its height, in the late 1920s, the literary fair was multi-ethnic. Ivan Kulyk, for example, was Jewish, spoke Yiddish, Russian, and Ukrainian, and headed the Writers' Union in Soviet Ukraine. Writer Leyb Kvitko, for another example, translated Tychyna's works into Yiddish (and Tychyna, in turn, translated Kvitko into Ukrainian). But the presence of Jews in a largely Ukrainian milieu did not mean that, as a group, these elites considered that Soviet Ukrainian culture itself should be multi-ethnic. The multi-ethnic reality of the region posed a challenge for the literary fair. After all, the literary fair was emerging from the multi-ethnic southwest provinces, they had all grown up in multi-ethnic spaces and institutions, whether the village, the city, or the imperial and Red Army. Yet this reality was in tension with the agenda for creating and promoting culture in Ukrainian and reflective of a Ukrainian sense of belonging, understood not regionally, but ethnically.[55]

The artistic creation of the literary fair reveals the perceived separateness of the Soviet Ukrainian cultural elite from their counterparts in Moscow. *Literary Fair*, Khvyl'ovyi's journal, was supposed to recall to the reader Gogol''s 1832 short story "Sorochintsy Fair" and specifically named Gogol'-Hohol' as its namesake. The editors referred to Gogol' as "our tragic countryman," thus placing themselves directly in Gogol''s lineage. Khvyl'ovyi himself advocated for a new Gogol' for Soviet times: "Our era has to be shown in all its manifestations ... we need a contemporary Gogol'." Nikolai Gogol', a.k.a. Mykola Hohol', was perhaps the premier imperial Russian writer of Ukrainian descent who revolutionized Russian literary life and created the fantastic world of noses, inspectors general, and dead souls.[56] Khvyl'ovyi's precise meaning remains vague – was he referring simply to a need for more talented writers of Ukrainian descent? A writer who used Ukrainian folk legends and realia to create the extraordinary? A writer not afraid of laughter and the grotesque? Gogol''s exploration of form – and the fact that this writer of Ukrainian descent found success on an imperial scale – may have been what Khvyl'ovyi had in mind. A statue to Gogol' erected in 1909 stood right in the heart of the literary fair across from the Berezil' theatre, so Gogol' constituted part of the spatial and cultural map of the literary fair, but not everyone approved.[57]

One denunciation of Khvyl'ovyi informed that he was not "alien" to anti-Semitism. When the Soviet Ukrainian Repertory Committee expressed hesitation over the character of the Jew in Lysenko's opera from Gogol''s *Taras Bul'ba*, Khvyl'ovyi (apparently) replied that they should leave the scene as written: "Let them at least get beaten on stage." The denunciation further slandered Khvyl'ovyi: "All his heroes are from a backwater place where it reeks of Gogol'. What do his heroes do? They drink, they whore it up chasing skirts ... in a word – a new petty bourgeoisie with Party cards." This particular denunciation is full of falsification, so we'll never know if Khvyl'ovyi ever expressed such anti-Semitism, but the GPU document does show a different understanding of Gogol': as a writer of "backwater" provincialism and anti-Semitism.[58] For some, then, Gogol' meant possibility in making use of outsider status to make great art; for others, however, Gogol' was a backwards Imperial-era anti-Semite. What was Soviet Ukrainian culture?

Smolych describes one joyous night when Mayakovsky visited Kharkiv. Mayakovsky, however, seems an outsider in Smolych's recounting, and the story of how Maik Iohansen bested Mayakovsky in a billiard tournament at the Blakytnyi Literary Club provides a platform for showing the essence of the literary fair. Following Iohansen's victory, Kurbas, Vyshnia, Smolych et al. drank ("vodka flowed like a river") and ended up at Vyshnia's apartment writing a congratulatory note to Oleksandr Dovzhenko, an early film of whose they had seen earlier that evening, and who was also a writer and caricaturist for *News* and one of their milieu. Berezil' actor Amvrosii Buchma drunkenly did a handstand on the balcony of Vyshnia's fifth-floor apartment and as he tottered on the edge there was much amusement over the Galician vs. Central Ukrainian words for sleep-walker (*snovyda* vs. *lunatik*). "It was, I remember, a happy night," writes Smolych. Mayakovsky fades out of the story and in Smolych's memory the great Russian-language poet's visit to Kharkiv became the night Buchma almost fell out of Vyshnia's apartment after Dovzhenko's film. The literary fair allowed *kozakuvannia*, behaving like a Cossack – and beating the Russians at billiards. But this kozakuvannia was not separate from the Party-state, but rather imbricated in the early Soviet institutions.[59]

Part IV: Bulgakov, Kulish, and Internal Transnationalism

The literary fair was inscribed in Kharkiv's urban space and the network of people and institutions making culture in early Soviet Ukraine. But one could find literary fair equivalents throughout the early Soviet Union: in Tbilisi, with the Blue Horn poets, or in Minsk, with the Jews making Soviet Yiddish culture, or, of course, backstage at the Moscow Art Theatre and at Bulgakov's apartment. Were these literary fairs connected?[60]

Indeed, the archipelago of literary fairs, each with its own figures, stories, and challenges, represented the continued fracturing of the Imperial cultural infrastructure. Yet as the cultural topography of the Soviet Union centred increasingly on Moscow, so, too, did the relationship between the islands of literary fairs transform, making Moscow a centre and Soviet Ukraine a periphery. Bulgakov and Kulish, from literary fairs in Moscow and Kharkiv, belong in the same story. Bulgakov, in his *Whistle* and later Moscow Art Theatre milieu, was making Soviet culture; Kulish, in the literary fair, was making Soviet Ukrainian culture. And one of the emerging characteristics of the literary fair in Kharkiv was its increasingly tense relationship with Moscow. I use the term "internal transnationalism" to highlight the exchange of peoples, goods, and ideas across the real – and imagined – borders inside the Soviet Union. Our two leading characters in this chapter, Mikhail Bulgakov and Mykola Kulish, are themselves a perfect case study of internal transnationalism in action.

In 1929, members of the literary fair went to Moscow for meetings with Russian writers and the Soviet leadership. During the trip they were treated to an evening at the Moscow Art Theatre, where they saw Mikhail Bulgakov's 1926 play, *Days of the Turbins*. *Turbins* was already a hit inside and outside the Soviet Union, and Stalin saw the Moscow production fifteen times. It was performed abroad, in Paris and London, and it was such a common piece of early Soviet culture that a fellow by the name of Bulgakov (and not the famous writer) working at the Soviet consulate in Canada was renamed by his colleagues "Days-of-the-Turbins." Consular officer Ivan Kulyk references this joke throughout his published account of his time abroad; the apparent incongruity of a celebrity name and an ordinary apparatchik seems to have amused the consular staff to no end, as well as Kulyk's readers in 1930s Kharkiv. The Moscow Art Theatre production, then, was probably meant to show the visitors the best of the new Soviet repertory at the best theatre in the Soviet capital.[61]

However, the writers took great offence, both as Soviets and Ukrainians, and they spent the majority of their meeting with Stalin the next day complaining about Bulgakov and his Turbins. They were offended that a play with such an ideologically dubious plot, that of the demise of a non-Soviet intelligentsia family, had garnered such support from the state and from Stalin himself. Unlike Bulgakov, many of these writers had fought in the Red Army, brought socialism to victory in the south, and considered themselves loyal and true Communists. It is not surprising, therefore, that the depiction of the revolution in Kyiv offended them because it ignored their own story, that of those loyal to Soviet Communism and to Ukraine. They were also, then, offended as Ukrainians. They expressed shock at how the Moscow Art Theatre actors presented the German characters with a flawless German accent, but caricatured the Ukrainian accent for laughs. Stalin countered their objections, however, by asserting that the play was good, and as the Soviet arts had as yet produced few good plays, everyone had to reconcile themselves with Bulgakov and his Turbins.[62]

Even after returning to Soviet Ukraine, Kulish continued to express displeasure at Bulgakov's play and the Moscow Art Theatre production. Kulish did not appreciate the "attempt from the Art Theatre to discredit, as it were, the national movement in Ukraine" and wondered why the Moscow Art Theatre did not "send their workers to Ukraine to at least acquaint themselves with the history of the national movement." The broad Ukrainian accents in the production made it seem like "all rebels in Ukraine were some kind of dimwits." Kulish even wrote a character who has a lengthy monologue about *Days of the Turbins* in his 1929 satire on Ukrainization, *Myna Mazailo*. Aunt Motia comes from Kursk to visit Kharkiv and regales her Ukrainophile brother with tales of "such luxury, such truth, that if you had seen how generally accursed, abominable on the stage your Ukrainians are, you would totally renounce this name." She ends the monologue with "edinaia nedelimaia," united and indivisible, a reference to the anti-Bolshevik ideology of the Civil War. Motia's obsession with *Turbins* and with anti-Soviet slogans suggest – in a humorous monologue set piece – that Bulgakov himself belongs not with those building socialism, but with the pre-revolutionary bourgeoisie.[63]

In fact, *Days of the Turbins* became such a bête-noire for Kulish that he later mentioned it as an exemplar of Russian chauvinism to his informer-cellmate in the concentration camp on the Solovetskii islands. Nor was Kulish alone. A certain Petrenko, an arts official representing Soviet Ukraine speaking at the All-Union Conference of Arts Workers in Moscow in 1929, also decried *Turbins* as a play that was "harmful" both from an ideological and national point of view, which presented the Ukrainian revolutionary movement as "wild banditism." Commissar of Enlightenment Anatolii Lunacharskii himself wrote to Stalin in 1929 to complain that the Moscow Art Theatre "continues to stage a play that distorts the Ukrainian revolutionary movement and offends Ukrainians. And the director of the theatre and the Commissariat of Enlightenment RSFSR do not understand the harm that this will bring in mutual relations with Ukraine."[64]

In response to Bulgakov and his Turbins, therefore, Kulish wrote his own play about the years of revolution and civil war. Although Kulish's play also took place in Kyiv in 1918 and also featured a young hero and his encounter with revolution, Kulish's work differed from Bulgakov's in every way. Instead of Bulgakov's cosy family home, Kulish placed his characters in the communal boarding house of a former monarchist. Instead of the charming Chekhovian figures in Bulgakov's drama, *Sonata Pathétique* (*Patetychna sonata*) presented a prostitute, a paraplegic war vet-turned-Bolshevik, a politically indecisive hero, and the Ukrainian nationalist *femme fatale* Maryna, who plays the Beethoven sonata after which the play took its name. While Bulgakov's play was a lyrical ode to the world lost in the revolution, *Sonata Pathétique* was more ambiguous in its political orientation. The nationalist Maryna, for example, was clearly responsible for the hero's demise, but hardly as one-note as Bulgakov's faithless Talberg; Bulgakov's Aleksei Turbin was unquestionably anti-Bolshevik and anti-nationalist, while Kulish's nameless hero waffled between Ukrainian patriotism, Bolshevism, and lovelorn ennui. Bulgakov wrote his *Turbins* for the psychological depths of the actors at the Moscow Art Theatre, while Kulish wrote *Sonata* for Les Kurbas' experimental Berezil' Theatre.[65]

Most significantly, however, Bulgakov's play was a story of revolution, while Kulish's was a story of national revolution. Bulgakov painted all Ukrainians as nationalists, while Kulish's characters represented Ukrainian nationalism in a variety of political flavours. If Bulgakov's play was anti-Ukrainian, Kulish's was pro-Ukrainian, and in a Soviet key. As he stated, he wished to focus on "unravelling the national question ... and not with kid gloves." Kulish intended *Sonata*

Figure 2.4. Berezil' company meeting in Odesa with Mykola Kulish. Kurbas is in the second row from the back, first on the right; Kulish is sitting next to him in the embroidered shirt (Shevchenko)

to show, *pace* Bulgakov, the depth of the Ukrainian nationalist movement in, around, and against the Bolshevik Revolution. He wanted his play to show the legitimacy of the Soviet Ukrainian project, and how it differed from the non-socialist Ukrainian nationalist movement, as well as from the non-national "Russian" revolution itself. For Kulish, the "national problem" was central to cultural production in Soviet Ukraine.[66]

The Repertory Committee in Soviet Ukraine did not approve the play, however. Although I have not been able to find accounts of their deliberations, the decision is not surprising given that officials frequently mentioned Kulish with frustration in Soviet Ukrainian Politburo and Central Committee protocols. Kulish was not only a prominent playwright but also a political elite, serving on the editorial boards of multiple literary journals and Party committees. His work carried political weight and authority, and any political ambiguity was therefore problematic. Kulish made himself few friends when he argued that plays should always make the audience "uneasy" and should "not name enemies abroad," but rather "uncover them here."[67]

However, like all Soviet artists, Kulish understood the cultural topography of the Soviet Union. He sent the play to a colleague in Moscow, who translated it, and Aleksandr Tairov opted to direct the play at his theatre in the capital. Like Kurbas' Berezil' Theatre in Kharkiv, Tairov's *Kamernyi*, or Chamber, Theatre was perfectly suited to Kulish's play because it presented a constructivist set that highlighted the symbolic nature of the play's characters. Tairov worked with excellent actors, including Alisa Koonen, who starred as Maryna. She made the character a "Medea," but her celebrity made the character one audiences loved to hate. She wrote in her memoirs that Raisa Azarkh, (who in Kharkiv reported to Kaganovich and assisted Khvyl'ovyi) came backstage after the performance and informed her that Lazar Moiseevich was displeased with her interpretation because her acting choices did not make it clear enough that the audience should not like Maryna. Koonen was such an attractive personality that it was hard for audiences not to like Maryna, even if they recognized the hero's love for her as his fatal flaw.[68]

Sonata Pathétique was also the first production for young actress Faina Ranevskaia, who had long wanted to work at Tairov's theatre. She wrote that she was terrified of the set, which showed audiences the entire multi-storey house in which all the characters lived; Ranevskaia's character, the prostitute, spent the entire play in a room placed high above the stage. She writes that she was so nervous during rehearsals that she could hardly act, and it was only Tairov's gentle encouragement that facilitated her eventual performance. Even so, she was not able to descend from the heights to take her bow during the premiere because of vertigo.[69]

The production ran for forty performances from December 1931 to March 1932. Although rejected by the cultural infrastructure in Soviet Ukraine, the play found a home in Moscow. *Pravda* gave the play a lukewarm review entitled "Unsuccessful Pathos," but the editors still praised Kulish's success at managing to frame the national question "correctly" and called it "one of the best plays of this season." The review suggests that while the Soviet Ukrainian officialdom may have feared Kulish's exploration of national revolution, in the context of the Soviet capital the play simply seemed – like Bulgakov's – a well-written contribution to the Soviet repertory and less politically provocative. Celebrated civil war general Semen Budenny watched the show in a loge box with Kulish and, according to Kulish's wife's memoirs, praised the production and invited the writer for tea. In fact, theatres across the Union picked up the play for their seasons: *Sonata* was scheduled for performance in Leningrad, Omsk, Irkutsk, and Kazan', and even translated into German and published in Berlin by fellow traveller Friedrich Wolff, who lauded its "atmosphere of the Ukrainian land."[70]

But in March 1932 an anonymous editorial in *Pravda* written by "I. Ukrainets" complained about the play's Ukrainian nationalism, the *Pravda* staff apologized for their previous review, and Tairov had to close down the production. "No, it would be better if Comrade Kulish, for whom this is not the first unsuccessful play, would work on himself for several years, simmer in the workers' pot, and then start to write, because he has talent, but he is not giving his talent to us," wrote the anonymous *Pravda* reviewer. All accounts point to Kaganovich as the writer of the review; not only was he – like Bulgakov and Kulish – from the southwest borderlands, he had also worked hard from 1925 to 1928 in Soviet Ukraine to wrangle the local intelligentsia and he was not one of Mykola Kulish's fans.[71]

This story of Bulgakov's *Turbins* and Kulish's *Sonata* reveals the importance of internal transnationalism in Soviet culture. Is the failure of *Sonata* a Soviet Ukrainian story? Certainly, its rejection in Soviet Ukraine and the Kremlin accusations of Ukrainian nationalism would suggest so. Or, is it a Moscow story? Certainly, the success of the play in the capital and the role of a major Politburo player in its shutdown would suggest so. Yet the dynamic between the two texts and their authors suggests a larger framework. In short, a play by a Kyiv native about Kyiv events found success in the capital, which provoked a Soviet Ukrainian writer to write a play about the same events; lack of support in the provinces led to success in the capital, but events from the provinces shut down the production. The influence of *Turbins* cannot be explained exclusively with reference to Stalin, the Moscow Art Theatre, or Bulgakov's milieu in Moscow because its reach both abroad and to other republics shows its cultural authority. Similarly, the narrative of Soviet Ukrainian culture that sees Moscow only as a force of oppression does not explain how Moscow could (at times) allow for more opportunities and success for artists. Ultimately, both Bulgakov's *Turbins* and Kulish's *Sonata* are Soviet cultural products that represent not only one place but also an internal transnational circulation between Moscow and Soviet Ukraine.

Circulation continued, in fact, beyond the Soviet space. Kulish was executed in 1937, but his wife and two children survived and remained in Nazi-occupied Ukraine during Second World War. Kulish's son Volodymyr preserved his father's texts and had *Sonata* published by a Ukrainian-language publishing house in Nazi-occupied L'viv (at the time, Lemberg). Later Volodymyr Kulish took the text with him to the displaced persons camps and thence to the United States. But as the text travelled, so did its reception and, consequently, its meaning shifted: the figure of its author, a Soviet Ukrainian writing of the chaos of revolution, became a Ukrainian anti-Soviet writing a play against revolution. The reception of *Sonata* illustrates how the category of "Soviet Ukrainian" lost the Soviet element and became exclusively Ukrainian. Now Kulish is largely known only in Ukrainianist circles, when in fact his pro-Soviet play exemplifies a dynamic between Moscow and Soviet Ukraine, was performed by leading artists in Moscow, and caused enough of a scandal at the highest Soviet levels to be shut down.[72]

The reception of *Sonata* and *Turbins* also shows how Soviet culture lost the Ukrainian element. *Turbins* was a Soviet phenomenon, but was also written by someone who was from the former Imperial Southwest, a region that became Soviet Ukraine, and that inspired an entire cohort of cultural elites. The content of the play came from the southern provinces; the *zemliachestvo* of early Soviet Moscow nurtured the play, and its greater resonance included a polemic written by a Soviet Ukrainian. Soviet culture is much more than the culture of Moscow and Leningrad, yet Moscow and Leningrad have come to constitute Soviet culture. Only a lens encompassing the internal transnationalism of the

Soviet space, Moscow and Kharkiv, centre and periphery, can reveal the entire Soviet story behind Bulgakov and Kulish.

The spatial map on which Soviet artists and officials operated comprised the entire Union; opportunities to work in either the centre or the republics, and relations between the two, shaped Soviet cultural production and reception. Many artists worked this cultural topography to their advantage. Kulish, in fact, was not too dispirited by *Sonata's* closure to attempt another production in Moscow. In 1933 the Soviet Ukrainian Commissariat of Enlightenment shut down Kulish's play *Maklena Grasa*, which had premiered at the Berezil' Theatre in Kharkiv. This led to the removal of the theatre's artistic director, Les' Kurbas, and the end (not long after) of the theatre itself. Despite the scandal, Kulish wrote his former mistress that he believed the play had a future in Moscow. Soviet Ukrainian playwrights Ivan Mykytenko, and, later, Oleksandr Korniichuk found success on the Moscow and Union stages. The entire Soviet Union, then, was always in the mind of Soviet artists, not as a blank slate of a vast expanse, but as a particular and changing map, with a rugged topography of opportunities and limitations.

Days of the Turbins and *Sonata Pathétique* both resulted from the literary fairs in Moscow and Kharkiv, by the overlap between artists and officials created by revolution. The literary fair was a space of play: a fair that was not capitalist and dependent on evil entrepreneurs and greedy managers, but one offering exchange and sociability and space for theatrical experiments. Yet revolution in the arts meant something different in Moscow than in Ukraine. Korenizatsiia infused the literary fair in Soviet Ukraine; the policies of privileging Ukrainian upturned the hierarchy, offering new opportunities for humour, for pathos, and for stories that had not yet been told. The literary fair in Ukraine strove to figure out what "Ukrainian" meant, and what the revolution was, in the borderlands far from Moscow and Leningrad.

Kharkiv's literary fair ended by 1934 when the GPU arrested most of its major talent and shipped them off to the camps of the north. Oleksandr Shums'kyi, Ostap Vyshnia, Mykola Kulish, Iosyp Hirniak, and Les' Kurbas were all arrested in 1933–4. Khvyl'ovyi and Skrypnyk had by then already committed suicide; Furer would commit suicide in 1936 in Moscow. Khvylia would be arrested in 1937 and shot in 1938. The literary fair may have vanished, but the links connecting the arts, with the Party-state, with the police, stood firm. The Soviet state now had a monopoly over the arts.

3 Comedy Soviet and Ukrainian? Il'f-Petrov and Ostap Vyshnia

Part I: Il'f-Petrov at the Circus

Evgenii Petrov, born Evgenii Petrovich Kataev, worked as a criminal investigator in the seamy seaside port of Odesa, in the seamy civil war years when the city was a haven for all those fleeing to or from the Bolsheviks. His first professional piece of writing was the police report on an unknown corpse. At the same time, Il'ia Fainzil'berg Il'f had moved from Odesa to Moscow and was staying with Petrov's older brother, whose apartment had become a crash pad for Odessity moving north to make it in the new Soviet metropolis. No one would guess that these two were destined to work together. One was Jewish, one Russian; one short, one tall; and after all, Petrov was working in the police – although he did move to Moscow by fall 1923. And apparently Il'ia Il'f was the only one to correspond with Evgenii Petrov when the latter joined the Red Army in 1925–6 and, whether for that reason or on the advice of Petrov's older brother, the two started writing together. Il'ia Il'f and Evgenii Petrov ceased their professional lives as individuals and became a permanent duet, no longer Il'f and Petrov, but Il'f-Petrov, one writer, and the creator of some of the most enduring classics of Soviet culture.[1]

But more than that – Il'f-Petrov solved the problem of Soviet entertainment. Unlike other countries in Europe and North America, the Soviet Party-state had a monopoly over the arts. Of course, other states besides the USSR supported the arts, and of course, securing state funding in the USSR was not always easy for artists. In the heady days of the New Economic Policy, artists competed for funding from various pots, whether from Party or state committees at the city, republic, or Union level, or from the Arts Workers' Union. But, by the late 1920s, artists had achieved what they had long desired: full state support for the arts. As artists had imagined, state support facilitated artistic production. Let's take one example: Il'f-Petrov's first co-effort in 1927 was *The Twelve Chairs*, a picaresque romp across Eurasia following conman Ostap Bender's attempt to locate a batch of diamonds stashed in the leg of one of a set of twelve pre-revolutionary dining-room chairs. Clearly, Bender was a smooth operator working on the edges of the Soviet state, but Il'f-Petrov, Bender's creator, operated firmly inside the state, living on state salaries, in state-sponsored housing, and catapulted to success based on their con-man's antics. When artists in the United States were standing in bread lines during the Great Depression, the Soviet state could fund Il'f-Petrov's travel to America in 1931. But a total state monopoly over cultural production had other – more unexpected – consequences.[2]

State monopoly on the arts meant that metrics of "popularity" needed recalibration. Artists could not depend on book or ticket sales to prove resonance with an audience. Competition among artists for financial support was still fierce, but artists focused not on soliciting interest from the audience members or private patrons, but rather from the Party-state. This non-capitalist art "market" transformed how artists, officials, critics, and audiences understood artistic hierarchies. The notion of qualitatively good avant-garde artists creating art that was not widely consumed vanished: according to Soviet ideology, shouldn't all art be for everyone? After all, too much focus on securing the hard-won rubles from lower-class audience members created art that was ostensibly "lower" in the artistic hierarchy of the Russian empire. But freedom from the necessity of securing audience funding, because all funding came from the state, meant that even the most obscure of the avant-garde artists could reach an audience. Could culture that reached a large audience also be critically evaluated as good? Could quantity equal quality?[3]

Somehow, Il'f-Petrov squared this circle of pleasing the audience, the critics, and their patrons. Soviet readers loved Il'f-Petrov; letters from far and wide confirm Il'f-Petrov's non-market popularity. One reader from Luhansk even wrote to the duo requesting – rather, demanding – that they explain to readers whether Ostap Bender was okay: "In Soviet literature there should not be heroes remaining in uncertainty – the chain of tragicomic situations ended but the person remained. Where is he now?"[4]

But it was theatre that constituted nineteenth-century entertainment in the Russian empire, and so it was in the domain of theatre that Soviets negotiated this thorny issue of what to perform and how the audience should react to it. Il'f-Petrov started their theatrical work by writing for the Moscow Music Hall, *Moskovskii Miuzik-Kholl*. Il'f and Petrov wrote several short vaudeville sketches. One, "Deputy King" (Vitse-Korol), involved the attempt made by several bourgeois to feign various kinds of madness in order to avoid arrests by the new Bolshevik regime. One bourgeois pretends to be a dog, one Julius Caesar, one the Deputy King of India. They are, of course, humorously discovered and uncovered by the female psychiatrist.[5]

Unlike other theatres, the Music Hall operated under the aegis of the GOMETS, the State Trust of Music, Estrada, and the Circus, as opposed to Narkompros, the People's Commissariat of Enlightenment, which dealt with education, health, and "academic" theatres, such at the Moscow Art Theatre or the Bol'shoi. In other words, Il'f-Petrov wrote for a different state institution, one that categorized their work as part of a different kind of cultural production than Bulgakov's *Days of the Turbins* at the Moscow Art Theatre.[6]

Bulgakov may have left the world of *The Whistle* for "academic" theatre with *Turbins*, but he would reconnect with the Moscow Music Hall in his famous novel, *Master and Margarita*. The Music Hall inspired the novel's Variety Theatre, *Teatr Var'ete*, where the Devil and his henchmen come to perform for a contemporary audience. To investigate and understand "real" Muscovites, the cabal does not attend the Moscow Art Theatre but rather the venue attended by people looking for entertainment. This audience, afflicted with the housing crisis and desperate for finery and escapism, enjoys the acrobats and fire-eaters brought together on stage by theatre managers seeking profit, even if in a Soviet context.[7]

Il'f-Petrov wrote *Under the Circus Tent* (Pod Kupolom Tsirka) in 1934 for the Moscow Music Hall.[8] *Under the Circus Tent* told of backstage life at the circus: an American woman with an African-American child, driven from racist and bourgeois America, finds comfort and professional fulfilment – and, of course, romance! – in the Soviet Union at the Soviet circus. A motley crew of characters surround her, and the script contains many "bits," sketches depending on comic timing, such as a character taking a taxi and never managing to pay for it, or romantic misunderstandings between two couples. In the script, the circus director admits that to his shame "up to this point we still cannot master this imported, foreign attraction … the mass production of tractors we have mastered, aviation motors we have mastered, Magnitogorsk we have mastered, the Arctic we have mastered, pork cutlets in cafeterias we have mastered, but somehow a certain lousy flying torpedo we cannot master!" The phenomenon of the flying torpedo, which the Director desires to obtain in order to improve the circus's quality, suggests a wider meaning: an attraction, a trick, a moment that delights and entertains. This evening at the Music Hall itself was, perhaps, intended to be just such a flying torpedo.[9]

Theatre was complicated, however, because the genre could never truly belong to mass culture. Quite simply, only so many people could fit into a theatre building; technological advances created forms of culture more effective at truly reaching the masses, such as the radio and the movies. Indeed, Il'f-Petrov ultimately left the Music Hall and wrote for the cinema. In 1937, *Under the Circus Top* became a movie, *Circus* (Tsirk), directed by Grigorii Aleksandrov. Il'f-Petrov, together with Kataev, who wrote the screenplay with the duo, disliked what Aleksandrov did with the film. Yet they still received their honorarium and the film does reflect their original script. With *Circus*, the Soviets mastered the flying torpedo, creating a truly Soviet artistic product that delighted and entertained.[10]

And Soviet entertainment did indeed entertain the entire Soviet Union. The novel *The Twelve Chairs* reached readers across the entire Soviet Union, oddly mirroring Ostap Bender's Union-wide search for the hidden diamonds. Although Ostap Bender was most likely Jewish, the novel was typically Soviet in its lack of focus on ethnicity. This lack of ethnic particularism proved typical for products aimed at an all-Union audience. There is a famous scene, in fact, in *Circus* where the small mixed-race child of the American heroine is passed around the entire audience of the circus, and everyone sings the child a lullaby in a different language of the Union, ending with Solomon Mikhoels singing in Yiddish. Of course, each audience member may have represented a different Soviet nationality, but the result made *Circus* a supra-ethnic and truly "Soviet" cultural product, not one reducible to any one ethnicity. Soviet culture, made on an all-Union level in Moscow, promoted cultural products – the flying torpedo, the con man, the lullaby – that spoke to and included everyone. Every language of the Union belonged in a Soviet song, in a Soviet story, and in a Soviet film. And this, of course, raises the question: What about the real Ostap Benders remaining in Soviet Ukraine? If Soviet culture was supposed to be urban and pan-ethnic, what should happen with Ukraine, which was largely rural, and the literary fair, which was largely Ukrainian?[11]

Part II: Ostap Vyshnia: The Cherry Elf

The nexus of theatrical production, audience reception, and entertainment posed a challenge for the literary fair in Soviet Ukraine. Ukrainian-language repertory had a long history in the southwest borderlands, but it consisted of melodrama and musical comedies aimed at precisely that traditional village audience that the younger generation despised. Instead, younger artists wanted to build on the new experiments in exploring the boundaries of what was permissible on stage; much of the literary fair involved itself with modernism. The challenge for Soviet Ukraine was not creating an avant-garde, but creating an urban culture for the masses. At the centre of the contestation over cultural hierarchies was Ostap Vyshnia, the Il'f-Petrov of Soviet Ukraine. Of course, he was one person, not two, and differed greatly from the Odessity, but both Il'f-Petrov and Vyshnia successfully created Soviet entertainment, the former in the centre, and the latter in the regions.

Ostap Vyshnia, or Ostap "Cherry," born Pavlo Hubenko, was rescued twice from prison, both times to serve Soviet Ukrainian culture. The first time, Blakytnyi brought him out of Bolshevik imprisonment in order to serve as a needed Ukrainian-language expert in 1921. The second time Vyshnia was rescued from prison was years later, in 1943, after he had served almost ten years in the gulag. Not Blakytnyi, long deceased, but secret police chief Lavrentii Pavlovich Beria scooped up the writer from the claws of death to raise morale for Soviet Ukraine during the war. This he did. Vyshnia's funeral in 1956 filled the streets of Kyiv's central street, Khreshchatyk.[12]

This is the story of the Cherry Elf. Vyshnia had a biography similar to that of his compatriots in the literary fair. He was born in 1889 in Poltava oblast to a large family. He went to school in Kyiv, like Mikhail Bulgakov, to study medicine and received training as an army medic. This would later save his life, as would the ulcer that plagued his health through the 1920s and 1930s. He served with the tsarist army as a medic, and then the UNR — the Ukrainian People's Army — and was rescued from Bolshevik prison by Blakytnyi to write for *News*. Hubenko, now permanently Ostap Vyshnia, joked in "And that's how I write" that what he spoke growing up was "not Little Russian, not Russian, but a little Russian"; his playfulness with the Ukrainian language served him and *News* quite well. Vyshnia soon became one of the major figures of the literary fair.[13]

Vyshnia's writing entertained Soviet Ukrainian readers, as the work of Il'f-Petrov did Soviet-wide readers. In a meeting with locals in the Donbas, famous writers such as Mykola Khvyl'ovyi, Mykola Kulish,

Arkadii Liubchenko, and Vyshnia, received written questions from the gathered audience. Vyshnia received the most audience interest, mostly requests for him to read his works aloud. Specifically, the writer received eleven signatures on a request to read aloud, two additional requests for him to read specific stories, and multiple further requests for information on how to find copies of his stories and play adaptations.[14]

The comparison between Vyshnia and Il'f-Petrov reveals the difference between the way that Soviet entertainment developed in Moscow and in Soviet Ukraine. Both artists produced works designed to attract an audience and make that audience laugh. Both, in fact, created protagonists who shared a common trait: the little man pulling one over on the establishment.

Yet there were differences. Il'f-Petrov's protagonist was the urban con man Ostap Bender, Vyshnia's the hick *idiot savant*. Il'f-Petrov did not engage in ethnic humour, while much of Vyshnia's humour rested on the category of "Ukrainian." The Cherry Elf captured the challenge of creating culture in Soviet Ukraine: Soviet culture was modern and urban, yet what resonated in Soviet Ukraine was a village narrator. In one of his sketches, Vyshnia describes the land of the "Scratchranians" (in Ukrainian, *Chukhraintsi*), and the five characteristics that "were so typical of them that whenever a Scratchranian lost himself in a million-sized crowd of humanity, anyone who had ever lived among the Scratchranians for even a short time could guess with certainty." Yet the traits themselves, of course, are the vaguest of the vague: "1. If only I knew. 2. I forgot (about it). 3. I was late. 4. It'll work itself out somehow. 5. I knew it would happen." In other words, Vyshnia pokes fun at the fact that these are hardly "national" traits that would distinguish a person, yet the comedy lies in the very necessity of defining the elusive Scratchranian. The audience had to wrestle with the identity of "Soviet Ukrainian," and that, it seems, was entertaining.[15]

Il'f-Petrov and Vyshnia, moreover, also wrote for different media: Il'f-Petrov ventured into cinema, while Vyshnia remained in the realm of the published text and live performance. Vyshnia wrote actively for the theatre – the Shevchenko Theatre, the Ivan Franko Theatre, and the Berezil'. Il'f-Petrov, by contrast, never wrote for the Moscow Art Theatre, or Meyerhold's theatre, or Vakhtangov's theatre. Bulgakov and Il'f-Petrov certainly knew each other socially in Moscow circles, but their successes unfolded in different performance spaces and genres.

Vyshnia also wrote for an audience that was not exclusively urban. He wrote a series entitled "Face to the Village"; in one sketch he joked about how a city visitor would only turn his face to the village ... every other body part would remain firmly turned towards the city. Vyshnia's wrote a series for *News* that involved reportage from Berlin, where he travelled in 1928 to heal his ulcer. One of Vyshnia's running jokes throughout the series was about how bewildering it was for the narrator that no one spoke Ukrainian. Naturally, then, the humour and observations of Il'f-Petrov, writing in the modern Soviet metropolis, and Vsyhnia, writing in the rural-yet-industrializing multi-ethnic Ukraine, differed. Ostap Bender and Vyshnia's *khokhol* may have been cut from the same cloth, but they took different paths and spoke to different publics – either an all-Union public, necessarily supra-ethnic, or a republican public, intended to be Ukrainian, to speak Ukrainian, and to recognize the characteristics of the Scratchranians – or at least acknowledge the importance of defining them.[16]

Hello from Radiowave 477!

Vyshnia occupied such a presence in the artistic landscape of Soviet Ukraine that he became a stage character. An actor playing the character of "Vyshnia" starred in *Hello from Radiowave 477!* the first-ever Ukrainian-language revue show, created at Les' Kurbas' Berezil' theatre in 1929. Although similar to Il'f-Petrov's comedy written for the Moscow Music Hall, the show highlights the theatrical environment of Soviet Ukraine. The show was performed not in the local Music Hall, but in the premier theatre of the republic, and it starred and referenced the premier cultural elites, the literary fair. *Hello* proved a unique cultural product in the Soviet Union, and one that still stands out in the trajectory of theatrical development in Soviet Ukraine. The year 1929 was a transitional moment Union-wide in in many spheres: the end of the New Economic Policy, the push towards class struggle, and collectivization in the countryside. Yet Soviet theatre, too, was in the midst of transformation; *Hello* is an exemplar of modern, urban Soviet and Ukrainian culture, which was – with few exceptions – never seen again.[17]

The literary fair constituted the engine of cultural production and reception in early Soviet Ukraine, and *Hello* was one of their most self-referential cultural products, written by the literary fair, referencing the literary fair, and starring the literary fair. Yet the production also served as an attempt to create entertainment that was qualitatively Soviet and Ukrainian. *Hello* was one of few examples of such entertainment, which suggests both its success and its inherent limitations: using theatre in the age of radio and film as mass entertainment, and ethnicity's inflection of comedy.

The title contained an inside joke: Kharkiv's local radio ran on frequency 477. The show, written by literary fair member Maik Iohansen with the assistance of the younger Berezil' generation, comprised three acts: act 1 was a "gallop" across Kharkiv with short comic sketches illustrating various situations characteristic of Soviet life; act 2, without words, showed a piano player and hotel bellboy cavorting in a luxury Western hotel; act 3 revealed an actor dressed in a mask of writer Ostap Vyshnia going on a hunt, encountering a line of dancing girls in the forest, and singing an aria in Café Hell (in Ukrainian, *Peklo*), peopled with actors dressed in masks signifying other figures from the literary fair: Iurii Smolych, Oles' Dosvitnyi, Maik Iohansen, and Mykola Khvyl'ovyi. At each of the forty-six Kharkiv performances in the spring of 1929, 1,000 spectators could observe actors masked as literary celebrities sing with dancing girls in a café called Hell.[18]

Figure 3.1. Café Peklo, *Hello from Radiowave 477!* (Shevchenko)

Hello was the latest manifestation of a career-long interest in small forms and estrada for Kurbas and his theatre. The cabaret trend had spread across Europe from Paris's Montmartre to Moscow in the early twentieth century. In the 1920s the popularity of jazz, music halls, and "small forms" (*malye formy* in Russian, *Kleinkunst* in German) continued to shape the European cultural scene, and Kurbas was no exception. Kurbas had spent time in the civil war cabarets of Kyiv, but these were performances in the Russian language, and the Ukrainian-language basement theatre offered poetry or more serious theatrical work. Kurbas' 1924 production of *Macbeth*, however, made use of contemporary humour; the Porter character, played by rising star Amvrosii Buchma, replaced Shakespeare's jokes with references to current events. In 1926 the Berezil created the comedy *Riff-Raff* (Shpana; written by Volodymyr Iaroshenko, directed by Ianuarii Bortnyk) as one of their last productions in Kyiv.[19]

Officialdom, too, took an interest in entertainment. At a special conference at the Commissariat of Enlightenment "on matters of estrada performances in food-related enterprises," the GPU official who was present argued that because "life itself calls out for the existence of estrada," they could "hardly forbid" the genre, but should simply try to "make sure there is no pornography." Although restaurant/cabaret acts differed from a full-length revue show performed in a theatre, the police official's concerns represented an increased recognition of the importance and prevalence of comedy, music, and "small forms" outside the genre of the dramatic play. In fact, in 1926 in Kharkiv, the All-Ukrainian Council of Workers' Unions (which managed Boba Lifshyts" *The Proletarian*) founded the Gleeful Proletarian Theatre (Veselyi Proletar) to explore estrada in the context of a theatre for workers. This was a theatre especially designated to entertain workers with variety acts, comic sketches, and satiric revues. The Arts Workers' Union hired former Kurbas protégé and Berezil' director, Ianuarii Bortnyk, as artistic director. Estrada, therefore, constituted a major interest of the literary fair, in the police, the Party-state, and the theatre.[20]

Kurbas advocated in the press for creating a new Ukrainian-language estrada tradition. Russification, he argued, occurred through the lack of Ukrainian-language alternatives to urban culture, slang, and *khorosho*. In other words, if Soviet culture were to exist in Soviet Ukraine in Ukrainian, Ukrainian-language culture had to catch up to the times. He wanted to use *Hello* to create an inexpensive revue show of comic sketches that could be repeated every year with slightly different content and would allow his company to explore this genre that would

"Ukrainianize the street." The Berezil' spent 8,000 karbovantsy on the production (the most on any production that season), so *Hello* hardly seems like a cheap show made for yearly renewal, but its characters and sketches do attempt to define a kind of urban, modern, comedy both Soviet and Ukrainian, a kind of theatre as mass oriented and modern as the radio.[21]

In a memo regarding a different (and unproduced) musical comedy entitled simply *Music Hall*, playwright-director-choreographer Borys Balaban, a member of the younger Berezil' generation who had directed and danced in *Hello*, articulated the play's goal: to "show two points of view" (that of a worker and non-worker) and show how each perceived the differences between the USSR and the West, to "laugh at fascist fears," and, along the way, to advertise aviation. Given the intricate nature of the script, Balaban may have wanted also to display his talents at set design, choreography and composition. Balaban's proposed show in this genre of mass-oriented theatrical entertainment carried multiple goals; similarly, Kurbas expressed multiple goals for *Hello*: to show that estrada could exist in Ukrainian, to bring the street into the theatre, and to create art without "serious and profound" themes that (presumably) would entertain. These were goals shared by the literary fair; the show expressed a multitude of influences, both from inside the fair and from Europe.[22]

It was trips to Berlin in 1927 and 1928 that inspired the literary fair's plans for an estrada production at the Berezil'. In 1927 Kurbas, Iosyp Hirniak (healing his colitis), and Mykhailo Datskiv, the Berezil''s managing director, visited Germany, where Kurbas and Hirniak saw theatre and Datskiv seems to have sought out stage lighting. A letter from "Schwabe and Co." in Berlin, dated August 1927, suggests that the equipment was purchased, giving the Berezil' modern stage lighting: coloured inserts for stage lamps of various sizes, equipment for various stage effects, including snow, rain, water, and clouds, and incandescent spotlights. Artist Vadym Meller's set design for *Hello* most certainly made use of the Schwabe order. But it was not only lights that travelled west to east, but artistic ideas. When Kurbas returned, he noted to his company a "Parisian revue" that he had seen; he wanted to create a similar revue at the Berezil, and *Zhovtnevyi ohliad*, or "October Review," was an early attempt at a variety show that sported both technological savvy (thanks to that lighting order) as well as artistic "numbers."[23]

The next year, in 1928, more members of the literary fair went to Germany. Iosyp Hirniak, for example, was accompanied by Fusia Furer,

whom Hirniak in his later memoirs accuses of informing to Kaganovich. Both Vyshnia and Hirniak mention a play they took in at Max
Reinhardt's Deutsches Theater, *Artists*. The production struck Hirniak
with the "several hundred" backstage personnel supporting the performance; Vyshnia, too, noted that the technical conditions in Kharkiv
were "slightly" worse, but suggested that the Berezil' could still turn
out "good, even wonderful" shows.[24]

Hirniak writes that Kurbas attended *Artists* with them, but he must
be mistaken because Kurbas was not in Berlin in 1928, only in 1927.
Still, that both Hirniak and Vyshnia remembered the show suggests
that it made an impression. In fact, Reinhardt's *Artists* was a German
version of the Broadway hit *Burlesque,* written by George Manker
Watters and Arthur Hopkins. The American influence, the backstage
"exposé" aspect to the show, and the vaudeville elements suggest that
it was indeed *Artists* that contributed to the literary fair's inspiration
for an estrada show in Soviet Ukraine. In other words, Soviet theatre
found its influences in an American Broadway play and a Weimar Germany smash hit.[25]

The American *Burlesque* focused more on the backstage antics of variety theatre actors than the variety show itself. The play told the story of
a couple, Skid and Bonnie, who perform in a variety show. Skid lands
a job in a big Broadway musical, which leads to alcohol, temptation,
and betrayal of Bonnie. All's well that ends well, however, and Skid
learns his lesson and returns to his loyal Bonnie and their variety show.
Played on Broadway in 1926, the show was of a piece with other variety shows showcasing the music styles of jazz as well as the American melodrama of the young Eugene O'Neill, whose *Anna Christie* and
Desire under the Elms had already graced Broadway. Hollywood made
three films based on the play: 1929's *The Dance of Life*, 1937's *Swing High,
Swing Low*, and in 1948, *When My Baby Smiles at Me*. The three remakes
attest to the dependable box office formula among American audiences
of backstage melodramas.[26]

Max Reinhardt, however, transformed *Burlesque* for his theatre in
Berlin. Reinhardt had become, by the 1920s, the major theatre innovator
in German-speaking Europe; among other achievements, he started the
Salzburg Festival with Hugo von Hoffmannsthal. Reinhardt ran several
of the major houses in Berlin, which received state and municipal funding, until 1933 when he emigrated to the U.S. after the rise of Hitler.
Reinhardt focused less on plot and more on using the play to display
technical innovation. Both Vyshnia and Hirniak remember Vladimir

Sokoloff (or Sokolov), a Russian émigré and former Moscow Art Theatre actor now famous in the Berlin scene and wowing audiences in
the production. Yet Hirniak's and Vyshnia's overwhelming reactions
to Reinhardt's technological prowess point to Emil Orlik's set design,
which featured filmed images of the theatre's backstage displayed for
the audience, giving the impression of taking the audience behind the
scenes and making them a part of the production itself.[27]

Weimar theatrical culture in the late 1920s was characterized by
cabaret, both in seedy underground clubs and in major theatres like
Reinhardt's. According to Hirniak, the Soviet Ukrainians also took in
a French revue (this could be confused with the 1927 trip with Kurbas), and Berlin nightlife cabaret, thanks to a taxi driver who knew
such locales, and was a former officer in the tsarist army happy to serve
"countrymen from Little Russia." Vyshnia noted that they took in a
play at "Skala," La Scala de Berlin, one of the most celebrated variety
theatres in the city, and Vyshnia was impressed by the multiple different acts, including the trapeze, presented during one evening's performance. La Scala was also, however, the current home of the Swiss
clown Grock. Grock, a tall clown with white pancake makeup and a
skull-cap, was a musical clown and could play – apparently – 24 instru-
ments. He combined brilliant musical and technical skill with the affect
of a naïf; he was famous for the way he drew out the words "warum?"
(why) and "nit moeglich!" (not possible!) to an increasingly frustrated
straight man. In 1927, in fact, Leonid Utesov himself travelled to Berlin
and studied Grock's clown acts intensively.[28]

Precisely how these 1927 and 1928 trips to Berlin shaped the production of the first-ever Ukrainian-language variety show remains a
mystery. Did Kurbas, like Utesov, see Grock at La Scala in 1927? Did
Vyshnia and Hirniak discuss the Reinhardt production of *Artists* with
Kurbas and their colleagues in the literary fair on their return to Soviet
Ukraine? The precise genealogy of artistic inspiration may remain
opaque, but the theatrical landscape in Berlin, with its technological
innovation and experimentation in form does seem to have shaped the
search for Soviet Ukrainian entertainment.

Kurbas now tried to solve the problem of entertainment unsolved by
Ukrainization: how should artists make the estrada form both Soviet
and Ukrainian and create urban culture for the masses? The State Publishing Company of Soviet Ukraine published the play in 1929, but
copies no longer exist. However, the archive-museum of the former
Berezil' Theatre contains drafts of *intermediia*, sketches and jokes from

the production. Some match the description of act 1 sketches detailed in Cherkashyn's or Hirniak's memoirs, or photographs of the production. Others do not, but exist in enough copies to suggest that they do indeed make up the production. Analysed together, these sketches suggest what was humorous and what was important for the literary fair.

Act I: Soviet Comedy

The production began with two actors, Iosyp Hirniak (playing Borys Arnoldovych Bream) and Marian Krushel'nyts'kyi (playing Panteleimon Panteleimonovych Piglet), emerging from the audience. This may have been a reference to the *hanamichi,* the arm extending from the stage on which characters entered and exited, characteristic of Japanese Kabuki drama. The hanamichi inspired many early twentieth-century artists, including Max Reinhardt, who had learned about the hanamichi from his stage designer Emil Orlik, who had spent a year in Japan studying woodblock prints. As *conferenciers* for the three-act revue, Bream and Piglet told jokes and their song, *Kharkiv, Kharkiv,* Maik Iohansen's parody of an ode by Pavlo Tychyna, always provoked laughter in the audience. Bream and Piglet led the audience on a "gallop around Kharkiv," a series of short sketches portraying Soviet Ukrainian life, including jokes about the lack of products in the General Store, and rhymed verses about bandits, drunks, and the sports-obsessed. These sketches could speak to any Soviet subject; other jokes were more specific to Soviet Ukraine.[29]

Several sketches involved the relationship between Soviet Ukraine and Moscow and reflected the importance of internal transnationalism in the construction of culture in the republic. One involved the definition of the acronym *URE*: did it refer to the Red Army, or to the Ukrainian Revolution? The character *Unwritten* explained that it referred to the Ukrainian Soviet Encyclopedia (*Ukrains'ka radians'ka entsiklopediia*). Character *Kopystka* responds, "That's, shoot (*mat'*), those books that have all those *soviet* words collected in them?" The word used was *sovetski,* the Russian word for Soviet versus *radians'ki,* the Ukrainian word – thus implying that this was a Russian project and pointing out the dissonance of a Ukrainian encyclopedia in Russian. Another sketch involved *Crocodile* (Krokodil'), the Moscow-based satire journal, and *Red Pepper* (Chervonyi perets'), the Kharkiv-based satire journal, together on a hunt. Introducing himself to a passerby *Crocodile* said, "I'm a special shock worker organ that bests bureaucrats, bunglers,

Figure 3.2. A Gallop around Kharkiv, *Hello from Radiowave 477!* (Shevchenko)

fools, wreckers, deviants, and other plagues." *Red Pepper*, in contrast, said simply, "And I'm *Red Pepper*, a satirical-humourist bi-weekly. Fifth year of publication. Cost – 15 kopecks." Like *Red Pepper, Hello* was supposed to offer a *radians'ki*, and not *sovetski* urban cultural product, and was intended to mark a contrast with Moscow-based *sovetskaia kultura*. The challenge of doing so must have provided part of the humour.[30]

Jokes on the relationship between Soviet Ukraine and Moscow included jokes on the police, the GPU. In another sketch making fun of the Gleeful Proletarian Theatre, Unwritten queried why the director (former Kurbas and Berezil protégé Ianuarii Bortnyk) should have shot himself: was it because he asked the state for a permanent space for his theatre and he did not receive one from the Party-state, or because he was ordered to go to Donbas and would rather die? Kopystka answered that the director must be an embezzler taking Soviet money and escaping away to Donbas. Unwritten rejected such an explanation; that could not be the case because "now the GPU arrests embezzlers before they even get to such a point." The joke contained several layers: on the lack of space for theatre; on Bortnyk's Gleeful Proletarian Theatre rivaling Kurbas' Berezil'; on the Donbas; on the GPU; on the situation in Kharkiv where a theatre director would potentially shoot himself. The jokes also operated on insider knowledge that, in fact, much of the personnel and even productions of the Gleeful Proletarian came from the Berezil'. These jokes about the relationship between Ukraine and Moscow highlight the cultural reorientation taking place between centre and periphery.[31]

Act II: Europe in Soviet Ukraine

While act 1 included multiple sketches and seemingly endless characters, act 2 took place in a Western-style hotel, in which a bellboy, played by director and choreographer Borys Balaban, and his friend, played by Kurbas' wife, Valentyna Chystiakova, cavorted in a luxury suite. According to memoirs, Chystiakova, an accomplished dancer and musician, performed a Chaplinesque mime sequence in which she "encountered" a piano for the first time, slowly began to play and eventually played like a virtuoso, which scared her so much that she retreated from the magical instrument. While she played the piano, Balaban performed various "American" dances, such as the Charleston, the tango, and the shimmy. Jazz and American dance styles were popular even in the Land of the Soviets, as were Chaplin movies. Chystiakova's physically expressive style of acting, and her costume and makeup, recalled Charlie Chaplin's iconic character of the Tramp. Act 2 of *Hello*, then, reflected the literary fair's interest in film, and the sounds and movements of the contemporary dance hall – as well as the West.[32]

However, the literary fair strove to create not Soviet culture, but Soviet *Ukrainian* culture. Could the contemporary dance hall, with its tangos and shimmies, belong to Soviet Ukrainian theatrical culture? This question of how modern urban culture could become a part of the theatrical performance culture of Soviet Ukraine plagued the literary fair. The journal *Literary Fair* not only recalled Gogol', whose *Sorochintsy Fair* took place right outside Poltava, but also the European fair focused on Vienna. The editors write that Vienna might be considered a "province compared with Berlin," until one takes into account the *iarmarok*, the market, the fair: the Prater, the carousel, the "proletarian entertainments." Europe offered a model of urban culture that they could transport to Soviet Ukraine.[33]

Of course, Europe offered more than inspiration. Several elites, such as Kurbas, or actor Iosyp Hirniak, grew up in Galicia; that is, they themselves were from "Europe." They travelled frequently to Germany or Poland, and their childhoods were shaped by influences different from those in the Russian Empire. As writer Iurii Shevel'ov notes in his memoirs, culture for many was *Kultur*, Germanic in origin. Kurbas grew up in the Austro-Hungarian Empire, studied in the imperial centre of Vienna, and spoke fluent German. Shevel'ov, years later, wrote that as a young teenager in Kharkiv he recognized Kurbas by his brown leather coat, which must have been from Germany because "no one had such a coat" in Soviet Ukraine.[34]

The cultural orientation of Soviet Ukraine was a point of tension, however. Of particular concern to the GPU and its informers was Mykola Khvyl'ovyi's long-term trip abroad in December 1927. His official *agentura* file, in fact, starts upon his return to Soviet Ukraine in 1928. Khvyl'ovyi and his family, noted informer "Literary Man," were dressed "in the latest fashion of Europe," and "laden down with seven suitcases and a new typewriter." The GPU and informers, then, objected to the European provenance of clothes, material objects, and styles that reeked of another world.[35] Nor did everyone agree that Europe should offer a source of inspiration. Futurist poet (and denizen of Cafe Pok and neighbour of Kurbas at Villa Zhatkina) Mykhail' Semenko found fault with Kurbas' European connections and wrote in an open letter in verse in his journal, *New Generation*, "Is it possible that your European-ness, which is well known to us, / has prevented / you / from carrying on with unenlightened Asiatics?" Despite the *New Generation*'s interest in German expressionism and Bauhaus architecture, Semenko painted Kurbas as bourgeois and anti-Soviet: "In your orangerie you are the only *pan*."[36]

The cultural orientation towards Europe also carried political conse-quences. In his polemical pamphlets arguing that Soviet Ukraine had to turn to European and not to Russian culture for direction, Mykola Khvyl'ovyi was careful to clarify that he meant a cultural Europe, not a political (i.e., bourgeois or capitalist) Europe: "Europe – it's the experi-ence of many centuries ... It's – the Europe of colossal civilization, the Europe – of Goethe, Darwin, Byron, Newton, Marx, et cetera and so forth." In his salvo, Khvyl'ovyi argued that if elites in Soviet Ukraine oriented themselves culturally on Moscow, they would end up as Little Russians, and Soviet Ukraine would sink into provincial status, a new Little Russia.[37]

Commissar of Enlightenment Oleksandr Shums'kyi, at the same time, discussed with Stalin the failures of Ukrainization and suggested that there were still too many ethnic Russians in the Party, a conversation provoking Stalin's now-famous letter to Lazar Kaganovich. Shums'kyi was duly removed – but there were political consequences with the Communist Party of Western Ukraine, in Poland. Communists fighting the good fight against the anti-Communist and anti-Ukrainian Polish government did not understand the political expediency of Moscow's removal of a Communist advocating Ukrainian nationalism. Politburo debates on Ukrainization and Khvyl'ovyi's pamphlet reflected the tense triangular relationship between Soviet Ukraine, Europe, and Moscow. Soviet Ukrainian state leader Hryhorii Petrovs'kyi clarified: "The question is not about national policy, but rather about authority." One member further noted, "Khvyl'ovyi opened such a deep question that I don't dare oppose him." As Petrovs'kyi implied, the issue was not really whether they held meetings in Ukrainian or in Russian; the issue was that authority, ultimately, was not in Soviet Kharkiv, but in Moscow. Khvyl'ovyi's pamphlet did not pose a problem and occupy space on the Soviet Ukrainian Politburo agenda because it was wrong, but rather because it touched on a nerve: the relationship between Soviet Ukraine and Moscow, which posed a problem that the literary fair as well as Politburo members were trying to solve.[38]

Act III: Elites and Mass Culture

The jokes of act 1 and the silent-movie tango of act 2 spoke to a general audience, but the insider quality to act 3 circumscribed *Hello's* audience, and not everyone was entertained. One had to be in the literary fair to decipher all the riddles. Act 3 showed an actor dressed as Vyshnia hunting in the forest and encountering a line of dancing girls in a café called Hell. There, he met other actors dressed as literary figures Iurii Smolych, Maik Iohansen, Oles' Dosvitnyi, and Mykola Khvyl'ovyi. At some point some of the girls sat on the laps of the masked literary figures. Memoirs point to an Owl appearing, and to either the Owl and/or Vyshnia singing an aria to alcohol. Vadym Meller's set design consisted of a series of huge, lighted, concentric rings that could move and create different shapes for each act. On the lighted rings now hung large disks creating the illusion of tables at a café. At these "tables" sat two-dimensional flat figures of blackfaced café visitors, a trope used often at this time to suggest an American or European *café chantant*.[39]

This act held many inside jokes; one critic of the time even went so far as to call the show a "rebus," and in fact, when the show went on tour to Kyiv, one reviewer complained because he did not understand all the "hints, however witty, on certain individuals known in Kharkiv literary circles." Informer "Young Guy" noted to the GPU that a series of fake questionnaires filled out by writers in a new literary journal were "senseless, filled with stupidities and the tendency, which is growing recently, of writing for themselves, just like *Hello from Radiowave 477!*"[40]

This exclusive show meant for the masses held many inside jokes. Vyshnia, in fact, did often go hunting, and often with his friends Khvyl'ovyi, Smolych, and Iohansen. Vyshnia (together with much of the literary fair) also drank a lot; his wife wrote that they were all lucky to make it home after meetings at *Red Pepper*. It may be a stretch, but Café *Peklo* (Hell) sounds remarkably like Café *Pok*, site of many literary fair rendezvous. There were more riddles in acts 1 and 2 for those in the know. The character of Kopystka was a clear reference to the hero of Mykola Kulish's play *97*. In fact, in one sketch, the *conferenciers* refer to the authors as "authors-plagiarists, that is, literary villains. They stole Kopystka from the play of Mykola Kulish *97*." In a later sketch Kopystka himself appears and introduces himself to Unwritten: "I'm Musii Kopystka." To which Unwritten replies, "I'm Unwritten, the hero of an unwritten worker's play." His interlocutor responds, "Oh, my brother, it'll be very tough for you, since you're still unwritten, to debut in this revue!" This wordplay would not make sense to anyone who did not know the history of Kulish and the Berezil.[41] Iosyp Hirniak's makeup as the *conferencier* Bream made him resemble a young Les' Kurbas. The show's opening tune had catchy lyrics by Maik Iohansen that parodied the poetry of Pavlo Tychyna; anyone who knew the two literary fair members would have been amused since they famously did not get along personally. Finally, the masked figures in act 3 would have appeared even more bizarre, presumably, if one did not recognize these literary figures by their faces – hardly a skill that everyone "turning the radio to frequency 477" possessed. Kurbas wanted to create a show that would "Ukrainianize the street," but one has to wonder how much a person off the street would understand *Hello from Radiowave*

477! The show seems more created for insiders than the Everyman of the Soviet mass audience.[42]

Of course, the literary fair constituted a significant sector of the audience. The journal *Literary Fair* – which was read by the literary fair – advertised *Hello* and noted that all tickets were sold out for the "joyful revue" for the current week, but urged readers to buy tickets for the next week at the box office. Readers of *Literary Fair* – themselves in most cases members of the literary fair – were those likely to see *Hello*. Yet, ironically, those readers were those least likely to actually purchase tickets. Those working for the Party-state and the newspapers enjoyed permanent seats in the theatre. In the Berezil', the local Commissariat of Enlightenment received seats 11–14 in the first row of the orchestra; in the second row of the orchestra sat members of the GPU and the Arts Workers' Union, and representatives and critics from the local newspapers – all in a row. Republic-level Party-state institutions received entire boxes of seats up in the loge levels.[43]

But who else attended the production? Audience statistics give us some sense of the non-insider audience of *Hello*. In this 1928–9 season, the Berezil' gave 165 performances of ten plays. They had almost 133,000 spectators over the season, although their numbers do not indicate repeat visitors. General attendance was at about 72 per cent, or 800 people per evening in the 1,000-person theatre. If we rely on the 1926 census that claimed 23 million people in Soviet Ukraine, then only about half a per cent of the population saw the Berezil' in action, and an even smaller fraction of that saw *Hello*.[44]

Still, the Berezil' remained a big deal for these 133,000 people. Students, Red Army soldiers, or members of Party committees could purchase subscription books. In the season of *Hello*, the Berezil' made 40,000 karbovantsy from student subscriptions alone. The subscription books cost about 5 karbovantsy, so this suggests about 8,000 students attended the theatre, which is no small matter. Iurii Shevel'ov speaks of how the "theatre debates" around Kurbas in early Soviet Kharkiv attracted young people who were from the village and initiating themselves to Soviet urban life. Bream and Piglet, who both emerged from the audience to run the show, were intended to be Kharkiv students, one from the village and one from the city. Buying a subscription book and attending the theatre, then, offered young people a path to insidership. Seeing *Hello* and learning what literary celebrities looked like and deciphering the inside jokes could serve as a key to the privileged world of elites.[45]

Figure 3.3. The Berezil' audience (TsDKFFA 10670-II)

Indeed, the literary fair who socialized at the Berezil' were elites. A female informant wrote in 1930 about a certain Ivan Purin, who divulged to her about the literary circles of Kharkiv. Purin, a worker in the state apparat who dreamed of becoming a writer, claimed friendship with such elites as Khvyl'ovyi, Kurbas, and star Berezil' actor Amvrosii Buchma. He had all the qualities of an insider: he proudly drank a lot, he was a Party member, he knew GPU workers, and he was part of a milieu, "where everyone feels very free, where they often gather in a bar ... with women and they drink a lot." Purin bragged to the female informant that these were "his own people" and that when they got together they spoke "in their own cultured language that only they understand." The world of *Hello from Radiowave 477!* then, was indeed a desirable milieu for those anxious to become insiders in early Soviet Kharkiv.[46]

Moreover, elites and non-elites alike loved comedy. Audience attendance for the 1928–9 season was highest for *Hello*, Gilbert and Sullivan's operetta *The Mikado*, and Mykola Kulish's satire on Ukrainization *Myna Mazailo*. In other words, these Soviet statistics, however doctored they may have been, do suggest general interest, on the part of insiders and outsiders purchasing tickets, in modern, urban, and comic theatre. There was a demand for this entertainment, and in *Hello from Radiowave 477!* the literary fair attempted to fulfil it.[47]

But the audience remained an enigma for the Berezil', as the production itself expressed. When asked about what kind of art he liked, the character Red-head explained, "I like it when there's, you know, beauty, comfort ... velvet chairs, blue light. I like it when it's naturalistic and there's something to look at. And when a play is a play, and the actresses are plump. Like for example, I really adore fights or sword-swallowers." *Hello* was an attempt to create a variety theatre production for Soviet Ukraine, that is, a production reflecting a performance reminiscent of "fights and sword-swallowers," albeit done in a more modern style. The performers made fun, in this moment, of philistine audience members, at the same time as they were creating a performance for the mass audience, many of whom must have loved watching sword-swallowers and plump actresses in luxurious velvet seats. The Berezil' wanted to attract precisely those audience members of whom they made fun.[48]

In one of the sketches of *Hello* an amateur photographer came on stage, looked directly out at the audience breaking the fourth wall, and commanded, in the Russian language, "Make a serious face! Merci!" as he snapped a picture. The moment collapsed the boundary between both the audience and artists, because the photographer-actor broke the fourth wall, and yet through language separated the spectators from the players, since *Hello* was a production at a consciously Ukrainian-language theatre. The moment threw the focus on the audience, as if those on stage wanted to capture those sitting in the theatre and laughing at the performance on the stage.[49]

Yet the barrier between those on stage and the non-literary-fair audience could be all too real. Kurbas' student, Vasyl' Vasyl'ko, was the artistic director of the Red Factory Theatre, designed to cater to Kharkiv's industrial working masses. He lamented at a 1929 meeting, "We have to work among spectators who at the end of last season threw ... not only apples, but also iron objects at the heads of the actors." The attempt to reach the masses was, in 1929, far from successful. Intriguingly, however, Vasyl'ko's diary continues with little concern over attempting to reach the masses, threatening his actors with iron objects and fruit, and focuses more on the ins and outs of Party politics in the theatre.[50]

And no wonder – after all, it was not the masses of individual ticket buyers that would ensure a theatre's success, but rather patronage extended by the Party and the state. The paradox of *Hello*, the representation of inside jokes for the masses, reflects the challenges of the audience in a system where the state had a complete monopoly over the arts. While the theatrical production may have been aimed at the masses, in reality it was not the general public but the literary fair that constituted the most important audience for theatre. After all, patronage came from within the web of personal and professional connections in Soviet Kharkiv: ties with Party-state institutions were crucial for repertory and financial stability, and reviews written by friends and colleagues kept the wheels of theatrical production running smoothly.

With audience input therefore removed, Party-state patronage became crucial to finance theatre, and local connections with officialdom provided the path to securing funds. Socialist theatre had no box office – or at least not a box office contributing in any significant way to a theatre's income. What mattered for success was not how many tickets a theatre sold, but how many seats its managers succeeded in "organizing" through Party connections. In a state-supported arts "market" of a state monopoly, funds came not from the public (i.e., the box office), but the Party-state. Theatre was (and is), quite simply, an extremely expensive art form, so companies depended on state subsidies to fund their seasons, which resulted in a turn away from the audience, and towards the patron, the Party-state. From where else could a theatre like the Berezil' acquire the cash and credit to mount a production except the Party-state? The company received the highest state subsidy for a theatre, 120,300 karbovantsy, almost twice as much as the second-highest theatre, the Ivan Franko Theatre in Kyiv. And in fact, in the 1928–9 season, the Berezil' was recorded as having received over 157,000 karbovantsy, since throughout the season theatres continually requested more funds.[51]

The Soviet Ukrainian Commissariat of Enlightenment then subsidized the theatre, and the theatre decided how to best spend the money. Subsidies combined funding from several sources, even in the case of the top theatres both republic-level and local-level institutions contributed to the budget. In the 1929–30 season, the theatre spent more money on *Hello from Radiowave 477!* than on any other show. The company spent almost 8,000 karbovantsy on preparation, including 763 karbovantsy for special electric equipment, 213 to hire a fencing instructor, and 21 to create a *papier-mâché* horse for a comic sketch in act 1. Most of the artists involved in the show were on yearly salary, ranging from under 100 karbovantsy a month for young artists like Roman Cherkashyn, to 500 a month for artistic director Les' Kurbas. Any artist involved in the show not on staff received an honorarium for work performed, such as composer Iulii Meitus, who received 400 karbovantsy for writing the show's music.[52]

Of course, the theatres' managing directors, Party officials appointed by the Commissariat, had to report clearly how theatres spent their subsidies. But these appointees had little to no authority. For example, the beleaguered Volodymyr Novits'kyi, the Berezil''s managing director in 1928–9, had to once personally travel to Odesa to track down Kurbas in order to clarify several matters for his report. The Berezil' – despite the hefty state funds – was continually in financial difficulty. The Commissariat's inspectors noted financial irresponsibility: actors used theatre props and set pieces to furnish their apartments, and the theatre lent money to individuals and even entire theatres (like the Soviet Ukrainian State Yiddish Theatre) unlikely to pay back the loans. Yet the failure to use state funds wisely never seems to have mattered for future support, and the money kept rolling in from the Party-state.[53]

The paradox of the Soviet audience remained: the mass audience constituted theatre's focus and goal, yet the very institutions of Soviet theatre and the state monopoly over the arts precluded truly including the audience in theatrical production. Theatre in Soviet Ukraine (and by extension in the Soviet Union) was a state theatre for the public that never reached the public but remained entrenched in the state. Those in the audience, those onstage, and those in the wings backstage largely belonged to the same milieu, one largely removed from the masses. The myth of theatre for the people remained, but the reality far from achieved this goal.[54]

Yet this paradox of a production created by insiders for the masses may have mattered less with modern technology. Theatre was a widespread form of mass culture in the nineteenth century, but advances in film production and distribution, as well as the spread of radio, meant that theatre became more exclusive. It simply could not reach the numbers of spectators that a film could. There may have been inside jokes in Il'f-Petrov's *Circus*, for example, but the film's distribution across the entire Soviet Union necessarily increased its resonance with a mass audience because the masses were able to see it. *Hello* may have attempted to be theatre that was radio, but it remained firmly a live theatrical performance unable to reach the masses.

Part III: Ethnic Entertainment

Most of the scholarship on non-Russian culture focuses on the positive effects of *korenizatsiia* (here, Ukrainization) because officialdom promoted and supported culture in non-Russian languages in a way that the state never had in the imperial period. Indeed, the years of korenizatsiia corresponded to years of artistic flourishing in Soviet Ukraine. The korenizatsiia-as-positive focus identifies oppression promulgated from Moscow as the cause of the demise of the 1920s renaissance in Ukrainian-language artistic culture, and there is no doubt that the murder of the top artists during two days in 1937 in Sandormorkh challenged the future creative output of Soviet Ukraine. In 1937 Khvyl'ovyi had committed suicide, Dosvitnyi, Kulish, Iohansen, and Kurbas were shot, and Hirniak and Vyshnia were imprisoned in the gulag. The Soviet state, without a doubt, took its toll on the talents of the borderlands.[55]

But korenizatsiia, more than a specific set of policies outlined in 1923, represented a more general practice of ethno-national categorization characterizing the entire Soviet period. For a multi-ethnic place, ethnic particularism posed particular challenges. Yuri Slezkine, in a famous article, used Lithuanian Bolshevik Juozas Vareikis' image of the "communal apartment" to analyse the paradox that the Bolsheviks, avowed enemies of nationalism, actually promoted nationalism in the form of ethnic particularism. But the communal apartment image breaks down when taken out of the context of Bolshevik ideology and placed in the concrete context of Soviet Ukraine.[56]

It is perhaps significant that Vareikis, a Lithuanian Bolshevik working in 1924 in the Central Asian apparat, used an image that focused on the universal inclusivity of Soviet nationality policy; put simply, there was room for everyone, from Balts to Central Asians, in the Soviet Union. Yet looking from the provinces, Vareikis' metaphor resonates differently: his metaphor has no room for republics, only for ethnicities. The space envisioned is a unitary one, and Soviet Ukraine as a separate region ceases to exist. The literary fair, in fact, understood Soviet nationality policy in an entirely different way. For them, ethnic particularism offered a means not to create universal Soviet culture, but rather to promote their own national culture locally in the complicated ethnic patchwork of Soviet Ukraine.

Moreover, "Ukrainian" was far from an objective cultural category. Korenizatsiia required articulating what precisely each ethnic culture would look like, and few agreed, either on form or content. When comparing cultural processes in Moscow and Soviet Ukraine, it is therefore striking that that Il'f-Petrov and Vyshnia were engaged in different cultural processes: while Il'f-Petrov, like Bulgakov, was creating Soviet culture, Vyshnia, like Kulish, was creating Soviet "ethno-national" (here, Ukrainian) culture. Categorization by ethnicity shaped cultural production and reception in Soviet Ukraine far more than in Moscow. Korenizatsiia presumes stable categories, and it is precisely these categories that were unstable in the 1920s.[57]

Soviet Ukraine posed a particular challenge for ethno-national categorization simply because its population comprised so many ethnic groups. According to the 1926 census, 80 per cent of the population declared themselves Ukrainian, but most of those respondents lived in villages. Cities displayed quite a different makeup; only 4 per cent of Odesa's population was Ukrainian, for example. Of the 12,000 artists registered with the Arts Workers' Union in Soviet Ukraine, 40 per cent were registered as Jews, 30 per cent as Russians, and 24 per cent as Ukrainian. Reflecting this diversity, Ukraine sponsored forty-eight theatres in eight languages: Moldovan (2), Russian (7), Ukrainian (33), Yiddish (2), German, Polish, Bulgarian, and Armenian (1 each). As a result, Soviet Ukraine sponsored more theatres in non-Russian languages than any other republic. These numbers show the monumental task facing Soviet Ukrainian elites who believed in the necessity of culture not only Soviet, but also Ukrainian.[58]

The literary fair solved this dilemma, like good Soviets, by organizing the arts according to ethno-national categories: Jewish audiences were assigned to the Jewish theatre with Jewish artists and Jewish plays; Ukrainian audiences to the Ukrainian theatre with Ukrainian artists and Ukrainian plays; Polish audiences to the Polish theatre with Polish artists and Polish plays; and so forth. Organization according to ethno-national units contained a specific hierarchy, whereby the theatres of the titular ethnos of the republic received the most funding from the Party-state, and theatres of ethnic minorities received significantly less support (such as allocation of funds for renovations or opportunities for touring). Soviet Ukraine accordingly privileged its Ukrainian-language theatres. In Soviet Ukraine, the Russian-language theatres,

Yiddish-language theatres, and the Polish-language theatre (in fact, the only one in the entire Union) competed for local support and funding.

These categories necessarily broke down in practice, both artistically and institutionally. The literary fair, as shown in chapter 2, may have aimed at creating artistic products not only Soviet, but also somehow Ukrainian, but this process of articulation and separation took place in a multi-ethnic landscape. Yet cultural and political elites still aspired to the full separation of cultural institutions by ethnicity and privileged Ukrainian-language culture. At an Artistic-Political Council meeting of 1929, the managing director of the Yiddish theatre in Kharkiv, Saul Guzhnovskii, expressed concern about the lack of Ukrainian-language plays available for translation and inclusion in his theatre's repertory. The Yiddish theatre could not produce Kulish's *Myna Mazailo* – a satire on Ukrainization – because "they [the Jewish audience] would not understand this play, the Ukrainian spectators would not react approvingly [to a Yiddish translation], and moreover the Jewish listener would not understand." Guzhnovskii's concern reflects the assumption behind ethno-national organization of complete difference between the Yiddish and Ukrainian theatre audiences. The "Ukrainian spectators" and the "Jewish listener" did not overlap for Guzhnovskii. However fluid these borders may in fact have been in practice, officials viewed these cultural institutions – and therefore the cultures represented inside – as separate.[59]

The ethnic separation of theatre institutions meant that theatrical culture was categorized by ethnicity and not by region. A speech by apparatchik Petrenko in 1929 reflected this rigid understanding of cultural categories. Although he declared himself in favour of "Ukrainian Soviet art," he still believed "that all the national minorities in Ukraine should be provided with their own national art." In other words, non-Ukrainian minority art was "national," in the same way that Ukrainian art was itself national. The arts of national minorities deserved protection in Soviet Ukraine, but were not included in the cultural category of "Ukrainian" Soviet art. This shows the dilemma of korenizatsiia in a multi-ethnic space: categorization by ethnicity prohibited the development of a particularly "Soviet Ukrainian" theatre that might incorporate other ethnic categories, focus on region as opposed to ethnicity, or highlight the cultural hybridity unique to the region. Put differently, Petrenko's declaration carried the assumption that Soviet Ukraine should support Yiddish theatre but not allow for the more localized cultural category of "Soviet Ukrainian Yiddish."[60]

Moreover, separating the arts by ethnos demanded clear differentiation between the various artistic cultures in the region: Ukrainian, Russian, Polish, and Jewish (among others). The content of "Ukrainian" culture itself was far from clear – to artists, to officials, and indeed, to audiences. Mykola Kulish declared in a meeting that "the national question is not such a trivial question, it is the question of an entire era of social revolution, the question of our party, etc., which has been solved in the Union, but not solved in its entirety." The stakes for creating Soviet Ukrainian culture were indeed high.[61]

Yet *Hello* was a product that defied korenizatsiia's categories. Ultimately, the production suggests some of the challenges posed by ethnic particularism for the development of modern, urban entertainment culture. *Hello* emerged from multiple influences, including Max Reinhardt's Berlin theatre and a French cabaret. The show expressed the quintessence of the literary fair, but was not reducible to ethnically particular culture. Act 1 operated on the internal transnationalism between Soviet Ukraine and Moscow; act 2's tango and silent-movie style had no "markers" to distinguish it as ethnically Ukrainian, but rather reflected global trends of modern and urban culture; act 3 depicted the world of artistic production and reception in early Soviet Kharkiv, but one defined not ethnically but rather by personalities, faces, and inside jokes. A theatrical product that demanded local knowledge (of poets' faces), a wide perspective (reaching to Moscow), facility with multiple languages (Russian and Ukrainian), and a cosmopolitan sensibility for the latest dance fads (tango) – *Hello* challenged the categories of korenizatsiia culture. It was a cosmopolitan cultural product that was entirely local – hardly just Ukrainian, yet also not just Soviet, it was "Soviet Ukrainian," reflecting the rich cultural landscape of the former southwest provinces and also the new Soviet modernity. Here was the challenge: korenizatsiia rested on ethnic categories, yet modern and urban entertainments challenged those categories, or were at least not circumscribed by them.

Part IV: Searching for Ukrainian Tangos

The attempt to bring estrada to a state-theatre stage continued with the Berezil'′s 1931 revue show, *Four Chamberlains*, also starring Bream and Piglet. But the trend did not last. Revue shows were relegated Union-wide to specifically designated musical comedy theatres and away from the larger academic theatres, like the Berezil'. Instead of estrada or revue shows as part of a theatre's repertory, the genre was categorized and classified away into its own theatres. In Kharkiv, the Gleeful Proletarian Theatre – the object of such jokes in *Hello* – was one such theatre designated specifically for revue shows. It functioned into 1932, but never enjoyed a permanent performance space, and largely toured around the area playing small venues. Rather than modern and urban mass-oriented culture, in the non-Russian regions mass-oriented culture was ethnicized: Soviet Ukrainian entertainment became folk.[62]

What did mass folk entertainment look like? Il'f-Petrov, in fact, offer a suggestion. Rather, Evgenii Petrov himself offers one. After Il'ia Il'f's untimely death from tuberculosis in 1937, Petrov continued to write screenplays, until his own death in a plane crash during the Second World War. In 1940 he completed *Quiet Ukrainian Night*, perhaps a reference to Pushkin's poem about the Battle of Poltava. Yet while *Hello* was theatre aiming to be radio, this screenplay of Petrov's was film presenting theatre.[63]

The story takes place in 1940 and focuses on two rival song-and-dance ensembles, one from Poltava and one from Kremenchuk. Petrov describes the first orchestra, *Zirka Kapella*: "It's the most ordinary kapella, such as you meet on the periphery and such as you would meet several decades ago. The chorus is singing one of the songs that kapellas of this kind always sing."[64] With this note Petrov highlights the traditional quality of this musical group, meant to represent many such groups that one would find "on the periphery" in the waning days of the Russian Imperial Southwest. Indeed, Petrov underscores the authenticity of these groups through the plot: each kapella has long been a family business, which creates a sense of continuity between the culture of the Russian Empire and that of the Soviet Union.

Of course, like any good romantic melodrama, the plot of *Quiet Ukrainian Night* hinges on a love story. Stars of the two rival ensembles fall in love, mirroring the love affair of the artistic directors of the rival ensembles, who also fall back into each others' arms after a resolved quarrel. Although it seems like all's well that ends well, disagreements over which group will move to which city – Poltava or Kremenchuk – break up the romantic pairs. Finally an apparatchik in the Soviet Ukrainian Commissariat of Enlightenment summons both the older and younger couples to his office and explains that there will be a *dekada* (festival) of Soviet Ukrainian art in Moscow and they must represent the republic to the best of their abilities. The apparatchik critiques them strongly:

Your collectives are stuck in place and don't move forwards. Old repertoire ...
you probably do not even suspect the repertory richness possessed by
Our Ukraine. The songs and dances of Donbas, the Black Sea region, the
Western Ukraine of Bukovina. Wonderful rituals, guessing games, dances,
and of course wedding traditions.[65]

The apparatchik promotes the importance of folk orchestras for representing Soviet Ukraine in Moscow, as well as reducing the "richness" of
the newly acquired Western territories to wedding rituals and rural traditions. Under pressure, the troupes join forces and create a production
of a Ukrainian wedding ceremony at the Kyiv Opera House. Intriguingly, Petrov adds one more red herring to the plot, when the young
heroine refuses to kiss her man – but it turns out that she is simply
shy in front of all the spectators. The wedding ritual, an "authentic"
rural tradition recreated in Soviet context, represented reality, since the
young couple has now reunited. The screen fades to black as we leave
our two ensembles, rivals no longer, hurtling in a train car from the
periphery to the capital to represent Soviet Ukraine with their *banduras*,
their wedding rituals, and their charming folkish kitsch.[66]

This film was never made. Perhaps it was soon overtaken by 1941 and
the need for more war-oriented screenplays. The young romantic lead
is noted as just returning from the Finnish War in 1940, a war in which
Petrov himself participated, which may have been a sensitive topic,
although the censor did not note that particularly character element.
Yet the film highlights official Soviet Ukrainian culture surprisingly
accurately and suggests what official mass-oriented Soviet Ukrainian
entertainment looked like, a particular recipe mixing elements of folk,
live theater, and cinema.

The moments described by Petrov in his screenplay – music and
dance ensembles refusing to work together, the state intervening, issues
over what to present in the Soviet centre – were not the creation of an
author trying to come up with a whimsical plot of charming artists.
Rather, they accurately represented a very real cultural landscape in the
regions, one dominated by folk song and dance troupes and concerned
over quality and allocation of resources. They also represented a very
real relationship with the centre: the apparatchik in Petrov's screenplay
has counterparts in real life as officials struggled to put together the
program to best represent the art of their republic in the Soviet capital.

There were, in fact, two folk orchestras, one from Poltava and
one from the Kyiv Philharmonic, which were forcibly joined by the

Party-state in 1935. Another choral ensemble, Kyiv's *Kapella Dumka*, performed its standard folk and nineteenth-century classic melodies at the 1936 *dekada* of Ukrainian art in Moscow. Indeed, it was precisely folk dance and classic nineteenth-century repertory that represented Soviet Ukraine at the ten-day event in Moscow. Four years later, if there had been a 1940 Ukrainian dekada, Petrov's musical groups would have fit right in at the Hall of Columns in the Kremlin. No modernism, no avant-garde, no jazz: there was no *Hello* represented Soviet Ukraine by 1936.[67]

Yet Petrov knew that the cultural landscape of the former southwest provinces had profoundly changed. Kapellas may have been a major component of late imperial culture, but they hardly represented the extraordinary theatrical flourishing that had taken place in Soviet Ukraine in the 1920s and early 1930s. The quaint world depicted by Petrov would have shocked the literary fair. Indeed, apparatchik Petrenko despaired that it was only the song-and-dance culture traditional to this region's repertoire that was presented as representing Soviet Ukrainian art: "In the RSFSR and in the other Union republics they are not well enough acquainted with our achievements in the sphere of art ... everything presented here is a legacy of the past. *Malorossiishchina* and the *hopak* have no place in Ukraine, and yet here are presented as Ukrainian art." Art in Soviet Ukraine, as Petrenko well knew, included the plays of the Berezil', but at the Union level art in Ukraine appeared as only folk dancing and nineteenth-century melodrama. Why would *Quiet Ukrainian Night* not include rival jazz orchestras, or tango dancers, or the latest stage lighting techniques, like *Hello*?[68]

This lack of modern, urban entertainment challenged Soviet Ukraine when the Soviets entered Eastern Poland in 1939. Evgenii Petrov's film apparatchiks may have been wrangling folk orchestras for a Moscow festival, but in reality, in 1940, apparatchiks were wrangling tangos and jazz for audiences in the lands they had just occupied thanks to the Hitler-Stalin Pact. In Poland, in contrast with Soviet Ukraine, modern and urban Ukrainian music already had a place, if admittedly minimal, in the artistic landscape. One of the successes of theatrical and musical interwar Lwów (today's L'viv) was Ukrainian tango. Bohdan Veselovs'kyi, a young conservatory student, wrote a Poland-wide hit, "Pryide shche chas," The Time Will Come Again, performed with several young friends and colleagues, violinist Leonid Yablons'kyi and accordionist Anatoly Kos-Anatols'kyi, all of whom made up the "Yabtso" jazz orchestra. Veselovs'kyi's hit played on the radio throughout interwar Poland, and so it must have resonated with more than a Ukrainian-speaking audience. For whom they played live remains a mystery; were their listeners largely Ukrainians, or young people in the city, whether Polish, Jewish, or Ukrainian, anxious for a catchy tune? Veselovs'kyi himself left in 1938, leaving the city bereft of modern urban Ukrainian culture. There was no such culture in Ukrainian for the Soviets to co-opt on their arrival, and they had nothing to bring to Eastern Poland except historical melodramas and folk orchestras.[69]

Yet audiences wanted entertainment. The Party-state had to turn to refugees from Nazi-occupied Warsaw to craft Soviet entertainment for the new territories. Soviet L'viv became a refuge for stars of the world of Polish cabaret, cinema, and popular song. The L'viv Philharmonic boasted a *tea-jazz*, theatricalized jazz, division. Run by famous Warsaw composer Henryk Wars, born Warszawski, the group was joined by several Polish-Jewish stars from the celebrated Warsaw cabarets. But this was not all; the most successful theatre in L'viv between 1939 and 1941 was the state-managed Polish-language *Teatr miniatiur*, the Theatre of Small Forms.[70]

It is worth dwelling on the statistics of this period because they show the audience's proclivity for entertainment, and highlight how the Soviet Party-state had to hire new artists to create that entertainment, because Soviet Ukraine did not have urban and modern popular culture to offer. Because the Party-state was unable to immediately organize the house, ticket sales in Soviet-occupied L'viv actually reveal a show's "popularity" because they reflected the tickets purchased by the general public. And ticket-buying audiences lapped up these Polish-Jewish estrada performances. In 1940, the exclusively Polish-language academic theatre and the Yiddish-language academic theatre brought in just over half of their "planned" income; the Theatre of Small Forms overfilled the plan by 150 per cent. In fact, the only questionable statistic (from the Soviet state's point of view) for the Theatre of Small Forms was that they did not create enough productions; this was explained by the popularity of each production and the audience pressure to see each production before it closed. Their products were like *Hello*, not reducible to ethnic particularism, not reducible to folk orchestras, not staid historical melodramas.[71]

And they did not stay long in L'viv. Both the tea-jazz ensemble of the Philharmonic and the Theatre of Small Forms toured throughout the Soviet Union creating cultural products in Russian for an all-Union audience. One of the little-known musical releases of the pre-invasion

1941 Soviet Union was a song called "Only in L'vov," on a disk entitled *A Little Farewell Song of L'vov Jazz*. Polish matinée idol Eugeniusz Bodo sings a Russian version of a Polish song, "Tylko we Lwowie," Only in Lwów, a famous hit written by Wars from a 1939 Polish film homage to Lwów called *Tramps* (Włóczęgi). Bodo, Wars, and the "L'vov Jazz" scene of Warsaw refugees from Warsaw recorded the song in Russian for all-Union distribution, not in Ukrainian for all-republic distribution.[72]

The interwar Ukrainian-language hit "Pryide shche chas" – had it been in Soviet Ukraine – would have been translated into Russian and the Iabtso group would have been transferred to perform at the Kremlin and record for all-Union distribution. Anatoly Kos-Anatols'kyi, Veselovs'kyi's friend from the L'viv Jazz Orchestra, stayed in occupied Soviet Ukraine to play in a revue cabaret called *Wesoły Lwów*, Happy L'viv, under Nazi occupation. After the war he continued to compose, but only classical and folk works – as befitted a Soviet Ukrainian composer.[73]

And what of *Hello from Radiowave 477!* and the attempt at making culture for the modern Soviet Ukrainian street? The mute tango danced in act 2 of *Hello from Radiowave 477!* resulting from cultural and professional trips West, a local product of urban mass-oriented culture, part of Soviet Ukraine but not ethnically necessarily Ukrainian, remained a thing of the past. What was the music of the quiet Ukrainian night? A reference to classic literature, hearkening back to a tradition of nineteenth-century folk and dance ensembles that carried through into the Soviet era and came to represent the region's culture. Yet the quiet Ukrainian night missed the burst of urban popular culture of early Soviet Ukraine; Soviet Ukraine was left with Petrov's duelling folk orchestras and without the tango.

4 The Official Artist: Solomon Mikhoels and Les' Kurbas

The state is able to domesticate the artist because the artist has already made the state his home.

– Miklos Haraszti, *The Velvet Prison*[1]

Part I: Solomon Mikhoels

From the early days of revolution in 1917, artists and officialdom worked together: artists made use of Party-state institutions, and in turn, Party-state officials made use of artists, in order to pursue their respective agendas. By the late 1920s leading artists received enviable amounts of Party-state support, and not only financial. The Soviet state also ensured that artistic achievements were duly recognized. In 1931 The State Jewish Theatre (*Gosudarstvennyi evreiskii teatr*, or GOSET) celebrated its tenth anniversary and received a plethora of telegrams wishing congratulations and continued success from across the Soviet Union. The two State Yiddish Theatres in Soviet Ukraine sent their congratulations to Moscow, and the Soviet Ukrainian Scientific Academy sent regards in Yiddish. Les' Kurbas, a member of the Union-level committee appointed to organize the celebrations, wrote to the company personally that he was unable to attend the ceremonies but sent his congratulations. As a theatre the Berezil' collective wrote to their fellow artists, "Only with the October Revolution did we receive the freedom to create art that was national in form and proletarian in content, Long Live GOSET!"[2]

As the Berezil' was associated with Les' Kurbas, so was GOSET associated with its leading actor and artistic director (from 1928), Solomon Mikhoels. Shlomo Vovsi grew up in a Yiddish-speaking religious family in Dvinsk, today's Latvian city of Daugavpils. His family was scandalized when his older brother, Leyb, left home to become an actor. As a child Shlomo saw one of the plays of Avrom Fishzon's itinerant troupe – *Koldunia*, The Witch – and loved it. Shlomo and his brother Chaim were involved in the cultural scene in Dvinsk: reporting for the local Hebrew-language newspaper, and not only convincing their parents to let them see the circus when it came through town but also creating their own version of a circus and performing it for their friends. Ever the good son and student, however, Vovsi-Mikhoels did not run away with the players like his older brother, but attended the Kyiv Commercial School in 1911 and in 1915 began to study law in St. Petersburg. In post-revolutionary Petrograd, however, fate struck and the law student met theatre director Aleksei Granovskii (born Abram/Abraham Azarkh). Granovskii, like Kurbas, Smolych, and many others from the Russian Imperial borderlands, was shaped not by Stanislavsky, but by Max Reinhardt and the expressionist physicality of the pre-war German-language theatre. Azarkh-Granovskii grew up in Riga and served as assistant director on Reinhardt's famous 1911 Oedipus tour, which led to study in Munich under Reinhardt himself. Except for touring companies, there had been no Yiddish-language theatre in Moscow or St. Petersburg, since these cities were located outside the Pale of Settlement, and Granovskii now wanted to take advantage of new opportunities and form a permanent troupe in the Soviet capital. Mikhoels was one of his first acquisitions. When, during GOSET's 1928 tour to Europe, Granovsky left the troupe to remain in Paris, for complex reasons, Mikhoels was appointed artistic director and the theater has ever since been associated with his prodigious talent.[3]

Kurbas and Mikhoels crossed paths frequently. There was a strong connection between Soviet Ukraine and the Moscow State Jewish theatre; Yiddish-language theatre and the Ukrainian-language theatre had both emerged from the Russian Imperial Southwest and enjoyed audience demand, a rich repertoire, and a deep bench of talent. Many of the GOSET artists were themselves from the former southwest provinces and had either gone north during the Civil War or joined the company when GOSET toured Soviet Ukraine and Soviet Belarus in the 1920s.[4] Indeed, the world depicted in much of the GOSET repertory was that of the former southwest provinces. On GOSET's 1925 tour to Soviet Ukraine, Granovskii made the film *Jewish Luck* (Evreiskoe shchast'e), inspired by Sholem Aleichem's Menachem Mendl, a hapless yet resilient entrepreneur and classic *luftmensch*. Granovskii made the film at the Odesa film studios; the film starred Mikhoels and featured other GOSET actors – as well as intertitles written by Isaak Babel'.[5]

The artists of the theatre companies felt this connection themselves, as Kurbas student and director Vasyl' Vasyl'ko noted in his diary. Vasyl'ko acknowledged that Granovskii's was a "good school." Yet Vasyl'ko also noted with some jealousy the comparative richness of the Yiddish-language company: actors had new shirts at every performance and did not have to help out with any of the backstage requirements because the troupe travelled with large numbers of technical personnel. Still, the two troupes apparently enjoyed a final banquet together.[6]

But the Ukrainian-language director and the Yiddish-language director most famously encountered each other through Mikhoels' 1935 production of *King Lear*. Legend has it that when Kurbas was thrown out of the Berezil' and into exile in Moscow in 1933 he found artistic solace with Mikhoels, and together they crafted Mikhoels' extraordinary performance of Lear, which GOSET finally performed two years later, in 1935, when Kurbas was already imprisoned at Solovki. Film clips and photo stills from this production show its exceptional quality, a product, so the story would suggest, of Ukrainian-Jewish relations in the best sense. The artists' lives continued to intertwine: Kurbas was shot in 1937, Mikhoels murdered in 1948. Two theatrical geniuses, two non-Russian minorities, one Ukrainian, one Jewish, both murdered by the Soviet state, yet the encounter between them resulted not in violence but in a work of great art.[7]

The story is beautiful, but not entirely true. Mikhoels did, in fact, help Kurbas, who was in exile in Moscow, after being removed from his theatre in Kharkiv, and essentially awaiting arrest. Most memoirists point to their fear in contacting (and therefore failure to contact) the Soviet Ukrainian director.[8] However, in Kurbas' arrest file, he is noted as working as a "temporary director" at Mikhoels' theatre. This means that Mikhoels extended to Kurbas official registration at his theatre (a choice that put Mikhoels in danger, too, of course). Theatre scholar Nelli Korniienko notes that Mikhoels' second wife, Asia Pototskaia, remembers Kurbas and Mikhoels talking about *Lear*. But according to Kurbas' file, the two artists worked not on *Lear* but on an anti-fascist play by German social critic Friedrich Wolf. Kurbas was also, apparently, in conversation with the Malyi Theatre for a production of Shakespeare's *Othello*, a play that was also performed in Moscow in 1935. In any case, Kurbas reached Moscow only in mid-October, and the GPU arrested him at the end of December, so he did not have much time to spend on artistic creation.[9] No one can ever know how much even informal discussions between the two artists shaped Mikhoels' *Lear* two years later, but certainly their performance styles, building on physicality, innovative set design, and working with a non-Russian canon, had much in common.

Highlighting the connection between Ukrainian-language and Yiddish-language theatre misses two significant stories, however. First, focusing on the interethnic connection misses the major difference between the two artists: Kurbas worked in the Soviet provinces, and Mikhoels in the Soviet centre. Both artists were murdered by the Soviet state, but their careers unfolded differently because of the topography of culture in the Soviet Union. In the early 1930s Kurbas was thrown out of his theatre and awaiting arrest, yet Mikhoels was then at the height of his career, one of the leading official artists of pre-war Moscow, with two of his greatest roles – Lear and Tevye the Milkman – ahead of him. Mikhoels' theatre was at that point *soiuznogo podchinenia*, under Union jurisdiction, a theatre that was managed and supported on the Union level, not the republic or municipal level. State support devolved in a hierarchy from the Union centre. The theatres deemed the best in quality were all located in Moscow or Leningrad and received the highest level of support and privileges. Republic-level support was reserved for the theatres deemed the best in the republics, like Kurbas' Berezil' Theatre. Other theatres depended on support from local Arts Workers' Union associations, or local Party or state committees. GOSET was the only non-Russian-language theatre supported at the Union level. Kurbas created theatre in the titular language of the republic, but his theatre would always be deemed secondary to Union-level theatres in Moscow and Leningrad, and as such, his theatre would always be funded only at the republic level. Such was the hierarchy of the Soviet cultural infrastructure, inscribed in the space of the entire Union, as it developed in the 1920s.[10]

Yet the focus on the Ukrainian and Jewish connection not only occludes the major difference in the artists' cultural topography, it also misses the profound similarity between Kurbas and Mikhoels, and between these two artists and all celebrated artists in the Soviet Union: their extraordinary status.

The Official Artist

The privileging of artists is one of the distinguishing features of the Soviet regime. In the early Soviet years there emerged what I call the *official artist*: a state employee allocated better housing, guaranteed audiences, a stable salary that could even rise with the awarding of various orders, prizes and titles, and often such luxurious perquisites as foreign travel, dachas, and access to automobiles. As discussed in chapter 1, artists in the Russian Empire were never fully accepted by high society regardless of celebrity status among the general population; by the 1930s artists in the Soviet Union had become some of the most respected, authoritative, and insider Soviet subjects. Dining until dawn at a hotel in Kyiv with actress Faina Ranevskaia and playwright Oleksandr Korniichuk, Mikhoels gave the waitress a 100-ruble note. In response to Ranevskaia's shocked face, Mikhoels urged his friend not to worry, "Let her think that I am crazy." This was the status of artists in the Soviet Union: they ate in hotels, they socialized with elites, and they had 100-ruble notes to give away to waitresses on a lark.[11]

While many artists were politically committed leftists in the interwar period (such as Bertolt Brecht or Erwin Piscator in Weimar Germany), few apart from those in the Soviet Union received such extensive state investment. Of course, states have, over the centuries, invested in many artists: from Louis XIV's absolutist court and Jean-Baptiste Poquelin, also known as, Molière, to the Meiji Emperor and itinerant kabuki troupes, to Britain's Royal National Theatre. It is not unusual for states to allocate financial resources to the arts, yet rarely have the perks accorded artists by states so separated artists from the general population and come with both such elevated cultural status and the possibility of oppression.[12] Rather than gauging to what degree artists like Mikhoels or Kurbas supported or protested the Soviet regime, the more interesting phenomenon may be that these artists had such high status in the Soviet state and society at all. Mikhoels even became part of officialdom; he famously represented the Jewish Anti-Fascist Committee during the Second World War and travelled to the U.S. to meet with Jewish leaders in the community and rally support for the plight of Jews dying in Nazi Europe.[13]

The focus on literature centres on the 1934 Writers' Conference and the proclamation of socialist realism as an officially mandated style.[14] However, the stylistic move from avant-garde to realism swept across Europe and America, not just the Soviet Union. In the United States in the 1930s, the Group Theatre worked with experimental acting techniques, but created productions in a realist style by playwrights like Clifford Odets, whose *Awake and Sing* or *Waiting for Lefty* (both 1935) hoped to fan the flames of class war, but in the form of family drama and light romance with a good plot. Odets was a politically committed leftist; had he been supported by the United States government, worked in some division of the New York State Legislature, and been given an apartment on Fifth Avenue, his would be a similar case to that of Kurbas. Style in the Soviet East was similar to the capitalist West. The striking oddity in the USSR may not have been the privileging of realism as an aesthetic but rather the privileging of the artist.[15]

Focusing on the transformation in artistic status as opposed to aesthetics offers a new chronology for Soviet culture of the pre-war period. The more experimental style of the 1920s did indeed shift to one more realist in the 1930s, but the more fundamental shift was in the place of the artist in relationship to the state and to the audience. A chronology that focuses on transformation in status as opposed to aesthetics is particularly important for the theatre. In the market-dependent West, theatre artists had to adapt to changing technologies, as they faced competition from the movies and the radio. Economic collapse post-1929 also meant that the general public often did not have the finances to pay for theatre tickets. Who would pay to support theatre when one could go to the cinema or listen to the radio at home (for those who had sets)? Poverty, unemployment, and bread lines did not spare theatre artists in the West during the Great Depression; theatre artists in the Soviet Union, by contrast, did not have to worry about food, living space, or the advance of technology making their craft irrelevant. State support for the arts, in fact, only increased from the 1920s to the 1930s.[16]

Total state support necessarily changed the relationship between artists, officials, and audiences. The literary fair was a marketplace of overlapping artists and officials: officials who patronized the arts and socialized with artists, and artists who served in Party or state committees. This overlap facilitated the explosion of experimental theatre in the early Soviet period, as chapter 2 showed. Yet this structural shift – the disappearance of any space between artists and officialdom – proved extremely consequential. Only in the Soviet Union was the state so thoroughly occupied with artists that it allocated the time, energy, and money to send them to the gulag, or shoot them in places whose names now resonate with new meanings, such as Bykivnia, Solovki, or Kolyma.

Although there was never a title of "official artist," the state awarded special categories of "People's Artist" (*narodnyi artist*) or "Distinguished Artist" (*zasluzhenyi artist*), and graced certain artists with Stalin and Lenin prizes. Artists attained "success" not only through talent but also their involvement in the Soviet cultural infrastructure and social-political organizations, negotiating the proper patronage, and perhaps receiving the requisite apartments, vacations, and awards. Sometimes state categories did not make sense to the artists. In one meeting Mikhoels objected to the privileging of only theatre youth as *udarniki*, shock workers. He asked himself the "Hamlet-esque question [*Hamletovskii vopros*]: Am I young or not young [*molodniak*]?" The underlying assumption was that younger artists were free of pre-revolutionary (i.e., capitalist and bourgeois) baggage, but Mikhoels' query pointed out, with a touch of irony, that there were plenty of aging artists who started acting professionally after the revolution, like himself. Mikhoels concludes that he was "of a Balzac-ian age."[17] Molodniak, Balzac, Hamlet? Whom should the Party-state privilege? In fact, it was not age, not talent, but connections that largely shaped an artist's possibility for success.

Mikhoels' world is the beau monde of the book's title: official artists, and as the next chapter will detail, arts officials. Through artists' involvement in the state, and the state's allocation of time and resources to artists, the contours of the official artist emerged.

Part II: Theatre of Collectivization: The Artist and the State

The place of the stage and the theatrical artist in relation to the state acquired a particular urgency in Soviet Ukraine, in the early 1930s with the advent of Stalin's Five-Year Plan pushing for full collectivization in the countryside. Two productions directed by Kurbas at the Berezil' Theatre, one created at the first signs of struggle with collectivization in 1929 and one during the height of its horrors in 1933, offer a powerful lens on the emergence of the official artist by tracing the contours of the artist's relationship with the state and with the audience. These two plays prove particularly significant because both deal with collectivization, Stalin's plan announced in 1927 to liquidate the *kulaks* (wealthy peasants) as a class and to consolidate individual farms into collective farms. In Soviet Ukraine, the breadbasket of the former Russian empire, this process unfolded particularly violently, leading to a massive human tragedy now called the Holodmor in 1932–3, when millions starved to death and those surviving dealt with immense trauma. The Ukrainian countryside would never be the same again.

Ivan Mykytenko's 1929 *Dictatorship* (Dyktatura) was an ode to collectivization and class warfare and intended to be the centrepiece of the 1929–30 season for every theatre in Soviet Ukraine. Collectivization was well underway, the state needed artistic support, and grain collections provided a plethora of material for playwrights. Yet the directorial choices in Kurbas' 1930 production of Mykytenko's play offer a vision of the artist's relationship with the state distinct from that proffered by Mykytenko and ultimately preferred throughout the Soviet space. Kurbas' 1933 production of Kulish's *Maklena Grasa*, in turn, highlights the new relationship between the artist, the state, and the Soviet audience. The artistic, official, and audience responses to plays about collectivization show how radically the function of the artist had changed by the early 1930s.

Mykytenko, Kurbas, and Dictatorship

At the first meeting of the new Artistic-Political Council in 1929 Kurbas claimed that his theatre, the Berezil', stood "between bayonets and knives," as most of the event involved colleagues, friends, and enemies denouncing him. His former best friend and current neighbour at the Villa Zhatkina, futurist poet Mykhail' Semenko, noted that Kurbas "has a persecution mania," and "we should send him to the hydrotherapy clinic [*vodolikarnia*]." The Berezil''s managing director, Mykhailo Datskiv, added, "Here we have a struggle between *Dictatorship*, and the dictatorship of the Berezil'." Nor did Kurbas refrain from responding to his accusers. He declared that Semenko was engaging in "so-called politics, politicking" and failed to understand that "his tasks were artistic." Kurbas ended his speech dramatically: "I did not want to provoke tears of mercy. I do not fear your blocs, I do not fear struggle, I fear only one thing. I fear that you will behave like counterfeiters, like tricksters at cards."[18]

Kurbas saw a dichotomy between arts and politics, between artists and the state. For Kurbas, Semenko's "politicking" had nothing to do with art. Kurbas may have been the artistic director of the theatre with the highest Party-state subsidy in Soviet Ukraine, but for him, the Party-state should remain exclusively a financial patron. Art belonged outside the state; any artist involved with the state was a trickster making counterfeit art. In Kurbas' opinion, to engage with the Party-state, to *politick*, was to cheat at the rules of the game for making art. The rules of the game, however, were changing.

In counterpoint to Kurbas, who advocated space between the arts and the state, stood Ivan Mykytenko, author of *Dictatorship*. A mediocre talent, perhaps, but vigorously embedded in Party-state institutions, Mykytenko gained extraordinary authority in the "artistic-political" world of Soviet Ukraine. Kurbas may have considered him a trickster making counterfeit art, but Mykytenko had figured out the new rules of the game and offers an exemplar of the emerging figure of the Soviet *official artist*.[19]

Mykytenko had made it by *Dictatorship*. The former medical student had become a denizen of Kharkiv's elite Blakytnyi Literary Club and had stopped wearing leather jackets and started wearing suits, according to later memoirs. In 1929 he even sported a khaki military uniform given him as a gift in Germany. Berezil' actor Roman Cherkashyn described him as a "person of great energy, not a little self-love, a temperamental social-political figure, a talented speaker," whose career took off – like that of Mykola Kulish – with his move from Odesa to Kharkiv. In 1928 Mykytenko wrote a friend about how he had gone to the countryside to participate in collectivization and the liquidation of the kulaks as a class: "In a word, life is glorious, extraordinary!" In 1933, the GPU sent the Commissariat of Enlightenment short descriptions of the major figures in the literary scene. Ivan Mykytenko: "secretary of the Orgkomitet [of the Writer's Union founded in 1932], playwright. His plays *Dictatorship*, *Girls of Our Country*, *Cadres* enjoy great success not only in Ukrainian theatres but also in the theatres of the whole Union, Party member, one of the leaders of [literary organization] VUSPP, member of the All-Union Secretariat of Writers." At the Literary Club in his suits, engaged in the Party, the police, running one of the major literary organizations and later the Soviet Ukrainian Writers' Union, Mykytenko was a major player in Kharkiv: an artist, an official, an emerging official artist.[20]

Kurbas noted laconically that Mykytenko's *Dictatorship* was "deprived of anything that could push our theatre to mistakes," but Kurbas' former student, Vasyl' Vasyl'ko, now artistic director of Kharkiv's Red Factory Theatre, hailed the play as "an event, a new era." The plot was simple: a Communist hero, Dudar, who comes from the city to the village to collectivize, conquers the local kulak oligarchy, fulfills and overfills the grain collection quota, and along the way meets a good *komsomol* girl, Oksana Nebaba. Photographs of the first productions, including that directed by Vasyl'ko, show thatched village roofs, simple peasant costumes, and realistic staging. In director Hnat Iura's production at Kyiv's Ivan Franko Theatre, apparently, actors tossed "Get the Grain!" signs out into the audience as a way of involving them in grain collections and underscoring the contemporary relevance of the play. For Mykytenko, who had found his experience in the countryside collectivization so "extraordinary," his play mirrored the goals of the state, his employer.[21]

Yet nowhere did Mykytenko write of the play as simple propaganda; in fact, he rewrote the play five times and sent directors new bits of dialogue and character notes during rehearsals. Director Marko Tereshchenko in 1931 was nervous about including Mykytenko's latest rewrites for his upcoming premiere, since the new text had not yet been approved by the Higher Scientific Repertory Committee. Mykytenko, however, assuaged his colleague: "I gave the play to *repertkom*, they will send you permission, and in the worst case, the local municipal *repertkom* will give you permission, while you are waiting from Kharkiv." How could the state refuse the play? Mykytenko saw no distinction between writing about grain collection and participating in grain collection because the practice of being an artist was indistinguishable from the practice of being an official.[22]

Kurbas' production of *Dictatorship* did not appear until the following May (1930), and when it did, it created a scandal. Kurbas had completely changed Mykytenko's play. First, Kurbas added a cinematic dream sequence. The audience watched as Dudar, the hero, fell asleep. His dream then played on a film screen lowered into the theatre: A suitcase sits on a table by the window in a small village hut, and a hand extends through the window and takes the suitcase. The screen goes black. Dudar wakes up. Cherkashyn suggested that this was a *prise de conscience* for Dudar, the collectivizer taking grain from peasants. Or was Dudar in fact the one stealing? Or was the hand stealing at all? The meaning of the dream was clear to no one and added ambiguity to a straightforward collectivization drama. The cinema screen appeared again during a scene in a train compartment showing scenery "passing by" behind the actors, giving the illusion of movement. This blending of new cinema technology in the theatre was nowhere in Mykytenko's text. While the early Soviet years certainly witnessed innovation in film techniques, no other theatre directors in Soviet Ukraine were experimenting with bringing film to the stage.[23]

Kurbas not only changed the play's form by adding film, he also changed the genre by adding music. Act 3's local village council meeting was now sung in aria form; Dudar sang his monologues in *recitative*. Comic scenes became duets of *chastushky*. Composer Iulii Meitus, as Cherkashyn recalled, worked together with Kurbas, who himself suggested many of the melodies. Cherkashyn described the music as "close to the composers of the twentieth-century Stravinsky, Prokofiev, Shostakovich." It may not be entirely clear what this music sounded like, but it suggests a kind of experimental style. An everyday story of a Soviet hero suddenly acquired operatic grandeur; a realist drama became a musical. Again, such experimentation in genre was characteristic of the 1920s across Europe, but turning a contemporary play into a musical was quite unusual for the Soviet Union, and unique for Soviet Ukraine.[24]

Kurbas also added powerful stage images not present in Mykytenko's written text, thereby highlighting the visual over the literary. Actress Sofia Fedortseva explained how Kurbas used his idea of "transformation" (*peretvorennia*) to help actor Iosyp Hirniak portray Worm (*Chyrva*), the head kulak. Hirniak and Kurbas created a physicality for Worm involving crawling on the ground and clutching at the earth. This image conveyed the idea of "grasping," which was central to Worm's character and to the portrayal of kulaks in the production. At the same time, notes Cherkashyn, Hirniak did not play Worm one-dimensionally, but rather Hirniak's Worm had a "long grey beard and looked rather like something in a biblical icon." A (mostly) stereotypical kulak suddenly acquired more dimensions than existed in the author's text.[25]

Figure 4.1. *Dyktatura*, Scene on the Train (DMTMKU inv. # F 65762)

Figure 4.2. *Dyktatura*, Scene of the Kulaks (DMTMKU inv. #F 61608)

One infamous reworking concerned the first scene in which the three kulaks discuss the imminent arrival of Dudar. Kurbas directed each actor playing a kulak to stand behind a small *maquette* of a house, each of which was placed on wooden planks. These formed the foundation of Vadym Meller's set design, which manipulated the planks to create various combinations and angles throughout the production. The kulaks then crouched around their "houses" and the lights dimmed so that the audience saw only three lit kulaks crouched over smaller-than-life houses. The image was so powerful that three years later in a cartoon in the humour biweekly *Red Pepper*, Kurbas was himself portrayed holding onto his "house," a small version of the Berezil'.[26]

Theatre vs. Literature

With new media, new genre, and new images, Kurbas had utterly transformed the play. Actress Natalia Uzhvii, who played *komsomol'ka* Nebaba, wrote that Mykytenko was "quite destroyed by such innovation – the unpleasant audacity of this work." Iosyp Hirniak, writing his memoirs in emigration, described the drama as pointing out the evils of collectivization; according to Hirniak the directorial changes transformed the meaning of the play. No other memoirs or reviews, however, point to an altered meaning. In other words, a pro-collectivization drama did not all of a sudden become anti-collectivization. But Mykytenko (and others) did consider Kurbas' production scandalous. Why? Although the theme of the rise of the proletariat against the village oligarchy may have remained the same, the changes in form challenged rising cultural norms of the early Soviet Union. Playing with medium, genre, and image reflected a tension in early Soviet artistic culture: between text and image, literature and theatre, and more fundamentally, over the position of the artist vis-à-vis the Party-state.[27]

Kurbas reduced the power of Mykytenko's writing and increased the power of the theatrical image. He changed the spoken text to song and assaulted the audience with images, music, even film, in addition to the actual script. It was no longer the text of the scene with the kulaks, but rather the image of the kulaks towering over their property that reached the audience. It was not Worm's text that dominated, but rather the image of "biblical" Worm crawling on the ground, an image created by Kurbas and Hirniak, not Mykytenko. Meyerhold in the 1920s created a series of productions, such as Gogol''s *Inspector General* and Ostrovskii's *The Forest*, which privileged the performed image over the literary text; Mikhoels, too, created the *Adventures of Benjamin III*, inspired by the character of Don Quixote, which used the literary text as a starting point for his creative vision. That was in Moscow, however, and this was Soviet Ukraine, a smaller world with fewer theatrical experimenters. Kurbas had always stood out, and his production of *Dictatorship* radically differed from those at other theatres.

The concept of "image" actually played a central role in Kurbas' theatrical methodology. Actors who worked with Kurbas generally recall less work with text and more with *peretvorennia*, transformation, a concept based in the visual. In fact, claimed actress Sofia Fedortseva, Kurbas originally conceived of calling the idea of *transformation* simply *obraz*, image, but he then rejected that term as too "everyday" and so opted for the more poetic "transformation." Throughout actors' memoirs of Kurbas the idea of transformation appears; essentially, the idea was to discover an action that conveyed the essence of the character and repeat that action in precisely the same way multiple times throughout the play to "reveal in front of the spectators the full depth" of the image; the action was not supposed to be realistic, but to create forms on stage to which the spectator was unaccustomed. Ideally, the selected image, performed with technical precision multiple times, would "provoke in the spectators the necessary number of associations" to convey the essence of the character and ultimately, the play. Worm's crawling and grabbing at the ground, then, was a transformation to convey to the audience the kulak's passionate attachment to the earth. Kurbas' transformation technique was similar to other acting methods of the day, such as Michael Chekhov's psychological gesture, Brecht's *gestus*, or Meyerhold's biomechanics, all of which created a level of extratextual meaning through physicality. For Kurbas, how the story was told, through film, through music, and image, became just as important as the story itself. The form conveyed the content; meaning arose through image, rather than text. For Kurbas' contemporaries, however, the form obscured the content, and they objected to the way Kurbas had played with Mykytenko's text. Soviet art was increasingly literary, and Soviet artists were increasingly literary figures: playwrights, not directors.[28]

The rejection of Kurbas' *Dictatorship* shows the rising dominance of literature versus theatre. No audience reviews of *Dictatorship* exist – as they are absent for nearly all productions of the time – but actor Cherkashyn wrote in his memoirs how audiences clapped at the image of the kulaks crouched over their houses and at a scene where actors mimed riding on horse-drawn wagons chasing Dudar. Audiences, according to Cherkashyn, were therefore clapping at the moments of live performance created by Kurbas, not at Mykytenko's play. Audiences enjoyed the stage images, and do not seem to have run out to join the fight against the kulaks in the countryside, as Mykytenko may have intended, after their evening at the Berezil'. Former Kurbas student Vasyl'ko wrote in his journal about the antagonism between literature and theatre: "This literature business will eat up the theatre, will kill its ... essence." In his opinion only "scenarized poems" now entered the Soviet Ukrainian stage, and he wanted a new Sophocles, Shakespeare, Molière, "for the new times, but our theatre has not made its own Sophocles. And meanwhile the theatre has been rented out to literature ... playwrights want to be dictators in the theatre ... the literary organizations are taking theatre hostage." Of course in the same entry Vasyl'ko congratulated himself with relief on the fact that Mykytenko was giving the Red Factory Theatre the next play after *Dictatorship*, *Cadres*: "This is positive, that we get attention from the secretary of VUSPP." Literary organizations controlled the fate of the theatre, and Vasyl'ko knew that he needed connection with a leading literary organization and its leader to achieve artistic success.[29]

Some scholars explain this textualization of theatre as caused by censorship and the necessity of monitoring performance.[30] Yet Hungarian dissident Miklos Haraszti offers a different view on socialist realism: "This art neither hates nor worships 'reality'; it merely denies reality the chance to be mysterious."[31] Equalizing the form with the content diminished the element of mystery in art; socialist realism, as it was emerging in theatrical production at least, may have been less about mimetic realism and more about a lack of mystery. Yet Kurbas' production of *Dictatorship* – with the film, with the images, and with the music – added an element of mystery. Texts, of course, could themselves be ambiguous, as Katerina Clark's *The Soviet Novel* argues. Kurbas' production so radically differed from Mykytenko's text, however, that the director showed the possibilities and the elasticity of the word and the power of live performance to transform the playwright's text. Mystery may have been absent from Mykytenko's original play, but the image of the kulaks lit in shadow crouching over their miniature houses, the film scene, and the experimental musical element all brought mystery to the performance.[32]

Figure 4.3. *Dyktatura*, Scene of the Wagon Chase (DMTMKU inv. # F 65752)

Kurbas vs. World

Kurbas' *Dictatorship* revealed the tension between Kurbas and other members of the cultural elite. At the first Artistic-Political Meeting after the Berezil''s premier, Hnat Iura, artistic director of Kyiv's Ivan Franko theatre and a former colleague of Kurbas', declared that *"Dictatorship* should be like a political act, but in Kurbas' design it sounded like the devil knows what." Stepan Bondarchuk, by contrast, a former Berezilite, defended the production by saying that Kurbas was the only one trying to shape what theatre could be in this new era. Yet director Marko Tereshchenko countered that the production had rightly been criticized for the "absolute dictatorship" of the director, which was "totally unacceptable." Kurbas may have been attempting to shape what theatre could be, but he was increasingly separated from the general trends.[33]

Kurbas even became at odds with his own company. Like all theatres and institutions the Berezil' had a *stengazeta*, a wall-newspaper. A tour to the Dnipro (then Dnipropetrovs'k) region that was less than successful sparked the 1930 issue. In the article "Evil in Ourselves," the editors blamed Kurbas: "We do not oppose the fact that Kurbas had to rest and heal himself for further work, but the collective still should have been prepared for the tour." As the newspaper described, the tour was so poorly organized that one performance of *The Mikado* started before several of the actors had even arrived at the theatre, which made the company look "provincial." The editors rejected what they perceived to be the philosophy of the Berezil': "A suit from abroad ... stockings of the best foreign labels ... skirts from contraband products, and the disgusting smell of foreign perfume, as well as a huge ring on the finger." "Take off the white gloves," remove the "remains of the dandy," urged the editors, even going so far as to suggest readers "burn the foreign suit in gasoline ... break the bottles of foreign perfume." The wall-newspaper reveals rifts in the Berezil': complaints against tardiness, drunkenness, and hooliganism, complaints about the wall-newspaper itself, and complaints against those complainers, "you have revealed yourself to be a wrecker ... You are an aristocrat. It's clear." While memoirs often suggest that working the Berezil' was the pinnacle of artistic fulfilment – and in some cases, of course, it must indeed have been – the wall-newspaper highlights backstage antagonism: between the technical personnel and the artists, between the "aristocrats" and the "non-aristocrats," between Kurbas and everyone else.[34]

Party apparatchik Andrii Khvylia explained in a meeting of the Arts Workers' Union in 1933, when discussing Kurbas' expulsion from the theatre, that "with his formalist methods" Kurbas "to a certain extent devalued the political meaning" of plays: "The best example of this is what Kurbas did with *Dictatorship*. The theatre does not show a real person. The plays about the Middle Ages and Mykytenko's play come out looking exactly the same." Ultimately, "Kurbas made from *Dictatorship* what a class enemy could make." Events on stage seemed "like those happening in Ancient Greece," not contemporary and relevant. How characters talked, moved, related was all "made bloodless." For Khvylia, "devaluing the political meaning" in theatre was a problem. Art was supposed to operate together with the Party-state; there was supposed to be no divide between art and politics. Yet, in fact, Cherkashyn remembered that at the end of the play Kurbas had an actor come on stage in contemporary dress and read the latest news on the victories of Soviet Communism, so either Cherkashyn remembered incorrectly or that moment of contemporary relevance did not impress Khvylia enough to make up for the rest of the production. Perhaps Khvylia sensed that, unlike Mykytenko, Kurbas strove for more than the mimetic goal of provoking the audience to get the grain.[35]

Kurbas' focus on art as separate from politics did not mean, importantly, that Kurbas did not understand politics. In a 1932 Arts Workers' Union meeting Kurbas skewered a local critic, Dmytro Hrudyna, who had accused him of a lack of political literacy: "I believe it is Comrade Hrudyna should first study up on political literacy and learn that dialectic is not a wolf's tail that you can spin as you wish." Yet Kurbas refused to talk further with the critic: "I believe that it is a lowering of my brain to discuss with him, let him not be offended." Kurbas believed that Hrudyna's comprehension of Marxism was weak, and suggested that "Marxist" was simply a term bandied about in public discourse when needed. Art, however, was something else. In the same meeting Kurbas critiqued a production at a different Kharkiv theatre, Mykytenko's new pet project, Theatre of the Revolution, for simply "pumping up the spectator with enthusiasm" and added that the show might have been better "if they had understood that artistic material was a much more complicated task ... you cannot compare how many tractors a factory puts out with how many plays a theatre puts out." Kurbas wanted to do more than engage the spectator in the task of collectivization and factory work, but Khvylia saw this as removal from the state. The official artist worked for the state, not for the theatre, nor for the audience.[36]

Part III: The Official Artist at Home

Kurbas may have considered his work outside the auspices of the Party-state, but the Party-state considered artists its employees. The Party-state was more than financial patron, it also housed its artists. Haraszti referred to the artist making the state its home metaphorically, but in the Soviet period the state gave artists an actual home.

In the Soviet system, state employees were furnished with housing, schools, healthcare, and all the sundry *accoutrements* of the welfare state. Official artists were no exception to this rule. In late 1929 – just in time to celebrate the arrival of 1930 – Kharkiv's literary fair moved into a new building north of Dzerzhinsky Square called Budynok "Slovo," the Building of the Word. Olga Bertelsen points out that the literary cooperative "Slovo" (so-called because its members were writers) began the lengthy process of gathering funds to build an apartment cooperative as early as 1926 but (as is not surprising with building projects) ran out of funds two years into the project, after a location and an architect had already been secured. The Soviet Ukrainian Politburo approved a request for 200,000 karbovantsy from Union funds (specifically, from the Union Sovnarkom's reserve funds) to support a cooperative building for Soviet Ukrainian writers in 1928. Stalin's right-hand, Lazar Kaganovich, signed off on the request. Moscow turned the request down, as Vdovychenko, the Permanent Representative of Soviet Ukraine in Moscow, reported in August. But the Radnarkom of Soviet Ukraine contributed to the building themselves, as did local Kharkiv organizations and the writers themselves. Writers could not move in, however, until late 1929 because of problems with the boiler, inspiring humour journal *Red Pepper* to print a cartoon of homeless writers at a construction site.[37]

Mykytenko and Kurbas were now neighbours, living in the same building that housed almost all the figures in the literary fair. The Slovo, a C-shaped five-storey building with five entryways surrounding a courtyard, occupied an entire block of Red Writers' Street north of the Derzhprom building. Kurbas was one of the few theatre artists to receive an apartment in the Slovo. Playwrights like Mykytenko and Kulish, of course, lived there, as did several actresses whose husbands were writers, and several leading set designers like Vadym Meller or

Anatol' Petryts'kyi. Yet other theatre directors like Vasyl'ko, or leading actors like Iosyp Hirniak or Amvrosii Buchma, did not move into the privileged building. Buchma, in fact, seems to have lived inside the Berezil' theatre itself for a long time. The Slovo was primarily a literary house, reflecting the dominance of the literary among cultural elites.[38]

The list of the inhabitants of the sixty-four apartments of the Slovo shows who had elite status in the late 1920s and early 1930s: Khvyl'ovyi, as well as Serhii Pylypenko, respected nemesis of Khvyl'ovyi who opted for massism; Iurii Smolych, who often borrowed books from Kurbas' extensive library; editor of *Visti* Evhen Kasianenko; the "two Ivans" – Ivan Mykytenko, of course, and Ivan, a.k.a. Israel Kulyk, friends with Mykytenko and also a rising official poet; poet Volodymyr Sosiura, whom Kulyk denounced to GPU chief Vsevolod Balyts'kyi as suffering from erotic psychosis; Kulyk had also worked in the Polish underground with prose writer Oles' Dosvitnyi, with whose old grenade his children played, a reminder of their father's heroic days in the Red Army; symbolist Pavlo Tychyna, who was so bothered by upstairs neighbour Maik Iohansen's raucous antics and barking dogs that the two switched apartments; Arkadii Liubchenko, married to actress Ol'ha Hors'ka; humourist Ostap Vyshnia, married to actress Varvara Masliuchenko; of course, Kurbas, married to actress Valentyna Chystiakova, and Kurbas' mother Vanda, who never learned Russian; Kurbas' former neighbour and former friend, Mykhail' Semenko, who was married to Berezil actress Natalia Uzhvii, and whose drinking nearly ended the marriage; Ivan Dniprovs'kyi, who died of consumption in 1934 and whose wife, a translator, stayed on in the Slovo until the 1960s; Leonid Pervomais'kyi (Huryovych), like Kulyk, a Ukrainian Jew choosing to write in Ukrainian; writers Leib Kvitko and Isaak Fefer, who wrote in Yiddish; and many others living in the sixty-four prime apartments.[39]

According to the memoirs of playwright Mykola Kulish's son, Volodymyr Kulish, all the apartments were outfitted with bathrooms and kitchens, but the stoves required heating with coal from a huge pile in the courtyard. Those on the upper floors had to trek up and down the stairs several times a day to fetch coal. Winters provided the opportunity for a skating rink in the Slovo's courtyard, and writer Mykola Khvyl'ovyi was especially talented on the ice. Many families had dogs: Maik Iohansen had two enormous dogs, and no one knew "who walked whom," Vyshnia had three hunting dogs and one other named Tsia-Tsia. Khvyl'ovyi had three dogs named Pom, Zav, and Bukh, for *pomichnyk* (assistant), *zaviduiushchyi* (head), and *bukhhalter* (accountant). Khvyl'ovyi gave the Kulish family an English setter, Joy (*Dzhoi*).[40]

The Slovo became a central institution for the elites of the literary fair. They now not only frequented the same cafes, the same editorial offices, the endless meetings and debates at the Commissariat of Enlightenment, but they also lived in the same building. The tricksters at cards, the bayonets and knives were all at home – for those lucky enough to have the right connections and cultural capital to secure an apartment in the Building of the Word. Living space marked status in the Soviet artistic-political landscape. In his diary aspiring official artist Vasyl'ko complained that his managing director, Oleksandr Boiars'kyi (a nothing, "nyshcho"), had recently garnered a new apartment on a central street, which had already become a centre where the "ruling theatrical elite" gathered to engage in "thea-politics" (i.e., theatre-politics) – and Vasyl'ko's apartment, alas, was no such milieu. In an interrogation another poet noted that when a friend of his wanted an apartment in the Slovo, he knew to talk to Mykytenko.[41]

With their housing in one building, official artists became yet more entrenched into officialdom: the institutions of Party and state and the police. The police received information from informers about the milieu of the literary fair at home and elsewhere. Informer "Careful" said in early 1931 that Kulish, Khvyl'ovyi, and Vyshnia had been dining at the Literary Club along with several other representatives of literary organization VAPLITE. Kulish got drunk and declared, "I acknowledge the Leninist policies of the Central Committee, but without Stalin," which riled up those from another literary group sitting at the neighbouring table. These men proceeded to attack the Kulish group with chairs and "demanded an apology." After what appeared to have been fisticuffs, both sides made peace and concluded that Kulish "just should not talk about politics in such places." Everyone continued to drink, and the writer Kirilenko (at the non-Kulish-Khvyl'ovyi-Vyshnia table) had to take a thoroughly soused Khvyl'ovyi home to Slovo. After all, they both lived there.[42]

The Official Artist and Moscow

But what might Kulish's comment about Stalin have concerned, if source *Careful* was indeed correct in what he heard? One possibility seems most likely: Soviet nationality policy. As the discussion of his play *Sonata Pathétique* showed in chapter 2, Kulish was deeply concerned with the national question, with creating a Soviet Ukraine that was socialist but also distinguished from Moscow and Russia. To be "at home in the state," in Miklos Haraszti's words, implied not only working in state-supported theatres and living in state-supported apartment buildings but also integrating into the hierarchy of the Soviet Party-state apparatus, which was centred in Moscow. The general contours of the official artist appear similar in Moscow, in Kharkiv, and in Tbilisi and Minsk. Yet, as chapters 2 and 3 showed, the topography of Soviet culture shaped the process of officialization. Mikhoels, Bulgakov, and Il'f-Petrov attained such status because they were talented and because they lived and worked in Moscow. Artists with the most authority were closest to Moscow; proximity to the Kremlin mattered.

The topography of culture reflected political authority in the Union. Artists needed to create and maintain a relationship with Moscow that did not challenge Moscow's authority or precedence in artistic production. This was a challenge for some members of the Soviet Ukrainian literary fair, such as Kurbas, Kulish, or Khvyl'ovyi, who considered their work influenced as much by Germany as by Russia and aimed to (and did) create artistic products equal in quality to those in the Soviet centre. Artists and officials in Soviet Ukraine, then, found themselves increasingly frustrated by the provincializing blows that came fast and furious in the 1930s. VUFKU transformed into *Ukrainfilm*, a provincial affiliate of Moscow; Soviet Ukrainian Politburo head Stanislaw Kosior even protested the matter with Stalin, to no avail. Later, the Soviet passport had the word "passport" written in many languages of the Union, but not Ukrainian. Last but not least, the Soviet Ukrainian elite felt continual pressure, via telegram and personal visits from Molotov and Kaganovich, to fill and overfill the grain collection quotas. As early as 1931 Moscow chastised the Soviet Ukrainian Politburo for not devoting adequate time or attention on grain collection and Stalin sent Molotov down to Kharkiv from Moscow to put personal pressure on the local Party elite.[43] In theatre, one provincializing moment was the 1930 All-Union Olympiad, organized to showcase the best theatres from the republics competing for prizes in Moscow during the 16th Party Congress.[44]

Kurbas refused to go to the Olympiad. He did not subscribe to the hierarchy of cultural quality based on geography as opposed to artistic merit. Why should he take part in a competition when Meyerhold – his equal in theatrical achievement – was not participating? Nor was this frustration simply from Kurbas' wounded pride; memos show the anxiety created by the Olympiad in the Soviet Ukrainian Party-state itself. Head of the All-Ukrainian Council of Workers' Unions Naum Rabichev wrote Feliks Iakovlevich Kon (his counterpart in Moscow) in April about the Olympiad and questioned why there were no theatres from Moscow or Leningrad taking part and why the competition was set to take place at an outdoor park inappropriate for professional theatre. In May, Rabichev followed up with a complaint that the jury would be composed exclusively of workers from the Russian-language theatre judging the "national minority" theatres. There were no representatives from the republics on the jury and no "serious theatres" from the Russian republic competing. The final insult for Rabichev was that the Union was not providing accommodation, and the Soviet Ukrainian Radnarkom therefore had to allocate 50,000 karbovantsy to send artists to compete. Yet as Rabichev noted, Soviet Ukraine had to send a delegation because the Olympiad was scheduled during the 16th Party Congress. Failure to participate would have political consequences. Some of Kurbas' students, including Vasyl' Vasyl'ko, saw only an opportunity – and indeed, the Red Factory Theatre won the 1930 Olympiad and was graced with accolades in the Union press. Kurbas, instead, took his theatre on a tour to the Georgian Republic. They went, quite simply, in the wrong direction. Artists were supposed to aim for the centre, and the centre was by 1930 most definitely Moscow.[45]

Soviet Ukraine was increasingly not at the centre of its own story. April 1932 brought not only increased collectivization in the countryside but also institutional collectivization among writers; by a decree from Moscow's Central Committee published in the newspaper, all literary organizations were liquidated to create one single Writers' Union, centred in Moscow with affiliates in the Union republics. All the literary politics of Soviet Ukraine – VUSPP vs. VAPLITE, vs. Prolitfront, vs. Pluh – vanished with one decree from Moscow. The question was now simply who was in the Union and who was not. Iurii Smolych described the morning of April 24 when the Slovo reeled from the decree that exploded "like a bomb." Everything was "buzzing" in the Slovo. The newly collectivized writers walked, stunned from the news, from the State Publishing Agency on Liebknecht Street (the new name of Sums'ka Street) to the editorial offices of News, then to Café Pok. By the first Writers' Congresses in 1934, Smolych notes, Stanislav Kosior and Pavel Postyshev, heads of the Soviet Ukrainian Central Committee, and Panas Liubchenko, head of Soviet Ukrainian Radnarkom, gave speeches. Writers were now firmly brought into officialdom, and officialdom was centralized in Moscow.[46]

The 1932 literary centralization and consolidation confirmed what Kurbas and Rabichev had sensed during the debacle over the Olympiad: artists in the republics were now institutionally lesser than those in Moscow (or Leningrad). Theatres from the regions could only compete with other theatres from the regions, not with those from Moscow; the assumption of the officials organizing the Olympiads was that the theatres in Moscow were of a higher quality than those in the regions. The consolidation of literary organizations meant that a writer in the Writers' Union in Moscow had a higher status than a writer in the affiliate organization in Soviet Ukraine, Soviet Belarus, or Soviet Georgia – because the centralization assumed that the best talent lived and worked in Moscow and lesser talents lived and worked in the regions. More resources, more prizes, more authority lay in Moscow than in the provinces. And ultimately, this centralized hierarchy would shape the quality of cultural production such that it was indeed more likely that the better artists worked in Moscow. Yet at this period, in the late 1920s and early 1930s, the literary fair was creating innovative cultural products in the regions far from Moscow, and they experienced the painful process of centralization. This hierarchy of presumed artistic merit did not reflect the actual artistic achievements by artists like Kurbas, or Kulish, or Vyshnia, who may have worked in the provinces but whose work was hardly provincial. From increased political control from the Kremlin ordering Party elites to up the grain quotas to the political necessity of competing against lesser theatres in the capital, the cultural topography of the former empire was shifting; the former Imperial Southwest was becoming the Soviet cultural periphery.

In January 1933 Mykola Skrypnyk was removed as Commissar of Enlightenment and Stalin sent in Pavel Postyshev, endowed with plenipotentiary powers, to wrangle the Kharkiv beau monde. Vsevolod Balyts'kyi, now heading the GPU, began arresting key members of the literary fair, beginning with Khvyl'ovyi's best friend, Mykola Ialovyi, who had married Blakytnyi's widow. This arrest, combined with the chaos in the countryside, seems to have led to one of the most central events among Kharkiv elite: the suicide of Communist writer Mykola Khvyl'ovyi on 13 May 1933. Khvyl'ovyi, one of the major players in the literary fair, was known for his political pamphlets, especially "Ukraine or Little Russia," which was not published but made the rounds of the Politburo, and for his advocacy of moving culturally away from Moscow and towards Europe. Although clearly a Communist believer, Khvyl'ovyi's turn away from Moscow did not fit with the increasing authority of Moscow in Soviet cultural topography.[47]

The "shot of Khvyl'ovyi" shocked the entire artistic and official community. Within two hours, the GPU was ensconced at the Slovo interrogating Khvyl'ovyi's wife, Iulia Umantseva, a Communist Party member at the State Publishing Organization of Ukraine. Umantseva claimed that Khvyl'ovyi was "shaken" by the arrest of his close friend and believed that the "speculators" new to literature were responsible for the "*poisoning* of the older generation": "Who gave them the right to blacken writer-Communists?" Umantseva claimed that Khvyl'ovyi, hearing of the arrest, tried to call Karl Karlson, head of the Kharkiv regional GPU and GPU chief Vsevolod Balyts'kyi's right hand, but Umantseva did not know the number and thought the arrest would soon be cleared up anyway. Umantseva's statement raises the intriguing point that Khvyl'ovyi, like others in the Slovo, owned a telephone and that Khvyl'ovyi believed that he could speak directly to Karl Karlson and had the clout to clear up the arrest. Umantseva explained that at 11:00 a.m. Mykola Kulish and Oles' Dosvitnyi came over to chat; Khvyl'ovyi stepped into the other room, then "we heard the shot, we ran up to him – he's lying there." A certain GPU agent, Zheleznogorskii, was responsible for gathering the many papers, which included Khvyl'ovyi's suicide note: "The arrest of Ialovyi – is the devastation of an entire generation ... for what? Because we were the most genuine Communists?" He ended the note with "long live Communism!" and bequeathed all his work to his wife's daughter. Umantseva underscored her separation from her husband's work: "I myself do not belong to the group of writers. I came home only to sleep."[48]

A dramatic event in the life of the literary fair and all artistic-political elites of Soviet Ukraine, Khvyl'ovyi's suicide underscored the changing relationship between Kharkiv and Moscow. The suicide was reported and investigated at the highest levels. GPU Officer Aleksandrovskii wrote a "completely secret special report" reporting all gossip and conversation around the Slovo, where writers gathered in the hallways, apartments, and the courtyard all night discussing the event. Writer Maik Iohansen complained that they could not make speeches during the funeral because the Writer's Union Organizational Committee, headed by Mykytenko, would control it – and indeed, noted Aleksandrovskii, no one from Khvyl'ovyi's circle paid any attention to Mykytenko's funeral peroration. Iohansen further declared Khvyl'ovyi's suicide was more significant than Mayakovsky's; while the former "died for social discontent in '33," the latter only died "of personal discontent in '30." Several Slovo residents, as suggested in

Aleksandrovskii's report, believed the suicide would result in positive changes towards Soviet Ukrainian literary scene. One writer commented that they should have asked Maxim Gorky long ago to use his authority to change policy towards "Ukrainian literature and Ukrainian writers"; another believed Stalin would now make policy changes to improve their work conditions. These references to Stalin show that the event was also a touchstone in the Moscow–Kharkiv relationship, and one that pulled Soviet Ukraine deeper into the centripetal force of Moscow. Writers and the GPU saw the event as significant on a Union scale – and believed that a suicide in Kharkiv could change Moscow's relationship towards Soviet Ukraine.[49] These comments suggest, moreover, that artists already understood that it was Stalin or Gorky, in Moscow, who could change their circumstances, not local officials. However, while Stalin had indeed expressed concern about Khvyl'ovyi in his famous letter to Kaganovich in 1926, this concern largely focused on Commissar of Enlightenment in Soviet Ukraine Shums'kyi and his propensity towards what Stalin believed was ethnic nationalism. There is no evidence that Stalin took any action in regards to Khvyl'ovyi's suicide.

The Party-state locally, however, was shocked and thrown off guard by the suicide, and it was unclear which institution, that is, the local militia, the local procuracy, or the GPU, which reported to the Union, should handle the matter. A certain Kusharskii of the Kharkiv regional procuracy was unwilling to let GPU agent Aleksandrovskii examine the materials. Sergei Pustovoitov, higher ranked in the GPU, asked Kusharskii, "Why are you behaving this way, one would think that you think we are on the 'other' side?" To which Kusharskii responded, "Don't prevent me from working." But then Mykytenko arrived – ever the official artist connected with all Party-state institutions, including the police – together with the militia, which brought Kusharskii a note that the GPU would actually be handling the investigation. This made sense: the GPU already had a file on Khvyl'ovyi, of course, and the death of such an important figure in the literary fair merited handling by the institution that had been handling him all along. After all, Aleksandrovskii and the GPU had already been following Khvyl'ovyi and his circle for years. They were prepared – and this was not a local event, but one that demanded the institutional clout of the GPU.[50]

GPU agents Sokolov and Sherstov had, in fact, set up an operation in May 1933 using informer "Vlas" who was formerly acquainted with a certain Halyna Kolesnyk, who worked at the radio. Via Kolesnyk's

acquaintance with writers, Vlas planned to infiltrate a group including Khvyl'ovyi and Kulish, who all "get drunk and make readings of
unpublished manuscripts with chauvinist content." The GPU finalized
preparation for the operation on 7 May and 11 May. While one cannot
say that Khvyl'ovyi discovered this particular bit of intrigue, it does
prove that, in fact, Khvyl'ovyi was correct that his group was betrayed,
that others were denouncing them, and that his generation and the literary fair was threatened with destruction. The Party-state was now
completely enmeshed in the life of the Slovo, the Slovo was enmeshed
in the Party-state, and the GPU and Khvyl'ovyi's own acquaintances
monitored his moves. Artists occupied the energy, time, paperwork
and man-hours of the police and the Party-state. Khvyl'ovyi exhibited many traits of the official artist: a believer in the Soviet project, a
"writer-communist" who felt entitled to call the head of the local GPU,
an artist so connected to the state that he had a telephone, a file, and
inspired a police operation and a slew of files after his death. However, the official artist ultimately had to express a different relationship
towards Moscow than that of Khvyl'ovyi.[51]

In many criminal files from the 1930s, Khvyl'ovyi's suicide served as
an explanation for and cause of alleged anti-Soviet organization; countless writers and cultural figures "confessed" to being so upset by the
"shot of Khvyl'ovyi" that they (allegedly) organized terrorist attacks on
GPU chief Vsevolod Balyts'kyi or Stalinist appointee Pavel Postyshev.
Khvyl'oyvi's suicide constituted a defining moment in the life of the
Kharkiv elite. Soviet Ukraine was increasingly not autonomous, neither
politically nor culturally; artists now had to negotiate a hierarchy in
which they were either in the centre or in the provinces, and the provinces would always be second to the centre.[52]

Part IV: The Official Artist and the Audience: Kurbas, Kulish, and *Maklena Grasa*

As the provinces continued to suffer from grain collection quotas in
1933, Kulish wrote his next play for the Berezil': *Maklena Grasa*. A note
in the Polish press about a bankrupt banker who paid a homeless man
to kill him so that his family would receive his life insurance inspired
the play; the homeless man in the real story gave the banker up to the
police instead of committing the murder. In Kulish's play, however,
Maklena, the young girl, does indeed shoot Zbrozek, the banker, and
then runs off to join Communist revolutionaries. Maklena agrees to

Zbrozek's deal – and runs off with the revolutionaries – because her family is starving in Poland. Kulish's play therefore critiques capitalist and bourgeois Poland where bankers pay starving girls to murder them, and so implicitly praises the Land of the Soviets. However, Kulish inserted a note of ambiguity into the play in the character of a Musician, a disillusioned dreamer, former Communist believer, artist, and revolutionary, now living in a doghouse and often too drunk to pluck out a melody. In act 3 as Maklena and the Musician discuss her desire to join the revolutionaries, he laments, "The revolutions, socialism, and communism have all passed. The land is old and cold. And bald. Not a blade of grass on it. The sun – is like the moon, and the moon – like a half a frying pan." Maklena responds that she will marry a Bolshevik in an airplane.[53]

Figure 4.4. The musician Padur, *Maklena Grasa* (Shevchenko)

Importantly, *Maklena* was a play about famine in Poland, yet performed in a time of famine in Soviet Ukraine. It simply could not have been more topical. Collectivization and famine in the countryside did not spare the city. The Berezil"s *mestkom*, or local trade union committee, for example, expelled a member for refusing to go on a grain collection campaign in the countryside – although it did turn out later that he was legitimately ill. Such absenteeism was a constant problem; even Politburo documents note high-level political elites claiming illness in order not to have to join countryside campaigns. Moreover, food came from villages, not from the city, and so Kharkiv's food supply suffered. In the fall of 1933, the Presidium of the Arts Workers' Union in Soviet Ukraine described deficiencies in cafeteria resources. For example, the Berezil' had their own cafeteria for their workers, serving 120 lunches per day, but the theatre had no rural production base of their own and was therefore dependent on distribution from other institutions' or state production bases. The State Yiddish Theatre in Kharkiv, by contrast, did possess two wagons of potatoes at the time of the memorandum, but no means with which or space in which to cook them, although there were promises of a cafeteria opening soon. Vasyl'ko notes angrily in his diary in late 1932 that the Red Factory theatre actors received no bread, while actors at other theatres did. Such details could prove to be life or death in 1933 Soviet Ukraine.[54]

The context of *Maklena*, needless to say, concerned officials. Furthermore, Kurbas cast the actor Marian Krushel'nyts'kyi as the Musician, which created a sort of "ghosting," in Marvin Carlson's concept. Krushel'nyts'kyi had played the lead character in Kulish's 1927 *The People's Malakhii* (Narodnyi Malakhii), a tragicomic tale of a postman who goes insane from his "blue dreams" of socialism that he could not make come true in the current socialist state. *Malakhii* and Kulish's "blue dreams" caused a scandal, divided cultural elites in Kharkiv, and provoked a flurry of newspaper articles and Politburo discussions. Casting Krushel'nyts'kyi as a similarly disillusioned former Communist may have created a resonance hearkening back to the previous production, which most people in the audience would have seen, or at least about which they would have heard rumours.[55]

Andrii Khvylia wrote a memo to the Soviet Ukrainian Central Committee warning about the play and promising to meet with Kulish and Kurbas as soon as possible. Khvylia detailed his objections: there was no "revolutionary fight" and no real Communists in the play. The play would seem to suggest that the proletariat of Poland/Western Ukraine

The Official Artist 155

was simply "begging for mercy from capitalists," which was a "slander on the revolutionary workers in Poland." Khvylia believed that Kulish was saying that capitalists could buy off revolutionary youth, like Maklena, and that in order to pursue revolutionary goals in capitalist lands, one had to perform "criminal misdeeds." The Musician's quote that the revolutions had all passed disturbed Khvylia deeply.[56]

Khvylia indeed soon met with Kurbas, and, as he reported to the Central Committee, warned Kurbas that *Maklena* was "ideologically harmful" and that the theatre never should have started working on the play without explicit sanction from the Commissariat, even though the Repertory Committee had already given their go-ahead. While Kurbas told Khvylia that he might consider the Berezil''s artistic methods, he declared that his company would never engage in "vulgarity" like Hnat Iura's Ivan Franko Theatre. Khvylia felt it was "important to inform the Central Committee about this conversation with Kurbas" because it had "deep cultural-political character" and showed that the Berezil' continued "to stand on its nationalist positions."[57]

Two days later Khvylia, Kurbas, and Kulish argued in a meeting for five hours until an exacerbated Khvylia finally concluded, "You just cannot take a thirteen-year-old girl, give her money, then make her kill for this money, and then go to socialism. It's a crazy thing, and our proletarian society will cry because of it." Khvylia spoke for proletarian society, that is, for the audience – or so he believed. His memoranda show that he was concerned that the play was "ideologically harmful" and that it would trouble the audience. Khvylia saw himself as protecting the audience from Kulish and Kurbas.[58]

Despite officialdom's reservations, the play was set to open the Berezil' season on 5 September 1933. Kulish was anxious about the reception of the play. His letter to his former mistress in the summer describes his stress: "I really want a rest from my unhappy profession. The word is torturing me. To speak more accurately, the word has so tortured me that I have started, of late, to flee from it." Kulish did leave Kharkiv and went to Kislovodsk for a cure during the premiere of *Maklena*, but he read every newspaper and asked his son to write a full report on opening night. He then actively followed the negative eruption in the Kharkiv papers: "I was ready for everything, I hoped for everything, but such a thing, I admit, I did not expect. The play is evaluated as anti-artistic, false, good-for-nothing." Kulish felt it was a sign of his "destruction" as an artist. When he read about Kurbas' expulsion from the Berezil' a month later, on 6 October, he lamented the "finale of Maklena" and described his sense of despair: "It's as if I'm losing my physical equilibrium, and as if the ground is shaking under me." Kulish appears to have been shocked and saddened by the response to his play.[59]

Hirniak's memoirs describe Kurbas and Kulish as truth-tellers testifying to the effects of the famine and crushed by the Party-state complicit in the destruction of Ukrainians in the famine of 1932–3; for Hirniak, the play was written to directly oppose officialdom and its violent policies. And indeed, at first glance the play does seem to reflect an anti-Soviet stance ... but any deeper examination reveals Kulish's goals and the play's reception as much more complex. Kulish's letters, for example, reveal a desire for approval from his peers and critics, who were all part of officialdom.

Yet Khvylia (representing officialdom) and Kulish had radically different views of the function of theatre. Khvylia was concerned for the play's noxious effect on "our proletarian society." Kulish may have been, *pace* Hirniak, a committed Communist, but he allowed a note of mystery into this play. In a different world, a play about famine performed in a time of famine could have been cathartic. Watching a character like the Musician disillusioned with Communism could have been meaningful for an audience, in which perhaps several members felt disillusioned themselves, or could have challenged audience members to see the revolution in a different light, or could have elicited an entirely different response. Had all the revolutions, in fact, passed? Was the earth cold, and entirely barren? The play could have sparked debate about socialism itself. In Solovki, Kulish told his informer cellmate that "to be a writer with proletarian ideology and an important artist – these are incompatible things ... All talented people ... were always in conflict with their society."[60]

Istvan Rev writes of socialist realism not as an aesthetic style, but as an "officially sanctioned way of making the world (available)." Rev implies that socialist realism is not (primarily) an aesthetic, but rather signifies a series of relationships between the artist and state authority mediating the experience of the work of art. Khvylia, as his memoranda suggest, saw his role as controlling and monitoring how the world was made available for the new Soviet audience. Rev's articulation highlights the changing function of art in the Soviet Union; artists were no longer witnesses involved in a project of self-expression or representation, but were absorbed into the larger Soviet project of changing the world. For all Kulish's radical political beliefs, his vision of theatre was quite traditional. Kulish spoke largely to a local audience with local concerns, and his play was supposed to spark debate, whereas the official artist – like Mykytenko, whose *Dictatorship* urged audiences to action in collectivization campaigns – should participate in the larger transformative project of making the world available in a Soviet style for a general Soviet audience. Haraszti writes that the "state" artist becomes "inseparable from his new public ... Artists, as a group, have become a part of the political elite." If officialdom had become the audience to the exclusion of local communities, then there was no place for the work of an artist like Kulish. The case of *Maklena Grasa* suggests that the Soviet audience had become officialdom, and when officials found ambiguity (in the figure of a disillusioned Musician) it was too unsettling to be allowed. For Kulish, art held the proverbial mirror up to nature; for Khvylia, the mirror should shift what was reflected. Kulish's target audience was local society; for Mykytenko and Khvylia, the target audience was officialdom, through which art would shape all-Union society.[61]

Official Artists and the Multi-Ethnic State

By actively mediating between artist and audience, officialdom became the primary audience, and officials always kept their eyes turned towards Moscow. Theatre was intended to speak to an all-Union audience centred in the Soviet capital, and Moscow did not want to hear about famine in Soviet Ukraine. Khvylia's defence of the proletarian audience, too, could also be considered a defence of himself and his fellow officials, who surely did not want Moscow to hear that they had allowed a play about famine to be performed.

The position of the non-Russian artist working in a non-Russian language was complicated. Such artists had to negotiate two hierarchies, both based on Soviet nationality policy and the Soviet cultural topography. First, artists had to negotiate their local ethnic hierarchy: Kurbas, working in Ukrainian, could attain official artist status in Soviet Ukraine, but only because he was working in Ukrainian, that is, the language of the titular nationality and language of the republic. Kurbas could not have become an official artist in Moscow; a Yiddish-language, or even Russian-language artist, could never become an official artist in a non-Russian republic. Dovzhenko and Korniichuk, too, attained official status working in Ukrainian, yet were connected to Stalin's patronage in the Kremlin. Their work could be translated into Russian and could speak to an all-Union audience; it was not specific to Soviet Ukraine. Mikhoels was unique – the exception proving the rule – in that he worked in a non-Russian language in the Soviet capital, and still he attained the highest status.

And yet, Mikhoels' theatre was struggling in the 1930s. In an Arts Workers' Union meeting in late 1933 (precisely when Kurbas was staying with Mikhoels, and covering the day he was arrested) the leaders of the multiple State Jewish Theatres of the USSR discussed the problems with Yiddish theatre. Mihkoels, Mikhail Rafalskii from Belarus, Boris Vershilov from Kyiv, and Rubinshtein from Birobidzhan talked primarily about a lack of audience. What was harming theatre was, in Mikhoels' words, "the theory of denationalization (assimilation) objectively being the expression of the discontent of the nationalist elements, the progressive growth of the cultural level of the Jewish working masses who live not only through interests in Soviet Jewish culture, but also in other cultures of the peoples of the USSR." In other words, the fact that Jews could go to other theatres meant that they did go to other theatres. To be sure, Mikhoels was part of the beau monde, and many members of the cultural and political elite attended his theatre. Elena Bulgakova notes that she did not love the *Lear*; Mikhoels overacted, for her taste, but Benjamin Zuskin was very good as the Fool. Her critique shows that she attended Mikhoels' *Lear*; Yiddish language did not circumscribe the audience. But GOSET's audience attendance statistics are indeed low. These numbers could always have resulted from a creative act on the part of theatre management, but it is striking that all the other Union-level theatres, such as the Moscow Art Theatre, the Vakhtangov, and Malyi, presented statistics of nearly full houses. *Turbins*, for example, always reached 99 per cent capacity. Mikhoels' theatre presented numbers of as low as 57 per cent capacity.[62]

Perhaps everyone was lying except Mikhoels. Perhaps 1937 was especially hard on the Mikhoels' Jewish audience. Or, perhaps, fewer people attended his theatre for reasons he himself diagnosed: the audience began to attend the supra-ethnic Soviet theatre, as opposed to the niche ethnic products, the "Jewish" stories, like Tevye the Milkman. As Yuri Slezkine has written, the assimilation of Jews into "Russian" culture meant that "Jewish" culture *qua* Jewish culture was lost. At one point Mikhoels questions why he would do *The Inspector General* when he has such "fat fingers" and other artists were already performing a good production at another theatre. In fact, Elissa Bemporad argues that the Yiddish theatre in Minsk was more successful because they could do any play they wanted; the audience was a Jewish audience who wanted shows in Yiddish, whether those were European classics, traditional Yiddish plays, or the latest Soviet offerings. In Moscow, regardless of his theatre's critical success, Mikhoels had to fit the niche of the "Jewish" theatre in order to secure an audience.[63]

Let us return to the legend of Kurbas and Mikhoels creating the *Lear*. Could Mikhoels, for example, have come to Soviet Ukraine to collaborate on a theatre piece? An answer to this counter-factual is provided by the example of Alexander Granach. Born Jessaja Shajko Gronoch in 1890 to a Jewish family in the shtetl of Werbowitz in Galicia – not far, in fact, from where Les Kurbas grew up in Staryi Skalat – he ended up in Austro-Hungarian Lemberg, where he fell in love with the Yiddish theatre. That passion led him, eventually, to Berlin, where he joined Max Reinhardt's company. Yiddish-speaking Jessaja Gronoch became German-speaking Alexander Granach and rose to fame as a German-language actor of stage and screen. With Hitler's rise to power, Granach escaped to Soviet Ukraine where he was hired as a director and leading actor at the Soviet Ukrainian GOSET.[64]

Granach effusively noted in his first letters to his wife how amazing it was that the Soviet Union sponsored minority-language theatre so generously and how excited he was about the upcoming production of Shakespeare's *Merchant of Venice*, in which he would reprise the classic role of Shylock, the Jewish moneylender. After a short time, Granach's letters expressed various frustrations. The hierarchy of ethnicities in Soviet nationality policy meant that although Granach was a celebrated actor of great talent, he was, in fact, now working in a theatre lower on the hierarchy in Soviet Ukraine. The Politburo paid less attention and invested less money and time to Granach's troupe. The new artistic director, Naum Loiter, arrived, whom Granach respected neither as a person nor an artist: "a really superficial, silly asshole who talks too much." With Loiter's arrival, the mood in the company seems to have changed. Granach, he writes, felt frustrated by the artistic limitations caused by the extreme difference not only in age but also in experience between himself and his colleagues. He describes one actress as "completely cold – without soul, without heart, and very cheeky ... a definite non-artist." Granach, it seems, was the most talented and experienced actor in the troupe. Although he threw himself into his Shylock, he planned to leave the troupe as well as the Soviet Ukraine as soon as possible. State-supported theatre that was not top-quality was not worth it.[65]

Granach wanted to meet with film innovator Oleksander Dovzhenko, but was unable to ever secure a meeting. Former artistic director of the Yiddish theatre, Boris Vershilov, suggested he transfer to the Russian-language theatre, but the official offer never materialized. Ultimately, Granach was arrested in 1937 and freed only thanks to the personal intervention of fellow-traveller Leon Feuchtwanger. Granach immediately fled the Soviet Union and ended up in Hollywood, where, joining the ranks of Eastern European Jewish refugees making their name in American cinema, he played in several films, including the 1939 Greta Garbo hit *Ninotchka*.[66]

The official artist had to speak to the entire Union, in the Union language, and with plots and characters that anyone could understand. *Hello from Radiowave 477!* for example, had no place on the all-Union stages because it operated on local jokes. *Sonata Pathétique*, which in Soviet Ukraine was too incendiary to be performed, became just another play of the season in Moscow – until Kaganovich shut it down. *Maklena Grasa*, too, had a powerful local resonance, and officials feared what the Kaganoviches in Moscow would make of it. Artists who attained what I'm calling "official" status – who won Stalin prizes and People's Artist titles and enjoyed dachas and performed at the Kremlin – performed in Russian and created products that spoke to an all-Union audience. Mikhoels proves an exception; and it might be no wonder that his attendance numbers were in decline.

Part V: The Official Artist in the Hands of the Party-State

Official artists were home in the Party-state, and this was a Party-state with a police. Connection with officialdom meant with the police, and in the Soviet regime these connections had consequences. Put bluntly, this was a state that cared so much about artists that it spent time and energy arresting them. In 1933 a group at the GPU headed by Vsevolod Balyts'kyi controlled the arrest, investigation, interrogation, and sentencing of many members of the Slovo and the cultural elite – all members of the literary fair. Vsevolod Balyts'kyi personally ordered the arrest of actor Iosyp Hirniak and humorist Ostap Vyshnia. Borys Kozels'kyi (a.k.a. Bernard Golovanevskii) was the highest-ranked officer controlling the GPU group, and a certain Bodron and Mykola Hrushevs'kyi performed the interrogations. It was Hrushevs'kyi who took the old grenade from writer Oles' Dosvitnyi's apartment as proof of a terrorist plot; Hrushevs'kyi's sister taught Dosvitnyi's daughter at school and informed the young girl that her father had had a psychological break-down under interrogation. A certain Sherstov, Isaak Sokolov, Semen Dolyns'kyi (a.k.a. Glazberg), and Pera Goldman worked on investi-gating the cases and often assisted in interrogations. Ivan Senchenko remembers how the arrests shook the Slovo; the Writer's Union build-ing became a place of huge alcohol-infused banquets, a feast in the time of plague. Writers would stay out late so as not to be home should the police show up to arrest them.[67]

The Soviet Ukrainian Commissariat of Enlightenment removed Kur-bas from his theatre on 5 October 1933. The Politburo confirmed the removal, but Kurbas was allowed to go to Moscow, where he made plans with Mikhoels to work on a play by Friedrich Wolf and with the *Malyi Teatr* to stage a production of Shakespeare's *Othello*.[68] Kurbas was arrested in Moscow on 26 December 1933 and held in the Lubianka for several months, giving no statements. Because he was arrested in Mos-cow, his apartment in Kharkiv was never searched.[69]

In March he was transferred to Kharkiv and wrote a confession to the Collegium of the GPU taken by Sokolov. Kurbas, in his confession, referred to the "organization" as composed of VAPLITE, Khvyl'ovyi, Ialovyi, and Kulish, in other words, his circle in the literary fair. Kurbas wrote this confession in Ukrainian, but one week later Sokolov inter-rogated him in Russian. Kurbas "confessed" that he wanted "to make revolution in Ukraine by organic means of Ukrainian culture and de-Russification of Ukraine." Later Sokolov manipulated Kurbas to admit to a dichotomy between the proletarian and the national: "We wanted to isolate the theatre from the proletarian in order to link it with the national." Kurbas was, of course, making a theatrical revolution. He was, of course, invested in de-Russification. However, as shows like *Hello from Radiowave 477!* show, he saw no dichotomy between the pro-letarian and the national; rather, he strove to find and shape an audi-ence that was both Soviet and Ukrainian. His comments reveal some of the complications in reading GPU files: they are based on invented plots, they result from physical and emotional duress, but they can con-tain elements of truth.[70]

Kurbas did not survive to either write any kind of memoir account of his experience or undergo reinterrogation as part of the post-Stalin rehabilitation process in the 1950s. However, two of his counterparts – Hirniak and Vyshnia – survived the interrogations and described them in detail. Bodron interrogated Vyshnia, who had been arrested at home in Budynok Slovo on 26 December 1933 (the same day as

Kurbas) on the "personal order of Balyts'kyi Vsevolod Apollonovich." Vyshnia was charged with 54–11, anti-Soviet conspiracy. His wife, former Berezil actress Varvara Masliuchenko, and the Slovo doorman were present at the arrest to serve as witnesses.[71] The following day, Bodron pointed to a thick folder on his desk and said that "in this folder is your whole life. We know everything." Vyshnia claimed to have smiled, joking that he was glad they knew everything because then he had nothing to fear.[72]

In his autobiographical statement written on 31 December from Room 15 at the GPU building in Kharkiv, Vyshnia noted that he did not like gambling and never used drugs, but that he drank a lot. He never drank while writing, and he had recently started "taking myself in hand" and was trying to drink less. He claimed that Mykola Khvyl'ovyi was his best friend. It was not until 9 January 1934 that Vyshnia wrote any "statements." Because Vyshnia did not "correctly" answer the questions posed by Bodron, the latter employed "physical measures." At one point, Vyshnia tried to help Bodron put together his case by pointing to his 1929 trip to Berlin, where surely the Germans might have turned him? Bodron rejected the idea: "There is nothing in the file about Germany." "As a result of the psychic and physical actions on me I had to slander myself and others," Vyshnia later explained. In other words, Bodron tortured Vyshnia, and the case against Vyshnia had already been created even before his arrest. When Vyshnia did not confess as Bodron wished, the stenographer wrote nothing down; when Vyshnia finally agreed to confess, Bodron ordered that he write his "statements" by hand, so that they seemed more genuine. Bodron gave Vyshnia a list of people to include in the handwritten testimony, and warned him "not to especially fantazise." Hirniak, who was also interrogated by Bodron, noted in his memoirs that the GPU agent would often point to a wall of weapons as a way of intimidating Hirniak and compelling him to confess to the crimes invented by the GPU.[73]

We have no idea how the confessions were ultimately created: did Bodron dictate? Did Vyshnia write himself, with or without "fantasizing"? Vyshnia's testimony points to a bloc including the Berezil' (especially Kurbas) and VAPLITE (especially Vyshnia, Kulish, and Khvyl'ovyi). In other words, Vyshnia points to the literary fair. Kurbas, in the words of the testimony, was "a genius, a leader in the Ukrainian theatrical process." Vyshnia "thought of all other theatres as provincial and not artistic." Khvyl'ovyi, explained Vyshnia, believed that just because the Russian republic played the dominant role in the Union politically, this should not mean that the Ukrainian republic could not be equal with Russia artistically. Russian writers, the testimony complained, had their own automobiles and better funding.[74]

These statements, perhaps surprisingly, do not seem to have resulted from especial "fantasizing" because they were similar to conversations recorded by informers to the GPU (like Kulish's outburst at the Literary Club). However, they were taking place in an interrogation cell in the GPU building and veer between the plausible (Vyshnia could have said that Kurbas was a genius and that the Ivan Franko Theatre was mediocre) to the patently implausible: Vyshnia was not preparing an attack on Balyts'kyi. Vyshnia was many things, but he was not a terrorist. Balyts'kyi, the supposed object of terror, may have in fact been responsible for saving Vyshnia's life. At the sentencing on 23 February, agents Bodron, Dolyns'kyi, and Kozels'kyi concluded that Vyshnia should be sentenced to death by shooting. On 3 March, however, the sentence was changed to ten years. No one except Balyts'kyi would have had the power to change the sentence, especially when it was he who had ordered Vyshnia's arrest in the first place. Vyshnia was sent in March 1934 to Ukhtpechlag, a camp complex in the far northeast near the Urals, where he served out his ten years and survived through work in the camp newspaper and dispensary, and through help from fellow literary fair member Iosyp Hirniak, who was managing the camp theatre. For some reason, Balyts'kyi cared enough to alter Vyshnia's sentence and (in a bizarre way) saved his life.[75]

Vyshnia's and Hirniak's experience of physical threats and duress of the creative act of weaving a confession based on a false plot without "fantasizing" suggest what Kurbas' experience may have been. GPU Prosecutor Krainyi interrogated Kurbas for the final time in April 1934 in the presence of Sherstov and Sokolov. Kurbas claimed that while in Moscow at the Lubianka he had denied his guilt, but under interrogation in Kharkiv he was able to confess through analysing his "entire past" as political. Kurbas explained, "If there is a lack of clarity, for example, in the question of national policy, so it is because my life has basically been filled with the questions of my profession and I engaged too little with the political life of the country." Krainyi countered, "So you only want to submit to Soviet power, you don't accept it?" Kurbas responded that he believed it was "not possible for me to think up dilettantish explanations of world policy." This issue over the national question led Kurbas to give – and Krainyi to allow – a lecture on Soviet Ukrainian Culture.[76]

Kurbas believed, as he stated to his audience of three GPU men in an interrogation room in Kharkiv, that in cultural questions, "language, the culture of language" had a huge significance because of the link between the clarity of language and the clarity of thinking. The level of development of the national language determined the level of the development of "scholarly and societal thinking." Several years previous there had been a huge growth in language, "but in recent times the Ukrainian language step by step" was beginning "to transform into *zhargon*, slang, which in this perspective threatens ... raising the cultural level of the working masses." Ukrainian culture was on "some sort of pathlessness ... it's as if the cultural process now is in some sort of crisis or illness." Kurbas finally concluded, that to "work in the cultural situation as it is in Ukraine is like death for an artist" and he told his interrogators that he wanted to keep working in Moscow: "I know that in the social sense I am an invalid, but as a political and artistic subject I feel healed and the matter of curing suggests to me a comparison: I feel like a hysteric after a very successful cure with Dr. Freud."[77]

While, again, we do not know the "author" and can assume that the text resulted from interrogators' suggestions as much as Kurbas' ideas, the speech reflects other statements of Kurbas' from the period. Kurbas did, indeed, worry about the Ukrainian language, Soviet Ukrainian culture, and the connection between theatre and politics. Kurbas was not wrong; Soviet Ukraine was at a difficult crossroads, and Moscow offered more opportunity for an artist at that time. He and his generation had attempted, as chapters 2 and 3 detail, to create an artistic culture in Ukrainian that was urban, that was modern, that equalled the best from Europe or Russia. Their task was extraordinary, but Kurbas and his fellows took it upon themselves. The project, however, was floundering, and Kurbas knew it. Plays might not be able to be turned out like tractors from a factory, but that seemed to be what the times demanded. In order to continue making art, an artist had to become an official artist. An official artist in a republic had fewer possibilities both for creative expression and for validation than official artists in Moscow. According to the interrogation transcript, Kurbas still hedged on the place of the artist in the state, which (in the form of the GPU) chastised Kurbas for not involving himself in the "political life of the country." For Kurbas, art should be separate from the state, because involvement in the Party-state necessitated involvement in "world policy" – and an artist's opinions on world policy would be, he thought, "dilettante-ish." World policy should remain in the Party-state, and theatre should remain in the arts, but by now the two spheres were dissolving into each other. Mykytenko's *Dictatorship* was a "political act," and Kulish's *Maklena Grasa* required Party-state intervention. Together with many of the cultural elites arrested in 1933 and 1934, Kurbas was sent to Belbaltlag, the camp complex at the White Sea-Baltic Canal based at the former Solovetskii monastery in the far north.[78]

Theatre director-scholar Les' Taniuk claims that Balyts'kyi's protection spared Kurbas from a death sentence in 1933. This implies that the artists arrested in the early 1930s would have gotten a good scare, but nothing more – had the momentum of purges not carried away all of officialdom in Soviet Ukraine, together with the artists whose arrests they had ordered. Actor Iosyp Hirniak's memoirs support this theory. Hirniak recalls his final interrogation when his investigator, Hrushevs'kyi, informed him that everything was *khorosho*, good, with his friend because Kurbas was not shot, only sent to a camp, and Hirniak should not worry: "You'll get two, three years. Soon you'll go home." Hirniak's memoir and Kurbas' lecture also point to the obvious: as artists were pulled into officialdom (meaning here, the GPU), the GPU involved themselves in the arts, in who would go to Kazakhstan, who should be shot, who could survive "two, three" years running a theatre in the gulag. Artists were now official artists; officialdom managed the arts.[79]

After the wave of arrests, in January 1934, the Soviet Ukrainian Central Committee of the CP(b)U learned that Stalin and the Central Committee in Moscow had other plans for them: Kyiv would be the capital, the Kharkiv era was over. The move shocked the Party-state elite, and Postyshev noted at the 12th Party Congress of Soviet Ukraine, "No one is happy about it," to which Balyts'kyi retorted, "They will be." Kharkiv was over. The Slovo was over, the countryside destroyed; the experiment in building a Soviet Ukrainian – socialist! urban! proletariat! – capital had, in a word, ended. The best talent of Soviet Ukraine was now sequestered in the gulag; the Soviet Ukrainian audience spared the results of their creativity.[80]

Kurbas later, in one of the camps of the gulag archipelago, explained his arrest in the following way: "I was too open and was not a politician-diplomat. I will never return to political life." Kurbas saw his work in Kharkiv as an "attempt to swim against the current" and the "great and strong" power of the Bolshevik Revolution, which would "mercilessly crush the smallest wavering." Kurbas was correct in his understanding that his work had gone "against the current," against the notion of "politician-diplomats" as artists, against the notion of literature reigning over theatre, against the notion of clear and fixed texts, and against the idea of art as something that can emerge from a factory, like a tractor, based on a template and according to a pre-arranged schedule.[81]

Soviet Beau Monde: Engineers of Human Souls?

In a speech at the Kharkiv County Party Committee in 1934, Mykytenko declared that Stalin had told the writers of the Soviet Union that they must become "engineers of human souls" and that there was "great responsibility" in that task. This "exceptional attention" of the Party to the matter of literature, theatre, and art guaranteed "further spirited development of these aspects of ideological work." The notion of writers, and more generally, artists, as "engineers of human souls" was widespread; Mykytenko called it a "responsibility," but it was certainly one that he willingly took on himself.[82]

Miklos Haraszti noted that this infamous phrase of Stalin's implied that the artist's job was "to make certain that trains run smoothly and on time, not to determine destinations." Kurbas, as we see with his production of Mykytenko's *Dictatorship*, wanted to determine destinations; Mykytenko, by contrast, wanted the trains to run on time. Official artists might excel at technique and artisanship, but rarely could an official artist think outside the box, challenging the nature of theatre itself. As Kurbas sensed, such creativity might have been possible in Moscow, but not at this moment in the provinces of Soviet Ukraine, and therefore he longed to return to Moscow.[83]

Perhaps in Moscow he would have rejoined Mikhoels, who was enjoying very different professional circumstances from Kurbas in 1934. Mikhoels rode the wave of high culture all the way to the Kremlin and would receive great accolades for his Lear and his Tevye. As an official artist, and therefore as an artist given duties of officialdom, he would head the Jewish Anti-Fascist Committee during the Second World War and even travel to the West in 1943 in order to rally support for the Jewish (and Soviet) cause. The two non-Russian artists' careers unfolded differently because Mikhoels worked in the Soviet centre and Kurbas in the Soviet periphery. Osip Mandel'shtam, in his journalistic sketches of 1920s Kyiv life, comments on GOSET's tour to Soviet Ukraine in 1926. "We are brothers by blood," he notes Mikhoels as declaring. Yet Mandel'shtam describes the differences in their theatres. GOSET, despite its status as one of the top theatres in the Soviet capital, was "on native soil" in Soviet Ukraine, since so many of its actors were born in the Russian Imperial Pale of Settlement. The Berezil', by contrast, could have emerged only in Ukraine, argues Mandel'shtam, suggesting that the GOSET was more universal in its reach than the Berezil. Yet really it seems that the expressionism of the Berezil' was not to Mandel'shtam's taste and the sketch unites Mikhoels and Kurbas more than divides them. And indeed, Mikhoels' fate ultimately aligned with that of Kurbas; he was murdered in a car accident rigged by the secret police in Minsk in 1948.[84]

Leszek Kołakowski's essay "The Priest and the Jester" posits that every age has philosophers of two kinds: the priest, defending absolutes, and the jester, mocking absolutes. Kołakowski's description of the situation of People's Poland suggests that artists in the Soviet space were more often priests, yet it was jesters who were truly needed: "The jester must stand outside good society and observe it from the sidelines in order to unveil the nonobvious behind the obvious, the nonfinal behind the final; yet he must frequent society so as to know what it holds sacred, to have the opportunity to address it impertinently."[85]

Where were the jesters in the Soviet space? Kulish's drunken musician in the doghouse? Kulish himself, maintaining that artists should be in conflict with society? Perhaps Kurbas was a jester, as he took the pieces of a hack play and created a memorable evening in the theatre, presenting *Dictatorship* with innovation and wit. Shakespeare's Fool in *King Lear*, portrayed in the Mikhoels production by Benjamin Zuskin (a performance eliciting praise from Elena Bulgakova), is the quintessence of impertinence. Was Mikhoels, then, himself a jester, as the central figure behind the production? Yet the official artist was (largely) not a jester; as in *Lear*, where the Fool vanishes after Lear's dark night in the storm, so, too, did the jester vanish from the Soviet artistic landscape. Artists, rather than standing outside good society, as they had done in the Russian empire, belonged to good society. Rather than unveiling the mysterious, like the kulaks in shadow in *Dictatorship*, they guarded the absolute: the printed word, the single genre, the mono-ethnic culture. The seductive pact between artists and officials created a class of official artists engineering human souls, but the Party-state was now deprived of jesters.

5 The Arts Official: Andrii Khvylia, Vsevolod Balyts'kyi, and the Kremlin

A state is never a utilitarian institution pure and simple. It congeals on the surface of time like frost-flowers on a windowpane, and is as unpredictable, as ephemeral and, in its pattern, as rigidly causal to all appearances as they.

– Johann Huizinga, *Homo Ludens: A Study of the Play Element in Culture*[1]

Part I: Soviet Shevchenkos

The statue of Taras Shevchenko, erected in 1935 in Kharkiv, marked the culmination of several years of work for Andrii Khvylia. Leningrad artist Matvei Manizer's design consisted of the nineteenth-century serf-poet in mid-stride, greatcoat tossed over his shoulders, towering over a series of figures spiralling upwards around the base of the statue. The figures depicted revolutionaries from different eras, such as tsarist-era peasants, *haidamaks* (eighteenth-century Cossack rebels and heroes of Shevchenko's verse drama, *Haidamaky*), Red Army soldiers and sailors, miners, *Komsomol* youth, and a figure of Kateryna, Shevchenko's serf-mother heroine here portrayed as a member of a collective farm. Despite Manizer's undisputed reputation at this period – he had created the design for all the Lenin statues now covering the Soviet Union – Khvylia had many concerns when he saw the bronze cast of the statue. For example, Khvylia believed Manizer should remove some of the chin because Shevchenko was surely not so portly. Manizer also needed to work on the boots, depicted as *choboty*, village work boots. Khvylia noted that while Shevchenko certainly must have worn work boots, he should tower over these revolutionary figures for eternity in his dress boots. Finally, Khvylia wanted the artist to "soften" Shevchenko's right arm and fix the back of the coat, which looked "dead." Given the need for these little tweaks, Khvylia suggested that the artists of the Berezil' Theatre pose for Manizer to improve the statue. Thus the Shevchenko statue links apparatchik Khvylia with the theatre artists of the Berezil'.[2]

Berezil' actors Natalia Uzhvii, Amvrosii Buchma, and Les' Serdiuk all posed for the sculptor. Uzhvii, posing as Kateryna on Khvylia's suggestion, cradled a baby, the model for whom was Uzhvii's son with futurist poet and Kurbas enemy, Mykhail' Semenko. The Kharkiv Shevchenko statue then carried two narratives: first, it told the story of Shevchenko's dreams of serfs rising to freedom finally realized, a narrative that cleverly ignored the Ukrainian nationalism of Shevchenko's works and inserted a bit more socialism than the poet may have intended; second, the statue immortalized a connection between artists and officials. By the time the statue was completed, the actors may have remained, but Kurbas, the director who had made their careers and brought the theatre to prominence, was already in the gulag, partly thanks to Khvylia. The Party-state used the ceremonial occasion of the unveiling to rename Kurbas' theatre to the Shevchenko Theatre. The monument immortalized other figures of the Kharkiv 1930s as well: apparently, Shevchenko himself resembled Pavel Postyshev, Stalin's plenipotentiary, who apparently walked around Kharkiv with his coat tossed over his shoulder and held by one hand, just as depicted in Manizer's statue. A photograph taken of the celebrations held at the statue's unveiling show a crowd of Party-state elite gathered, including Karl Karlson, the deputy to the secret police chief Vsevolod Balyts'kyi. Karlson was responsible for spearheading the invention of nationalist plots that caught up many members of the literary fair, including Kurbas, Kulish, Vyshnia, and Hirniak. It was that very same Karlson that Khvyl'ovyi wanted to call after his friend Ialovyi was arrested.[3]

The Kharkiv Shevchenko resulted from artists and officials coming together to make art; its connections with Balyts'kyi, Postyshev, and the Berezil' show the involvement of officialdom in the arts, opening a window on a creative milieu. This was a creative milieu not of artists but of officials contributing to cultural production and reception by coming up with solutions to problems in arts administration through transferring knowledge from one sphere to another. Using experience from their work in the apparat, they solved the problem of managing the entire artistic system of the Soviet Union and its constituent republics. Like artists' involvement with officialdom and the emergence of the official artist, the extent of officialdom's involvement in the arts

Figure 5.1. Shevchenko statue, Kharkiv, 1951 (TsDKFFA 2-058677)

and the emergence of the *arts official* is one of the striking features of the Soviet system. Yet those who managed, supported, and organized the vast Soviet cultural infrastructure remain understudied, the links between them, artists, and audiences not apparent at first glance. Yet the archives themselves reveal the shocking quantities of paper, time, and energy that officialdom spent on the arts and artists.[4]

There were two kinds of arts officials in the Soviet Union: first, there were the career workers in arts administration, who climbed the Party-state ladder through managing culture. Working at the local or Union level in the in the Commissariat of Enlightenment, Arts Workers' Union, or later the Ministry of Culture, these arts officials spent their lives managing a complex system of arts institutions and artists. The arts and artists occupied the docket frequently for apparatchiks in the Party-state, both because the state fully managed the arts and because artists drew the state into their agendas.

Second, the work of many officials influenced the development of the arts, although they themselves worked in other fields. In the centre, of course, this was largely Stalin and his fellows at the Kremlin. Stalin's bodyguard, Nikolai Vlasik, notes that the Great Leader enjoyed patronizing the arts because "he liked things he could do for his country." He gave prizes in his name, the coveted Stalin Prizes, which were "his money, his initiative," and, like anyone, he had his own tastes: the actress Liubov Orlova, the films of Grigorii Aleksandrov, the Bolshoi Theatre, and of course, Bulgakov's *Days of the Turbins*.[5] The Kremlin lay at the centre of a network of arts officials stretching over the entire Soviet Union. These officials, working in the institutions of the Party-state or secret police and tasked with managing cultural production and reception, doled out patronage to artists at all level of the artistic hierarchy. It was not only Stalin supporting the career of Bulgakov, for example, but legions of lower-level officials managing careers, advocating for titles, apartments, and vacations, and signing off on arrest warrants. The more informal patronage exerted by the literary fair transformed into the more formal management of the official arts administration. Patronage became official.

Part II: Andrii Khvylia: Career Arts Administrator

Khvylia, a lifetime employee of the Party-state, had worked his way up through the Soviet Ukrainian *apparat* before securing the post of head of the Department of Arts Affairs in 1936. He may never have made a career in the arts himself, but he had found incredible success in arts administration. By the time of his arrest, Khvylia was one of the central figures shaping the arts in Soviet Ukraine in the 1930s, and he was a prime example of the Soviet arts official managing a variety of artists in a multi-ethnic landscape and negotiating a complex hierarchy of artistic institutions reaching all the way up to the Kremlin. He was a career arts administrator whose tastes, actions, and agenda shaped the emergence of culture both Soviet and Ukrainian.

Andrii Khvylia was born Andrei Olinter in 1898 in Bessarabia, in the far southwest of the Russian empire. Young Andrei attended school in Russian Imperial Poltava, and then, like so many others, fought in the Civil War and involved himself in revolutionary activities. Although he began with the Borot'bisty, the Ukrainian Left Socialist Revolutionaries, he switched over early to the Bolsheviks, and by 1920 he had renamed himself Khvylia and ran the Vinnytsia Party Committee. Given the wild nature of Vinnytsia in the civil war years, this post shows that Khvylia had already amassed a great deal of trust among the upper echelons of the Communist elite. His revolutionary *nom de guerre*, *khvylia*, could have meant "wave" or "moment," and was perhaps meant to suggest the young activist's involvement in riding the proverbial wave of the revolutionary moment and bringing to fruition the new society brought about by civil war.[6]

Humour journal *Red Pepper* may have published a caricature poking fun at Khvylia (that he personally was carrying books to the masses), Communist cultural hero Mykola Khvyl'ovyi may have disparaged Khvylia in both public pamphlets and personal correspondence (that Khvylia was finally starting to write much more "literately," *hramotnishe*), but Khvylia gathered more and more authority in the Party-state of Soviet Ukraine. He ran the Party's Agitprop Committee, which became the Committee for Culture and Propaganda, and in 1933 he moved to the state side of the Party-state apparat as deputy to the Commissar of Enlightenment Volodymyr Zatons'kyi. From there, in 1936, he became head of the Administration of Arts Affairs and managed the arts in all of Soviet Ukraine. His success was both professional and personal: Khvylia's wife, Party member Anna Terezanskaia, worked in the Institute of History, and the power couple had four children. By the time of his arrest in summer 1937, Khvylia had built up his own circle that spread throughout Soviet Ukraine. From the small-town far western reaches of the Russian empire to a high position in the capital of Soviet Ukraine, Khvylia's life path was a model success story, achieved through arts management.[7]

Arts officials like Khvylia were unique to the Soviet system. While other countries supported the arts, Soviet officials not only managed artists but also crafted and maintained the proper ideological line. They partnered with artists in creating Soviet culture. Khvylia concerned himself deeply in the arts in Soviet Ukraine, as his numerous memoranda to the Central Committee and Politburo attest. In fact, Khvylia's letters, petitions, and memoranda constitute one of the major sources of information about the early Soviet Ukrainian Party-state involvement in culture. He involved himself in the Shevchenko monument as well as in projects involving the renovation of Kyiv's famous Monastery of the Caves, the recording of folk songs across Soviet Ukraine, and, of course, the theatre. The fall of the Berezil' left Soviet Ukraine without a top-quality theatre. In February 1934 Khvylia notified the Soviet Ukrainian Central Committee that the move of the capital city to Kyiv would demand "raising the level of artistic service in Kyiv" – and consequently Khvylia requested 3,700 rubles to spiff up the theatres. He further recommended moving the Berezil' troupe to Kyiv. As the best theatre in the republic, it should serve the capital.[8]

Eventually, the Berezil' stayed in Kharkiv, but operated under its new name, the Shevchenko Theatre (in Ukrainian, "Theatre in the Name of Shevchenko"). But the top artists, including Natalia Uzhvii and lead actor Amvrosii Buchma, left Kharkiv to join the Ivan Franko Theatre in Kyiv, with the idea that the Franko could now become the better theatre in the republic with the infusion of new talent. Trouble ensued. In May 1935, Khvylia wrote to Soviet Ukrainian Party leader Stanislav Kosior and Soviet Ukrainian state leader Panas Liubchenko asking for help. He accused Kharkiv Regional Party head Mykola Demchenko of inviting the two former Berezil' actors back to Kharkiv for one production – Oleksandr Korniichuk's *Platon Krechet* – and then plying them with dachas, higher salaries, and access to automobiles, all in hopes that they might stay. So Khvylia now begged the Central Committee to ask the managing director of the former Berezil' Oleksii Lazoryshak to officially send Buchma and Uzhvii back to Kyiv.[9]

Uzhvii's and Buchma's place of work was not simply the obsession of one rogue apparatchik. The 1936 interrogation of Demchenko's deputy (Ivan Musul'bas) attests to Lazoryshak's reluctance to return the stars to Kyiv and to Demchenko's willingness to spend untold sums on gifts, just to keep the actors in the former capital. Patronage was personal, and having prized artists in one's stable afforded officials a measure of authority.[10]

Nor was Khvylia, it seems, paranoid in his judgment that the Franko needed fresh talent. In fact, after Kurbas' arrest and the move of the capital to Kyiv, the artistic situation of theatres in Kyiv seemed quite dire. Postyshev and Liubchenko wrote to Stanislaw Kosior in 1936 informing him that the collective of the Moscow Art Theatre's Second Studio was being dissolved, and that Pavel Kerzhentsev, who headed the All-Union Committee for Arts Affairs in Moscow, had suggested moving the troupe to Soviet Ukraine. Kosior immediately telegrammed back his approval; the company would be "useful for all theatres" in Soviet Ukraine as a model. Was the quality of theatre in Soviet Ukraine truly so poor that they should have to import a company from Moscow? Liubchenko, Postyshev and Kosior felt that it was an honour Kerzhentsev had thought of them and wanted the troupe in their republic. It turns out, however, that Kerzhentsev himself was not at all concerned about the quality of theatre in Soviet Ukraine, but rather about space and salaries for a group of actors. By moving the Second Studio into a former cinema he was able to keep the troupe in Moscow and avoid sending them south to the provinces. Of course, this back and forth between officials ultimately reveals how much they worried about artistic quality, and how much time and energy they spent on the arts.[11]

Khvylia's Circle

Khvylia, quintessential Soviet arts official, succeeded in shaping the cultural landscape of Soviet Ukraine through a network of Party-state appointees making their political careers through arts administration. Khvylia's circle emerges from the files of NKVD interrogations of key arts officials in the apparat: Khvylia's secretary, his protégé running the opera, and managers in the central theatres in Kyiv, Kharkiv, and Odesa. These officials ran the theatre behind the scenes, and all are linked to Khvylia, who managed the arts in Soviet Ukraine in the 1930s. All of these officials were career officials who had worked their way up the apparat through Party appointments. A career in the arts, their lives show, could unfold through the Party just as much as through the arts. Just as artists had moved into official posts in the late civil war years, now officials moved, if not into artistic posts, at least into posts that carried artistic responsibility. Officialization occurred through officials managing the arts. Who were some of these people?

Volodymyr Slatin met Khvylia in the fall of 1931 when working as one of Khvylia's secretaries in the Committee of Culture and Propaganda in the Party side of the Party-state. When Khvylia was named deputy to the Commissar of Enlightenment, he hired Slatin as his secretary. Slatin, as he stated under interrogation by the GPU in 1937, received a nicer apartment, a raise in salary, and a subsidy from literary honoraria – it remains unclear for which works of literature precisely – because of his promotion. Slatin claimed under interrogation that his boss was "very interested" in the Shevchenko monument, and detailed Khvylia's involvement in all aspects of cultural production and reception. For example, in his capacity as head of the Institute of Folklore, Khvylia supervised Dmitrii Al'tschuler's research on folk songs from the villages of Soviet Ukraine. For Slatin's GPU interrogators this focus on folk suggested a hindrance in developing "Soviet Ukrainian" classical music, such as symphonies. Slatin continued that estrada, "the most popular kind of art among the masses," remained completely underdeveloped and suffered from a lack of repertoire and experienced directors. Of course, we have no idea what Slatin really thought about his boss's activities, but the file underscores the fact that Khvylia was a mover and shaker in the arts.[12]

Khvylia promoted and managed the careers of his protégés. Khvylia took an interest in Ivan Ianovs'kyi in 1933 when the Kharkiv Regional Party Committee named Ianovs'kyi head of the Kharkiv Opera Theatre. Khvylia, according to Ianovs'kyi's interrogations in 1937, actively campaigned for Ianovs'kyi to take over the Kyiv Opera when Kyiv became the capital in 1934. Ianovs'kyi worried about currying favour with the opera's Party cell and mestkom (trade union committee) in order to encourage the opera's chances of winning a coveted Order of Lenin. Khvylia reprimanded him: such awards were always decided in Moscow, and that's where Khvylia would go to ensure the award. Khvylia made good on his promise, and the opera received an Order of Lenin in 1934. At the same time, however, Khvylia, as portrayed by Ianovs'kyi's interrogations, chafed under the Moscow yoke: he complained that Moscow's (i.e., the Union's) Commissariat of Finance had taken all their money, and that they would have to "show what Ukrainians are capable of" when they took the classic nineteenth-century opera, *Natalka from Poltava*, to Moscow.[13]

Khvylia's network covered the central performing arts institutions of the republic, and his clients had clients of their own. For example, Khvylia appointed a certain Sobolev to head the Division of Theatre in the Administration of Arts Affairs in Kyiv. Sobolev, Khvylia's appointee, then brought Kirill Hetman, from the Odesa Regional Administration of Arts Affairs, all the way up to managing director at the prestigious Ivan Franko Theatre in Kyiv. Hetman, in turn, sent Fedor Hopak to manage the Ukrainian-language Theatre of the Revolution in Odesa. Khvylia then had "his people" in Kyiv at the Party-state and the leading theatre, and at the leading theatre in Odesa. Moreover, the post of managing director at the theatres, which had always been in the purview of the "red experts" of the Party-state, now allowed elite officials like Khvylia to have certain theatres in their own spheres of authority.[14]

As a patron, Khvylia protected those in his network. Ianovs'kyi told his interrogators that when his brother-in-law was arrested, he expressed a desire to leave his job. After all, he was now related to an "enemy of the people." Khvylia, however, assured Ianovs'kyi that he would take care of the matter and that Ianovs'kyi's career was safe since Khvylia was Ianovs'kyi's patron.[15] When Ianovs'kyi suggested that Anatol' Petryts'kyi, a painter considered by some "formalist," might not be a good choice to design the opera's production of *Taras Bul'ba*, Khvylia told Ianovs'kyi that he "did not understand anything and that right now Petryts'kyi was at [Radnarkom Chairman Panas] Liubchenko's dacha painting his portrait." Petryts'kyi, in fact, was painting portraits of just about everyone who was anyone in the 1920s and 1930s elites, from Soviet Ukrainian Commissars of Enlightenment Mykola Skrypnyk and Oleksandr Shums'kyi, to Communist writers Mykola Khvyl'ovyi, to artists like Les' Kurbas. If Liubchenko wanted his portrait painted by Petryts'kyi, it not only ensured Petryts'kyi's well-being, it also ensured Khvylia's well-being, since Khvylia – via his protégé Ianovs'kyi – offered Petryts'kyi work in the opera. For a while everyone was winning with the system of Party-state patronage in the arts – but when Liubchenko and Khvylia ran into trouble, the entire group was at risk. Indeed, information about Khvylia's circle emerges from the interrogations of its members after Liubchenko fell into political disfavour.[16]

Patronage involved responsibility. Ultimately Khvylia had to answer to the Soviet Ukrainian Central Committee, the Soviet Ukrainian Politburo, and Moscow. On 12 March 1934, for example, in the Berezil' during an evening performance, the blade from a prop sword flew from the stage, over the heads of the parterre, and lodged in the loge of the third level. Thankfully, in this case, since Kurbas' removal the previous October, the Berezil' was marked as a dangerous theatre, which discouraged attendance. Therefore the loge was completely empty. On 13 March, the very next day, Khvylia ordered Lazoryshak, the current managing director, to fully investigate the matter and find the guilty party. All theatres, noted Khvylia in a republic-wide memo, ought to check on the condition of their props and "special attention must be paid to the conditions of weapons and the ability to use them properly." Khvylia notified the Central Committee of the matter and of his handling of it on 14 March. Had someone been injured, of course, the fault would have been Lazoryshak's, and ultimately, Khvylia's for hiring him. A blade flying from stage to audience could be interpreted as anti-Party, anti-Soviet, or nationalist, and again, since Khvylia managed the arts, the fault would have been his. His swift handling of the affair shows the stakes involved.[17]

Indeed, when the tables turned, not only Khvylia himself but also his entire patronage network came under question. On the night of 7–8 August 1937 there was a meeting in the Party cell of the Administration of Arts Affairs to discuss the Khvylia affair. Members found anti-Soviet meaning in Khvylia's patronage choices and pet projects, such as supporting Ianovs'kyi or restoring the Monastery of the Caves. They also accused him of still supporting the "old theories of Kurbas." The day after Khvylia's arrest, the Party cell forwarded the protocol of the meeting to the NKVD (that is, the former GPU, the secret police). Of course, Khvylia had hardly supported Kurbas, and indeed was one of the central figures behind his arrest. Yet the accusations show how arts officials' activities could be used against them as a weapon; and when networks collapsed, the ties of patronage could destroy. Khvylia declared, in an interrogation of August 1937 in Lefortovo Prison in Moscow, that Liubchenko – his former patron – had complained to him that the grain requisition levels were too high. Khvylia was sentenced on 8 February 1938 and shot on 10 February 1938.[18]

Like Petryts'kyi painting Liubchenko's portrait, artists secured their careers not through the "official" Party-state channels and proper ideological style but through official patronage of officials. At a Party conference in 1930, Stanislaw Kosior noted, "You know time and again, five to six writers meet and among them there are five to six different views and they want us to go to them, to go to their little groups, to judge them, select them, divide them into those who belong in Communist heaven and those who don't. We will not do that."[19] However, artists' negotiation of unofficial networks is only part of the story. Officials made use of such networks as well. Zatons'kyi stated under interrogation that Panas Liubchenko "held in his hands [his] connection with writers through [playwright Ivan] Mykytenko." Officials patronized artists, it seems, to maintain influence with artistic circles, and it seems that artistic patronage gave actual clout in the institutional hierarchy of the Soviet apparat. That Liubchenko had his portrait painted by Petryts'kyi may have helped him as much as it helped Petryts'kyi himself.[20]

Mykytenko, unlike the portrait painter Petryts'kyi, seems to have been pulled into the vortex of the NKVD with his patrons Liubchenko and Khvylia. He left his apartment in Kharkiv one day and never came back. He was found shot, whether by suicide or murder remains unclear.[21]

Part III: Managing the Multi-Ethnic State

One of the challenges for Andrii Khvylia and his circle was managing arts institutions and artists in a multi-ethnic region. When Khvylia was arrested at home in Kyiv on 13 August 1937, on his desk lay a petition from the actors of the Kyiv State Yiddish Theatre, a memorandum about theatres in Dnipro (then Dnipropetrovs'k), and a copy of the *Internationale* translated into Ukrainian. The petition, most likely, concerned the fate of Iakov Libert, an elderly Jewish actor arrested in 1937; Liubchenko had put the search for an adequate translation of the Communist anthem on the Politburo docket earlier that year. Khvylia's desk testifies to the multi-ethnic nature of his work, which demanded managing not only Ukrainian-language theatre but also Yiddish-language theatre and Russian-language theatre, among others.

Yiddish-language theatre posed a particular problem for Khvylia and his apparat. Tikhon Medvedev, a Khvylia appointee, headed the Kyiv Regional Administration of Arts Affairs until September 1937. Like Khvylia, his boss, he had worked his way up through the Party inside cultural institutions: VUFKU (the All-Ukrainian Photo-Cinema Administration), various photography and cinema journals, the Radio and Telegraph Agency in Kyiv, and finally the Kyiv arts apparat.[22]

Accusations against Medvedev centred on his alleged anti-Semitism. David Volskii, who ran the state circus in Kyiv, recalled meeting him. Volskii was Jewish, and always spoke Ukrainian with Medvedev, who commented one day on how amazing it was that "such a good theatrical worker" ran the circus: "You're not a Jew [using *zhyd*, the Ukrainian word for *Jew* taken from the Polish, which in Soviet Ukrainian had the tint of *kike*, vs. the more Russian *evrei*] but a Ukrainian and you could direct the Ukrainian Opera or the Franko Theatre." The assumption was that only Ukrainians spoke Ukrainian, Jews would speak Russian, and only ethnic Ukrainians should run the "Ukrainian" cultural institutions. Life in Medvedev's good graces was short-lived, however. Medvedev's deputy, Isaak Harold, requested two permanent seats in the circus for his boss, but Volskii refused because the circus, as he explained, was under the direct administration of Moscow and so "could not submit to local ruling." Khvylia and Medvedev, as Volskii described later, discredited him and removed him from work in the circus – because of the ticket debacle. Years later, under reinterrogation in 1955, Volskii claimed that Medvedev always knew he was Jewish and that he had heard that Medvedev "did not like it that the circus was headed by a Jew and not a Ukrainian." While Volskii in 1955 claimed not to remember if Medvedev was an anti-Semite, his testimony seems to suggest the opposite.[23]

Anti-Semitism as an accusation occurs fairly frequently throughout secret police files, generally signifying "bourgeois Ukrainian nationalist." It could also, of course, refer to "great Russian chauvinism," hearkening back to the legacy of the Black Hundreds and those imperial pogromists who did not support non-Russian cultures. Yet it was also an easy accusation; but in this case it seems Medvedev really was anti-Semitic. Three times, and with slight variations, witnesses repeated a story of attempts by the managing director of the Soviet Ukrainian State Yiddish Theatre, Aron Dymarskyi, to organize a tour to Soviet Ukraine in 1936 for Klara Jung, a famous Yiddish actress popular throughout the Russian empire from before the First World War and now living in Moscow. Medvedev denied Dymarskyi's request declaring that he would not "allow that Jewess" to tour Kyiv. When Dymarskyi countered that Moscow's Central Repertory Committee had already signed off on the tour, Medvedev snapped, "Go on to Berdichev," a historically Jewish town. Dymarskyi wanted to speak to Khvylia, Medvedev's boss, but he was told that Medvedev was Khvylia's protégé and Khvylia would never oppose him. "All of theatrical Kyiv knew," claimed Dymarskii, that Medvedev was an anti-Semite. In fact, Dymarskyi did manage to take the Klara Jung troupe to Zhytomyr, a city near Berdichev with a large Jewish population. When Medvedev found out about this, he tried to fire the managing director of the Zhytomyr theatre, but in vain. Whether adequately representing Medvedev's views or not, the accusations of anti-Semitism are so prevalent as to suggest that for Medvedev promoting Soviet Ukrainian culture really meant an ethnically

Ukrainian culture that did not include Jews or Yiddish-language cultural productions.[24]

The Medvedev file speaks to the challenge of managing the arts in a multicultural Soviet republic. The discomfort, whether real or imagined, with a multi-ethnic Soviet Ukrainian culture appears also in the turn towards nineteenth-century Ukrainian musical classics, the kind performed by the Theatre of Luminaries and beloved by their pre-revolutionary audiences. On the one hand, the NKVD accused Medvedev of producing Mykola Lysenko's 1899 *Marusia Bohuslavka*, which was, like *Natalka from Poltava*, from the classic nineteenth-century Ukrainian repertory that – for the NKVD – could smack of bourgeois nationalism. Yet, at the same time, Andrii Khvylia wanted to send *Natalka from Poltava* to Moscow to show "what Ukrainians could do." The problem of the form and content of "Soviet Ukrainian" culture was vexing, and the talented artists most capable of solving it – such as Kurbas, Vyshnia, or Kulish – were awaiting execution in the gulag. What theatrical production would have the right proportions of Soviet and Ukrainian for Moscow's evaluation? Like the beleaguered apparatchik in Petrov's *Quiet Ukrainian Night* who wrangled the two folk ensembles to best represent Soviet Ukraine, so did Khvylia hope that the old repertory would serve the republic well on the Union stage. The simultaneous support and oppression of nineteenth-century Ukrainian-language operetta suggests a lack of clarity over its place in Soviet Ukrainian culture. Kurbas and other members of the literary fair fought against nineteenth-century melodrama, and against "Soviet Ukrainian" as comprising only the old repertory; yet with the demise of the literary fair, the folkish melodramas returned as Soviet cultural products.[25]

Managing Yiddish Theatre

Khvylia and his circle managed the arts, but the flip side is that artists had to get Khvylia and his circle to manage them. Without officialdom's involvement, a theatre stood little chance of survival. In April 1937 Maks Iudovskii, a coat checker and ticket taker at the Kyiv State Yiddish Theatre, turned to Politburo member Mendel Markovych Khataevych with a memorandum in which he complained about the poor state of his theatre. Iudovskii believed that the Kyiv GOSET was better in quality than Mikhoels' Moscow GOSET, but he blamed Khvylia and the theatre's managing director for not paying the workers on time and for the general run-down nature of the company. Oddly, Iudovskii also blamed Khataevych himself, so it's unclear whether Iudovskii had all his marbles, but he ended by begging the Politburo member to come to the theatre and complained that Postyshev had not yet attended. The Kyiv State Yiddish Theatre could not get officialdom to the audience – and Iudovskii knew the consequences.[26]

The coat checker seems to have sized up the situation adequately. Pavel Postyshev received a memorandum in the fall of 1934 from the Kharkiv State Yiddish Theatre artists expressing their shock that the Party-state was "not sufficiently informed about the sad state of affairs of the creation of the Yiddish theatre," but this memorandum does not seem to have translated into policy. The artists detailed the situation: Commissar of Enlightenment Volodymyr Zatons'kyi wanted to join the two theatres, Kharkiv and Kyiv State Yiddish Theatres, after the move of the capital back to Kyiv. Although the two troupes were technically joined, work had yet to start and the opening of the season in fall 1934 was fast approaching. Actors were sitting around doing nothing and as yet unpaid. Furthermore, the actors complained about the financial mismanagement and "provincialism" of the theatre's administration. The Kyiv City Council had decreed that the Jewish theatre would take the stage of the Communal Farm Workers' Club, a decent space that could hold about 800 spectators. But the theatre's management for some reason exchanged this space for the space of the Construction Workers' Club, which was secluded in a courtyard, held only 450 people, and was not equipped "for a powerful theatre of all-Ukrainian significance." The company was also headed towards a huge deficit of 97,000 rubles because the management was planning on 90 per cent attendance, which was unrealistic. The actors proposed that the most they could hope for was 66 per cent attendance, which would amount to about 1,500 rubles an evening in the box office. Actor Dmitrii Zhabotinskii called the union of the two theatres a "tragedy."[27]

They finally demanded financial assistance, a better theatre, and "more Bolshevik objectivity in direction, guaranteeing us a really healthy joining of two collectives and fruitful friendly work to realize the high political importance of a Ukrainian GOSET." If, according to the memorandum, the actors could anticipate only 66 per cent attendance of 450 seats, then they were only planning on about 297 spectators a night. The insistence on the 1,500 rubles (about 5 rubles a ticket, then) suggests that the State Yiddish Theatre managed to achieve very few "organized" houses and remained dependent on single-ticket sales. Dependence on the box office meant that a theatre lacked

Party-state patronage because it was the bulk ticket sales to Party, state, or union committees that largely filled houses. The State Yiddish Theatre's lament shows that without officialdom, a theatre would struggle to survive.[28]

Still, the State Yiddish Theatre had big plans. Apparently, the Kyiv City Council in 1936 had allocated 15,000 karbovantsy and secured 40,000 from the Soviet Ukrainian republic's reserve funds to build the company a new theatre space. The company was preparing *Shylock*, based on Shakespeare's *Merchant of Venice*. The production, directed by former Stanislavsky student Boris Vershilov, would star German Jewish refugee Alexander Granach. The Granach production offered possibilities: the Land of the Soviets sheltering and supporting a German refugee promoting Jewish theatre! But then the Soviet Ukrainian Council of People's Commissars reprioritized, the Russian drama theatre got the funds, and the Yiddish theatre's request was postponed. Everyone was demoralized, lamented the managing director, and Vershilov was considering moving back to Russia.[29]

Khvylia worked hard to raise the standard of Ukrainian-language theatre in Kyiv and fought for Uzhvii and Buchma, but, as coat checker, Iudovskii noted, Khvylia did not advocate for the Yiddish stage. As the actors noted, the theatre had "political importance" – but the difficulties faced by the State Yiddish Theatre show the extent to which political importance did not translate into state investment. In short, the State Yiddish Theatre enjoyed little involvement of arts officials. Rather than the dependence on the box office, theatre was now dependent on arts officials in the Party-state. But the hierarchy of ethnicities placed the State Yiddish Theatre outside Party-state priorities, and therefore the Politburo paid less attention and invested less money.

Managing Polish Theatre

Even more challenging was the situation with the Polish-language theatre. Kyiv boasted the one and only Polish-language theatre in the entire Soviet Union, but the institution was a disaster. Lacking any suitable Polish-speaking candidates in the whole of Soviet Ukraine, or the Soviet Union, the Soviet Ukrainian Commissariat of Enlightenment hired Polish revolutionary theatre artist, Witold Wandurski, in mid-1929 for the post of artistic director. Wandurski had tried to found an experimental theatre company in Poland, but the Polish police shut it down and arrested Wandurski, who emigrated to Berlin after his stint

in a Polish jail. Wandurski later described the chaos of the theatre company at his arrival in Kyiv. One could "hardly call it a theatre, especially
a state theatre." Students spoke Polish badly and were "basically bourgeois and foreign to revolutionary ideology and far from grasping the
foundations of Soviet society." Wandurski was horrified after a production (prepared before his arrival) of a Soviet Ukrainian play, Sofia Levi-
tina's *The Sentence* (*Wyrok*, in Polish, *Vyrok*, in Ukrainian), an agitprop
vehicle about the Polish–Bolshevik war intended to show the domi-
nation of the Bolsheviks over the bourgeois Poles. The cast radically
misunderstood the play to such an extent that the Polish-speaking spectators expressed their "gratefulness" that finally someone had "unmasked
the base intrigues of the cunning Bolsheviks" and shown an example of
"our" fine Polish military.[30]

Struggling with the "risk of anti-Semitism" and "bohemian studio
atmosphere" took its toll on Wandurski's kidneys and psyche to such
an extent that he begged the state to send him a managing director.
The problem was that the Commissariat could not find anyone in
the Soviet Union who was both a qualified administrator and a fluent Polish speaker. They finally tracked a fellow down in Russia, but
the candidate replied that he had not spoken Polish since 1915 and felt
ill-equipped for the job. Wandurski sent the Commissariat a telegram:
"The situation of the Polish theatre is altogether serious / no space / no
budget / no managing director / no cadres. Please come personally."[31]

The Commissariat sent an inspector to investigate and concluded
that Wandurski was "waging a struggle against the Party." They
claimed that Wandurski was not accepting the Party workers sent to
politically educate the actors, and that Wandurski's wife was hindering
the advancement of other actresses by taking the best roles. The much
longed-for new managing director informed the state that Wandurski
had cursed when speaking about the Party and had explicitly said he
wanted "dictatorship" in the theatre, understood "as nothing less than
liberating from Party leadership." One wonders if the director was
referring to Mykytenko's play (*Dictatorship*), and the managing director simply misunderstood. Wandurski – who had been so passionately
begging for Party-state intervention – was removed by the Party-state
on 5 February 1931, his file was handed over to the Control Commission; he was arrested, and eventually executed in Moscow.[32]

Wandurski gave a series of interviews to the Kyiv papers in early 1930
touting the accomplishments of Soviet Ukraine in managing its multicultural landscape. Polish and Yiddish resounded throughout the hall

where the Polish State Theatre and Yiddish Theatre of Working Youth rehearsed; such warm relationships between Poles and Jews could not, implied Wandurski, exist in Poland. Outside the official press, however, Wandurski's file shows absolutely no interaction between the Polish and Jewish theatre scene, or between the Polish and Ukrainian or Russian theatres. Wandurksi was very much alone. The situation with Poland – right across the border – was a cause for concern, and so supporting Polish culture was politically tricky. Essentially, Wandurski was tasked with creating Soviet Polish culture in a Soviet Ukrainian context. This turned out to be a tall order, and to create Soviet-style Polish culture would ultimately take an occupation, a devastating war, and the creation of People's Poland.[33]

After the removal of Wandurski in early 1931, the Commissariat of Enlightenment in Soviet Ukraine petitioned to include the theatre on an all-Union budget, but the Union's Central Executive Committee in Moscow turned down their request. Funding the one and only State Polish Theatre in the Soviet Union remained in Soviet Ukraine's bailiwick, and the theatre was desperate for funds.[34] After the demise of their theatre in 1933, Berezil' actors Lesia Datsenko and her second husband, actor Borys Drobins'kyi, moved to Kyiv where Drobins'kyi took a job at the State Polish Theatre. Datsenko revealed later in a letter to her former Berezil' colleagues that her husband actually "absolutely did not know the Polish language, the actors translated for him throughout the play." She even admitted that the work at the theatre "was not very successful." Actors Miriam Livshits and Henrikh Tarlo, who transferred from the Yiddish-language theatre to the Polish-language theatre, joined Drobins'kyi. They were all arrested and shot as Poles in 1937 as part of Stalin's anti-Polish, and anti-minority, campaigns.[35]

Only complaint letters and accusations within the Party-state propped up the State Polish Theatre. In 1935, the company toured to Odesa and Marchlevsk, where as per protocol they should have been supported financially by the local Party-state apparat. Apparently, they were not. Iwan Lipinski, the managing director from Poland (not enough cadres in the Soviet Union!) had written Kosior at the Central Committee of the CP(b)U personally about the lack of Party-state help accorded the theatre in preparation for their tour to the Marchlevsk region. Marchlevsk was a Polish-speaking area incorporated as an autonomous region into Soviet Ukraine, so supplying the local population would be an important political goal in the Soviet calculus. Kosior followed up in a note to Veger, the head of the Odesa Regional Party Committee, in late April chastising the Odesa Regional Executive Committee for dragging their feet on assisting the theatre with preparations for their tour to "serve the Polish population." In turn, Fedor Holub, the head of the Regional Executive Committee – who must have heard about this from Veger – wrote immediately to Kosior to defend himself. He explained that Odesa county had 100,000 rubles to support the tours of four theatres: the Belorussian, two troupes from Moscow, including that of celebrity Vsevolod Meyerhold, and the State Polish Theatre in question. "Your direction about the Polish Theatre has been fully carried out, without any *buts*," assured Holub, "but I thought it was necessary to inform you of certain circumstances in the general situation in these matters." The State Polish Theatre was not on the top of anyone's list of priorities.[36]

In 1938 Khrushchev's Politburo decided to liquidate the State Polish Theatre "because the theatre in Kyiv has a limited base of Polish spectatorship, is of poor ideological-artistic quality, and has not proved itself in its seven years of existence." A month earlier, 107 members of the theatre had gathered and discussed (in the Russian language) low attendance, their failure to attract an audience, and their financial difficulties – they were only were able to stay in business by renting out the space for conferences and meetings. If the theatre were solely dependent on the *kassa*, the box office, it would have long ago shut down, concluded the theatre artists. Furthermore, the State Polish Theatre lacked "the culture of the word," since 45 per cent of the troupe was not Polish and many of the artistic workers did not even know Polish. No city would accept the theatre on tour and cities were "even offering the theatre money to stay in Kyiv." The general consensus was that there were no "spectators in our theatre, despite all efforts on the part of the direction to attract them." It was "painful," complained artists, to perform to "half-empty houses," and the actors wanted the state to liquidate the theatre so that they could work at better companies.[37]

The failure of the Polish State Theatre, even more than the struggles with Yiddish-language theatre, shows the importance of official engagement for theatre to function. Certainly, the Russification policies of the late Russian empire, combined with the mass exodus of Poles during the First World War conjuncture, led to *de facto* de-Polonization; that the Party-state struggled to find cadres would suggest a vanishing of the Polish-language artistic layer. Certainly, too, cities may have refused to take the theatre on tour because the entire Party-state apparat could get accused of pro-Polonism. This makes sense; why would a professional union or Party organization purchase a performance at a theatre where many of the personnel had been condemned as enemies of the people? Indeed, the Polish theatre appears in the interrogations of Volodymyr Zatons'kyi; his interrogators make him write that he and Khvylia developed the theatre and subsidized it more than the Ukrainian-language theatre and allowed the Polish theatre to become a hotbed of anti-Soviet propaganda. Clearly, this was not at all true; the interrogations do show, however, the way that choices made by arts officials could prove fatal.[38]

However, regions such as Marchlevsk were indeed Polish-speaking, and presumably there was a Polish-language audience eager for theatre that would offer a competitive alternative to that produced in Poland itself. Witold Wandurski came to Soviet Ukraine with the desire to create culture in Polish that he could not create in Poland. Presumably, he was not the only theatre artist interested in pursuing Polish culture in a Soviet context. The achievements in Polish-language theatre in the interwar period, such as the directing triumphs of Juliusz Osterwa, not to mention the popular genres of the Warsaw cabarets, could have provided a stimulus to create equally quality Polish-language culture in Soviet Ukraine. The demand for Polish-language culture may have been there, but the Party-state was unable to create adequate supply. The Soviet Ukrainian Party-state did not invest in searching out this potential audience, nor did they care to develop the theatre.[39]

Part IV: Vsevolod Balyts'kyi, NKVD Arts Patron

Together with Andrii Khvylia, NKVD chief Vsevolod Balyts'kyi was one of the central movers and shakers in the arts in the 1930s in Soviet Ukraine. Khvylia may have served as a career apparatchik in the arts administration, but Balyts'kyi shaped the artistic landscape through his work in the GPU and NKVD, the institutions of the secret police. While Khvylia had been a major figure in the first wave of terror sweeping through the Ukrainian intelligentsia and literary far in 1933–4, Balyts'kyi's entire network, including Khvylia, fell under the weight of Ezhov's house-cleaning and Stalin's terror sweeping through Soviet elites in 1937–8. Ivan Karbonenko, codename "Svidomyi," claimed under interrogation that in March 1935 he had presented the GPU with information about painter Mykhailo Boichuk preparing to blow up the Kharkiv Shevchenko monument. Karbonenko-Svidomyi, born 1893 near Poltava, ethnic Ukrainian, professor of linguistics, arrested in April 1937, had started to inform for the GPU in May of 1933 after his arrest as a Ukrainian nationalist; in the 1950s the Soviet Ukrainian KGB noted that Karbonenko had written several petitions to the then GPU "admitting nationalist activity," throwing himself on their mercy, and naming names. It was Karbonenko, noted the KGB, who gave testimony against both Andrii Khvylia, as well as against Khvylia's patron, Panas Liubchenko. The idea of modernist painter Boichuk exploding Shevchenko, who embodied nineteenth-century realism, is oddly suggestive. Karbonenko, however, probably meant to suggest that Boichuk would explode the statue at its unveiling, when all the Party-state elite would be at the statue. When Karbonenko first gave the (false) testimony against Boichuk, Khvylia, Liubchenko and Balyts'kyi were in power; just several years later, all of those elites were themselves arrested. And much of the investigation and interrogation centred on their work as arts officials.[40]

In her memoirs, Agnessa Mironova-Korol describes Balyts'kyi, the charismatic NKVD chief. Agnessa's second husband, Sergei Mironov, worked in the Dnipro (then Dnipropetrovs'k) GPU-NKVD from 1936. Balyts'kyi, apparently, paid for Agnessa and Sergei's wedding from NKVD funds: "Well, of course, government money, what other kind?" Balyts'kyi also provided his dacha on the banks of the Dnipro for the celebration, and it was a success: "What didn't we have! His employees organized everything in a flash – everyone wanted to have a good time!" Carrying a tray of vodka shots, Agnessa approached every (presumably male) guest, who would each take a shot and give her a kiss. When she approached Balyts'kyi – "and he was handsome, tall, stately, blonde, a real Siegfried" – the guests held their breath in expectation. Balyts'kyi downed his shot, but, as Agnessa explains, could not kiss her with his wife ("small, pitiful, evil, never dropped her eyes from him") looking on, so he placed a silver ruble (which "at that time was a rarity") on the tray.[41]

Balyts'kyi had already taken notice of the flirtatious Agnessa during a vacation at a seaside sanatorium: "As always, where Balyts'kyi was, there was it cheerful." Balyts'kyi hosted many parties, including Party-state elites, such as Postyshev, Vlas Chubar, Hryhorii Petrovs'kyi, Anastas Mikoian, and of course, all his subordinates and all their pretty wives. When Balyts'kyi responded to her coquettish displeasure over the seating arrangements, he placed her chair right next to his own. Mironov took a chair and edged himself between his wife and Balyts'kyi protesting, "I don't like this." Two servants, however, at Balyts'kyi's command removed Mironov together with his chair to another table – all the guests laughed until they cried. At another party Agnessa went too far: dancing with "Siegfried," she provocatively opened a Chinese parasol and covered their faces. Balyts'kyi's wife refused to kiss her goodbye: "I bit my lip, I was ashamed in front of everyone."[42]

Agnessa Mironova clearly valued her youth as a flirtatious NKVD wife, but her description of Balyts'kyi seems not overly exaggerated. At one Party conference, a Comrade Nikolaevksii was giving a report referring to Mikoian's comments on American light industry. Apparently, Mikoian had reported that in America no one "let a meal go by" without drinking tomato juice, and "if they're wealthy, of course they drink orange juice." To which Balyts'kyi piped up, "And in Europe they drink wine!" This "real Siegfried" had his own circle of guys working throughout the GPU-NKVD in the late 1930s through whom he operated as an unofficial minister of culture.[43]

Balyts'kyi's Circle

Sergei Apollonovich Pustovoitov, born 1893, an ethnic Russian with a gentry background and some higher education, was arrested with most of Balyts'kyi's circle during the summer of 1937. Pustovoitov explained that around the May and October holidays his group would give orders to writers in their employ to write something about planned terrorist attacks: "We always said that the terrorist attacks were against Postyshev and Balyts'kyi ... to show that Balyts'kyi was a leader (*vozhd'*), after whom terrorists hunt." Pustovoitov and his group tried to portray "the Ukrainian intelligentsia as the real danger" so that "by repressing this intelligentsia we would provoke their moving away from Soviet positions and push them into battle with Soviet authority."[44]

Pustovoitov and company made great use of Volodymyr Iurynets', a forty-six-year-old Galician academic who belonged to the literary fair in Kharkiv and himself wrote for the journal *Literary Fair*. Iurynets' told a crazy story under a series of interrogations in late July 1937. He claimed to have written reports denouncing various writers and artists, including literary fair members Mykhail' Semenko and Mykola Kulish, on the demands of the NKVD. In October 1934, for example, Pustovoitov approached Iurynets' and suggested that there might be a terrorist event under preparation for the October days in Kharkiv. When Iurynets' remarked on how odd that should be, since the capital was now in Kyiv, Pustovoitov accused him of disinformation. Iurynets' was pressured to name names, and he did, including playwright Mykola

Kulish, who was arrested in December. "Entirely made up," noted Iurynets' in 1937 about the plots. Iurynets' wrote a 162-page report on how certain elites in the Writers' Union, "held fascist views." One document, supposed to resemble a conversation he had had with Mykola Kulish, was handed to NKVD officer Borys Kozels'kyi on 14 September 1933 (according to the interrogation of Iurynets' on 28 July). Or it may have been handed over to Sherstov, who said it would not do because the "ends did not come together" and the prosecutor would never sanction arrest (according to the interrogation of 22 July). Was this two documents, or the same document?[45]

In any case, the tale continues: Balyts'kyi, Iurynets' later found out, had used the false document(s) in a presentation to Postyshev. Kozels'kyi then demanded that Iurynets' translate the document(s) into German, so that Kozels'kyi would have both (fake) German- and Ukrainian-language documents linking writers with underground émigré and fascist organizations. When Iurynets' was less than enthusiastic about writing a report, Kozels'kyi threatened that he "could not answer" for Iurynets' "in front of Balyts'kyi and maybe the question of your work will come up and we will arrest you."[46] Iurynets'' interrogations speak to the difficulty of continually inventing fake plots. While writing one document, Iurynets' referred to Trukhaniv Island, an island in the middle of the Dnipro in Kyiv. It turned out Iurynets' had spent the summer of 1935 relaxing and swimming in the Dnipro with a friend, and these blissful summer days were on his mind when he had to write the report, and so the report included (mis)information about terrorist cells on Trukhaniv Island. Iurynets'' interrogations show how the literary fair was now intertwined with Balyts'kyi's clan in the police.[47]

Mykola Hrushevs'kyi was another member of the Balyts'kyi circle arrested in 1937. This was the same Hrushevs'kyi who had investigated Hirniak and Vyshnia in 1934 and admitted to "running" a certain Antin Onyshchuk, called "Antonenko," to implicate artists in terrorist plots. Onyshchuk, aged fifty-four at the time of his arrest and, like Iurynets' hailing from Galicia, worked as a paid secret agent of the GPU-NKVD from 1929. The NKVD found a list of counter-revolutionary organizations and names at his apartment, which Hrushevs'kyi explained as necessary in order to keep straight who was in which organization in his invented reports. Making up stories was a complex and potentially fatal business.[48]

Hrushevs'kyi, ethnically Ukrainian, was born in 1905 and had only elementary-school education. In a fourteen-page typed interrogation on 12 August, he implicated Kozels'kyi, Pustovoitov, Iurynets', and Onyshchuk (among others) in falsifying evidence. If Iurynets' describes the process of falsifying evidence, Hrushevs'kyi's interrogation details the inner workings of the Balyts'kyi circle inside the GPU-NKVD. This is how he described it: They had a system of agents, largely taken from "writers' circles and run by Balyts'kyi and Zinovyi Katsnelson and including Iurynets' and [Ivan] Karbonenko and Onyshchuk." These academics would write reports-to-order about terrorist organizations. GPU expert Solomon Bruk could extract testimony from truculent arrestees and often "directed" the confessions: "It was enough that Bruk wanted something, and the confession of the arrested person was secured and the investigator had success," noted Hrushevs'kyi. The agents gave those who confessed better food, allowed meetings with relatives, passed on packages from loved ones, and made vague promises, all of which helped carrying out the investigations. Hrushevs'kyi kept personal copies of testimony in a burn-proof safe in Kyiv and later took it with him when he was moved to Dnipro (Dnipropetrovs'k). This was the logic of the GPU: in case those arrested recanted, Hrushevs'kyi needed "proof" that he had not been making up the testimony. The method of self-defence could backfire, however: Kozels'kyi actually demoted Hrushevs'kyi to Dnipro (Dnipropetrovs'k) in 1935 because Hrushevs'kyi had lost a real testimony (i.e., the real document that detailed a fake plot!) and had to invent a new one, which did not quite match up with other elements in the file in question; after Kozels'kyi shot himself in his office in January of 1936, however, Hrushevs'kyi was forgiven and returned to work in Kyiv.[49]

The carousel continued, with invention and interrogation. Samuil Isaakovich Samoilov, a not-yet-forty Jewish Kyiv native with some secondary-school education, performed all of these interrogations of NKVD agents. In turn, Samoilov was himself arrested and sentenced to death in September 1938, having confessed that he was part of (yet another) counter-revolutionary organization embedded in the NKVD that "systematically broke Soviet laws by arresting innocent Soviet citizens."[50]

A möbius strip emerges – where's the truth and where's the fabrication? Where are the real networks and the fake networks? Samoilov interrogated the interrogators, creating false evidence against those who had created false evidence. Nothing in these documents was true, and everything was a lie; peel away the layers of the onion and nothing remains except paper and fake plots inspired by summer days sunning on Trukhaniv Island. But still, the police arrested and shot writers, artists, and officials. The documents themselves speak to a certain kind of truth because they reveal the way that officialdom functioned, how they exercised incredible authority over artists' lives, and how connected the secret police was with artists. As Ostap Vyshnia's file and Iosyp Hirniak's file both show, Balyts'kyi himself ordered arrests of certain cultural elites – but he also could personally turn a death sentence to a stint in the gulag. Moreover, Balyts'kyi, or someone inside the GPU-NKVD, had to make sense of all the evidence woven together on various artists. Why write a denunciation on Kulish, why on Vyshnia, why on Khvyl'ovyi? The GPU-NKVD had to understand the world of the literary fair in order to figure out whose arrest would have significant consequence.

Balyts'kyi's authority as head of the NKVD extended not only into the world of arts and letters but also into officialdom, even after his own removal in summer 1937. The web of lies could be so thick that officials believed the plots, often plots that they themselves had ordered. In an exchange at a tense Party plenum on 30 August 1937, after Khvylia's and Balyts'kyi's arrest, Liubchenko told Kosior that Balyts'kyi had protected certain former Politburo members who had already been arrested. In other words, if these officials were indeed enemies of the people, and Balyts'kyi had protected them by withholding information, then how could they trust him? "And look, he fabricated something on me. I said then that he was making it up, and I say that he is making it up now," professed Liubchenko. So Liubchenko believed the files on his former colleagues (he assumed that they were guilty and Balyts'kyi had protected them), but still believed that Balyts'kyi had fabricated information on him, Liubchenko. Liubchenko had lost the strand of truth: his own file must be invented, but surely others' files were not. At the plenum, Liubchenko tried to get Kosior to side with him against Balyts'kyi (i.e., to agree that the information provided by Balyts'kyi, now declared an enemy of the people, must have been false). Liubchenko related a story to the plenum: During a boat cruise on the Dnipro River, Balyts'kyi had told Liubchenko's wife that he "had a file" on her husband, and Liubchenko had related the story the next day to Kosior with the conclusion that Balyts'kyi was "a bandit and not a Bolshevik." Liubchenko's attempt to win over Kosior with this anecdote failed. Kosior expressed no sympathy towards Liubchenko, who saw where the plenum was headed. At a recess, Liubchenko went home and shot his wife and then himself.[51]

This plenum may have taken place well after Balyts'kyi had been arrested, but the traces of his work and the work of his network still remained. Natalia Uzhvii, former Berezil' actress desired by both Kyiv and Kharkiv, was forever suspected of having betrayed her husband, Mykhail' Semenko, to the NKVD, leading to his arrest and execution in 1937. Semenko's children by his first wife never believed the actress's innocence even after shown Semenko's arrest file, which never mentioned Uzhvii or in any way suggested that Uzhvii had betrayed Semenko. But still the rumours persisted. Semenko's son even wrote to the KGB objecting to a 1990 book describing the Kharkiv Taras Shevchenko monument. The book's author had claimed (correctly, in fact) that Uzhvii was Semenko's wife and that the baby depicted with her in the Shevchenko statue was her child with Semenko. For the remaining Semenko children, however, the rumours were more real than the truth.[52]

Balyts'kyi was known well among Kyiv locals. In a bizarre 1936 case among young dancers at the opera, two boys accused a third of not only pornographic jokes but also of recounting "anti-Soviet" anecdotes about the "horrors" of the GPU, about how Jews like Balyts'kyi lived near cemeteries. Unusual for the times, the accused boy was released following his desperate mother's contacting the head of the chorus to find out who in the company would have denounced her son to the GPU. "Personal grievances" were discovered, and the accused, who confessed only to pornography, was freed. Balyts'kyi did not live near a cemetery, nor was he Jewish. The incident shows the shadow world of the police: rumours of horrors, rumours of denunciation, rumours about the infamous head of the police at the centre of a house of mirrors. But the GPU-NKVD was not a shadow world, but very real, one of the unique characteristic of the Soviet artistic landscape. This was a state that took culture seriously, and a culture that took the state seriously, and winding between culture and the state was the police, whose leaders, like Balyts'kyi, supervised a world of fabrication and rumour. Balyts'kyi's agents had real influence on the arts and culture of Soviet Ukraine, as represented by Karl Karlson standing in front of the Kharkiv Shevchenko statue, which fixed Natalia Uzhvii and her child in bronze.[53]

In April 1935, the Council of People's Commissars of Soviet Ukraine declared a need to celebrate the memory of the great Ukrainian "poet-revolutionary-democrat" Shevchenko, and they decided to build a memorial to Shevchenko in "the capital of Ukraine, Kyiv." After all, much time and effort had gone into the Kharkiv statue, before anyone knew that Moscow would transfer the capital from Kharkiv to Kyiv in mid-1934. The Council wanted the project headed by Manizer, who had also designed the statue in Kharkiv.[54]

But the two statues reflect their construction at different times. The Kharkiv variant: dynamic, swirling ribbon of revolutionaries, peasants, and Shevchenko characters, wrapping up to the central podium where Taras stands in mid-stride. The Kharkiv statue demands that the spectator walk around the statue to see each figure and contains inside stories for those in the know – famous Berezil' actors trained by Les' Kurbas, Postyshev's coat, the scandal over Semenko and Uzhvii, the dress boots advocated by Khvylia. The Kyiv statue, finally erected only in 1939, differs from the Kharkiv statue. The poet-serf stands tall on a simple podium. His eyes are downcast, his hands clasped behind his back: dynamism to stasis, a multiplicity of narratives to one narrative, the poet among many figures, Taras alone. The sculptor may have been the same, but officialdom behind the sculptor was utterly different: Khvylia, Balyts'kyi, and their entire circles were gone. Apparently, it was Nikita Khrushchev himself who ruled against the multi-figured serf-poet Taras and opted for a simpler design. The Kyiv statue represents, then, a change in aesthetics and a change in leadership. In the years after the Second World War, over seventy statues of Shevchenko sprang up all over Soviet Ukraine. Each of these statues was a product of a sculptor and of an equally creative milieu of Soviet arts managers.[55]

"The less official in art, the more creative," wrote Iurii Smolych in his memoirs in the late 1960s, as he lamented the passage of a certain type of patronage. Waxing nostalgic about the Golden Age of Kharkiv's 1920s, Smolych gives the example of literary fair patron Fusia Furer: "Why are those same newspaper editors or directors of other cultural institutions not *habitués* [zavsidnyk] of the theatres – not people who attend the official run-throughs, but namely – habitués, who have their own people backstage at the theatre, who are friends with actors' circles?" Why, he continues, are art exhibits, or concerts prepared only by the creative unions or the Ministry of Culture, and not the "private initiative" of individuals who happen to take a liking to certain artists? Furer, who supported Kulish's play, or Blakytnyni, who hired Ukrainian native-speaker Vyshnia, or Shums'kyi, who protected Khvyl'ovyi, were indeed all habitués of the Berezil' Theatre, socializing at the buffet, backstage, or in their reserved seats. These patrons were "friends with actors' circles," but they were not involved in arts administration per se. Yet it was this initial literary fair, this deep involvement of those in officialdom with those in the arts, that congealed – like Huizinga's snowflakes on the windowpane – into a system of official artists and arts officials. As artists involved themselves in the Party-state, official-dom took greater control of the arts. The Soviet Party-state appears as if it causes cultural products, but in fact, it was the deep involvement of the Party-state in the arts, not the state itself by itself, that shaped cultural production and reception.[56]

6 The Soviet Beau Monde: The Gulag and Kremlin Cabaret

Part I: Theatre in the Gulag

Iakov Moroz, former head of the secret police in Baku now running the Ukhtpechlag complex in the far Soviet north, was a patron of the arts. Moroz had great plans for his fiefdom: he had a 1,000-person "summer" theatre built, which was never used because it was never summer weather, constructed a pioneer palace, and hired actor Iosyp Hirniak to run the camp theatre company. Moroz's patronage kept the actor alive during his three-year sentence. Hirniak describes his arrival on 30 August 1934 at Chibia, the camp complex's capital in the Komi Autonomous Region. He was thrilled to find fellow Kharkiv literary fair member Ostap Vyshnia already acknowledged among camp authorities and inmates as a famous writer; Vyshnia's jokes, personality, and fame seem to have helped his situation in Moroz' fiefdom. Artistic talent could provide a lifeline for a camp inmate; just as in the non-gulag Soviet world, talent and patronage could allow access to better living conditions.[1]

Thanks to Vyshnia's influence and contacts, Hirniak managed to get himself removed from "general labour" extracting oil and coal and placed as head of the club tasked with creating entertainment for the entire camp population with a motley group (criminals both male and female, street kids, two professional actresses, and a young student of Vsevolod Meyerhold's). As the GPU-NKVD arrested artists, artists and gulag officials negotiated to create entertainment for prisoners and guards – much of which, because of the talent level of the inmates, was highly professional. The gulag became an important stop on the Soviet theatrical network, linking the regions, including Soviet Ukraine, with the centre. The gulag's role as a significant node on the Soviet theatrical network marks a rupture with the Russian empire. Although of course there were theatrical productions in labour camps under the tsars, the professionalization and privileging of such theatrical culture was a new phenomenon under Soviet rule.[2]

As Hirniak found Vyshnia, so did Kurbas find fellow Kharkiv artist, playwright Myroslav Irchan, in another camp of the gulag archipelago. Irchan had been a cultural elite in Kharkiv after his return to Soviet Ukraine in 1929. He had spent a period of six years attempting to sow socialism in the Canadian steppes. Irchan recounted to a camp informant that he had enjoyed a lot of money in Kharkiv, which allowed him to support a high lifestyle. The doors of his apartment "were always open for everyone. At my place gathered well-known writers, actors, artists." Irchan worked on the editorial board of a newspaper, *Zakhidna Ukraina* (Western Ukraine), and when the entire editorial board was arrested, he had to run the journal by himself. He went to Pavel Postyshev at the Central Committee to request help for the journal after the arrests, and Postyshev assured him that "he would help in everything." When Irchan walked out of the building, however, he felt someone take his arm, the fellow asked his name, and "when I said my name, he took me to the GPU." Irchan was a member of the literary fair, ran a journal, lived in the Slovo, and had enough connections with officialdom to walk straight into Pavel Postyshev's office and request help.[3]

Kurbas, Irchan, and Mykola Kulish, among over 100 other members of the Soviet Ukrainian elite, had all been sent to *Belbaltlag*, the White Sea-Baltic Canal camp complex centred at the former Solovetskii monastery. The monastery had long ago been a hotbed of the *raskol*, the Schism, home for those monks who refused to follow the church reforms of Patriarch Nikon in the seventeenth century. In the early Soviet years the monastery became a prison camp filled with Mensheviks and Socialist Revolutionaries who had opposed the Bolsheviks. Now it housed those who became caught up in the chaos of the consequences of the revolution, even the most loyal communists, of all nationalities. Kulish, in fact, was imprisoned in isolation, and it is not clear whether Kurbas and Irchan even knew that Kulish was with them until their removal to execution in Karelia in late 1937. Reports from prisoners at Solovki informing the III Division (the GPU-NKVD section of the GPU-NKVD camp) at the camp offer an insight into the life of the literary fair after Kharkiv.[4]

Camp conditions were terrible, but one could survive if one could escape the physical labour. In June 1934 – soon after his arrival – Kurbas managed to get himself assigned to kitchen work. He also, reportedly, found books (he was once caught reading Shakespeare in German), as well as conversation partners (albeit those who reported to the camp authorities). With one such "Source," Kurbas declared that he was entirely innocent, but nevertheless sentenced to five years. The Source replied that surely Kurbas had friends or acquaintances who could use their popularity to help him clear his name. Kurbas replied that, on the contrary, "It was these people who put me here, and the Party people are also 95 per cent arrested in this same affair, so there is no one from whom to seek protection." Yet Kurbas had connections, reported the Source, which allowed him to work at "cultural-enlightening" work, such as giving lectures on current political topics.[5]

Kurbas, like other inmates, remained connected to the world back home. Kurbas received postcards and letters from his wife, who wrote of her theatre performances with the former Berezil' (now Shevchenko) Theatre, both in Kharkiv and on tour. His mother wrote letters as well and sent packages containing canned goods, *salo*, sausage, and sugar. Kurbas, along with many others, kept up with current events and often went to the reading room to read the Soviet Ukrainian Party-sponsored newspaper, *Komunist*. Kurbas got very upset one day upon reading in the paper that Khvylia had called him a fascist; the Source reported that Kurbas even started speaking out loud to himself and the Source was concerned for Kurbas' sanity. Through the news, the letters, and the packages, camp inmates were hardly completely cut off from the world of the literary fair back home. Mykola Kulish even wrote to his wife requesting that she send him a postcard of the Shevchenko statue, newly erected in the former Soviet Ukrainian capital.[6]

By August, the camp administration gave Irchan and Kurbas a chance to leave physical labour entirely to focus exclusively on creating theatrical productions appropriate for the mass population. Kurbas, apparently, talked "about himself in the barracks and about his past, as about a great master of Soviet theatre. He says that he was a director of state theatres and a People's Artist of the Republic."[7] And indeed, one would assume that the camp administration would make use of the resources at their disposal to create entertainment, as Moroz was doing with Hirniak at Ukhtpechlag. Yet, while Hirniak appears to have been successful in entertaining the camp audience, Kurbas and Irchan were not. Sources noted that Irchan's and Kurbas' attempt was a failure. Their work "did not arouse any interest in the camp inmates" because Kurbas "carried himself higher than the masses surrounding him." Apparently, Kurbas and Irchan "showed a total lack of understanding" of the requirements of their artistic work. The texts of the *chastushki*, rhyming ditties, written by Irchan lacked any rhythm, claimed the Source, and touched only topics like the camp food and drunk collective farmers. There was a number titled "A Spoiled Breakfast" written by Irchan and performed by, it seems, Kurbas and Irchan. The sketch told the story of a rich foreigner eating breakfast whose mood is spoiled by reading the Soviet newspaper detailing the successes of the USSR. The other numbers were "the most ordinary," like music from the *balalaika* (a stringed instrument like a lute), various folk dances, poor reading of verse, and "Ukrainian anecdotes." One wonders if the silent tango or the broader comedy of *Hello from Radiowave 477!* would have gone over better, and perhaps Kurbas and Irchan were trying too hard to please their audience.[8]

The performance material was all pre-approved, of course, by the III Division, so the problem was not that it was not politically correct. Yet somehow the material failed to entertain the audience, at least according to the Sources reporting to the III Division. What might have caused this failure in reception? Later in 1936, a Source noted that when the masses of inmates gathered in the theatre and in meetings, the atmosphere especially depressed Irchan: "In the camps he first encountered this element and it strongly affected him, especially the fact that Soviet authority considers this element closer to it that those judged by counter-revolutionary articles."[9] The various denunciations and reports suggest a class hierarchy in the camp, one in which artists were judged critically for their elite status in the world outside the gulag. There may have, then, been prejudice against Kurbas and Irchan from the beginning; also, however, Soviet artists were not accustomed to focusing on the needs of the audience. They were accustomed to speaking to Party elite to secure patronage, so perhaps the Source was correct in that Irchan did not have extensive experience with the rank-and-file Soviet subjects who were now his audience and whom he had to reach so that they would respond positively to his theatrical work.

Hirniak explains that – at least for the theatre at Chibia – the theatre received portions of the camp's cultural subsidy. Camps received subsidies from Moscow to support the camp artistic infrastructure: theatre, lectures, dances, and other performances. But the subsidy was never enough, and so the camp theatre actually depended on ticket sales to boost revenue and secure their existence. Unlike the non-gulag world, where the lack of money was made up for by "grants" throughout the season from local Party or state patrons, here in the gulag there were no additional subsidies and camp artists were dependent on the camp "market," the audience. Artists like Hirniak had to think about which plays would be interesting to a camp audience and think about how to draw a camp audience to a production – concepts unfamiliar to Soviet artists. Because of their failure with *A Spoiled Breakfast*, camp authorities transferred Kurbas and Irchan back to felling trees, but they were allowed to continue some work in the cultural division. Kurbas even offered to translate foreign radio programs from the German for all those interested – if the camp authorities would let him listen to foreign radio programming.[10]

In late September 1934, the expedition headed by Maxim Gorky to view the successes of the White Sea-Baltic Canal visited the Solovki camp complex. An actor from a Moscow theatre told a Source that he wanted "to see and to talk to Kurbas, who is one of the most important directors of the Soviet Union." Kurbas had tried to talk to the actor three times, but their discussions were always swiftly interrupted. Another visitor wanted to chat with Irchan, but, just as with Kurbas, a camp official interrupted the conversation. The III Division had given camp officials strict instructions to prevent any conversation between the artist-visitors and artist-inmates. Members of the expedition complained to Sources about the "harsh regime and discipline in the camps," where "great artists" like Kurbas and Irchan were working at physical labour in the forest and not making use of their talents. In October 1934 – perhaps because of the severity of comments from the Gorky expedition – Kurbas' dream came true and he was transferred to head the theatre in Medvezhia Gora.[11]

Once again, however, Kurbas was removed from his theatre. Irchan told the Source that Kurbas was "in an extremely downtrodden mood" and "felt that he was losing control over himself." Kurbas wondered why he had been fired: "In the theatre I worked the entire time honestly, with great satisfaction, and never did I even have thoughts of taking even a single provocative step." Kurbas claimed that someone had asked him several times to try to get money from home sent illegally. Kurbas (wisely!) refused. Was his refusal to engage in underground activity the cause of his removal? Was it from another denunciation? "I know that a part of the elites in the theatre were against me because they feared competition. I also know that in the theatre I was really needed as a director ... because they don't have serious, cultured directors." Kurbas was now, according to the Source, "worried" for himself because his "spiritual situation was horrible." He had been able to tolerate the physical labour since he assumed that "sooner or later" he would be allowed to work in theatre, but now he saw "that it's not like that. The fact that without any reason I have been arrested and judged for the second time in my life" proved that he would not be allowed to make theatre: "I am becoming more and more convinced that they have decided to utterly destroy us slowly, but physically, according to plan. They gave me five years, but my life is being shortened by twenty years. For the first time in my life I come to think – is it worth it to draw out such a pitiful existence and poison the life of myself and my family."[12]

Kurbas did somehow still work in the theatre, but it is not clear precisely when or in what capacity. A poster shows his name as the director of a production of Nikolai Pogodin's *Aristocrats*, a contemporary play about former bourgeoisie toiling away their sins through labour, from the 1936–7 camp season. In May 1937 big changes rocked the Solovki camp, and all the women and theatrical workers were sent away. The description of Kurbas' fall in NKVD documents reads as if it were from Kharkiv: a certain Andronnikov had informed the authorities that Kurbas' program for the First of May was too similar to an operetta. Because of the accusation of operetta style, Kurbas was removed from directing the First of May spectacle, and Andronnikov himself got the job. For this betrayal, claimed the Source, a certain Privalov and Kurbas, in turn, denounced Andronnikov. But this was all rumour. Others – the Source dutifully reported – believed that Andronnikov was "taken away" not because of Kurbas' denunciation but because of his "untactful behaviour with women" in the club building for free labourers (i.e., those who worked in the camps, but were not incarcerated). Yet all was not over – still another theatrical worker managed to remove Kurbas and Irchan, but for some reason "had mercy on Privalov." Why? In the Financial Section there was talk that the "Ukrainian group" in the theatre had to go. Yet one Source noted that actually the Soviet Ukrainians had turned on each other, that one group accused the other of denouncing their fellows under interrogation back in Soviet Ukraine. Rumours from the shadow world of the police persisted even in the camps. The world of theatre functioned on rumour, on denunciation, on egos bruised, and on ideology, just like in Kharkiv, or in Moscow. Irchan, apparently, noted that he believed that "Soviet authority was killing creative force." Irchan's comment could refer not only to the world back home, wracked by arrests of the most talented cultural creators, but also to the world of the camps.[13]

On 9 October 1937, a Leningrad *special troika* sentenced 134 of the Soviet Ukrainian artists imprisoned in the Solovki camps to death. Kulish, Kurbas, and Irchan were all shot on 3 November 1937 in Sandormorkh forest in Karelia, as a note from NKVD agent Matveev attests.[14] The project of modern, urban Ukrainian culture ended with the death of the best talent, the cultural elite, the literary fair. Also executed in the purges of 1937–8 were Andrii Khvylia, Vsevolod Balyts'kyi, Stanislaw Kosior, Pavel Postyshev, and the majority of the Soviet Ukrainian Politburo. From a shtetl on a hill in Galicia, to the Soviet constructivist landscape of Kharkiv, to the islands of Solovki and the forests of the north, Kurbas' was a quintessentially Soviet path. From a unique confluence of imperial cultures shaping modern and urban Soviet Ukrainian culture, which turned out both very Soviet and very Ukrainian, the literary fair bridged the worlds of artists and officialdom. They created new forms of patronage that created great art, yet they were also a part of the processes of officialization and the vortex of provincialization pulling them into orbit with Moscow politically and culturally. A Leningrad court sentenced the elite of Soviet Ukraine, a Soviet official supervised their execution far from home, and those remaining banished them from Soviet Ukrainian memory. Art, as Iurii Smolych later noted, was now firmly in the official sphere, and what of creativity?[15]

Ostap Vyshnia was supposed to be shot with the group of his friends and enemies from Kharkiv's literary fair. During his transfer, however, he fell ill and those guarding him dropped him off to recover at a camp medical facility on the way. While he was recovering, the "meat grinder" turned on and the purges claimed all those who had ordered him to be shot; the local doctor then allowed him to stay on at the camp working in the medical wing, since, after all, Vyshnia did have medical training and the camp needed assistance. He survived and was freed ten years later, thanks to official artists Mykola Bazhan and Oleksandr Dovzhenko, both serving in the Soviet Ukrainian government-in-exile in Moscow and tasked by Beria with selecting writers currently in camps whose talents could be used in the war effort. Smolych writes that Vyshnia was the first name on their list, and Beria freed the Cherry Elf in early 1943.[16]

Iosyp Hirniak worked at the camp theatre his entire sentence, and even returned to Chibia after he was technically able to leave the gulag; he turned down a directing position in Soviet Ukraine because he was concerned that he would be set up, sentenced, and forced to return to the camps as an inmate. Better, he concluded, to remain at the camp theatre by choice. Waiting offstage before one performance he ran into one of his investigators from Kharkiv: "Well, as you can see, slapped with seven years!" Hirniak, as he describes in his memoirs, expressed his shock that the investigator had not received more and declared that he, Hirniak, would gladly have killed him. The investigator shrugged off the threat, saying, "Oh Iosyp Iosypovich, why? Hey, give me a cigarette." And the two men smoked backstage at a theatre in the gulag. A Soviet Ukrainian artist and a NKVD officer from Soviet Ukraine at a theatrical production in a camp of the far north: Soviet theatre as its essence.[17]

Part II: Official Soviet Ukrainian Culture

Most accounts of culture in Ukraine – understandably – end with the demise of the literary fair, either with the arrest of Kurbas and Kulish in 1933–4, or with the execution of most Soviet Ukrainian elites in 1937–8. After all, theirs was the work that still holds an interest today. Yet not all of the literary fair was shot on those two days in November 1937; Soviet Ukrainian culture continued, but it continued firmly entrenched on the Soviet theatrical network, and firmly entrenched as (largely) either folk or high melodrama. Kurbas' former theatre company, for whom Kulish had written his great plays, where Hirniak had acted, where Vyshnia and Khvyl'ovyi had socialized, continued to work in Kharkiv. Under its new name, the Shevchenko Theatre, the group toured Moscow in summer 1939. The star of the tour was rising official artist Oleksandr Korniichuk.

Korniichuk did not merely dominate culture in Soviet Ukraine, or exemplify culture in Soviet Ukraine, but rather he himself was Soviet Ukrainian culture in the late 1930s through 1940s. He was the most celebrated official artist, most active arts official, and his plays constituted the bulk of the repertory in Soviet Ukraine. In 1940, Korniichuk's *Bohdan Khmelnyts'kyi*, *Platon Krechet*, *Death of the Squadron*, *The Banker*, and *Elita* were all playing at the same time at various theatres throughout the Soviet Union. Korniichuk's screen version of his *Bohdan Khmelnyts'kyi* was filmed outside L'viv and would reach cinemas in 1941.[18]

Korniichuk was a Soviet wunderkind. Born in 1905 in Khrystinivka, Korniichuk was a generation younger than the literary fair; he actually saw Kurbas perform outside Kyiv in the chaotic days of civil war. His began his professional career with an ode published in a newspaper to Lenin on the first anniversary of the leader's death, but Korniichuk's first success was 1933's *Death of the Squadron*, written for an all-Union competition to honour the fifteen-year anniversary of the revolution. The play was a panegyric to the sailors of the Black Sea Fleet who sank themselves and their ships "in order to perish with honour for the sake of the proletarian revolution and not give in to the Central Rada or German imperialism" (in the words of one character). Walking to his death, the hero Haidai, reformed through his love for the staunch and plucky Communist Oksana, declaims, "I will carry this flag through fire and death. Farewell, sea! We will stir up on the land such a fire that even you will boil with a red flame. Farewell!" The play received second place together with Vladimir Kirshon's *The Miraculous Fusion*. No one took first place.[19]

The role of official artist fit Korniichuk like a glove. With Mykola Kulish's arrest and Ivan Mykytenko's death, Korniichuk was the most powerful and prolific playwright to remain standing in Soviet Ukraine. At the same time, Korniichuk's patron, Nikita Khrushchev, was one of the only members of the Soviet Ukrainian political elite still alive. In fact, the late 1930s were great years for Korniichuk. He followed up *Death of the Squadron* with the equally successful factory melodrama, *Platon Krechet*, which was such a hit that the rising star wrote to *Pravda* on invitation to a closed competition. Korniichuk even received the attention of Stalin himself.

Of course, things were not all smooth sailing. Moscow theatres did perform the young Soviet Ukrainian's works, but the celebrated Moscow Art Theatre proved intransigent. Vladimir Nemirovich-Danchenko honoured Korniichuk with an opportunity to stage his latest work, *The Banker*, and the play went into rehearsals and design preparation in 1937. But when the venerable artistic director saw the final product, he pulled it from the repertoire and claimed that in no way was this play up to the artistic level demanded by the traditions of the Moscow Art Theatre. Now, this may be a legend told in a memoir by a Ukrainian actor that could have spread simply through jealousy of the rising star from the borderlands. The Moscow Art Theatre never did stage the play, however, and the rumour could also reflect an unfortunate truth: making it big in Soviet Ukraine was one thing, but success in Moscow on an all-Union level was quite a different matter. "Moscow is the theatrical, as well as political centre of the Soviet Union," wrote one theatre critic in 1934. "The theatres of other cities and the national republics reflect what is happening on the stage of the Moscow theatres, and by the achievements of the latter the Soviet theatre as a whole may be judged."[20]

The Soviet Theatrical Network

Soviet Ukrainian official culture thus existed in a certain hierarchy with the other theatres of the Union. Generally, during the "off-season" after the theatre season closed in the spring, theatres traversed the Soviet Union bringing their work to another city or series of cities. Touring reinforced hierarchy, by marking out the cultural topography of the USSR into places audiences, officials, and artists deemed important and those deemed undesirable backwaters. Touring was nothing new, of course. During the Russian empire, artists and entrepreneurs had travelled extensively along the roads and railways to bring theatrical culture to multiple audiences; in the Soviet Union, however, the Party-state organized and managed which theatre went where, when, and for how long.

The Soviet theatrical network, then, fixed the centre of all theatrical activity as Moscow – with Leningrad a close second – and the provinces as peripheral. In fact, officials referred to the regions as the "periphery" (or the "peripheral regions"), reflecting the assumption that the cultural production of Soviet Ukraine, for example, would always be lesser than that of Moscow. As one apparatchik wrote: "Theatrical culture and any new work came from Moscow and Leningrad. Here was the centre of theatrical culture, here the line and direction was dictated to our enormous network of peripheral theatres." The Party-state hoped that "the appearance on the periphery of independent and serious work" would mean that such theatres would not "repeat what has already been done by other others," but rather follow their own paths. This notion that "independent and serious work" happened in the regions only after 1917 is, as this book has shown, quite simply false. Early professional Ukrainian-language theatre and Yiddish-language theatre, not to mention the experimental explosion in Soviet Ukraine and throughout the borderlands, reveals the incorrectness of this statement. However, this kind of thinking reified the hierarchy of the Soviet theatrical network: Moscow (and Leningrad) as the centre, the provinces as the periphery.[21]

Organizing the touring itineraries of various theatres posed complications both logistic and ideological. Theatres from the regions wanted to perform in Moscow or Leningrad, and theatres in the centre wanted to control to which far-flung locations the Party-state might send them. As one apparatchik noted, during a tense meeting where the details of the summer season were under negotiation, they had to focus on the "task of political and artistic exchange, the organization of a close connection between the peoples, and not just that everyone gets to go where he wants." Party leaders from the constituent republics – like all good arts officials – clamoured and negotiated to book certain theatres, complained vociferously about the quality of the theatres eventually assigned to them, and advocated for their local audiences.

A representative from Soviet Ukraine, for example, requested that the Kyiv State Jewish Theatre be assigned to tour Leningrad, and that one of the "leading theatres of Moscow and Leningrad," in turn, travel south to tour Soviet Ukraine. Indeed, part of the goal of the summer tours was for the leading theatres of Moscow and Leningrad to grace the regions with their presence, as it were, and for regional theatres to benefit, so it was suggested, from the opportunity to perform in the capital. During their performances in the capital, each theatre's work was discussed and debated in the Committee on Arts Affairs. "The peripheral theatres' trip to Moscow according to the state plan of touring is a big event in the life of our theatre," noted a representative for the Shevchenko Theatre in summer 1939 during their tour to Moscow.[22]

Discussions at the Committee on Arts Affairs focused on the quality of the productions, as well as the choice of repertory. The former Berezil' had performed Korniichuk's historical melodrama, *Bohdan Khmelnyt'skyi*, as well as a classic nineteenth-century melodrama, *Give the Heart to Freedom and It Will Lead You into Slavery* by Marko Kropyvnyts'kyi. A certain Zalesski, deputy for the head of the Committee for Arts Affairs, expressed his view that he was struck by the very existence of Ukrainian-language theatre: "The fact that you have your own language, expressing your own feelings, your own emotions, your own thoughts, ideas, ideals, in whichever costumes your heroes are, whatever epoch they belong to, speaks to the fact that you, as a theatre, as a Soviet, Ukrainian theatre, are building your own performance." Indeed, it may have been a compliment, but one that seems remarkably resonant of the nineteenth-century criticism, painting Ukrainians as lyrical "Little Russians" negotiating the fluid border between Russian and Ukrainian. The commentary successfully "others" the Soviet Ukrainian theatre by expressing shock at its quality; in fact, many of the artists in the Soviet Union came from the southwestern provinces, and in fact, a rich theatrical culture existed there long before 1917. Yet this analysis on the part of the Committee on Arts Affairs shows just how fixed the hierarchy of culture was by the late 1930s. That there could be innovation happening on the periphery was unthinkable.[23]

Korniichuk, of course, responded to this critique carefully by thank-ing Zalesskii and expressing pleasure that the show had pleased the "Moscow spectator." Marian Krushel'nytsk'yi, who had been assigned the position of artistic director of the troupe after Kurbas' removal, had to walk a fine line in responding to the debate. He (cautiously) acknowl-edged any rumours about the theatre by admitting that (now-deceased) Khvylia was "our special friend, in 'quotes.'" He then observed that many in Soviet Ukraine respected the theatre, but always mentioned it with a "between us": "between us, it's a good theatre," or "between us, in this theatre the shows are better than at the Franko," referring to the theatre in Kyiv that effectively took the Berezil"s place when Kur-bas was removed and the capital transferred to Kyiv. "We are still in a cloudy position back home in Ukraine," concluded Krushel'nyt'skyi, and expressed his hope that their success in Moscow could perhaps improve their image back home. Indeed, internal transnationalism of the sort experienced by Bulgakov and Kulish was still a driving force in the creation and reception of Soviet culture. Success in Moscow could certainly add prestige to a theatre's home audience; the dynamic did not work the other way, however, by the 1930s. There do not seem to have been similar sessions of criticism for theatres from Moscow and Leningrad visiting the regions, for example. And why would there be, since the hierarchy between the centre and periphery was already so entrenched in the Soviet theatrical network?[24]

Still, working the dynamic between centre and periphery was a method of working one's own way up the hierarchy of Soviet theatrical network. Any artist from the regions who wanted to attain the highest status, similar to that of artists working Moscow or Leningrad, had to somehow work at the Union level. In that sense, the 1939–41 Soviet occupation of Eastern Poland was a great moment of opportunity for Korniichuk. In newly Soviet L'viv, formerly Polish Lwów, he affirmed his status not just as an official artist but also as an arts official. Arriving in L'viv just behind the Red Army, the thirty-five-year-old took up his position as official patron and met with writers, journalists, and artists in L'viv both publicly and privately in his hotel room. The newspa-per, which showcased his picture next to that of Nikita Khrushchev, advertised his speeches given in the early days of the occupation: for students at the university, for the intelligentsia, and for writers.[25]

Polish writer Aleksander Wat describes his interview with Korni-ichuk in his "office" at the Hotel George, where all the freshly-arrived Soviet elite were residing. Wat notes Korniichuk "wearing silk pajamas, acquired in Lwów of course, and a lot of cologne." Decadence aside (Wat also writes of "ample-bottomed girls" emerging from the hotel room-office), Korniichuk fixed up Wat with a post at *The Red Banner*, Czerwony Sztandar, the new Soviet Polish-language paper. One could no longer simply be an artist, of course, but had to have a position in a state-run cultural institution, such as a newspaper, theatre, or orchestra in order to have the opportunity to make art. Korniichuk proved central in organizing newly Soviet artists into such collectives – making them into official artists, as it were. During the early years of the war, Korniichuk would marry his second wife, Polish Communist writer and activist Wanda Wasilewska, and together they would serve as the ultimate power couple in politics and the arts in wartime and postwar Soviet Ukraine. His performance during the war years secured and solidified his authority in the postwar artistic and political landscape. If Korniichuk himself shows the degree to which artists had become arts officials, the touring network shows just to what extent the region of Soviet Ukraine, the former Russian Imperial Southwest, had become a cultural periphery.[26]

Snapshots of the Literary Fair in the Soviet South

The literary fair scattered during the Second World War. Oleksandr Korniichuk and poet Pavlo Tychyna solidified their status as official artists and arts officials by taking up posts in the government-in-exile in Moscow. Many official artists went on trains to the Soviet interior away from the frontlines and continued to write and to perform in Central Asia. Young actor Roman Cherkashyn remembers arriving at the theatre in Kharkiv one morning to discover that the leading lights of the theatre, including actress Valentyna Chystiakova, Kurbas' wife, had left the night before on a train specially designated for "the leading figures of science, medicine and art." Vyshnia, when he was released from the gulag, first stayed in Moscow with Iurii Smolych, who was keeping Soviet Ukrainian culture alive in the Soviet capital. Mykola Khvyl'ovyi's daughter by his first marriage joined the Red Army with her step-sister and made it all the way to Berlin, where the two girls wrote their names on the walls of the Reichstag.[27]

Yet not all members of the literary fair stayed in Soviet space; the Nazi invasion offered an opportunity to some, hoping to make Ukrainian culture under a different regime. Arkadii Liubchenko, writer and friend to Khvyl'ovyi and Kulish, wrote in his wartime diary of the conversation he had with a friend sitting on a bench in Kharkiv opposite the Shevchenko Theatre in the summer of 1941. As other official writers were scrambling for seats on the trains to the interior, Liubchenko and his friend, in euphemisms, debated whether to stay or to go. Should they stay with the Soviet Union, or try their luck under Nazi Germany? With several Soviet Ukrainian artists, Liubchenko decided to stay under Nazi occupation. Joining Liubchenko were Iosyp Hirniak and his wife, as well as the family of Mykola Kulish.[28]

Under Nazi occupation, Liubchenko and the members of his milieu pursued the project of Ukrainian-language culture. But what was that culture? For Liubchenko, it was reminiscences of the heydey of the literary fair. His diary is full of a series of bizarre and evocative dreams of his friends:

> Dream from night before last: Khvyl'ovyi, Kurbas and I are by some church, it seems, in Chernihiv, by a white wall on a green spring hill. We decide to drink and have some snacks. Sun ... Warmth. Joy. I get closer to them, they're already sitting on the grass, and as I walk over I uncork a litre of vodka ... I get the bread and I complain that it is today's German-Ukrainian bread made from whatever. I cut off a bit, and it is white bread, like a good bun! ... I go to them and they are amazed that I have such amazing bread.[29]

Most of Liubchenko's dreams involve eating, drinking, or elliptical conversations with his friends, especially Khvyl'ovyi and Kulish. Liubchenko, however, seems to have been quickly disillusioned about the opportunities for culture in Ukrainian under the Nazis: "Who are we going to arrange these Ukrainian writer evenings for, the Gestapo?" While the Nazis allowed Ukrainians theatre, journals, and opera (with approved repertory), the Nazi project did not include building any kind of Ukrainian "Nazi" culture, and officialdom was consequently less invested and involved in cultural production. The extensive financing, management, and meeting time spent on the arts so characteristic of the Soviet regime had no place in the Nazi state. Of course, Joseph Goebbels may be legendary as a patron of the arts creating Nazi culture, but he stood alone. There was no equivalent of Khvylia, for example, under Nazi occupation. Performances of Ukrainian-language culture mushroomed in quantity, but radical theatrical experimentation did not occur under the Nazis. Theatre scholar Valerii Haidabura estimates that 70 per cent of all productions were of nineteenth-century Ukrainian-language classics.[30]

Perhaps the one exception was the Ukrainian-language production of Shakespeare's *Hamlet* directed by Iosyp Hirniak, which was performed twenty-five times from 1943 to 1944 at the L'viv Opera House. Hirniak, who had first refused the position of artistic director of the Ukrainian-language theatre in L'viv under the Soviets, took up the position under the Germans. Liubchenko described the production as "provincial ... wooden in places," but overall was "moved" by what Hirniak was able to do with such limited wartime resources. Like many others, Hirniak and his wife fled at the war's end, spent time in displaced persons camps, and made their way slowly to the United States, where they created Ukrainian-language theatre in New York and Philadelphia. Volodymyr Kulish, Mykola Kulish's son, would join them in the United States. Arkadii Liubchenko died alone during a medical operation in Germany in 1945.[31]

Part III: Kremlin Cabaret

The literary fair falls out of the larger story of Soviet culture.

At the opposite end of the Soviet theatrical network from the gulag was the Grand Kremlin Palace, the centre of the Soviet beau monde. While artists have for centuries entertained rulers, and while the Russian imperial tsars and tsarinas certainly enjoyed the high culture that St. Petersburg offered, Stalin transformed court culture. Official artists and arts officials filled the ranks of attendees, from Politburo elite and patrons of the arts, like Stalin and Molotov and Voroshilov, to artists like Mikhoels and the leading lights of the central theatres. Of course, theatres from the periphery performed only during their *dekada*, their ten days of festival in Moscow, when they presented folk dances and operatic melodramas – just as depicted in Evgenii Petrov's *Quiet Ukrainian Night*. Nights spent at the Kremlin among Stalin and his guests reveal an evening's entertainment made up of various numbers of different media, sketches, dances, music, with no particular overarching plot. The evenings suggest, in fact, a new kind of estrada, a cabaret for the Kremlin. This genre of entertainment was a consequence of Soviet nationality policy in the arts: high culture (opera and serious drama) in all the languages of the USSR, folk culture (dances and village-inspired songs) in all the languages of the USSR, and popular culture (popular songs and entertainment) for the masses in Russian for all-Union distribution. At the Kremlin there was no Soviet Ukrainian jazz, although the jazz singers largely came from the region that was now Soviet Ukraine; from Soviet Ukraine there was only folk music and dance, Korniichuk's dramas, and opera from the nineteenth-century classical canon.[32]

Official artists were naturally involved in the Kremlin entertainment. Il'f-Petrov's comic sketches were performed by the most celebrated actors of the Moscow Art Theatre, together with classical music written by Russian composers (such as Tchaikovsky and Rimsky-Korsakov) and composers of foreign descent (such as Rossini). Yet as much as classical music was heavily represented, so, too, were Ukrainian folk songs, even more than folk songs from non-Russian nationality groups. Mikhoels was a guest and represented, with the Romen Gypsy Theatre, only one of two non-Russian-language theatres. There is one mention of Oleksandr Korniichuk, invited to a banquet on 22 April 1941.[33]

Such evenings were unique to the Kremlin. Neither in Kharkiv nor in Kyiv, neither at Kosior's, nor at Balyts'kyi's, did artists perform for the elite in the space of a government institution. The literary fair was not a part of this performance space, not a part of the Kremlin, neither as artists, nor as guests. From multiple literary fairs, from Tbilisi to Kharkiv to Tashkent, there formed one Soviet beau monde. A hierarchy centred in the Kremlin, at performances for Stalin, his cronies, and their guests, characterized this beau monde. And the literary fair of Soviet Ukraine did not belong in this space, the centre of Soviet culture and the world of Stalin's court.

Part IV: The Afterlife of the Literary Fair

when you decide to separate words
into those you used at least once and those you've never touched
you will feel the silence that ripped apart
the heart of that night – the tortured circle
you sense each time you return to this place

because long ago fragments of hot lexemes
grew cold in mouths filled with fear
and the man with the serious expression
with his dark notebook and lead pencil
left behind only silence
                    that fell like a dead bird

simply, such buildings exist
where the final border is particularly grim
where hell and veins of underground ore are unexpectedly close

where time sticks out like lumps of coal from the ground
where death begins, and literature ends
> – From Serhiy Zhadan, "The End of Ukrainian
> Syllabotonic Verse"[34]

Serhiy Zhadan uses the image of Budynok Slovo, the Building of the Word, to describe the "end of Ukrainian syllabotonic verse." For Zhadan, the death of the inhabitants of the Slovo had terrible consequences, namely, the end of innovative poetry in Ukrainian. The murder of those artists left, for Zhadan, a silence. Now the poet can only "separate words into those you have touched at least once and those you have never touched." The legacy of the Slovo means that later generations of poets, like Zhadan, do not possess the words with which to express themselves. "Simply," Zhadan concludes, "such buildings exist ... where death begins and literature ends." Zhadan, of course, refers specifically to the story of the literary fair in Ukraine, but in fact, the Slovo is a Soviet phenomenon. "Such buildings exist" all over the former Soviet Union, and the story of the Slovo is not unique, rather representative of a peculiar intertwining of the arts and the state in the Soviet Union.

The Slovo, too, was part of a larger early Soviet world outside Zhadan's lament. The inhabitants of the Slovo were the elites making Soviet Ukrainian culture. The Slovo was not removed from this world, but part of it: a short walk from the Soviet Ukrainian Central Committee, from the GPU-NKVD, from the constructivist Derzhprom building housing the apparat, from the Berezil' Theatre. This built environment, this sociability, this new infrastructure bubbling with creativity constituted their success. The Slovo could not have anticipated the increasing political and cultural centralization in Moscow, nor that organizing and ordering the chaotic multicultural imperial landscape of their childhoods would challenge cultural production. The inhabitants of the Slovo faced the Soviet challenge of creativity.

Fundamentally, *creativity* itself meant something quite different in the Soviet case than elsewhere in the world, because creative production in the Soviet Union carried a different relationship to the audience and to the state. Creativity was tied to planning. Mihaly Czikszentmihalyi, following Pierre Bourdieu, argues that "creativity" can only be construed contextually and results from power relationships among those negotiating what is and what is not creative. The Soviet case takes this "relative creativity" to the extreme. Evgeny Dobrenko has rightly pointed to the necessity of examining not the "objective" aesthetic value of Soviet cultural production (to the extent that objective aesthetic value could possibly exist), but rather figuring out what particular works of cultural production meant to their creators and those experiencing them. Soviet audiences, officials, and even artists had difficulty distinguishing between good and bad art when the metrics of distinction were radically shifting.[35]

Leszek Kołakowski wrote devastatingly about the way the Soviet socialist system thwarted creativity: "There have been – and I stress the past tense – some specifically communist works of art, literature and thought, unambiguous in their political content, that have nevertheless endured as part of our cultural heritage. But one can safely say that the longer the communists have been in power, the fewer such works there have been."[36] The story of the beau mode on the borderlands attempts to explain Kołakowski's critique; the Soviet cultural infrastructure, created and experienced by the literary fair, ultimately challenged local creative production. Kołakowski, too, suggests that ideology – and politics – has no place in art. Agendas of changing the world might inspire cultural production but ultimately complicate its development. Yet the arrest of the inhabitants of the Slovo did not end the story. Death did not end literature; rather, literature ensured that the literary fair of the Building of the Word continued after death.

In the 1960s, Smolych wrote his memoirs, three volumes about the people and places from his youth: *A Tale of Uncertain Times; A Tale of Uncertain Times Continues; A Tale of Uncertain Times Has No End.* Kurbas, Kulish, Vyshnia – as well as Blakytnyi, Khvyl'ovyi, Kulyck, and Mykytenko, all found their way into Smolych's memoirs. "It's truly terrible," he wrote, "that this most important ... period – the period of beginning – has become almost a 'blank spot' for the following literary generations." Smolych became obsessed with filling in this blank spot. He wrote to writer Konstantin Paustovskii, now living in Moscow, in 1966 that memoirs "for writers of our generation" were the most important genre. "Soviet literature was born on the barricades of October, in the battlefields of the Civil War, caught the great wave – the first post-October generation of young writers – right after the end of the Civil War and the start of peaceful construction," Smolych writes in his memoirs, reminding future generations that it was the experience of revolution and civil war that shaped the choices he and his friends made. "We – the first of this generation – in the 1920s and 1930s, in the years of the beginning, we erred, and were wrong, we made not a few mistakes," he admits. He never goes into detail about what those mistakes were, or how he later perceived those mistakes, but many of those remembered warmly in his memoirs did not die natural deaths, and the world he recalled was full of dynamism, but also of violence, failure, and dramatic change. Smolych's memoirs are exhaustive, covering each and every person who made the literary fair what it was – and many of the places in which they socialized and worked. Sava Holovanivs'kyi, a young writer in the 1930s, noted later in his own memoirs that what was significant about Smolych's memoirs was that every person, as seemingly inconsequential as an administrator to as seemingly consequential as a major poet, figured in the creation of the world of the literary fair with equal weight. Moreover, Smolych's world was created generally by people, with the exception of a few singular places, such as Parfishka's billiard club or the Blakytnyi Literary House – but mostly it was the people themselves and the ties between them that composed the literary fair.[37]

Yet the afterlife of the literary fair remains not only in the word, in poems like Zhadan's, or memoirs like Smolych's. The literary fair has an afterlife in the built environment of post-Soviet Ukraine. Plaques commemorating Kurbas dot the landscape of buildings across the now-independent state. Khvyl'ovyi, Vyshnia, and Kulish are all republished, commemorated, and reinvoked, but perhaps they are misunderstood. Their lives were larger than Ukrainian nationalism. They tried to reimagine what theatre could be, what art could do, how it could move people politically, emotionally, and socially. They rejected Moscow, but they also rejected the capitalist West. They believed in Ukraine, but a Ukraine that was not a part of the village, that was not anti-modern, but that was of the streets, and revelled in technology, jokes, and jazz melodies. The challenges of the literary fair did not vanish. They did not solve the problem of culture in a multicultural space – even with Jews murdered and Poles deported, Soviet Ukraine remained a multicultural space, with Ukrainians, Russians, Crimean Tatars, as well as Ukrainian speakers, Russian speakers, new people from the East, and new people from the West. It was still a borderland region on the edge of People's Poland, the Black Sea, and Russia proper. There were still no tangos in Ukrainian; folk tunes like the 1968 "Chervona Ruta" (Red Rue), to be sure, played the television and air waves, and contributed to a Soviet Ukrainian pop culture of sorts in the late Soviet period. That pop culture awaits further investigation, but it was based in village tropes and not the urban street, as Kurbas had attempted with *Hello from Radiowave 477!* Embroidered shirts, statues of Shevchenko, and a cult of the village seemed to shape postwar Soviet Ukrainian culture.[38]

The word remains. Vyshnia's sketches, Khvylvoyi's manifestos, and Kulish's *Sonata Pathétique* remain. With a renewed focus on exploring and solidifying the culture of Ukraine, the names of the literary fair resonate again. The topography of culture is shifting yet again, as international transnationalism has become external transnationalism, and as the relationship between Russia and Ukraine transforms. Where are the new centres and where are the new peripheries? Where are the new Kurbases, not those imitating him or worshipping him, but smashing, destroying, and therefore creating the stories that we tell ourselves? Theatre is about representation and about reflecting, but also about the audience, the lives they lead, and what they bring to the theatre. Actors in the post-Soviet space have now joined actors in the West who have to defend the artisanal power of live performance. What is the purpose of theatre and why must a story be told in the genre of live performance? Who, in the end, is the new post-Soviet audience? To see people experience joy, grief, sadness, representing the world mutually inhabited, to be entertained, to laugh, to cry, to experience what it is to be human: this is the experience in the audience. It is about the people sitting in the chairs, breathing with the actors, who have given three hours of their lives to sit in a dark space and dream.

The curtain rises.

Notes

Foreword

1 For more on this subject, see my thoughts in the discussion forum, "Diskusiinyi forum: Ukrains'ka revoliutsiia ta ii istoriohrafii: lokal'na, transnatsional'na i hlobal'na perspektyvy," *Ukraina Moderna* vol. 29 (Winter 2020): 31–60, and "The Geography of Revolutionary Art," *Slavic Review*, vol. 78, no. 4 (Winter 2019): 957–64.

2 Markian Dobczansky and Simone Bellezza organized a conference at the University of Toronto on precisely this topic: the resulting issue of *Nationalities Papers*,edited by them, includes my essay "What Was Soviet and Ukrainian about Soviet Ukrainian Culture?: Mykola Kulish's *Myna Mazailo* on the Soviet Stage," *Nationalities Papers*, vol. 47, no. 3 (May 2019): 355–65.

3 For information on Kurbas's productions, the current best source is Natalia Iermakova, *Berezil"ska Kul'tura: istoriia, dosvid* (Kyiv: Feniks, 2012). There is also a wonderful new project called Open Kurbas at the DMTMKU, https://openkurbas.org (accessed 1 March).

4 See my article, "Comrade Actress: The Everyday Life of the Theatrical Avant-Garde," *Ukraina Moderna* vol. 29 (Summer 2021): 289–312; see also Hanna Veselovs'ka, "Prostir zhinky v ukrains'komu avanhardnomu teatri," *Suchasne Mystetstvo* 14 (2018): 107–13; Hanna Veselovs'ka, "Persha zhinka – ukrains'kyi teatralnyi rezhyser Iryna Deeva," *Suchasne mystetsvo* 15 (2019): 69.

5 Olena Palko, *Making Ukraine Soviet. Literature and Cultural Politics under Lenin and Stalin* (London: Bloomsbury, 2020); Bohdan Tokarskyi, "The Un/Executed Renaissance: Ukrainian Soviet Modernism and Its Legacies," *Forum Transregionale Studien*, no. 8 (2021); for more primary source documents, see Olga Bertelsen, ed., *Arkhiv Rozstrilianoho vidrodzhennia. Les' Kurbas i teatr "Berezil'": Arkhivni dokumenty (1927–1988)* (Kyiv: Smoloskyp, 2016).

6 Virlana Tkacz, Anna Pohrivna, Anastasia Haishenets, eds.. *Kurbas: New Worlds*, (Kyiv: Mystetskyi Arsenal, 2019); Adeeb Khalid, *Making Uzbekistan: Nation, Revolution, and Empire in the Early USSR* (Ithaca: Cornell University Press, 2016), 21.

7 The Ukrainian translation was largely funded by a Ukrainian Cultural Fund grant for their educational platform, which includes my course "The Money and the Muse: An Introduction to Cultural History," which requires students to read my book; see the course at the Center for Urban History, Lviv, Ukraine: https://edu.lvivcenter.org/en/courses /money-and-muse-2/

Introduction

1 On the phone call, see Anatoly Smeliansky, *Is Comrade Bulgakov Dead? Mikhail Bulgakov at the Moscow Art Theater*, trans. Arch Tait (New York: Routledge, 1993), 170–3, and Juri Jelagin, *Taming of the Arts*, trans. Nicholas Wreden (New York: E.P. Dutton, 1951), 102–3; on the fifteen times, see Simon Sebag Montefiore, *Stalin: The Court of the Red Tsar* (New York: Vintage, 2005), 98, and Iurii Shapoval, "Oni chuvsvuiut sebia, kak gosti ..." (nad storinkamy stenohramy zustrichi Stalina z ukrains'kymy pys'mennykamy 12 liutoho 1929 roku), in Iurii Shapoval, *Ukraina XX stolittia: osoby ta podii v konteksti vazhkoi istorii* (Kyiv: Heneza, 2001), 93–130.

2 Work on Soviet culture in the pre-war period is staggering. The visual arts have produced nuanced analyses of the infrastructure producing Stalinist visual art, perhaps because so many of the objects under question are still available. For a review of work on the visual arts, see Oliver Johnson, "Alternative Histories of Soviet Visual Culture," *Kritika: Explorations in Russian and Eurasian History* 11, no. 3 (2010), 581–608; Susan Reid has written an impressive series of articles illuminating the greater context to the Stalinist visual arts, see "Socialist Realism in the Stalinist Terror: The Industry of Socialism Art Exhibition, 1935–41," *Russian Review* 60, no. 2 (2001), 153–84; on how avant-garde artists embraced consumer culture, see Christina Kiaer, *Imagine No Possessions: The Socialist Objects of Russian Constructivism* (Cambridge, MA: MIT Press, 2005); on the Stalinist context, Jan Plamper, *The Stalin Cult: A Study in the Alchemy of Power* (New Haven: Yale University Press, 2012); on music and connections with officialdom, see Kiril Tomoff, *Creative Union: The Professional Organization of Composers, 1939–1953* (Ithaca, NY: Cornell University Press, 2006); on literature, the classic analysis of socialist realism remains Katerina Clark, *The Soviet Novel: History as Literature* (New Haven: Yale University Press, 1984); on film, see Yuri Tsivian, *Lines of Resistance: Dziga Vertov and the*

1920s (Pordenone: Le Giornate del Cinema Muto, 2004). Theatre has produced fewer analyses and more document collections, production reconstructions, and narrative descriptions; on theatre see Laurence Senelick and Sergei Ostrovsky, eds., *Soviet Theater: A Documentary History* (New Haven: Yale University Press, 2014).

3 Document collections include the following: in Ukrainian, Vasyl' Vasyl'ko, ed., *Les' Kurbas: Spohady suchasnikiv* (Kyiv: Mystetstvo, 1967); in Russian, Natalia Kuziakina, Mykola Labins'kyi, and Les' Taniuk, eds., *Les' Kurbas: stat'i i vospominaniia o Lese Kurbase* (Moscow: Iskusstvo, 1987); published in the diaspora, Valerian Revuts'kyi, ed., *Les' Kurbas u teatral'nii diial'nosti, v otsinkakh suchasnykiv* (Toronto: Smoloskyp, 1989). The most comprehensive is now Mykola Labin's'kyi, ed., *Les' Kurbas: Filosofiia teatru* (Kyiv: Osnova, 2001), although Labin's'kyi has included both memoirs and archival documents without clarifying which is which. The earliest published memoir of Kurbas is Iosyp (Yosyp) Hirniak, "The Birth and Death of the Modern Ukrainian Theater," in *Soviet Theaters 1917–1941*, ed. Martha Bradshaw (New York: Research Program on the USSR, 1954), 250–388; Hirniak's more complete memoir has been an all-too-frequently used source, see Iosyp Hirniak, *Spomyny* (New York: Suchasnist', 1982); in Ukrainian, see Nelli Korniienko, *Les' Kurbas: Repetytsiia maibutn'ioho* (Kyiv: Fakt, 1998) and *Rezhisserskoe iskusstvo Lesia Kurbasa: Rekonstruktsiia* (Kyiv: Tsentr Lesia Kurbasa, 2005); Korniienko and Natalia Kuziakina were the two theatre scholars who brought Kurbas to academic attention in the 1960s, see Korniienko, "Les' Kurbas," *Teatr* 1968/4, 65–75, and Korniienko, "Teatr preobrazheniia," *Teatr* 1987/9, 60–70, and, Natalia Kuziakina, "Vospitat' uchenika!" *Teatr* 1968/9, 71–9; the most recent works are Bohdan Kozak, ed., *Zhyttia i tvorchist' Lesia Kurbasa* (L'viv: Litopys, 2012); Natalia Iermakova's monumental *Berezil's'ka kul'tura: istoriia, dosvid* (Kyiv: Feniks, 2012). In English, the only book on Kurbas is Irene R. Makaryk, *Shakespeare in the Undiscovered Bourne: Les Kurbas, Ukrainian Modernism and Early Soviet Cultural Politics* (Toronto: University of Toronto Press, 2004); see also the articles by Virlana Tkacz, "Les Kurbas and the Actors of the Berezil Artistic Association in Kiev," *Theater History Studies* 8 (1988), 137–55, and "The Birth of a Director: The Early Development of Les Kurbas and His First Season with the Young Theater," *Journal of Ukrainian Studies* 12, no. 1 (1987), 22–54. The publication of Irena Makaryk and Virlana Tkacz, eds., *Modernism in Kyiv: Jubilant Experimentation* (Toronto: University of Toronto Press, 2010) greatly increases the material available on Kurbas in English.

4 Natalia Kuziakina, *Dramaturh Mykoly Kulisha. Literaturno-krytychni narys* (Kyiv: Radians'kyi pysmennyk, 1962), and *Traiektorii dol'* (Kyiv: Tempora, 2010).

218 Notes to pages 6–11

5 Ostap Vyshnia, *Tvory vchotyr'okh tomakh*, vol. 2, *Usmishky, feiletony,*
humoresky 1925–1933 (Kyiv: Dnipro, 1974); Ivan Vasyl'ovych Zub, *Ostap*
Vyshnia: rysy tvorchoi individual'nosti (Kyiv: Naukova dumka, 1991); Serhy
Yekelchyk, "No Laughing Matter: State Regimentation of Ukrainian
Humor under High Stalinism," *Canadian-American Slavic Studies* 40, no. 1
(2006), 99.

6 Khvylia has not sparked much scholarship, but he did publish texts
on culture, see Khvylia's early work, a published collection of his
newspaper salvos: *Antysemityzm* (Kharkiv, 1930) and *Ukrains'ka narodna*
pisnia (Kyiv, 1935).

7 Iurii Shapoval and Vadym Zolotar'ov, *Vsevolod Balyts'kyi: osoba, chas,*
otochennia (Kyiv: Stylos, 2002).

8 Here I take inspiration for the idea of cultures in a region from Joseph
Roach, *Cities of the Dead: Circum-Atlantic Performance* (New York: Columbia
University Press, 1996), 183. Taras Koznarsky, "Three Novels, Three
Cities," in Makaryk and Tkacz, eds., *Modernism in Kyiv*, 108, argues that
the geographic terms suggest that the region disappears into the empire,
but Serhy Bilenky, *Romantic Nationalism in Eastern Europe: Russian, Polish,*
Ukrainian Political Imaginations (Stanford: Stanford University Press, 2012),
shows how contingent those geographic terms are on perspective, that is,
what was east to the Poles was west to the Russians; the specific history
of this region is well described in Faith Hillis, *Children of Rus': Right-*
Bank Ukraine and the Invention of the Russian Nation (Ithaca, NY: Cornell
University Press, 2013), esp. chap. 1.

9 Liliana Riga, *The Bolsheviks and the Russian Empire* (Cambridge: Cambridge
University Press, 2012).

10 Michael David-Fox, "Implications of Transnationalism," *Kritika:*
Explorations in Russian and Eurasian History 12, no. 4 (2011), 885–904;
Michael David-Fox, *Showcasing the Great Experiment: Cultural Diplomacy*
and Western Visitors to Soviet Russia, 1921–1941 (New York: Oxford
University Press, 2011); Katerina Clark, *Moscow the Fourth Rome:*
Stalinism, Cosmopolitanism, and the Evolution of Soviet Culture, 1931–1941
(Cambridge, MA: Harvard University Press, 2011). Erik R. Scott examines
circulation inside the Soviet Union as well, by arguing that the Soviet
Union was an empire of diasporas and showing how Moscow emerged
as a cosmopolitan capital precisely because of the empire's diasporas, in
Familiar Strangers: The Georgian Diaspora and the Evolution of Soviet Empire
(New York: Oxford, 2016).

11 Transnationalism is notoriously difficult to define. Isabel Hofmeyr writes,
"The claim of transnational methods is not simply that historical processes

are made in different places but that they are constructed in the movement between places, sites, and regions." Hofmeyr, "AHR Conversation: On Transnational History," *American Historical Review* 111, no. 5 (2006), 1444; Philip Ther, "The Transnational Paradigm of Historiography and its Potential for Ukrainian History," in Georgiy Kasianov and Ther, *Ukraine: Laboratory of Transnational History* (Budapest: Central European University Press, 2009), 100; David L. Ransel, "Reflections on Transnational and World History in the USA and its Applications," *Historisk tidskrift* 137 (4), 625–42.

12 I refer here to Dipesh Chakrabarty, *Provincializing Europe: Postcolonial Thought and Historical Difference* (Princeton: Princeton University Press, 2000), but I am not employing a post-colonial framework to prove that the centre was a colonizing force and the periphery was colonized. Rather, I build on the ideas of circulation developed by Kapil Raj, *Relocating Modern Science: Circulation and the Construction of Knowledge in South Asia and Europe, 1650–1900* (New York: Palgrave Macmillan, 2007), to focus on the cultural construction of the centre and the periphery.

13 I take here Serhii Plokhy's argument that Ukraine, or the region that is today Ukraine, has consistently driven Russian politics for the past 300 years, see Plokhy, *The Last Empire: The Final Days of the Soviet Union* (New York: Basic Books, 2015); Hillis, *Children of Rus'*, shows how the borderlands drove the creation of the idea of the Russian nation.

14 Terry Martin, *Affirmative Action Empire: Nations and Nationalism in the Soviet Union 1923–1939* (Ithaca, NY: Cornell University Press, 2001); for how korenizatsiia was intimately bound up with urbanization in Soviet Ukraine, see George O. Liber, *Soviet Nationality Policy, Urban Growth and Identity Change in the Ukrainian SSR, 1923–1934* (New York: Cambridge University Press, 1992). Some scholars have questioned the authenticity of Ukrainization. In the realm of the arts, the struggle to build culture at once Soviet and Ukrainian was real, here I build on the work of Matthew Pauly, who shows the policy-practice divide in Ukrainization in schools, *Breaking the Tongue: Language, Education and Power in Soviet Ukraine, 1923–1931* (Toronto: University of Toronto Press, 2014).

15 Eugen Weber, *Peasants into Frenchman: The Modernization of Rural France 1870–1914* (Stanford: Stanford University Press, 1976); Linda Colley, *Britons: Forging the Nation, 1707–1837* (New Haven: Yale University Press, 1992).

16 Francine Hirsch, in *Empire of Nations: Ethnographic Knowledge and the Making of the Soviet Union* (Ithaca, NY: Cornell University Press, 2005), has taken up the idea of the construction of the Soviet "national" identity, but the notion that Soviet Ukrainian identity could also be constructed

is little explored. Serhy Yekelchyk has taken on this exploration with *Stalin's Empire of Memory: Russian-Ukrainian Relations in the Soviet Historical Imagination* (Toronto: University of Toronto Press, 2004); Tarik Cyril Amar, *The Paradox of Ukrainian Lviv: A Borderland City between Stalinists, Nazis, and Nationalists* (Ithaca, NY: Cornell University Press, 2015), also shows how today's Ukrainian culture is a product of Soviet policies. For recent work on the construction of other Soviet identities, see, on Soviet Minsk Jews, Elissa Bemporad, *Becoming Soviet Jews: The Bolshevik Experiment in Minsk* (Bloomington: Indiana University Press, 2013), and on Soviet Gypsies, Brigid O'Keeffe, *New Soviet Gypsies: Nationality, Performance and Selfhood in the Early Soviet Union* (Toronto: University of Toronto Press, 2013); on why "Jewish" meant Yiddish-language and not Hebrew-language, Kenneth Moss, *Jewish Renaissance in the Russian Revolution* (Cambridge, MA: Harvard University Press, 2009); on Kyrgyzstan, see Ali Igmen, *Speaking Soviet with an Accent: Culture and Power in Kyrgyzstan* (Pittsburgh: University of Pittsburgh Press, 2012); on how young Muslim culturalists used socialism to further their agendas of modernization, see Adeeb Khalid, *The Politics of Muslim Cultural Reform: Jadidism in Central Asia* (Berkeley: University of California Press, 1998); and on culture in Uzbekistan, see Adeeb Khalid, *Making Uzbekistan: Nation, Empire, and Revolution in the early USSR* (Ithaca, NY: Cornell University Press, 2015). There is new work on unpacking the ethnic categories of Soviet culture, see Naomi Caffee, "Russophonia: Towards a Transnational Conception of Russian Literature" (PhD diss., UCLA, 2013), and Isabelle Kaplan, "Cultures and Politics in Soviet Turkic Republics: Canon-building and Nation-building under Stalin" (PhD diss., Georgetown University, in process). Taken together, this work challenges our conception of the monolithic quality of Soviet culture. It was monolithic, but in different ways at different times.

17 Literary scholars have focused more on Ukrainian literature as a defined category and traced its development over time and how it contributed – or not – to nation building, see Oleh Ilnytzkyj, *Ukrainian Futurism 1914–1930: A Historical and Critical Study* (Edmonton: University of Alberta Press, 1997), and Myroslav Shkandrij, *Modernists, Marxists, and the Nation: The Ukrainian Literary Discussion of the 1920s* (Edmonton: Canadian Institute of Ukrainian Studies, 1992). I build on this work by placing the cultural output of the literary fair in its Soviet and multi-ethnic context and by focusing on its constructed quality.

18 E.A. Evtushenko, *Sobranie sochinenii v 3 tomakh*, vol. 1 (Moscow: Khudozhestvennaia literatura, 1983), 443.

19 Charles A. Ruud, *Fighting Words: Imperial Censorship and the Russian Press, 1804–1906*, 2nd ed. (Toronto: University of Toronto Press, 2009), 52–67; Daniil Zavlunov, "Opera as Policy during the Reign of Nicholas I: The First Decade" (presentation at Stetson University, March 2016).

20 Leszek Kołakowski, "Communism as Cultural Formation," *Survey* 29, no. 2 (1985), 136–48; Czesław Miłosz, *The Captive Mind*, trans. Jane Zielonko (1953; reprint, New York: Vintage, 1990); Miklos Haraszti, *The Velvet Prison: Artists under State Socialism*, trans. Katalin and Stephen Landesmann with Steve Wasserman (New York: Basic Books, 1987).

21 I take the notion of beau monde from William Weber, see "Musical Culture and the Capital City: The Epoch of the *beau monde* in London, 1700–1870," in *Concert Life in Eighteenth-Century Britain,* ed. Susan Wollenberg and Simon McVeigh (Aldershot, UK: Ashgate, 2004), 71–2, 75–6, 86; for memoirs on the beau monde, Juri Jelagin, *Taming of the Arts*, trans. Nicholas Wreden (New York: E.P. Dutton, 1951); a good example is Iurii Elagin's descriptions of the parties at Vsevolod Meierkhol'd's Moscow apartment: "There ruled an atmosphere that was very relaxed, slightly frivolous, with a rich shade of the bohemian, entirely in the Moscow style of the NEP times. High-ranked Bolsheviks, military commanders and Chekists paid court to ballerinas, and at the end of the evenings – to Gypsy songs, foreign correspondents and writers had a bit of vodka with caviar and wrote ecstatic notes in their notebooks about the brilliant blossoming of the new communist society, attempting to challenge Kremlin commissars and Lubianka gentlemen with four stars on their crimson lapels to heart-to-heart conversations," in Elagin, *Vsevolod Meierkhol'd: Temnii Genii* (Moscow: Vagrius, 1998), 246.

22 In other geographic regions scholars have analyzed the relationship between artists and officialdom, see Jeffrey Ravel, *The Contested Parterre: Public Theater and French Political Culture* (Ithaca, NY: Cornell University Press, 1999); Michael Steinberg, *The Meaning of the Salzburg Festival: Austria as Theater and Ideology* (Ithaca, NY: Cornell University Press, 1990); Peter Lake, *The Anti-Christ's Lewd Hat: Protestants, Papists and Players in Post-Reformation England* (New Haven: Yale University Press, 2002).

23 For a smattering of the books on the oppositional relationship between artists and power, see Vitalii Sintalinskii, *KGB's Literary Archive*, trans. John Crowfoot (London: Harvill 1995); Vsevolod Sakharov, *Mikhail Bulgakov: Pisatel' i vlast'* (Moscow: Olma, 2000), V.S. Zhidkov, *Teatr i vlast': ot svobody do 'oznachennoi neobkhodimosti'* (Moskva: Moscow, 2003), Benedikt Sarnov, *Stalin i pisateli* (Moscow: Osma, 2008); Boris Frezinskii, *Pisateli i sovetskie vozhdi* (Moscow: Ellis Lak, 2008); Frank Westerman, *Engineers of the Soul: In the Footsteps of Stalin's Writers*, trans. Sam Garrett

(London: Harvill, 2010); Christina Ezrahi, *Swans of the Kremlin: Ballet and Power in Soviet Russia* (Pittsburgh: University of Pittsburgh Press, 2012). For an excellent review pleading for ending the binary, see Jan Plamper, *Vlast' i khudozhestvennaia inteiigentsiia. Dokumenty TsK RKP(b)-VKP(b), VChK-OGPU-NKVD o kul'turnoi politike. 1917–1953 gg*, and: *Stalin: vlast' i iskusstvo*, and: *Sum bur vmesto muzyki. Stalinskaia kul'turnaia revoliutsiia 1936–1938* (review), *Kritika: Explorations in Russian and Eurasian History* 2, no. 1 (2001), 211–18.

24 Jan Gross, *Revolution from Abroad*, 2nd ed. (Princeton: Princeton University Press, 2002), esp. chap. 3, on the importance of analysis vs. description; Stephen Kotkin, "The State – Is It Us? Memoirs, Archives, and Kremlinologists," *Russian Review* 61 (2002), 35–51. If the state is us (*gosudarstvo – eto my*), then artists are the state, too.

25 Lawrence Levine, *Highbrow/Lowbrow: The Emergence of Cultural Hierarchy in America* (Cambridge, MA: Harvard University Press, 1990); for an extended discussion of the intelligentsia and "popular" culture, see Michael David-Fox, *Crossing Borders: Modernity, Ideology, and Culture in Russia and the Soviet Union* (Pittsburgh: University of Pittsburgh Press, 2015), esp. chap. 2.

26 The best overview of Imperial theatre legislation is S.S. Danilov, "Materialy po istorii russkogo zakonodatel'stva o teatre," in *O teatre. Sbornik statei*, ed. S.S. Danilov and S.S. Mokulskii (Leningrad: Iskusstvo, 1940), 177–200. On early theatre, see G.Z. Mordinson, *Istoriia teatralnogo dela v Rossii: osnovanie i razvitie gosudarstvennogo teatra v Rossii XVI–XVIII veka*, 2 vols. (St. Petersburg: Sil'van, 1994). In English, see Robert Leach and Victor Borovsky, eds., *A History of Russian Theater* (Cambridge: Cambridge University Press, 1999).

27 Exceptions include Ira Petrovskaia, *Teatr i zritel' provintsial'noi Rossii* (Leningrad: Iskusstvo, 1979); E. Anthony Swift, *Popular Theater and Society in Tsarist Russia* (Berkeley: University of California Press, 2002); Gary Thurston, *The Popular Theater Movement in Russia 1862–1919* (Evanston, IL: Northwestern University Press, 1998); Murray Frame, *School for Citizens: Theater and Civil Society in Imperial Russia* (New Haven: Yale University Press, 2006), and Murray Frame, *The St. Petersburg Imperial Theaters: Stage and State in Revolutionary Russia* (Jefferson, NC: McFarland, 2000); Elise Wirtschafter, *The Play of Ideas in Russian Enlightenment Theater* (DeKalb: Illinois University Press, 2003).

28 Harsha Ram, "The Sonnet and the Mukhambazi: Genre Wars on the Russian Periphery," *PMLA* 122, no. 5 (2007), 1548–70, and Harsha Ram,

"Modernism on the Periphery: Literary Life in Post-Revolutionary Tbilisi," *Kritika: Explorations in Russian and Eurasian History* 5, no. 2 (2004), 367–82.

29 Kenneth Moss, *Jewish Renaissance in the Russian Revolution* (Cambridge, MA: Harvard University Press, 2009); Jeffrey Veidlinger, *The Moscow State Yiddish Theater: Jewish Culture on the Soviet Stage* (Bloomington: Indiana University Press, 2000); Gennady Estraikh, *In Harness: Yiddish Writers' Romance with Communism* (Syracuse: Syracuse University Press, 2005).

30 I build here on the work of literary historians working on hybridity and culture, see Stephen Greenblatt, ed., *Cultural Mobility: A Manifesto* (Cambridge: Cambridge University Press, 2006), and Peter Burke, *Cultural Hybridity* (Cambridge: Polity, 2009), as well as the classic Homi Bhabha, *The Location of Culture* (London: Routledge, 1991).

31 For an overview of the audience problematic, see Susan Bennett, *Theatre Audiences: A Theory of Production and Reception* (London: Routledge, 1990). Work on the audience in the French case has been extremely productive, see F.W.J. Hemmings, *Theater and State in France, 1760–1905* (Cambridge: Cambridge University Press, 1994), and Roger Chartier, *Forms and Meanings: Texts, Performances, and Audiences from Codex to Computer* (Philadelphia: University of Pennsylvania Press, 1995), 43–83; Labin's'kyi, ed., *Les' Kurbas: Filosofiia teatru*, 178. On popular culture, see Paula Backscheider, "The Paradigms of Popular Culture," *The Eighteenth-Century Novel*, vols. 6–7 (2009), 19–59.

32 The literature on governmental involvement in the arts is extensive, see the classic William J. Baumol and William G. Bowen, *Performing Arts: The Economic Dilemma* (Cambridge, MA: MIT Press, 1968); Dick Netzer, *The Subsidized Muse: Public Support for the Arts in the United States* (Cambridge: Cambridge University Press, 1978); Milton C. Cummings, Jr. and Richard Katz, *The Patron State: Government and the Arts in Europe, North America and Japan* (New York: Oxford University Press, 1987); Ruth Towse, ed., *Recent Developments in Cultural Economics* (Cheltenham, UK: Edward Elgar, 2007); and Bruno Frey, *Arts and Economics: Analysis and Cultural Policy* (Berlin: Springer Verlag, 2013).

33 See, for example, Fitzpatrick, "Intelligentsia and Power: Client-Patron Relations in Stalin's Russia," *Stalinismus vor dem Zweiten Weltkrieg: Neue Wege der Forschung / Stalinism before the Second World War: New Avenues of Research*, ed. M. Hildemeier and E. Müller-Luckner (Munich: Oldenbourg, 1998), 35–53; the February 2002 issue of *Contemporary European History* is devoted to Soviet networks, including essays by Kiril Tomoff, Barbara Walker, and Vera Tolz, all based on Fitzpatrick; see, for example, Kiril Tomoff, "'Most Respected Comrade...': Patrons, Clients, Brokers and

Unofficial Networks in the Stalinist Music World," *Contemporary European History* 11, no. 1 (2002), 33–65, and his book, Tomoff, *Creative Union.*
34 Les' Kurbas, *Shchodennyk,* in Mykola Labin's'kyi, ed., *Les' Kurbas: Filosofiia teatru* (Kyiv: Osnova, 2001), 63.

Chapter One

1 Anton Chekhov, *Sochinennia v 4-kh tomakh,* vol. 2 (Moscow: Pravda, 1984), 391.
2 Chekhov grew up in Ekaterinoslav guberniia; see Donald Rayfield, *Understanding Chekhov: A Critical Study of Chekhov's Prose and Drama* (Madison: University of Wisconsin Press, 1999), 1–2.
3 Mikhail Bulgakov, "Kiev-gorod," in *Sobranie sochinenii v 5 tomakh,* vol. 2 (Moscow: Khudozhestvennaia literatura), 307; Dmitri Zhabotinskii, *Instytut Iudaiky* (Kyiv), f. 21, op. 1, s. 8 ("lebns-bletlach fun a jidishn aktior"); Aleksandr Vertinskii, *Dorogoiu dlinnoiu* (Moscow: Pravda, 1991), 43–9; Konstantin Paustovskii, *Kniga o zhizne. Dalekie gody,* Konstantin Paustovskii, *Povest' o zhizni,* vol. 1, *Dalekie gody,* http://lib.ru/PROZA/PAUSTOWSKIJ/lifebook1.txt
4 For the plays, see Ivan Kotliarevs'kyi, *Poetychni tvory, dramatychni tovry, lysty,* ed. M. T. Iatsenko (Kyiv: Naukova dumka, 1982); Hryhorii Kvitka-Osnov'ianenko, *Povisti ta opovidannia, dramatychni tvory,* ed. O.I. Honchar (Kyiv: Naukova dumka, 1982); on the overlaps of concepts of nation and empire, see Stefan Berger and Alexei Miller, eds., *Nationalizing Empires* (Budapest: Central European University Press, 2015), 30.
5 On Russification in Opera, see Ostap Sereda, "Nationalizing or Entertaining? Public Discourses on Musical Theater in Russian-Ruled Kyiv in the 1870s and 1880s," in *Oper im Wandel der Gesellschaft: Kulturtransfers und Netzwerke des Musiktheaters im modernen Europa,* ed. Sven Oliver Müller, Philipp Ther, Jutta Toelle, and Geze zur Neider (Vienna: Böhlau, 2010), 34–5; Jarosław Iwaszkiewicz, *Książka moich wspomnień* (Cracow: Wydawnictwo literackie, 1968); Mariusz Korzeniowski, *Za Złotą Bramą: działalnosc społeczna kulturalna Polaków we Kijowie w latach 1905–1920* (Lublin: Wydawnictwo Uniwersytetu Marii Curie-Skłodowskiej, 2009), 458–67.
6 Moshe Rosman, *Founder of Hasidism: A Quest for the Historical Ba'al Shem Tov* (Berkeley: University of California Press, 1996).
7 On Hassidism and art, see Steven Muir, "Hasidism and Mitnagdism in the Russian Empire: The (Mis)use of Jewish Music in Polish-Lithuanian Russia," *Journal of Synagogue Music* 38 (2013), 193–212; Joel Berkowitz and

Jeremy Dauber, eds., *Landmark Yiddish Plays: A Critical Anthology* (Albany, NY: SUNY Press, 2006).

8 Michael Hamm, *Kiev: A Portrait 1800–1917* (Princeton: Princeton University Press, 1993); Natan Meir, *Kiev, Jewish Metropolis: A History, 1859–1914* (Bloomington: Indiana University Press, 2010); Faith Hillis, *Children of Rus': Right-Bank Ukraine and the Invention of a Russian Nation* (Ithaca, NY: Cornell University Press, 2013); Patricia Herlihy, *Odessa: A History, 1794–1914* (Cambridge, MA: Harvard University Press, 1986); Steve Zipperstein, *The Jews of Odessa: A Cultural History, 1794–1881* (Stanford: Stanford University Press, 1985); Tanya Richardson, *Kaleidoscopic Odessa: History and Place in Contemporary Ukraine* (Toronto: University of Toronto Press, 2008); Jarrod Tanny, *City of Rogues and Schnorrers: Russia's Jews and the Myth of Old Odessa* (Bloomington: Indiana University Press, 2011); Charles King, *Odessa: Genius and Death in a City of Dreams* (New York: Norton, 2011).

9 On Belarus, see Elissa Bemporad, *Becoming Soviet Jews: The Bolshevik Experiment in Minsk* (Bloomington: Indiana University Press, 2012).

10 Anne Dwyer, "Revivifying Russia: Literature, Theory and Empire in Viktor Shklovskii's Civil War Writings," *Slavonica* 15, no. 1 (2009), 24; Rebecca Stanton, *Isaac Babel and the Self-Invention of Odesan Modernism* (Evanston, IL: Northwestern University Press, 2012), see esp. 152–3n30.

11 Zipperstein, *The Jews of Odessa*, 32, notes about 35,000 Ukrainians in a city of about 400,000; here I build on Tanya Richardson's argument that Odesa can be considered Ukrainian, "if Ukrainian is understood spatially – or territorially – as a multiethnic borderland"; see Richardson, *Kaleidoscopic Odessa*, 6.

12 Iurii Smolych, *Ia vybiraiu literaturu* (Kyiv: Radians'kyi pysmennyk, 1970), 252; Antonina Kulish, "Spohady pro Mykoly Kulisha," in Kulish, *Tvory v 2-kh tomakh*, ed. Les' Taniuk (Kyiv: Dnipro, 1990), 696–707; Ostap Vyshnia, *Tvory* (Kyiv: Naukova Dumka, 1984), 439; SBU, s. 38 353 fp "Andrei Ananievich Khvylia," vol. I, ark. 1, 4–5; Iurii Shapoval, Volodymyr Prystaiko, and Vadim Zolotar'ov, *ChK-GPU-NKVD v Ukraini: osoby, fakty, dokumenty* (Kyiv: Abris, 1997), 22; Dmitri Zhabotinskii, *Instytut Iudaiky* (Kyiv), f. 21, op. 1, s. 8 ("lebns-bletlach fun a jidishn aktior"), 117.

13 Aleksandr Deich, *Golos pamiati* (Moscow: Iskusstvo, 1966), 10–24.

14 Richard Stites, *Serfdom, Society, and the Arts in Imperial Russia: The Pleasure and the Power* (New Haven: Yale University Press, 2008); exceptions include Natalia Zvenigorodskaia, *Provintsial'nye sezony V. Meierkhol'da* (Moscow: URSS, 2004), and Ira Petrovskaia, *Teatr i zritel' provintsial'noi Rossii* (Leningrad: Iskusstvo, 1979); on provincial theatre in France, see Lauren Clay, *Stagestruck: The Business of Theater in Eighteenth-Century France and Its Colonies* (Ithaca, NY: Cornell University Press, 2014).

15 I have taken the idea of "imperial theatrical network" from E. Anthony Swift, *Popular Theater and Society in Tsarist Russia* (Berkeley: University of California Press, 2002), 18, who uses the term to designate specifically the imperial theatres, and Stites, *Serfdom, Society, and the Arts in Imperial Russia*, 280, who writes of the "cultural network" emanating from Moscow travelled by "nomads of a performing empire."

16 I build here on the most concise summary of theatre through the eighteenth century in Elise Wirtschafter, *The Play of Ideas in Russian Enlightenment Theater* (DeKalb, IL: Northern Illinois University Press), 2–28; on the early theatre in the Polish Lithuanian Commonwealth, see Paulina Lewin, *Ukrainian Drama and Theater in the 17th and 18th Centuries* (Edmonton: Canadian Institute of Ukrainian Studies, 2008).

17 Joel Berkowitz and Jeremy Dauber, eds., *Landmark Yiddish Plays: A Critical Anthology* (Albany: SUNY Press, 2006), 5–6; Bertha Malnick, "The Origin and Early History of the Theater in Russia," *The Slavonic and East European Review* 19, nos. 53–54 (1939–1940): 203–27.

18 The Directorate began with exclusive control over all balls (*maskarady*) in 1803, then over the printing of playbills in 1804, then all performers in imperial houses were forbidden from working elsewhere in 1808, and finally an 1827 ukaz gave the Directorate full *de jure* control over all theatrical life in the capitals, see Frame, *School for Citizens*, 27, from Danilov, "Materialy po istorii russkogo zakonodatel'stva o teatre," 178–9.

19 Stites, *Serfdom, Society, and the Arts in Imperial Russia*, 132–5; Frame, *School for Citizens*, 25–6. On theatre size: the Aleksandrinskii had 1,790 seats, the Mikhailovskii had 1,151, and the Mariinskii had 1,625 seats; see Frame, *The St. Petersburg Imperial Theaters*, 10.

20 I build my understanding of imperial regulation from Danilov, "Materialy po istorii russkogo zakonodatel'stva o teatre"; Anthony E. Swift, "Fighting the Germs of Disorder: The Censorship of Russian Popular Theater, 1888–1917," *Russian History/Histoire Russe* 18, no. 1 (1991), 1–49, and Anthony Swift, "Russia," in *The Frightful Stage: Political Censorship of the Theater in Ninetheenth-Century Europe*, ed. Robert Justin Goldstein (New York: Berghahn Books, 2009).

21 Swift, "Fighting the Germs of Disorder," 5–6, and "Russia," 134–9.

22 Swift, "Russia," 139–54, on post-1865 censorship.

23 Andre Antoine's *Théâtre Libre* operated as an amateur society, which was yet another way around regulation; see Sally Debra Charnow, *Theater, Politics, and Markets in Fin-de-siecle France* (New York: Palgrave Macmillan, 2005), 16–95; Swift, *Popular Theater and Society in Tsarist Russia*, 1–2; Stanislavsky and Nemirovich also eventually secured the backing of

magnate Savva Morozov to gain financial security, see Nick Worrall, *The Moscow Art Theater* (New York: Routledge, 1996), chap. 6.

24 Maria Szydłowska, *Cenzura teatralna w Galicji w dobie autonomycznej, 1860–1918* (Cracow: Universitas, 1995); for a more general story of Austrian bureaucrats negotiating centre and periphery, empire and nation, see Iryna Vushko, *The Politics of Cultural Retreat: Imperial Bureaucracy in Austrian Galicia, 1772–1867* (New Haven: Yale University Press, 2015).

25 W.E. Yates, *Theatre in Vienna: A Critical History, 1776–1995* (Cambridge: Cambridge University Press, 1996), 30; Frame, *School for Citizens*, 107.

26 Ted Weeks, *Nation and State in Late Imperial Russia* (DeKalb: Northern Illinois Press, 1996), and "Russification and the Lithuanians," *Slavic Review* 60, no. 1 (2001), 96–114.

27 Marko Kropyvnyts'kyi, *Zbirnyk statei, spohadiv i materialiv*, ed. P. Dolyna (Kyiv: Mystetstvo, 1955), 48; Sofiia Tobilevych, *Moi stezhky i zustrichi* (Kyiv: Derzh.vyd. obrazotvorchoho mystetstva i muzychnoi literatury, 1957), 96, 140.

28 Vasyl Vasyl'ko, *Mykola Sadovs'kyi ta ioho teatr* (Kyiv: Derzhavne vydavnytstvo obrazotvorchoho mystetstva i muzychnoi literatury, 1962), 8–9; Dmytro Antonovych, *Trysta rokiv ukrains'koho teatru* (1928; reprint, Kyiv: VIP, 2003), 140; Tobilevych, *Moi stezhky i zustrichi*, 60–1; Nina Warnke, "Going East: The Impact of American Yiddish Plays and Players on the Yiddish Stage in Czarist Russia, 1890–1917," *American Jewish History* 92, no. 1 (2005), 4.

29 John D. Klier, "Exit, Pursued by a Bear: Russian Administrators and the Ban on Yiddish Theater in Imperial Russia," in *Yiddish Theater: New Approaches*, ed. Joel Berkowitz (Oxford: Oxford University Press, 2003), 159–74, and Barbara Henry, "Jewish Plays on the Russian Stage, St. Petersburg, 1905–1917," in *Yiddish Theater: New Approaches*, ed. Joel Berkowitz (Oxford: Oxford University Press, 2003), 61–75; on Kaminska, see Michael Steinlauf, "Jewish Theater in Poland," *POLIN: Studies in Polish Jewry* 16 (2003), 80–2. Although Ida Kaminska notes that they could not check into the hotel in St. Petersburg because they were outside the Pale and lacked the proper paperwork; see Ida Kaminska, *My Life, My Theater,* trans. Curt Leviant (New York City: Macmillan, 1973), 5.

30 Zbigniew Raszewski, *Trudny Rebus* (Wroclaw: Wiedza o kulturze, 1990), 16–19.

31 Arnold Szyfman, *Labirynt teatru* (Warszawa: Wyd artystyczne i filmowe, 1964), 48; and Adam Grzymała-Siedlecki, *Świat aktorski moich czasów* (Warszawa: Państwowy instytut wydawniczy, 1973), 276.

32 I base my narrative of the genesis of professional Ukrainian-language theater on the following sources: Sadovskii, "Iz Vospominaniia," *Sovetskii*

teatr 12 (1931), 28; Mykola Sadovs'kyi, *Moi teatral'ni zhadky*, ed. Maksym Ryl's'kyi (Kyiv: Derzhavne vydavnytstvo obrazotvorchoho mystetstva i muzychnoi literatury, 1956), 10–13; Tobilevych, *Moi stezhky i zustrichi*, 60–2; Antonovych, *Trysta rokiv ukrains'koho teatru*, 140; Liudmila Staryts'ka-Cherniakhivs'ka, "25 rokiv ukrains'koho teatru," in Antonovych, *Trysta rokiv ukrains'koho teatru*, 305.

33 See note above.

34 A.I. Miller, *The Ukrainian Question: The Russian Empire and Nationalism in the Nineteenth Century* (Budapest: Central European University Press, 2003), 267–9; note Ems *ukaz* published in Fedir Savchenko, *Zaborona Ukrainstva 1876* (Kyiv: Derzhavne vydavnytstvo, 1930), 381–3.

35 The stage names come from personal references: Khlystova-Adasovs'ka was born in the town of Zanky; the Toblievych's mother was from Saksahanyi and Sadovs'kyi was her maiden name; and Karpo was the given name of the Tobilevych's father.

36 Antonovych, *Trysta rokiv ukrains'koho teatru*, 140, makes the point about how the Ems was strict, but not fully enforced; S.N. Durylin, *Maria Zan'kovetskaia: zhizn' i tvorchestvo* (Kyiv: Mystetstvo, 1982), 427, notes the Loris-Melikov/Tolstoi discrepancy; for details on the Ems amendments, see Miller, *The Ukrainian Question*, 241–2, and 246n80, and Maksym Ryl's'kyi, ed., *Ukrains'kyi dramatychnyi teatr*, 2 vols. (Kyiv: Naukova dumka, 1967), 135.

37 Tobilevych, *Moi stezhky i zustrichi*, 116; Sadovs'kyi, *Moi teatral'ni zhadky*, 22, 106–7.

38 Sadovs'kyi, *Moi teatral'ni zhadky*, 61–2; Stepan Chornyi, *Karpenko-Karyi i teatr* (Munich: Ukrains'kyi vil'nyi universytet, 1978), 33, 51.

39 Tobileyvich, *Moi stezhky i zustrichi*, 130–1; Vasyl'ko, *Mykola Sadovs'kyi ta ioho teatr*, 7; Karpo's story inspired his son's plays – through a spelling error in his documents, the tsarist state would not approve his family's former nobility status.

40 For the plays, see Mykhailo Staryts'kyi, *Poetychni tvory, dramatychni tvory* (Kyiv: Naukova dumka, 1987), Ivan Karpenko-Karyi, *Dramatychni tvory* (Kyiv: Naukova dumka, 1989), and Marko Kropyvnyts'kyi, *Dramatychni tvory* (Kyiv: Naukova dumka, 1990).

41 Richard Stites, "The Misanthrope, the Orphan and the Magpie: Imported Melodrama in the Twilight of Serfdom," in *Imitations of Life: Two Centuries of Melodrama in Russia*, ed. Louise McReynolds and Joan Neuberger (Durham, NC: Duke University Press, 2002), 25–54; Peter Brooks, *The Melodramatic Imagination* (New Haven: Yale University Press, 1978), 43, 54–5.

42 See, for example, TsDIAU f. 442, op. 852, ark. 1–180; TsDIAU f. 442, op. 853, s. 2, ark. 1–207; and TsDIAU f. 442, op. 854, s. 2, ark. 1–205.

43 Alice Freifeld, "The De-Germanization of the Budapest Stage," *Yearbook of European Studies* 13 (1999), 148–73; Norbert Bachleitner, "The Habsburg Monarchy," in *The Frightful Stage: Political Censorship of the Theater in Ninetheenth-Century Europe*, ed. Robert Justin Goldstein (New York: Berghahn Books, 2009), 251–4.

44 On the Besida, see introduction to Olena Bon'kovs'ka, *L'vivs'ke teatr tovarystvo Ukrains'ka Besida 1915–1924* (L'viv: Litopis, 2003); Hugo Lane, "The Ukrainian Theater and the Polish Opera: Cultural Hegemony and National Culture," *Harvard Ukrainian Studies* 24 (2000), 149–70.

45 There are many such files, for example, TsDIAU, fond 442, opys 637, sprava 139, ark. 1, 3, 10, 18, 23, 26, and f. 442, op. 638, s. 54, ark. 12, 15, 22; *Derzhavnyi arkhiv Kyivs'koi oblasti* [DAKO] f. F-1, op. 141, s. 662, ark. 1–2.

46 Vasyl'ko, *Mykola Sadovs'kyi ta ioho teatr*, 91; Panas Saksaganskii [Saksahans'kyi], *Iz proshlogo ukrainskogo teatra* (Moskva: Iskusstvo, 1938), 74, 83; Ivan Mar'ianenko, *Stsena, aktory, roli* (Kyiv: Mystetstvo, 1964), 82.

47 Moshe Beregovskii, "The Interaction of Ukrainian and Jewish Folk Music, 1935," in *Old Jewish Folk Music: The Collections and Writings of Moshe Beregovski*, trans. and ed. Mark Rubin (Philadelphia: University of Pennsylvania Press, 1982), 513, 524–6; and Moshe Beregovskii, *Jewish Instrumental Folk Music: The Collections and Writings of Moshe Beregovski*, ed. and trans. Mark Slobin, Robert Rothstein, and Michael Alpert (Syracuse: Syracuse University Press, 2001), xii, 21, 27; Walter Zev Feldman, "Remembrance of Things Past: Klezmer Musicians of Galicia, 1870–1940," *POLIN* 16 (2003), 37–8n25.

48 Zhabotinskii, *Instytut Iudaiky*, 4, 9, 15–18, 22–3, 29, 32; Aleksandr Vertinskii, future estrada singer, used to do "Jewish anecdotes" based on his "own observations in Podol" at the Jewish pharmacists' club during their open-mic nights on Saturdays, Vertinskii, *Dorogoiu dlinnoiu*, 43–5.

49 Leonid Utesov, *Zapiski aktera* (Moscow: Iskusstvo, 1939), 11, 19–20, 28, 36–7.

50 Beregovskii, "The Interaction of Ukrainian and Jewish Folk Music, 1935," 513, 524–6.

51 Zhabotinskii, *Instytut Iudaiky*, 69–70.

52 On the contact zone, see Mary Louise Pratt, *Imperial Eyes: Travel Writing and Transculturation* (London: Routledge, 1992).

53 Natalia Kuziakina, "Les' Kurbas," in *Stat'i i vospominaniia o L. Kurbase*, ed. M. Labin's'kyi and Les' Taniuk (Moscow: Iskusstvo, 1988), 15.

54 Saksaganskii, *Iz proshlogo ukrainskogo teatra*, 16; Danilov, *Ocherki*, 169, 350; Petrovskaia, *Teatr i zritel' provintsial'noi Rossii*, 30; S.S. Danilov and M.G.

Portugalova, *Russkii dramaticheskii teatr XIX-ogo veka*, vol. 2 (Leningrad: Iskusstvo, 1978), 169, 350; Hamm, *Kiev: A Portrait 1800–1917*, 155.

55 The Russian *antrepren'er* signifies both "impresario" (i.e., troupe manager) and "entrepreneur" (i.e., theatre building proprietor).

56 Veniamin Nikulin, *Zapiski teatral'nogo direktora* (New York: Sovetskii pisatel', 1942), 350. GARF f. 5508, op. 1, d. 972, l. 45.

57 Mar'ianenko, *Stsena, aktory, roli*, 80; Maria Velizarii, *Put' provintsialnoi aktrisy* (Leningrad: Iskusstvo, 1938), 257; Tobilevych, *Moi stezhky i zustrichi*, 66–7; N. Sobol'shchikov-Samarin, *Zapisky* (Gor'kii: Gor'kovskoe oblastnoe izdatel'stvo, 1940), 67; Saksaganskii, *Iz proshlogo ukrainskogo teatra*, 71.

58 On Savina, see Catherine Schuler, *Women in Russian Theater: The Actress in the Silver Age* (London: Routledge, 1996), chap. 3, and Louise McReynolds, *Russia at Play: Leisure Activities at the End of the Tsarist Era* (Ithaca, NY: Cornell University Press, 2003), chap. 4.

59 Sadovs'kyi, *Zhadky*, 154–5; Iu. Kostiuk, "Z istorii pershoho ukrains'koho statsionarnoho teatru," *Teatral'na Kultura* (1968), 103–9; Ivan Marianenko, "Teatr Mykolu Sadovs'koho v Kyievi," in *Spohady pro Mykolu Sadovs'koho*, ed. R. Pylypchuk (Kyiv: Mystetstvo 1981), 73, 81; Hryhorii Hryhoriiev, "Ukrains'kyi teatr Mykoly Sadovs'koho," in *Spohady pro Mykolu Sadovs'koho*, ed. R. Pylypchuk (Kyiv: Mystetstvo 1981), 123–39; Smolych, *Ia vybiraiu*, 249–50.

60 Mark Von Hagen, "The Great War and Mobilization of Ethnicity," in *Post-Soviet Political Order: Conflict and State-Building*, ed. Barnett Rubin and Jack Snyder (New York: Routledge, 1998), 34–57.

61 Kurbas was drafted into the Austrian imperial army in 1911 but was discharged for medical reasons, see SBU "Aleksandr Kurbas" s. 75608fp, ark. 4zv; on how Sadovs'kyi knew Kurbas, see Bon'kovs'kaya, *L'viv'skyi teatr*, 218; on the changing scene on the Eastern Front in the First World War, see Mark Von Hagen, *War In a European Borderland: Occupations and Occupation Plans in Galicia and Ukraine 1914–1918* (Seattle, WA: Donald W. Treadgold Studies on Russia, East Europe and Central Asia, 2007), 23–8, and A. Iu. Bakhturina, *Politika Rosiiskoi imperii v Vostochnoi Galitsii v gody pervoi mirovoi voiny* (Moskva: AIRO-XX, 2000).

62 Labin's'kyi notes a letter from 1914 to K.L. Luchyts'ka in which Kurbas outlines his dream for a theatre in Labin's'kyi, ed., *Filosofiia teatru* (Kyiv: Osnovy, 1995). On the Molodyi, see Mykola Labin's'kyi, ed., *Molodyi teatr* (Kyiv: Mystetstvo, 1991), which is a compilation of memoirs and documents; Virlana Tkacz, "The Birth of a Director: The Early Development of Les Kurbas and his First Season with the Young Theatre," *Journal of Ukrainian Studies* 12, no. 1 (1987), 22–54.

63 Derzhavnyi arkhiv Kyievs'koi oblasti [DAKO] fond R-1, op. 1, s. 108, ark. 306, notes that the "Polish Young" theatre was at 19 Prorizna and the Kultur-lige at 15/1 Prorizna; Hanna Veselovs'ka, "Kyiv's Multicultural Theatre Life," in *Modernism in Kyiv: Jubilant Experimentation*, ed. Irena Makaryk and Virlana Tkacz (Toronto: University of Toronto Press, 2008), 249.

64 On Wysocka, see Grigorii Kryzhitskii, *Dorogi teatral'nye* (Moscow: Iskusstvo, 1976), 68–72; Aleksandra Smirnova-Iskander, *O tekh, kogo pomniu* (Leningrad: Iskusstvo, 1989), 92–103; Jarosław Iwaszkiewicz, "Stanisława Wysocka i jej kijowski teatr 'Studya': Wspomnenie," in *Teatralia* (Warszawa: Czytelnik, 1983), 7–72.

65 Iwaszkiewicz, "Stanisława Wysocka i jej kijowski teatr 'Studya'," 15, 44.

66 On Jewish theatre in Russia, see Jeffrey Veidlinger, *Jewish Public Culture in the Late Russian Empire* (Bloomington: Indiana University Press, 2009), chap. 6; on the anti-shund trajectory of Yiddish theatre, see Nahma Sandrow, *Vagabond Stars: A World History of Yiddish Theater* (New York: Harper and Row, 1977); Zhabotinskii, *Instytut Iudaiky*, 73–4, 77; Kaminska, *My Life, My Theater*, 11–13.

67 The Lige included modernist prose writers Dovid Bergelson and Der Nister (Pinchas Kaganovitch); poet and playwright Perets Markish; future editor of the Soviet Yiddish newspaper *Der Emes* (Pravda, The Truth) Moshe Litvakov; the visual artists Nissin Shifrin, El Lissitsky, Aleksandr Tyshler, and many others. Shifrin went on to design for Moscow's Theatre of the Red Army, while Tyshler worked with Solomon Mikhoels for the Moscow GOSET. On the Lige, see Kenneth Moss, as well as the excellent illustrated companion book to the exhibition, *Kultur-Lige: Khudozhnii avan-hard* (Kyiv: Dukh i litera, 2007); Aleksandra Podoprigorova, "Puti stanovleniia evreiskogo professional'nogo teatra v Ukraine v 20e gody XX stoletia," in *Evreis'ka istoriia ta kul'tura v Ukraini – materialy konferentsii u Kyevi* (Kyiv: Asotsiatsiia iudaiky, 1996), 154–60; and Hillel Kazovskii, "The Art Section of the Kulture Lige," *Jews in Eastern Europe* (1993), 5–23.

68 Bulgakov, "Kiev-gorod," 308.

69 DAKO f. R-142, op. 1, s. 151, ark. 1–2; TsDAMLM f. 988, op. 1, s. 33 [manuscript of Iona Shevchenko, *Suchasnyi ukrains'kyi teatr*], 14–16.

70 Inna Kozii, "Kyidramte v teatral'no-mystets'komu prostori Umani," *Kurbasivs'ki chytannia* 2 (2007), 176–85; Natalia Iermakova, *Berezil'ska kul'tura: istoriia, dosvid* (Kyiv: Feniks, 2012), 113–31.

Chapter Two

1 Iurii Smolych, *Rozpovid' pro nespokii* (Kyiv: Radians'kyi pysmennyk, 1968), 135.

2 Mikhail Bulgakov, *Sobranie Sochinenii*, vol. 1, *Zapiski pokoinika; avtobiograficheskaia proza* (St. Petersburg: Azbuka Klassika, 2002), 11.

3 Aleksei Kapler, *Dolgi nashi* (Moscow: Sovetskaia rossiia, 1973), 297, 322–35; Grigorii Kozintsev, *Glubokii ekran* (Moscow: Iskusstvo, 1971), 10, 21–3; Sergei Iutkevich, *Sobranie sochinennia*, vol. 1, *Molodost'* (Moscow: Iskusstvo, 1990), 32–53.

4 Leonid Utesov, *Spasibo serdtse!* 88; Iutkevich, *Sobranie sochinennia*, 32–53; Miron Petrovskii, *Gorodu i miru* (Kyiv: Dukh i litera, 2008), 245–82; Boris Efimov, *Moi vek: kak eto bylo* (Moscow: Agraf, 1998), 33–5, 92; letter from Babel' to Livshits, 17 April 1923, in Isaak Babel', *Sobranie sochinenii*, vol. 4, *Pis'ma* (Moscow: Vremia, 1996), 9–10; Konstantin Paustovskii, *Povest' o zhizni* (Moscow: Sovetskaia Rossiia, 1966); N.A. Lunacharskaia-Rozenel', *Pamiat' serdtsa* (Moscow: Iskusstvo, 1997), 225–8; Natalia Rozenel' was the sister of composer Ilia Sats, and thus the aunt of Natalia Sats, who founded Moscow's celebrated *Teatr iunykh zritelei*; on Bulgakov, see Marietta Chudakova, *Zhizneopisanie Mikhaila Bulgakova* (Moscow: Kniga, 1988).

5 Natalia Vovsi-Mikhoels, *Moi otets' Solomon Mikhoels* (Moscow: Vozvrashenie, 1997), 18–21.

6 Evgenii Petrov, *Moi drug Il'f. Sostavlenie i kommentarii. A. I. Il'f* (Moscow: Tekst, 2001), 93–106; Maria Kisel', "Literacy and Literary Mastery in Early Soviet Russia: The Case of Yuri Olesha," *Ulbandus Review* 11 (2008), 23–45; Kisel' points out that gudok.ru is still an online journal that prints transport information as well as cultural developments and connects itself to the Gudok founded in 1917.

7 E.S. Bulgakova, *Vospominaniia o Mikhaile Bulgakove* (Moskva: AST, 2006), 314, 325, 337.

8 Iurii Smolych, *Rozpovid' pro nespokii tryvae* (Kyiv: Radians'kyi pysmennyk, 1969), 8. The literary journal *Literaturnyi iarmarok* ran from 1928–9, published by the *Derzhavne Vydavnyts'tvo Ukrainy*, DVU, State Publishers of Ukraine.

9 Iurii Smolych, *Ia vybiraiu literaturu* (Kyiv: Radians'kyi pysmennyk, 1970), 252. Mark Von Hagen touches on the prevalence of amateur agitprop troupes operating under the aegis of the Red Army and shows how intertwined institutionally the Red Army and the Commissariat of Enlightenment were during the Civil War; see Von Hagen, *Soldiers in the Proletarian Dictatorship: The Red Army and the Soviet Socialist State, 1917–1930* (Ithaca, NY: Cornell University Press, 1990), 111–14, 154n62.

10 TsDAHOU Vyshnia, tom XII, ark. 6–9.

11 Antonina Kulish, "Spohady pro Mykoly Kulisha," in Mykola Kulish, *Tvory v 2-kh tomakh*, ed. Les' Taniuk (Kyiv: Dnipro, 1990), 696–707.

12 DA SBU Kulish, 93a-96.

13 Kulish, "Spohady pro Mykoly Kulisha," 712–22.

14 Ibid., 723–4; SBU Kulish 93a-96.

15 Letter from Kulish to Dniprovs'kyi, 30 July 1924, in Kulish, *Tvory*, 499;
    TsDAMLM f. 941, op. 1, s. 5 (letter from Kulish to Korneeva-Maslovaia, 2
    December 1924); Kulish, "Spohady pro Mykoly Kulisha," 723–4; Smolych,
    Rozpovid', 52–5.

16 Letter from Kulish to Dniprovs'kyi, 12 August 1924, in Kulish, *Tvory*, 504.

17 Letter from Mykola Kulish to Ivan Dniprovs'kyi, 29 April 1925, in Kulish,
    Tvory, 531; letter from Kulish to Dniprovs'kyi, 16 September 1924, Kulish,
    Tvory, 509; TsDAMLM f. 941, op. 1, s. 26 (letter from Kulish to Korneeva-
    Maslovaia, 29 May 1925); letter from Kulish to Dniprovs'kyi, 13 October
    1924, Kulish, *Tvory*, 511; letter from Kulish to Dniprovs'kyi, 29 April 1925,
    Kulish, *Tvory*, 531.

18 Letter from Kulish to Dniprovs'kyi, 12 August 1924, 505.

19 Letter from Kulish to Dniprovs'kyi, 16 February 1925, Kulish, *Tvory*, 524.

20 TsDAMLM f. 941, op. 1, s. 12 (letter from Kulish to Korneeva-Maslovaia, 5
    May 1925).

21 TsDAMLM f. 941, op. 1, s. 26 (letter from Kulish to Korneeva-Maslovaia, 22
    October 1925).

22 *Literaturnyi iarmarok* #1 (December 1928), ark. 240.

23 Letter from Kulish to Dniprovs'kyi, 12 August 1924, Kulish, *Tvory*, 505.

24 Smolych, *Rozpovid'*, 52–6. For the story of the Borot'bisty, see Jurij Borys,
    *The Sovietization of Ukraine, 1917–1923: The Communist Doctrine and the
    Practice of National Self-Determination* (Edmonton: Canadian Institute of
    Ukrainian Studies, 1980); on the Borot'bisty and cultural elites, see George
    Luckyj, *Literary Politics in the Soviet Ukraine, 1917–1934*, 2nd ed. (Durham,
    NC: Duke University Press, 1990), 20–2, and George O. Liber, *Total Wars
    and the Making of Modern Ukraine* (Toronto: University of Toronto Press,
    2016), 117. General Secretary Stanislaw Kosior makes the point himself
    that the Borot'bisty were not anti-Bolshevik in the 1937 Party Plenum
    defending his colleagues, see TsDAHOU f. 1, op. 1, s. 491, ark. 96–7.

25 Smolych, *Rozpovid'*, 27, 39.

26 TsDAHOU f. 1, op. 20, s. 1852, ark. 73–80.

27 SBU S-183 "Khvylevyi N. G," ark. 18–19.

28 Khvyl'ovyi, "Ukraina chy Malorossia," in Khvyl'ovyi, *Sanatoriina Zona:
    Opovidannia, novely* (Kharkiv: Folio, 2007), 359; TsDAHOU f. 1, op. 6, s. 102,
    ark. 125.

29 Smolych, *Rozpovid'*, 19; Luckyj, *Literary Politics in the Soviet Ukraine, 1917–
    1934*, 43–7.

30 Smolych, *Rozpovid'*, 222–3; Ostap Vyshnia, *Tvory* (Kyiv: Naukova Dumka,
    1984), 439; TsDAHOU f. 1, op. 6, s. 58, ark. 107-zv.

31 Smolych, *Pro teatr*, 180; this was Hnat Iura's Ivan Franko Theatre.
32 TsDAHOU f. 1, op. 20, s. 2018, ark. 38–41.
33 Iurii Shapoval, *Ukraina 20-50-kh rokiv: storinky nenapisanoi istorii* (Kyiv: Naukova dumka, 1993), 20, 32. Veniamin Iakovlevich Furer worked in Kharkiv, was promoted to Donbas, and from there catapulted to a post in the Moscow Party organization. Nikita Khrushchev remembers him as cheerful, and was shocked when he committed suicide in 1936; see N.S. Khrushchev, *Vospominaniia: vremia, liudi, vlast'* (Moscow: Moskovskie novosti, 1999), 156–9. Furer's wife was Galina Lerkhe, a dancer in Kharkiv whom Kaganovich had transferred to Moscow with Furer. She spent many years in the gulag after her husband's suicide; see A.N. Pirozhkova, *Vospominaniia o Babele* (Moscow: Knizhnaia palata, 1989), for her memories of Furer and Lerkhe, who were friendly with Babel'; TsDAHOU f. 1, op. 6, s. 67, ark. 60–1.
34 Smolych, *Rozpovid'*, 37.
35 The literary field was complicated. There was also Serhii Pylypenko, head of *PLUH*, the Plough, which wanted to encourage the masses making culture. Pylypenko et al. were in opposition to Khvyl'ovyi and Blakytnyi and called them *Olimpisty*, the Olympians. Shkandrij makes the valid point that Pylypenko wanted to make peasants into Ukrainians, while Khvyl'ovyi wanted to make Ukrainians into intellectuals; see Myroslav Shkandrij, *Modernists, Marxists, and the Nation*, 180; for the debates, see Luckyj, *Literary Politics in the Soviet Ukraine, 1917–1934*, and Mykola Khvyl'ovyi, "Kamo hriadeshy," in *Rozstriliane vidrodzhennia: Antolohiia 1917–1933*, ed. Iurii Lavrinenko (1959; reprint, Kyiv: Smoloskyp, 2007), 805.
36 On VAPLITE, see Iurii Liuts'kyi, ed., *Vaplitians'kyi zbirnyk* (Edmonton: Canadian Institute of Ukrainian Studies, 1977). Recently, Iryna Tsymbal' has elucidated some of these connections, see "Istoriia VAPLITE u 3D," *Spadshchyna*, vol. 7 (Kyiv: Laurus, 2012), 128–44.
37 Smolych, *Rozpovid'*, 264–70.
38 Kulish, "Spohady pro Mykoly Kulisha," 726, 728, 734.
39 On the zvanie, TsDAVOV f. 166, op. 4, s. 109, ark. 533; on the celebrations, DAKO f. R-111, op. 1, s. 378, ark. 94, 125, 185; DAKO f. R-112, op. 1, s. 1336 is a file dedicated to the preparations for the Berezil' celebration. In April 1926 the Kyiv Commissariat approved the Ukrainian Commissariat's decision to move the Berezil' (ark. 1), ark. 16 lists those institutions giving speeches.
40 Kurbas, "Lektsii z praktyki stseny," in *Filosofiia teatru*, ed. Labin's'kyi (Kyiv: Osnovy, 1995), 181.
41 Smolych, *Rozpovid'*, 135.

42 I base this idea on Jean-Christophe Agnew, *Worlds Apart: The Market and the Theater in Anglo-American Thought, 1550–1750* (Cambridge: Cambridge University Pres, 1986); *iarmarok* is Ukrainian; *iarmarka* is Russian. On the market as topos, see Amelia Glaser, *Jews and Ukrainians in Russia's Literary Borderlands: From the Shtetl Fair to the Petersburg Bookshop* (Evanston, IL: Northwestern University Press, 2012).

43 Smolych, *Rozpovid'*, 99–101, 104–5; TsDAHOU f. 1, op. 20, s. 6218, ark. 102. Most of Petryts'kyi's portraits did not survive, but those that did are compiled in V.V. Ruban, ed., *Anatol' Petryts'kyi: Portrety suchasnykiv* (Kyiv: Mystetstvo, 1991); on Semenko, see Myroslava Mudrak, *The New Generation and Artistic Modernism in the Ukraine* (Ann Arbor: UMI Research Press, 1986); and Oleh Ilnytzkyj, *Ukrainian Futurism: A Historical and Critical Study* (Cambridge, MA: Harvard University Press, 1997).

44 TsDAVOV f. 166, op. 9, s. 6390, ark. 26–8; TsDAHOU f. 1, op. 20, s. 2691.

45 *Literaturnyi iarmarok*, March 1929, ark. 170; Smolych, *Pro teatr*, 181.

46 On Furer, see Smolych, *Rospovid'* 102, and Iosyp Hirniak, *Spomyny* (New York: Suchasnist', 1982), 303–4.

47 Smolych, *Rozpovid' pro nespokii nemae kintsia*, 124–5; Roman Cherkashyn and Iuliia Fomina, *My-Berezil'tsi* (Kharkiv: Akta, 2008), 73; Liudmila Petryts'ka writes of her youth in TsDAMLM f. 237, op. 3, s. 47; on Semenko as a neighbour, TsDAVOV f. 166, op. 9, s. 247, ark. 44.

48 On *Red Pepper*, TsDAHOU f. 1, op. 6, s. 165, ark. 59; memoirs flesh out these various connections, see Cherkashyn and Fomina, *My-Berezil'tsi*; Hirniak, *Spomyny*; Hryhorii Kostiuk, *Zustrichi i proshchannia*, 2 vols. (Kyiv: Smoloskyp, 2008); Iurii Smolych, *Rozpovid' pro nespokii* (Kyiv: Radians'kyi pymennyk, 1968); as well as *Shchodennyk Arkadiia Liubchenka*, ed. Iurii Luts'kyi (L'viv-New York: M. P. Kots', 1999), and Volodymyr Kulish, *Slovo pro Budynok Slovo* (Toronto: Homin' Ukrainy, 1966).

49 SBU Khvyl'ovyi, 27, 45–6, 70; "Dysput 'Zelena Kobyla'," *Literaturnyi iarmarok* #2 (January 1929), 238–55.

50 Theatre director Witold Wandurski, for example, was imprisoned not for his avant-garde productions but for his Communist politics; see TsDAVOV f. 166, op. 6, s. 2001, ark. 265–7. Timothy Snyder shows how Polish interwar Volhynia tolerated a multi-ethnic artistic culture, but Volhynia was the exception in interwar Poland; Timothy Snyder, *Sketches from a Secret War: A Polish Artist's Mission to Liberate Soviet Ukraine* (New Haven: Yale University Press, 2005). For GPU officers in meetings, see TsDAVOV f. 166, op. 6, s. 2632 in its entirety.

51 Kulish, "Spohady pro Mykoly Kulisha," 734; letter from Dniprovs'kyi to Kulish, 28 June 1927, in Liuts'kyi, *Vaplitians'kyi zbirnyk* (Edmonton: Canadian Institute of Ukrainian Studies,, 1977), 223.

52 Johan Huizinga, *Homo ludens: A Study of the Play Element in Culture* (Boston: Beacon Press, 1950), 1–15, 120–4.

53 Khvyl'ovyi, "Kamo hriadeshy," 829.

54 For Der Nister, see *Literaturnyi iarmarok* #2 (February 1929), 157–60; Ostap Vyshnia, *Usmishky* (Kyiv: Dnipro, 1969); DMTMKU "Vasyl'ko," inventory #10242 (Shchodennyky t. 8), 190–1; Dmitri Zhabotinskii, *Instytut Iudaiky* (Kyiv), f. 21, op. 1, s. 8 ("lebns-bletlach fun a jidishn aktior"), 69–70; TsDAVOU f. 166, op. 6, s. 2001, ark. 255.

55 Myroslav Shkandrij, *Jews in Ukrainian Literature: Representation and Identity* (New Haven: Yale University Press, 2009), 100; Gennady Estraikh, "The Yiddish Kultur-Lige," in *Modernism in Kyiv: Jubilant Experimentation*, ed. Irena Makaryk and Virlana Tkacz (Toronto: University of Toronto Press, 2010), 197–217, argues that Soviet structures actutally facilitated interethnic collaboration; Yohanan Petrovsky-Shtern, *The Anti-Imperial Choice: The Making of the Ukrainian Jew* (New Haven: Yale University Press 2009), argues that there was a "Ukrainian Jew," but see my "Yiddish Theater in Soviet Ukraine: A Re-evaluation of Jewish-Slavic Relations in the Arts," *Ab Imperio* 2011/3 (December 2011), 167–88, in which I suggest that it was not that Jewish writers chose to write in Ukrainian, but rather that they invested in the category of Soviet Ukrainian, which could have not been ethnically Ukrainian.

56 TsDAHO f. 1, op. 20, s. 1852, ark. 79.

57 Donald Fanger, *The Creation of Nikolai Gogol* (Cambridge, MA: Harvard University Press, 1979); for a nuanced exploration of Gogol' as imperial and national, see Edyta Bojanowska, *Nikolai Gogol: Between Ukrainian and Russian Nationalism* (Cambridge, MA: Harvard University Press, 2007).

58 SBU Khvyl'ovyi 24–5. For example, the denunciation claims that Khvyl'ovyi, though passing himself off as uneducated, actually attended Kharkiv University. Scholar Iurii Shapoval and documentary filmmaker Iryna Shatokhina have exhausted the records and found no evidence that Khvyl'ovyi had anything more than a village education.

59 Smolych, *Rozpovid'*, 132–5.

60 On Minsk, see Elissa Bemporad, *Becoming Soviet Jews: The Bolshevik Experiment in Minsk* (Bloomington: Indiana University Press, 2012); on Georgia, see Harsha Ram, "Introducing Georgian Modernism," *Modernism/ Modernity* 21, no. 1 (2014), 283–8.

61 Iurii Shapoval, "Oni chuvstvuiut sebia, kak gosti …" (nad storinkamy stenohramy zustrichi Stalina z ukrains'kymy pys'mennykamy 12 liutoho 1929 roku), in Iurii Shapoval, *Ukraina XX stolittia: osoby ta podii v konteksti vazhkoi istorii* (Kyiv: Heneza, 2001), 93–130; Ivan Kulyk, *Zapysky konsula* (Kharkiv: DVO, 1929); for more on Ivan Kulyk, see Petrovsky-Shtern, *The Anti-Imperial Choice*, chap. 2.

62 Shapoval, "Oni chuvstvuiut sebia, kak gosti …," 107.

63 Mykola Kulish, *Vybrani tvory* (Kyiv: Smoloskyp, 2014), 383.

64 Mykola Kulish, "Vystup na teatral'nomu dysputi 1929 roku," in Mykola
    Kulish, *Tvory*, ed. Les' Taniuk (Kyiv: Dnipro, 1990), 464; *Derzhavnyi arkhiv
    Sluzhba bezpeky Ukrainy* [SBU] 36546 fp. v. III [Kulish Nikolai Gurovich],
    203; on Petrenko, *Gosudarstvennyi arkhiv Rossiiskoi Federatsii* [GARF] f. 5508
    "TsK Rabis," op. 1, d. 1307, l. 135; *Rossiskii gosudarstvennyi arkhiv sotsial'noi-
    politichieskoi istorii* [RGASPI] f. 142 "Lunacharskii," op. 1, d. 461, l. 8ob.

65 Mykola Kulish, *Sonata Pathétique*, ed. and trans. George and Moira Luckyj
    (Littleton, CO: Ukrainian Academic Press, 1975), based largely on Mykola
    Kulish, *Patetychna sonata* (L'viv: Ukrains'ke vydavnytstvo, 1943), but there
    is also the Russian version, Kulish, *Pateticheskaia sonata* (Moscow, 1931),
    copies of both are available at Harvard's Widener Library. Taras Koznarsky
    draws a comparison between *Turbins* and Valerian Pidmohil'nyi's *The City*,
    see Taras Koznarsky, "Three Novels, Three Cities," in *Modernism in Kyiv:
    Jubilant Experimentation*, ed. Irena Makaryk and Virlana Tkacz (Toronto:
    University of Toronto Press, 2010), 136n77.

66 Kulish, "Vystup na teatral'nomu dysputi 1929 roku," 460.

67 *Tsentral'nyi derzhavnyi arkhiv vyshchykh orhaniv vlady Ukrainy* [TsDAVOV]
    f. 166, op. 9, s. 247, ark. 99; *Literatura i mystetstvo* (Kharkiv) 22 June 1929,
    2–3; examples of Kulish's appearance at the highest republican discussions
    include TsDAHOU f. 1, op. 6, s. 142, l. 54–6.

68 Alisa Koonen, *Stranitsy zhizni* (Moscow: Iskusstvo, 1975), 340–3.

69 RGALI f. 2788, op. 1., d. 71, l. 45–6.

70 Mykola Kulish, *Die Beethovensonata: ein Stück aus der Ukraine*, ed.
    Friedrich Wolf (Berlin: Fischer, 1932); on Kaganovich in Soviet Ukraine,
    see TsDAHOU f. 1, op. 20, s. 2695 ["obshchii otdel 1928"], which details
    all of Kagnovich's dealings with the literary intelligentsia; B. Reznikov,
    G. Vasil'kovskii, and I. Erukhimovich et al., "Neudavshaiasia Patetika,"
    Pravda, 9 February 1932 (No. 39).

71 I. Ukrainets, "O Pateticheskoi sonate Kulisha," *Pravda*, 24 March 1932
    (No. 63). A review in *Sovetskii teatr* put it bluntly, "The talented artist
    needs to seriously take himself in hand to reconsider his own ideological
    baggage." See Boris Alpers, "Sud'ba liricheskoi dramy," *Sovetskii teatr*
    1932/2, 14–19.

72 See the introduction to Kulish, *Sonata Pathétique*. Kulish would benefit from
    the work that Istvan Rev did for Imre Nagy. By peeling away the layers
    of interpretation, Rev was able to recuperate the original Nagy: a reform
    Communist. As Rev points out for Nagy, the irony is that by categorizing
    Kulish as anti-Soviet, one simply reifies the (fake) secret police accusations.
    Kulish was not anti-Soviet, but rather practised "engaged social criticism,"

in Marko Stech's words, to improve his surrounding society; see Istvan Rev, *Retroactive Justice: A Prehistory of Post-Communism* (Stanford: Stanford University Press, 2005), and Marko Stech, "Kulish and the Devil," *Journal of Ukrainian Studies* 32, no. 1 (2007), 2. This aporia may explain why *Sonata Pathétique*, a very good play, has not been promoted and staged: for Ukrainians, Kulish is too Soviet, but for others, he is too Ukrainian.

Chapter Three

1 Aleksandra Il'f, *Dom, milyi dom: Kak zhili v Moskve Il'f i Petrov* (Moscow: Lomonosov, 2014), 28, 42, 80, 83, 87; Pavel Valer'evich Kuznetsov, "Svoeobrazie fel'etonistiki 1920-kh gg. v gazete *Gudok*" (PhD diss., A.S. Griboedov Institute of International Law and Economics, 2011); Evgenii Petrov, *Moi drug Il'f*, ed. Aleksandra Il'f (Moscow: Tekst, 2001); Viktor Shklovskii, "Iugo-zapad," in *Gamburgskii schet: stat'i, vospominaniia, esse* (Moscow: Sovetskii pisatel', 1990), 470–5.
2 Ilya Ilf and Evgenii Petrov, *The Twelve Chairs*, transl. Anne O. Fisher (Evanston, IL: Northwestern University Press, 2011); Il'ia Il'f and Evgenii Petrov, *Sobranie sochinenii*, vol. 1 (Moscow: Khudozhestvennaia literatura, 1994).
3 I build here on the excellent overview of popular culture in Russia by Richard Stites, *Russian Popular Culture: Entertainment and Society since 1900* (Cambridge: Cambridge University Press, 1992), 1–8, and the analysis of "popular culture" in Kristin Roth-Ey, *Moscow Prime Time: How the Soviet Union Built the Media Empire that Lost the Cold War* (Ithaca, NY: Cornell University Press, 2013); for an overview of popular culture, see Paula Backscheider, "The Paradigms of Popular Culture," *The Eighteenth-Century Novel*, vols. 6–7 (2009), 19–59.
4 RGALI f. 1821, d. 151, l. 21.
5 RGALI f. 656, op. 1, d. 1312, 1–22.
6 On the circus and institutions, see Miriam Neirick, *When Pigs Could Fly and Bears Could Dance: A History of the Soviet Circus* (Madison: University of Wisconsin Press, 2012), 7, 69; David MacFayden, *Red Stars: Personality and the Soviet Popular Song* (Montreal: McGill-Queen's University Press, 2001), 17. Today the *Moskovskii akademicheskii teatr satiry* is in the location of the former Music Hall.
7 Mikhail Bulgakov, *Master i Margarita* (Moscow: Azbuka Klassika, 2004).
8 Il'f, *Kak zhili*, 155.
9 RGALI f. 656, op. 2, d. 380, l. 5.
10 RGALI f. 1821, op.1, d.16, l. 13–14.

11 For a short clip of the lullaby scene, see YouTube, https://www.youtube.com/watch?v=jyzBOxODV90.

12 Ivan Vasyl'ovych Zub, *Ostap Vyshnia: rysy tvorchoi individual'nosti* (Kyiv: Naukova dumka, 1991); Serhy Yekelchyk, "No Laughing Matter: State Regimentation of Ukrainian Humor under High Stalinism," *Canadian-American Slavic Studies* 40, no. 1 (2006), 79–99.

13 Ostap Vyshnia, "Moia avtobiohrafiia," *Tvory vchotyr'okh tomakh,* vol. 2, *Usmishky, feiletony, humoresky 1925–1933* (Kyiv: Dnipro, 1974). Thanks to Iryna Vushko for suggesting the term "Cherry Elf."

14 George Luckyji, ed., *The Vaplite Collection* (Edmonton: Mosaic Press for the Canadian Institute of Ukrainian Studies, 1977), 64.

15 Ostap Vyshnia, "The Scratchranians," trans. Anatole Bilenko, Electronic Library of Ukrainian Literature, http://sites.utoronto.ca/elul/English/Bilenko/Vyshnia-Scratchranians.pdf

16 Ostap Vyshnia, " Vyshnevi usmishky zakordonni," in *Tvory vchotyr'okh tomakh,* vol. 2 (Kyiv: Dnipro, 1988), 17–18, and Vyshnia, "Zakordonni usmishky," in *Tvory vchotyr'okh tomakh,* vol. 2 (Kyiv: Dnipro, 1988), 309–10.

17 On the show, see Natalia Iermakova, "Allo na khvyli 477: pershe ukrains'ke reviu," *Protsenium* 17, no. 1 (2007), 7–13; Myroslava Mudrak, "Vadym Meller, Les Kurbas, and the Ukrainian Theatrical Avant-Garde," *Russian History/Histoire Russe* 8 (1981), 199–218; Roman Cherkashyn and Iulia Fomina, *My-Berezil'tsi* (Kharkiv: Akta, 2006), 55–64; Natalia Ermakova, *Berezil's'ka kul'tura: istoriia, dosvid* (Kyiv: Feniks, 2012), 382–90.

18 The play was published by DVU in Kharkiv in 1929, but no one, to my knowledge, has located a copy. I base my description of the play on Cherkashyn and Formina, *My-Berezil'tsi,* 55–64, as well as reviews (Leonid Skrypnyk, "Allo na khvyli," *Robitnycha hazeta Proletar,* 11 January 1929, 9), memoirs (DMTMKU Vasyl'ko, shchodennyk IX, 174), and the photographs and texts from the arkhiv-muzei at *Kharkivs'kyi derzhavnyi akademichnyi dramatychnyi teatr im T. H. Shevchenka* [Shevchenko], papka 29, "Allo na khvyli 477." Note these texts are not paginated for archival purposes, so I have done my best to note which sketch was on which page; the younger generation included directors Borys Balaban, Volodymyr Skliarenko, and Kost' Dikhtiarenko.

19 On *Macbeth*, TsDAVOV f. 1738 "Biuro Druku," op. 1, s. 49, and Irena Makaryk, *Shakespeare in the Undiscovered Bourn: Les Kurbas, Ukrainian Modernism, and Early Soviet Cultural Politics* (Toronto: University of Toronto Press, 2004), 100–1; on cabaret in general, Harold Segel, *Turn-of-the-Century Cabaret* (New York: Columbia University Press, 1987), and on cabaret in the Russian Empire, David MacFayden, *Songs for Fat People: Affect, Emotion,*

and Celebrity in the Russian Popular Song, 1900–1955 (Montreal: McGill-Queen's University Press, 2002); on *Shpana* (Riff-Raff), Iryna Chuzhynova, "Peredmova (zamist paradu-alle)," *Kurbasivs'ke chytannia* 7 (2012), 226–30.

20 TsDAVOV f. 166, op. 6, s. 10776, ark. 212–14.

21 Kurbas in *Radians'kyi teatr* 2–3 (1929), 83–113; TsDAVOV f. 166, op. 9, s. 270, ark. 6–7.

22 *Derzhavnyi arkhiv Kharkivs'koi oblasti* [DAKhO] f. R-2755, op. 1, s. 52, ark. 102.

23 TsDAVOV f. 166, op. 6, s. 6389 l. 11–13zv; TsDAVOV f. 166, op. 7, s. 1003, l. 12-zv; Hirniak 254–8. Uvarova describes the Soviet understanding of estrada, or a revue show, as a production comprised not of concert pieces, not of an overarching plot, but of a series of numbers that could involve dance, music, song, gymnastics, or acting, see E. Uvarova, *Russkaia sovetskaia estrada: ocherki istorii* (Moskva: Iskusstvo, 1976).

24 Iosyp Hirniak, *Spomyny* (New York: Suchasnist', 1982), 254–8; Vyshnia, "Berlin uvecheri," *Tvory vchotyr'okh tomakh*, vol. 2 (Kyiv: Dnipro, 1988), 371–6.

25 George Maker Watters and Arthur Hopkins, *Burlesque* (New York: Samuel French, 1926).

26 Ibid.

27 Hirniak, *Spomyny*, 254–8; Vyshnia, "Berlin uvecheri." Hirniak remembers Sokolov playing Bozo the Clown, but photographs of Emi Orlik's set design clearly show Sokolov playing Skid; see Birgit Ahrens, *Emil Orlik und das Theater* (Kiel: Ludwig Verlag, 2001), 238. Interestingly, later Hollywood star and teacher Michael Chekhov played Skid in Vienna; Michael Chekhov, *The Path of the Actor*, ed. Andrei Kirillov and Bella Marlin (London: Routledge, 2006), 140; on Grock, see Louise Peacock, *Serious Play: Modern Clown Performance* (Bristol: Intellect, 2009), 67–8, and Grock's memoir, *Grock: King of Clowns* (London: Methuen, 1957).

28 Hirniak, *Spomyny*, 254–8; Vyshnia, "Berlin uvecheri"; Leonid Utesov, *S pesnei po zhizni* (Moskva: Iskusstvo, 1961), 112.

29 See previous note for sources on the text itself; Cherkashyn and Fomina, *My-Berezil'tsi*, 57; Iermakova, "Allo na khvyli 477: pershe ukrains'ke reviu," 7–13.

30 Shevchenko, papka 29, "Allo na khvyli 477," ark. 7–8; page for the second sketch starts with "Krokodil i Chervonyi perets'."

31 Rather dark humour considering Bortnyk was, like many, shot in 1937; Shevchenko, papka 29, "Allo na khvyli 477," ark. 5, 7–8, GPU joke labelled *Antre 5*; on the Gleeful Proletarian, see Halyna Botunova, "Kharkivs'kyi teatr Veselyi proletar (1927–1931): uroky istorii," *Naukovyi visnyk Kyivs'koho*

natsional'noho universytetu teatru, kino, telebachennia imeni Karpenko-Karoho, 6 (2010), 65–90.

32 See, for Chaplin and the West, Stephen Kotkin, "Modern Times: The Soviet Union and the Interwar Conjuncture," *Kritika: Explorations in Russian and Eurasian History* 2, no. 1 (2001), 111–64; on jazz, Frederick Starr, *Red and Hot: The Fate of Jazz in the Soviet Union* (New York: Oxford University Press, 1983); Chystiakova's costume, *Instytut mystetstva imeni Ryl's'koho* f. 42 "Materialy teatru Berezil," s. 55, ark. 2, photo of Chystiakova and Balaban backstage; Chystiakova could have been inspired by the clown Grock as well.

33 Intermediia, *Literaturnyi iarmarok* #1 (December 1928), 45.

34 Iurii Shevel'ov, *Vybrani pratsi*, vol. 2, *Literaturoznavstvo* (Kyiv: Kyiv Mohyla Akad, 2008), 272.

35 SBU Khvyl'ovyi 30, 15; Shevel'ov, ibid., 272.

36 Shevel'ov, ibid., 272; Mykhail' Semenko, "Odvertyi lyst do tov. L. Kurbasa," *Nova Generatsiia* #9 (1929), 137–41.

37 Khvyl'ovyi, "Kamo hriadeshy," 813; the entirety of "Ukraina chy Malorossiia" is in TsDAHOU f. 1, op. 20, s. 2257, ark. 1–53.

38 Letter from Stalin to Kaganovich, Marxist Internet Archive, https://www.marxists.org/russkij/stalin/t8/t8_11.htm; letter from Shums'kyi to Kaganovich, TsDAHOU f. 1, op. 20, s. 2894; TsDAHOU f. 1, op. 6, s. 102, ark. 127, 135, 144.

39 See photos in Shevchenko, papka 29, "Allo na khvyli 477."

40 Iu. Mezhenko, "Allo na khvyli 477," *Proletars'ka Pravda* (Kyiv), 18 May 1929; SBU Khvyl'ovyi 71.

41 Shevchenko, papka 29, "Allo na khvyli 477," ark. 6 ("avtory-plagiatory"). In "Peredmova (zamist paradu-alle)," Chuzhynova points out that the "hell" reference could also refer to Jaques Offenbach's Orpheus in the Underworld and Gogol's Envy, both of which Vyshnia had adapted for the stage – clearly, the image was multilayered.

42 On Red Pepper, TsDAMLM f. 188 "Pavlo Hubenko-Ostap Vyshnia," op. 2, s. 8, ark. 5; on Hirniak's makeup, "Allo na khvyli 477," sheet music for the opening song, Shevchenko papka 29, "Allo na khvyli 477"; on Tychyna, DMTMKU f. "Les' Kurbas," inv. 9960 (Iulii Meitus spohady), ark. 5.

43 TsDAVOV f. 166, op. 6, s. 10783, ark.119; *Literaturnyi iarmarok*, January 1929, 258.

44 Also performed that season was an adaptation of Gilbert and Sullivan's *The Mikado*; Kurbas' revived production of Taras Shevchenko's verse drama *Haidamaky*; the nineteenth-century koryfei classic *Sava Chalii*; a Berezil company-created piece about 1905 entitled *Proloh*; Somerset

Maughm's *Sadie*; Ivan Dniprovs'kii's Civil War drama *Iablunevyi perelon*; Friedrich Schiller's *Fiesco, or the Genoese Conspiracy*; Prosper Merrimee's *La Jacquerie*; and Kulish's new comedy *Myna Mazailo*. Kurbas directed only *Myna Mazailo* and *Haidamaky* – the others were directed by his students, but heavily supervised by Kurbas, on the repertory, see TsDAVOV f. 166, op. 6, s. 6387, ark. 53–9; on the statistics, see TsDAVOV f. 166, op. 9, s. 557, ark. 40.

45 TsDAVOV f. 166, op. 7, s. 1003, ark. 107; copy of a coupon book, *talonna khyzhka*, TsDAVOV f. 166, op. 6, s. 6387, ark. 107; TsDAVOV f. 166, op. 9, s. 557, ark. 40–1; Shevel'ov, *Vybrani pratsi*, 242.

46 SBU Khvylovyi 75.

47 TsDAVOV f. 166, op. 9, s. 557, ark. 40.

48 Shevchenko, ark. 7–8, ark. 7, starts with "Matematyky ne khvatalo," and ark. 8 starts with "Ia liubliu."

49 Shevchenko, ark. 8, starts with "Ia liubliu… "

50 TsDAVOV f. 166, op. 9, s. 247, ark. 23; DMTMKU "Vasyl'ko," shchodennyky, for example, inv. #7849s.

51 TsDAVOV f. 166, op. 9, s. 1177, ark. 91.

52 TsDAVOV f. 166, op. 9, s. 1177, ark. 91; ibid., s. 557, ark. 21–4.

53 TsDAVOV f. 166, op. 7, s. 1003, ark. 69–81; ibid., op. 8, s. 333, ark. 5–8; ibid., op. 8, s. 624, ark. 30.

54 I build these ideas of the public and state on Ekaterina Pravilova, *A Public Empire: Property and the Quest for the Common Good in Imperial Russia* (Princeton: Princeton University Press, 2015).

55 On the murder of elites from Soviet Ukraine, see Serhii Bohunov, Volodymyr Prystaiko, and Iurii Shapoval, eds., *Ostannia adresa*, 2 vols. (Kyiv: Sfera, 1999).

56 Yuri Slezkine, "The USSR as Communal Apartment, or How a Socialist State Promoted Ethnic Particularism," *Slavic Review* 53, no. 2 (1994), 414–52.

57 On the constructivism of Soviet nationality policy, see Terry Martin, *Affirmative Action Empire: Nations and Nationalism in the Soviet Union 1923–1939* (Ithaca, NY: Cornell University Press), 20, and Francine Hirsch, *Empire of Nations: Ethnographic Knowledge and the Making of the Soviet Union* (Ithaca, NY: Cornell University Press, 2005). Matthew Pauly shows how teachers simply did not always know Ukrainian to Ukrainianize, and anyways, they lacked materials, see, *Breaking the Tongue: Language, Education and Power in Soviet Ukraine, 1923–1931* (Toronto: University of Toronto Press, 2014), 85

58 Census mentioned in, for example, TsDAHOU f. 1, op. 20, s. 2894, ark. 14–15 ("Pismo A. Ia. Shumskogo na imia L. M. Kaganovicha s osuzhdeniem ranee zaniatoi im pozitsii po voprosam ukrainizatsii. 11-20 December 1929"). Contemporaries did not miss the disparity between census data and cultural production. See, for example, director-actor Vasyl' Vasyl'ko's obsession with the data in *Derzhavnyi muzei teatral'noho, muzychnoho, ta kino-mystetstva Ukrainy* [DMTMKU] f. "Vasyl' Vasyl'ko," inventory #10374 (Shchodennyky), v. IX, ark. 56; *Rossiiski gosudarstvennyi arkhiv literatury i iskusstva* [RGALI] f. 962, op. 7, d. 12, "Svodki o sostoianii teatral'noi seti i kolichestve rabotnikov iskusstv s 1917-1936," ll. 1–3.

59 TsDAVOU f. 166, op. 9, s. 247, ark. 43.

60 GARF f. 5508 "TsK Rabis," op. 1, d. 1307, l. 97. Elissa Bemporad importantly shows that in the case of Minsk, *Yidishizatsiia* created a Soviet Yiddish culture alternative to Moscow. Indeed, she argues that the centre of Yiddish culture was not in Moscow but in Soviet Belorussia and Soviet Ukraine, where most Jews lived. Elissa Bemporad, *Becoming Soviet Jews: The Soviet Experiment in Minsk* (Bloomington: Indiana University Press, 2012), esp. chap. 4.

61 TsDAVOU f. 166, op. 9, s. 247, ark. 114.

62 Iryna Chuzhynova, "Kost' Burevii i politychne reviu 'Chotyry Chemberleny," *Protsenium* 1–3 (2012), 33–7; T. H Honcharenko, "Nevesela istoriia teatru Veselyi proletar," *Kraeznavstvo*, nos. 1–4 (2003), 171–4; Hanna Veslovs'ka, "Ukrains'kyi muzychnyi teatr malykh form pershoi polovyny XX stolittia," *Naukovyi visnyk Natsional'noi muzychnoi akademii Ukrainy imeni P. I. Chaikovs'koho* 89 (2010), 110–25.

63 RGALI f. 1821, op. 1, d. 52.

64 Ibid., 1.

65 Ibid., l. 42.

66 Ibid., l. 51–2.

67 GARF 5508, op. 1, d. 2136, l. 163; Volodymyr Nevezhin, "Dekady respublikans'koho mystetstva u Moskvi," *Kraieznavstvo* 4 (2011), 263–74; RGALI f. 962, op. 3, d. 672, l. 79, 82.

68 GARF f. 5508, op. 1, d. 1307, l. 97.

69 M.M. Hereha, "Fortepianna ipostas' tvorchoi osobistosti Bohdana Veselovs'koho," *Naukovi zapysky: seria Mystetstvoznavstvo* 1 (2010), 44–8; O. Zelins'kii, "Bohdan Veselovs'kii chy tango zi Stryia," *Chasopys' "i"* 70 (2012), 122–3; Bohdan Nahaylo has put many of these songs on YouTube, see, for example, "Old Ukrainian Tango," YouTube, https://www.youtube.com/watch?v=nfeBROvc8Sw&feature=related, and Bohdan

Nahaylo, "All that Jazz in L'viv: Capturing the Best of Ukrainian-Polish-Jewish Predicaments in Western in 1930s-1940s" (paper presented at the Danyliw Seminar, Ottawa 2013). For a more complete picture of non-Soviet Ukrainian national literature in diaspora, see Myroslav Shkandrij, *Ukrainian Nationalism: Politics, Ideology, and Literature, 1929–1956* (New Haven: Yale University Press, 2015).

70   It was also joined by Iryna Jarosiewicz / Iarosevych, star of Veselovsy's troupe, who refashioned herself as Renata Bogdanska and began singing for Warsaw cabarets in new Soviet L'viv; see Grzegorz Hryciuk, *Polacy we Lwówie 1939–1944: Życie codzienne* (Warszawa: Książka i Wiedza, 2000), 110; Michal Borwicz, "Ingenierowie dusz," *Zeszyty historyczne* (1962), 128.

71   DALO f. R-145, op. 1, s. 46, ark. 1.

72   For the recorded song, see "Eugeniusz Bodo & Henryk Wars Orchestra," YouTube, http://www.youtube.com/watch?v=tjNLz3jD0Gg; on Bodo, Ryszard Wolański, *Eugeniusz Bodo: Już taki jestem zimny drań* (Poznan: Rebis, 2012); on the cabaret scene, Marian Melman, "Teatr żydowski w Warszawie w latach międzywojennych," *Warszawa II Rzeczypospolitej,* ed. Emilia Borecka, Marian Drozdowski, and Halina Janowska, vol. 1 (Warsaw: Panstwowe wydawnictwo naukowe, 1968), 381–400.

73   DALO R-1479, op. 1, s. 38, ark 89; ibid s. 77, ark. 3, 12.

Chapter Four

1   Miklos Haraszti, *The Velvet Prison: Artists Under State Socialism*, trans. Katalin and Stephen Landesmann with Steve Wasserman (New York: Noonday Press, 1989), 5.

2   RGALI f. 2307, op. 2, l. 30 (Berezil), 16 (GOSET), 65 (Kyiv GOSET), 75 (Soviet Ukrainian Academy of Sciences).

3   On Mikhoels and GOSET, Jeffrey Veidlinger, *The Moscow State Yiddish Theater* (Bloomington: Indiana University Press, 2000); Natalia Vovsi-Mikhoels, *Moi otets' Solomon Mikhoels* (Moskva: Vozvrashchenie, 1987), 9–11, 18, 47. On Granovskii, see V.V. Ivanov, *GOSET: Politika i iskusstvo, 1919-1928* (Moscow: GITIS, 2007), 20.

4   Vovsi-Mikhoels, *Moi otets' Solomon Mikhoels*, 57, 60.

5   J. Hoberman, *Bridge of Light: Yiddish Film between Two Worlds* (New York: Schocken Books, 1991), 92; the film is available at the National Center for Jewish Film.

6   DMTMKU f. Vasylko, 10342, ark. 8–10, 15.

7   Clips from the production can be found, for example, on YouTube, "Mikhoels Playing King Lear 1935," https://www.youtube.com/

watch?v=AU838zh5ysw; Susan Tumarkin Goodman, ed., *Chagall and the Artists of the Russian Jewish Theater* (New Haven: Yale University Press, 2008). It is hard to overestimate how frequently one comes across this myth, from memoirs to scholarship, including Valentina Chistiakova, "Glavy iz vospominanii," *Teatr*, no. 4 (1992), 86; Aleksandr Matskin, *Po sledam ukhodiashchego veka* (Moskva: Aslan, 1996), 250; Irena Makaryk, *Shakespeare in the Undiscovered Bourn: Les Kurbas, Ukrainian Modernism, and Early Soviet Cultural Politics* (Toronto: University of Toronto Press, 2004), 192–5.

 8 Aleksandr Deich, "Chelovek, kotoryi byl teatrom," in *Les' Kurbas: stat'i i vospominaniia o Lese Kurbase*, ed. M. G. Labins''kii and L. S. Taniuk (Moscow: Iskusstvo, 1987), 190–1; Iurii Smolych, "Bilia dzherel," in *Les' Kurbas: Spohady suchasnikiv*, ed. Vasyl' Vasyl'ko (Kyiv: Mystetstvo, 1969), 49–50; Matskin, *Po sledam ukhodiashchego veka*, 250.

 9 Haluzevyi derzhavnyi arkhiv Sluzhby bezpeky Ukrainy [SBU] 75 608 *fond prypynennykh* "Kurbas Aleksandr Stepanovich," ark. 64; Nelli Korniienko, *Rezhisserskoe iskusstvo Lesia Kurbasa. Rekonstructsiia, 1887–1937* (Kiev: Gosudarstvennyi tsentr Lesia Kurbasa, 2005).

10 For a list of the theatres soiuznogo podchineniia, see RGALI f. 962, op. 7, d. 50.

11 RGALI f. 2788, op. 1, d. 71, l. 10.

12 John Willett, *The Theater of the Weimar Republic* (New York: Holmes and Meier, 1988), and Michael Schwaiger, ed., *Bertolt Brecht und Erwin Piscator: Experimentelles Theater in Berlin der Zwanzigerjahre* (Wien: Brandstalter, 2004); James R. Brandon and Samuel L. Leiter, eds., *Kabuki Plays on Stage: Restoration and Reform, 1872–1905* (Honolulu: University of Hawaii Press, 2003); for a good overview, see Bruno S. Frey, *Arts and Economics: Analysis and Cultural Policy*, 2nd ed. (New York: Springer, 2013).

13 Joshua Rubinstein and Vladimir Naumov, eds., Laura Esther Wolfson, trans., *Stalin's Secret Pogrom: The Postwar Inquisition of the Jewish Anti-Fascist Committee* (New Haven: Yale University Press, 2005).

14 See, for example, the classic Regine Robin, *Socialist Realism: An Impossible Aesthetic*, trans. Catherine Porter (Stanford: Stanford University Press, 1992); Katerina Clark, *Moscow, the Fourth Rome: Stalinism, Cosmopolitanism, and the Evolution of Soviet Culture, 1931–1941* (Cambridge, MA: Harvard University Press, 2011), esp. chap. 2, "Moscow, the Lettered City"; or the work of Evgenii Dobrenko, such as *The Making of the State Writer: Social and Aesthetic Origins of Soviet Literary Culture* (Stanford: Stanford University Press, 2001) and *The Making of the State Reader: Social and Aesthetic Contexts of the Reception of Soviet Literature* (Stanford: Stanford University Press, 1997).

15 See Harold Clurman, *The Fervent Years: The Group Theater and the Thirties* (New York: Da Capo Press, 1983); in other words, I avoid here the notion of "NEP culture" as examined in, for example, Sheila Fitzpatrick, Alexander Rabinowitch, and Richard Stites, eds., *Russia in the Era of NEP: Explorations in Soviet Society* (Bloomington: Indiana University Press, 1991), or Sheila Fitzpatrick, *The Cultural Front: Power and Culture in Revolutionary Russia* (Ithaca, NY: Cornell University Press, 1992). The NEP was a hindrance to socialist culture, for the figures in this story, and it was not less government intervention that directly caused an experimental style; rather, the style was experimental while government intervention, as intended by artists, increased. Government intervention was supposed to increase artistic innovation and facilitate creative production. The reverse was an unintended consequence.

16 Lisa Jensen, Katie Hamlin, and Dave Henning, "The Screwball and Its Audience" (Fall 2001), http://xroads.virginia.edu/~ug03/comedy/historicalcontext.html, note that movie ticket prices averaged 27 cents.

17 GARF f. 5508, op. 4, d. 14, 22ob.

18 The Artistic-Political Council, *Khudpolitrad*, was a Soviet Ukrainian version of a similar institution in the RFSFR, the Russian Republic in 1927; A.Z. Iufit, ed., *Sovetskii teatr: dokumenty i materialy* (Leningrad: Iskusstvo, 1982), 48–9; TsDAVOV f. 166, op. 9, s. 247, ark. 17, 114; the Ukrainian is *shulery pry kartakh*, which I have translated as *tricksters at cards*. A *shuler pry kartakh* in American English is a *cardsharp(er)*, or just a *cheater at cards*, while a *shuler* broadly speaking is a *grifter, swindler*, or *hustler*. The word *trickster* captures, in my mind, some of these other meanings.

19 On Mykytenko, see his collected works, *Teatral'ni mrii* (Kyiv: Mystetstvo, 1968); Mykytenko's son, Oleh Ivanovych, is a writer in the Ukrainian Academy of Sciences and has written circumspectly about his father's milieu, see his *V chervonykh lavakh: z istorii internatsionalnykh zviazkiv ukrains'koi radians'koi literatury 20-kh rokiv* (Kyiv: Dnipro, 1974); and also Sava Holovanivs'kyi, *Memorial: Spohady* (Kyiv: Radians'kyi pysmennyk, 1988), 60–1.

20 Roman Cherkashyn and Iulia Fomina, *My-Berezil'tsi* (Kharkiv: Akta, 2006), 66; TsDAMLM f. 657 "Mykytenko Ivan Kindratovych," op. 1, s. 191; TsDAHO f. 1, op. 20, s. 6218, ark. 134.

21 TsDAVOV f. 166, op. 9, s. 247, ark. 23 (Kurbas), 82 (Vasyl'ko); names: *Dudar* comes from the verb *dudaryty*, to call forward, and *Nebaba* comes from *not a baba*; photos: see *Radians'kyi teatr* in 1930 and *Nova Generatsiia* #11 (1929); Cherkashyn and Fomina, *My-Berezil'tsi*, 64.

22 Ivan Zaets', *Ivan Mykytenko* (Kyiv: Radians'kyi pysmennyk, 1987), 78. One version of the play is in Ivan Mykytenko, *Tvory*, vol. 3 (Kyiv: Dnipro, 1982), but note there is no record of the various changes Mykytenko made over the several seasons *Dyktatura* played in Soviet Ukraine. For Tereshchenko, TsDAMLM f. 657, op. 1, s. 132, ark. 5.

23 Cherkashyn and Fomina, *My-Berezil'tsi*, 68, 72. On film in the Berezil' production of *Jimmie Higgins*, see "Virlana Tkacz, Les Kurbas' Use of Film Language in His Stage Productions of *Jimmie Higgins* and *Macbeth*," *Canadian Slavonic Papers* 32, no. 1 (1990), 59–76; on film in Kurbas' production of *Macbeth*, see Irena Makaryk, "Dissecting Time / Space: The Scottish Play and the New Technology of Film," in *Modernism in Kyiv: Jubilant Experimentation*, eds. Irene Makaryk and Virlana Tkacz (Toronto: University of Toronto Press, 2010), 443–77.

24 Cherkashyn and Fomina, *My-Berezil'tsi*, 67; on Meitus, DMTMKU arkhiv "Les Kurbas," inv. #9960 (Iulii Meitus *spohady*), ark. 2–3.

25 TsDAMLM f. 173 "Fedortseva Sofiia Volodymyrivna," op. 1, s. 19, ark. 149, 18–19; Cherkashyn and Fomina, *My-Berezil'tsi*, 72.

26 Cherkashyn and Fomina, *My-Berezil'tsi*, 68–9; *Chervonyi perets'* #4 (1933); photos from arkhiv-muzei at *Kharkivs'kyi derzhavnyi akademichnyi dramatychnyi teatr im T. H. Shevchenka* [Shevchenko], papka 32 "Dyktatura."

27 TsDAMLM f. 657, op. 1, s. 199; Yosyp (Iosyp) Hirniak, "Birth and Death of the Modern Ukrainian Theater," in *Soviet Theaters 1917–1941*, ed. Martha Bradshaw (New York: Research Program on the USSR, 1954), 326–36.

28 TsDAMLM Fedortseva 18; see also Valentyna Chystiakova's description of her use of peretvorennia later in her career, DMTMKU Vasyl'ko, inv. #7164, letters Chystiakova to Vasyl'ko 4 October 1961 and 8 October 1961; Ihor Ciszkewycz, " Transformation – a Discovered Form: Berezil Theater, 1922–1934" (PhD diss., Southern Illinois University at Carbondale, 1988).

29 Cherkashyn and Fomina, *My-Berezil'tsi*, 69–70; DMTMKU Vasyl'ko inv. #103669, ark. 150–2.

30 Lynn Mally, *Revolutionary Acts: Amateur Theater and the Soviet State* (Ithaca, NY: Cornell University Press, 2000); Inna Solovyova, "The Theater and Socialist Realism, 1929–1953," in *A History of Russian Theatre*, ed. Robert Leach and Victor Borovsky (Cambridge: Cambridge University Press, 2000), 325–57.

31 Haraszti, *The Velvet Prison*, 110.

32 Katerina Clark, *The Soviet Novel: History as Literature* (New Haven: Yale University Press, 1984). On ambiguity, see Jan Plamper, "Abolishing Ambiguity: Soviet Censorship Practices in the 1930s," *Russian Review* 60, no. 4 (2001), 526–44.

33 TsDAVOV f. 166, op. 9, s. 1142, ark. 36–9, 61.

34 DAKhO f. R-2755, op. 1, s. 67.

35 TsDAHO f. 1, op. 20, s. 6229, ark. 27–31; TsDAVOV f. 2708, op.1, ark. 86; Cherkashyn and Fomina, *My-Berezil'tsi*, 67.

36 TsDAVOV f. 2708, op. 3, s. 735, ark. 400–5.

37 TsDAHOU f. 1, op. 6, s. 142, ark. 100; TsDAHOU f. 1, op. 6, s. 150, ark. 78; TsDAHO f. 1, op. 20, s. 2695, ark. 33–4, 37; *Chervonyi perets'* #8–9 (1929).

38 Olga Bertelsen's exhaustive study of Budynok Slovo focuses on its unique position as the first cooperative building in the USSR and on the spatial aspects of terror created by the majority of the literary elite living in one building. While I agree with Bertelsen that the fact that writers were in one place shaped how the terror unfolded, I think there is a larger aspect to housing. There ended up being many such buildings, the Dom pisatelei in which Ilf-Petrov lived, for example, and the famous Dom na naberezhnoi, House on the Embankment, for the government elite. These buildings acquired a reputation, but Soviets were still lucky to receive housing; see Bertelsen, "Spatial Dimensions of Soviet Repressions in the 1930s: The House of Writers (Kharkiv, Ukraine)" (PhD diss., University of Nottingham, 2011), and "The House of Writers in Ukraine, the 1930s: Conceived, Lived, Perceived," *Carl Beck Papers in Russian and East European Studies*, No. 2302 (2013).

39 Kulik on Sosiura, TsDAHO f. 1, op. 20, s. 6442, ark. 13–14; on Kulik, TsDAHOU f. 263, op. 1, s. 44 228, vol. XII, 82zv; on the Slovo, see the memoirs, Volodymyr Kulish, *Slovo pro Budynok "Slovo"* (Toronto: Homin' Ukrainy, 1966), and Natal'ka Dukyna, *Na dobryi spomny: povist' pro bat'ka* (Kharkiv: Vydannia zhurnalu *Berezil'*, 2002).

40 When Kulish was arrested in December 1934 the family had to give Joy to an actor from the musical comedy theatre; Kulish, *Slovo pro Budynok "Slovo,"* 10, 19, 21, 59–60.

41 DMTMKU "Vasyl'ko" inv. #10343s, ark. 9–10; SBU 36546 fp., vol. IV, ark. 37–9.

42 SBU Khvyl'ovyi 73.

43 TsDAHOU f. 1, op. 6, s. 204, ark. 45.

44 On Ukrainfilm, TsDAHOU f. 1, op. 6, s. 150, 192–4, on passport, TsDAHOU f. 1, op. 6, s. 407, ark. 53.

45 For Kurbas not wanting to go to Olimpiad, see Tamara Tsulukidze, "Les' Kurbas," in *Les' Kurbas: Stati'i i vospominaniia o Lese Kurbase*, ed. Labins'kyi and Taniuk (Moskva: Iskusstvo, 1987), 105; TsDAVOV f. 166, op. 6, s. 10776, ark. 17, 18, 34–5; "Ukrainskii gosudarstvenii Krasnozavodskii teatr," *Sovetskii teatr* 10 (1930), 10–11.

46 TsDAHOU f. 1, op. 6, s. 204, ark. 45; Smolych, *Rozpovid' pro nespokii tryvae*, 6–20.

47 The 1932–3 terror-famine, or Holodomor as it is now called, is extensively covered, including in contemporary document collections, such as the exhaustive V.K. Borysenko, ed., *Rozsekrechena pamiat': Holodomor 1932–1933 rokiv v Ukraini v dokumentakh GPU-NKVD* (Kyiv: Stylos, 2007), and the online collections at the Sluzhba Bezpeky Ukrainy website, www.ssu.gov.ua/sbu.

48 SBU f. 60, s. 183 "Khvilevoi N. G.," ark. 100–1, 98–9.

49 SBU Khvyl'ovyi, 112–115, 129.

50 SBU Khvyl'ovyi 135-zv.

51 SBU Khvyl'ovyi 123.

52 See, for example, interrogations in the files of Mykola Kulish, SBU 36 546 fp, volume III, ark. 162–8, and Iosyp Hirniak, TsDAHOU f. 263, op. 1, s. 33 467, ark. 31–3.

53 Mykola Kulish, *P'esy* (Kyiv: Naukova dumka, 2001), 221.

54 GARF, f. 5508, op. 1, d. 1922, l. 29–30, 78ob; DMTMKU f. Vasyl'ko, inv. no. 10343, ark 20.

55 Marvin Carlson, *The Haunted Stage: Theater as Memory Machine* (Ann Arbor: University of Michigan Press, 2003).

56 TsDAHOU f. 1, op. 20, s. 6218, ark. 71–5.

57 TsDAHOU f. 1, op. 20, s. 6229, ark. 27–31; also note that the Berezil' started work on the play before sanction from Narkomos, which shows the relatively low position of repertkom boards in the early 1930s in Soviet Ukraine; TsDAVOV f. 2708, op. 3, s. 740, ark. 83.

58 TsDAVOV f. 2708, op. 3, s. 740, ark. 83; TsDAHOU f. 1, op. 6, s. 285, ark. 97; note the cartoon of Khvylia in *Chervonyi perets'* 9 (1928), 9.

59 O. Borshchahivs'kyi, "5 veresnia vidkryttia sezonu v Berezoli," *Komunist*, 22 August 1933, ark. 4; TsDAMLM Kulish, s. 46, s. 47, s. 48.

60 SBU 36 546 fp, vol. III, ark. 211–18; this document is published in Bohunov, Prystaiko, and Shapoval, eds., *Ostannia adresa*, vol. 1, 175–9.

61 Istvan Rev, *Retroactive Justice: Prehistory of Post-Communism* (Stanford: Stanford University Press, 2005), 263; Haraszti, *The Velvet Prison,* 19. Here I differ from Boris Wolfson, "Fear on Stage: Afinogenov, Stanislavsky and the Making of Stalinist Theater," in *Everyday Life in Early Soviet Russia: Taking the Revolution Inside*, ed. Christina Kiaer and Eric Naiman (Bloomington: Indiana University Press, 2006), 92–119.

62 GARF f. 5508, op. 1, d. 2050, l. 6–12; RGALI f. 962, op. 7, d 50, 34, 43, 49, 63; E. Bulgakova, *Dnevnik Eleny Bulgakovoi* (Moscow: Knizhnaia palata, 1990), 138.

63 Bemporad, *Becoming Soviet Jews*; Yuri Slezkine, *The Jewish Century* (Princeton: Princeton University Press, 2004).

64 Alexander Granach, *There Goes an Actor*, trans. Willard Trask (Garden City, NY: Doubleday and Doran, 1945), 1, 6. For biographical information, see Angelika Wittlich and Hilde Recher, eds., *Du mein leibes Stück Heimat: Briefe an Lotte Lieven aus dem Exil* (Augsburg: Ölbaum verlag, 2008), 7–9, 369–70, and *Alexander Granach und das jiddische Theater des Ostens* (Berlin: Akademie der Künste, 1971); Shelly Zer-Zion, "The Shaping of the *Ostjude*: Alexander Granach and Shimon Finkel in Berlin," in *Jews and the Making of Modern German Theater*, ed. Jeannette R. Melkin and Freddie Rokem (Iowa City: University of Iowa Press, 2010), 174–96.

65 Dmitri Zhabotinskii, *Instytut Iudaiky* (Kyiv), f. 21, op. 1, s. 8 ("lebns-bletlach fun a jidishn aktior"), 122; Wittlich and Recher, *Du mein leibes Stück Heimat*, 130–1; letter from Granach to Lieven 4 April 1936, ibid., 164–5; letter Granach to Lieven 14 December 1936, ibid., 187; letter from Granach to Lieven 9 November 1937, ibid., 178–9; letter Granach to Lieven 25 June 1937.

66 Wittlich and Recher, *Du mein leibes Stück Heimat*, 369–70.

67 TsDAHOU f. 263, op. 1, s. 44 228, vol. I., ark. 1–2, 6-zv; Dukyna, *Na dobryi spomny*, 280, 295.

68 SBU 75 608 fp "Kurbas Aleksandr Stepanovich," ark. 64.

69 SBU Kurbas, 2–3, 31, 32, 34, 35. This also gave rise to the conclusion that Chystiakova was responsible for her husband's arrest (i.e., otherwise why would the apartment not have been searched?), a notion the arrest file does not support.

70 SBU Kurbas 40–51.

71 TsDAHOU f. 263, opys 1, s. 33 467, 65313 fp., ark. 58; on the Balyts'kyi circle, see Iurii Shapoval, Volodymyr Prystaiko, and Vadym Zolotar'ov, *ChK-GPU-NKVD v Ukraini: osoby, fakty, dokumenty* (Kyiv: Abris, 1997), 21–79.

72 TsDAHOU f. 263, op. 1, s. 44 228, vol. XII, ark. 41–2.

73 TsDAHOU f. 263, op. 1, s. 44 228, vol. I, ark. 29–32zv, vol. XII, 17–37.

74 TsDAHOU f. 263, op. 1, s. 44 228, vol. I, ark 8, 14.

75 TsDAHOU f. 263, op. 1, s. 44 228, vol. I, ark. 45, 49.

76 SBU Kurbas 61–6.

77 Ibid.

78 Ibid., 67–8, 69–70.

79 Les' Taniuk, "S pulei v serdtse," *Sovetskaia kultura*, 2 March 1989, 6, cited in Shapoval, Prystaiko, and Zolotar'ov, *ChK-GPU-NKVD v Ukraini*, 70; Iosyp Hirniak, *Spomyny* (New York: Suchasnist', 1982), 383.

80 TsDAHOU f. 1, op. 1, s. 446, ark. 3.

81 Bohunov, Prystaiko, and Shapoval, eds., *Ostannia adresa*, vol. 1, 368.

82 DAKhO f. 2, op. 1, s. 117, ark. 149–52.

83 Haraszti, *The Velvet Prison*, 129–31.

84 V.N. Gusarev, *Moi papa ubil Mikhoelsa* (Frankfurt: Posev, 1978); O. Mandel'shtam, "K ocherki Berezil'," *Sobranie sochinenii v chetyrekh tomakh* (Moscow: Art-Biznes Tsentr, 1993), 557.
85 Leszek Kołakowski, "The Priest and the Jester," in *Marxism and Beyond: On Historical Understanding and Individual Responsibility*, trans. Jane Zielonko Peel (London: Pall Mall, 1969), 53–4.

Chapter Five

1 Johann Huizinga, *Homo Ludens: A Study of the Play Element in Culture* (Boston: Beacon Press, 1950), 175.
2 TsDAHOU f. 1, op. 20, s. 6457, ark. 130–3.
3 On renaming, TsDAHOU f. 1, op. 6, s. 281, ark. 194; on Postyshev, Vadim Pavlovs'kyi, *Shevchenko v pam'iatnykakh* (New York: Ukrains'ka vil'na akademiia nauk u SShA, 1966), 26; on Karlson, see Iurii Shapoval, Volodymyr Prystaiko, and Vadym Zolotar'ov, *ChK-GPU-NKVD v Ukraini: osoby, fakty, dokumenty* (Kyiv: Abris, 1997), 117–43.
4 I base some of my understanding of the "arts official" as described by Richard Taylor, "Ideology as Mass Entertainment: Boris Shumyatsky and Soviet Cinema in the 1930s," in *Inside the Film Factory: New Approaches to Russian and Soviet Cinema*, ed. Richard Taylor and Ian Christie (London: Routledge, 1994), 193–216, and Martina Hessler and Clemens Zimmerman, eds., *Urban Creative Milieus: Historical Perspectives on Culture, Economy and the City* (Frankfurt: Campus, 2008), 17.
5 N.S. Vlasik, *Riadom so Stalinym* (Moscow: Algorithm, 2013), 174–5.
6 SBU 38 353 fp "Andrei Ananievich Khvylia," vol. I, ark. 1, 4–5.
7 SBU Khvylia, I, 6-zv; *Chervonyi perets'* #8–9 (1929); on Khvyl'ovyi's disparagement of Khvylia, see "Ukraina chy Malorossia" in Khvyl'ovyi, *Sanatoriina Zona: Novely, opoviadannia* (Kharkiv: Folio, 2007), 334–81, and Khvyl'ovyi's letter to Misha Ialovyi in SBU f. 60, s. S-183 "Khvilevoi N. G.," 17–20.
8 SBU Khvylia, vol. I, 183–4, 196–7; TsDAHOU f. 1, op. 20, s. 6457, ark. 1–2.
9 TsDAHOU f. 1, op. 20, s. 6652, ark. 84–6.
10 SBU 38 348 fp "Tkach Mark Petrovich," ark. 74, 86–8.
11 TsDAHOU f. 1, op. 20, s. 6873, ark. 7–8.
12 SBU Khvylia, vol. I, 183–4, 196; Slatin was shot in Kyiv on 25 October 1937, SBU Khvylia, vol III, 15; Moshe Beregovskii, *Jewish Instrumental Folk Music: The Collections and Writings of Moshe Beregovski*, trans. and ed. Mark Slobin, Robert A. Rothstein, and Michael Alpert (Syracuse: Syracuse University Press, 2000), shows how the Beregovskii expeditions to record klezmorim

could be counted as one of Khvylia's achievements; Dmitrii Al'tshuler, arrested in 1937, died in the camps of the Baikal-Amur Mainline in 1947, see SBU 44 983 "Getman Kirkii Andreevich," 74–7.

13 The organization charged with running the arts was the *Narkomos*, Commissariat of Enlightenment, but in 1936 an *Upravlinnia v spravakh mystetstv* was formed, translated here as Administration of Arts Affairs, which was located directly under *Radnarkom*, the Council of People's Commissars; SBU 44 240 fp "Ianovskii Ivan Ivanovich," 29, 34, 41.

14 SBU Khvylia 197; SBU Getman 15, 32–3.

15 SBU Ianovskii 38–40.

16 Ibid., 47.

17 TsDAHOU f. 1, op. 20, s. 6457, ark. 13–14; Ivan Ianovs'kyi was shot 26 October 1937, his wife, Lidia, was also arrested in 1937, served out her sentence in Karaganda, and stayed there, SBU Ianovskii 147, 148–9.

18 SBU Khvylia, volume II, 35–38zv, volume I, 91, 270–1; Khvylia's wife, Anna Terezanskaia, was shot on 24 October, 1937, SBU Khvylia, volume II, 67–8.

19 TsDAHOU f. 1, op. 1, s. 339, l. 44.

20 SBU 49 834 fp "Zatonskii Vladimir Petrovich," volume I, 145; for more on networks, see note 33 in the introduction. John Armstrong, *The Soviet Bureaucratic Elite: A Case Study of the Ukrainian Apparatus* (New York: Praeger, 1959), remains a classic.

21 George Luckyj, *Literary Politics in the Soviet Ukraine* (Durham, NC: Duke University Press, 1990), 235, 247.

22 SBU 37 137 fp "Medvedev Tikhon Alekseevich," vol. II, 44–5zv, 68–9zv.

23 SBU Medvedev, vol. II, 22–7, 79–80zv.

24 Ibid., vol. I, 62-zv, vol. II, 28, 29–30, 31–4.

25 Ibid., vol. II 39–40, 59, vol. I, 63–7.

26 TsDAHOU f. 1, op. 20, s. 7099, ark. 59.

27 Ibid., s. 6457, ark. 38–42; Zhabotinskii, *Instytut Iudaiky*, 115–16.

28 Ibid., s. 6457, ark. 38–42.

29 Ibid., s. 6873, ark. 5-zv; TsDAHOU f. 1, op. 6, s. 375, ark. 153, 168.

30 TsDAVOV f. 166, op. 6, s. 2001, ark. 265–7; for more on Wandurski, see Marci Shore, *Caviar and Ashes: A Warsaw Generation's Life and Death in Marxism, 1918–1968* (New Haven: Yale University Press, 2006), 120–2.

31 TsDAVOV f. 166, op. 6, s. 2001, ark. 304, 298; ibid., op. 9, s. 1179, ark. 222.

32 Ibid., op. 9, s. 1183, ark. 120–7.

33 Ibid., op. 6, s. 2001, ark. 224, 243, 254–5.

34 Ibid., op. 11, s. 6, ark. 25.

35 DMTMKU f. "Datsenko," s. R37793, inventory #16533 [letter from Datsenko to Fomina, 23.10.1989]; Moisei Loev, *Ukradennaia Muza: vospominaniia o kievskom gosudarstvennom evreiskom teatre imeni Sholem-Aleikhema* (Kiev: Dukh I litera, 2004), 39, 42.

36 On Marchlevsk, see Kate Brown, *A Biography of No Place* (Cambridge, MA: Harvard University Press, 2005). TsDAHOU f. 1, op. 20, s. 6652, ark. 60–1, 62–3.

37 TsDAHOU f. 1, op. 6, s. 463, ark. 42, 51; ibid., s. 477, ark. 208–11.

38 SBU Zatonskii, vol. II, ark. 25.

39 Piotr Horbatowski, *W szponach polityki: Polskie zycie teatralne w Kijowie 1919–1938* (Warszawa: Oficyna naukowa, 1999), 187–8.

40 SBU 69 860 fp "Anton Krushelnitskii i drugie," 83, 111–14; SBU Krushelnitskii 120; for a different argument see, Myroslav Shkandrij and Olga Bertelsen, "The Soviet Regime's National Operations in Ukraine, 1929–1934," *Canadian Slavonic Papers* 55, nos. 3–4 (2013), 417–47.

41 Agnessa Mironova-Korol, *Agnessa: Ustnye rasskazy* (Moskva: Zvenia, 1997), 64–5.

42 Ibid., 72–3.

43 TsDAHOU f. 1, op. 1, s. 516, ark. 208.

44 SBU Krushelnitskii, vol. VIII, 93, 99, 96.

45 SBU 36 546 fp, vol. XI, 74–7, 78–85; SBU Krushelnitskii, vol. VIII, 130.

46 SBU Krushelnitskii, vol. VIII, 127.

47 SBU 36 546 fp, vol. XI, 76.

48 SBU Krushelnitskii, vol. VIII, 84–92; SBU 46 293 fp "Boichuk Mikhail Lvovich," vol. II, 62–3, 64–5.

49 SBU Krushelnitskii, vol. VIII, 80–92.

50 TsDAHO f. 263, op. 1, s. 56 034 "Lopatinskii Favst Lvovich," 67–72zv.

51 TsDAHOU f. 1, op. 1, s. 535, ark. 60, 127.

52 SBU 44 961 fp "Mikhail Vasilievich Semenko," 231, 246; Miron Petrovskii, *Gorodu i miru* (Kyiv: Dukh i litera, 2008), 170–94.

53 SBU 33 573 fp "Liubarskii Valentin Grigorievich," 62–70zv. Karlson, after his career running Kharkiv oblast GPU and rising to Moscow, was arrested and shot in 1938; see Iurii Shapoval, Volodymyr Prystaiko, and Vadim Zolotar'ov, eds. *ChK-GPU-NKVD v Ukraini: osoby, fakty, dokumenty* (Kyiv: Abris, 1997), 484–5.

54 TsDAHOU f. 1, op. 6, s. 386, ark. 5–6.

55 Ibid., s. 408, ark. 184; Pavlovs'kyi, *Shevchenko v pam'iatnykakh*, 26–9.

56 Iurii Smolych, *Rozpovid' pro nespokii* (Kyiv: Radians'kyi pysmennyk, 1968), 108.

Chapter Six

1 SBU 75 608 fp "Kurbas Aleksandr Stepanovich," 70; Iosyp Hirniak, *Spomyny* (New York: Suchasnist', 1982), 391–401, 407; for more on those running the gulag, see Fyodor Vasilievich Mochulsky, *Gulag Boss: A Soviet Memoir*, ed. and trans Deborah Kaple (New York: Oxford University Press, 2011).
2 For examples of the productions created by prisoners described by Fedor Dostoevsky in *Memoirs from the House of the Dead*, see Fedor Dostoevskii, *Zapiski iz mertvogo doma. Rasskazy* (Moskva: EKSMO, 2005).
3 Serhii Bohunov, Volodymyr Prystaiko, and Iurii Shapoval, eds., *Ostannia adresa*, vol. 1 (Kyiv: Sfera, 1999), 368, 321. Note that all this volume's *operativne povidomlennia* are cited from volume III of file 0–21515, the criminal file on Myroslav Irchan located at SBU Kharkiv; however, Irchan's file *now* contains only two volumes, and volume III is missing, or has a different security level, or has been renumbered during an inventory. Until such time as SBU Kharkiv finds the file, or researchers get access to the file, we will have to make do with the published versions.
4 For an overview of the theatre in the gulag, see Natalia Kuziakina, *Theater in the Solovki Prison Camp*, trans. Boris M. Meerovich (Newark, NJ: Harwood, 1995); Tamara Petkevich, *Memoir of a Gulag Actress*, trans. Yasha Klots and Ross Ufberg (DeKalb: Northern Illinois University Press, 2010); and M. M. Korallov, ed., *Teatr GULAGa: Vospominaniia, Ocherki* (Moskva: Memorial, 1995), available at http://www.memo.ru/history/teatr/
5 Bohunov, Prystaiko, and Shapoval, eds., *Ostannia adresa*, vol. 1, 313.
6 Ibid., 313, 318, 368; letter from Kulish to Kulish 20 April 1936, Kulish, *Tvory*, vol. 2 (Kyiv: Dnipro, 1990), 683.
7 Bohunov, Prystaiko, and Shapoval, eds., *Ostannia adresa*, vol. 1, 364.
8 Ibid.
9 Ibid.
10 Hirniak, *Spomyny*, 320–1.
11 Bohunov, Prystaiko, and Shapoval, eds., *Ostannia adresa*, vol.1, 365–6, 320–1. Note that there were several theatrical groups at the Solovki camp complex, but the theatre at Medvezhia Gora seems the largest, see Kuziakina, *Theater in the Solovki Prison Camp*, and on the Gor'kii expedition, Michael David-Fox, *Showcasing the Great Experiment: Cultural Diplomacy and Western Visitors to Soviet Russia, 1921–1941* (New York: Oxford University Press, 2011), chap. 4, "Gorky's Gulag."
12 Bohunov, Prystaiko, and Shapoval, eds., *Ostannia adresa*, vol. 1, 328–9.
13 Ibid., 331–2, 336–7.
14 Ibid., vol. 2, 714–730; SBU 75 160 fp, vol. I, 385–6, 388–9, 386–7.

15 Iurii Smolych, *Rozpovid' pro nespokii* (Kyiv: Radians'kyi pysmennyk, 1968), 108.

16 Ibid., 207; Hryhorii Kostiuk, *Zustrichi i proshchannia*, vol. 1 (Kyiv: Smolosky, 2008), 143.

17 Hirniak, *Spomyny*, 419.

18 RGALI f. 962, op. 7, d. 715, l. 3.

19 Oleksandr Korniichuk, *Dramatychni tvory*, with an introduction by D.T. Vakulenko, ed. I.O. Dzeverin (Kyiv: Naukova Dumka, 1990), 9, 12, 81–3; George Luckyj, *Literary Politics in the Soviet Ukraine, 1917–1934*, 2nd ed. (Durham, NC: Duke University Press, 1990), 224–5.

20 V. Tikhonovich, "The Theater of the Soviet Union: The Moscow Theater Season of 1933–1934," *International Theater* (1934), 3–4, 45.

21 RGALI f. 962, op. 7, d. 293, l. 4.

22 Ibid., d. 456, l. 28, 159.

23 Ibid., d. 456, l. 45.

24 Ibid., d. 456, l. 36, 76–7.

25 *Vil'na Ukraina* 2 (26 September 1939), 2; "Pochinaet'sia nove zhyttia bez paniv-pomishchykiv, bez hnitu i nasyl'stva," *Vil'na Ukraina* 5 (29 September 1939), 2.

26 Aleksander Wat, *My Century: The Odyssey of a Polish Intellectual*, trans. Richard Lourie (New York: NYRB books, 2003), 99–100; Michał Borwicz, "Ingenierowie dusz," *Zeszyty historyczne* (1962), 128; Volodymyr Svidzins'kyi, "Robitnyky v rezhysers'kii laboratorii," *Tvory*, vol. 2, ed. Eleonora Solovei (Krytyka: Kyiv, 2004), 405–14.

27 Roman Cherkashyn and Iuliia Fomina, *My-Berezil'tsi* (Kharkiv: Akta, 2006), 174.

28 Iurii Liutskyi, ed., *Shchodennyk Arkadia Liubchenka* (L'viv: M.P. Kots', 1999), 369.

29 Ibid., 99.

30 Valerii Haidabura, *Teatr mizh Hitlerom i Stalinom 1941–1944* (Kyiv: Fakt, 2000) and *Teatr, zakhovanyi v arkhivakh: stsenichne mystetstvo v Ukraini periodu nimets'koi-fashysts'koi okupatsii, 1941–1944* (Kyiv: Mystetstvo, 1998).

31 Liutskyi, ed., *Shchodennyk Arkadia Liubchenka*, 185–6; on the production details, see Irena Makaryk, "A Wartime *Hamlet*," in *Shakespeare in the Worlds of Communism and Socialism*, ed. Irena Makaryk and Joseph Price (Toronto: University of Toronto Press, 2006), 119–35; Bohdan Kozak, "Palimpsest Ukrains'koho Hamleta: pereklad i praprem'era 1943 roku," *Visnyk L'vivs'koho Universytetu* (2003), 52–75; and V. Blavats'kyi, *V orbiti svitovoho teatru*, ed. V. Revuts'kyi (Kyiv, Kharkiv, New York: M. P. Kots', 1995), 25.

32 Boris Nevezhin, *Otechestvennaia istoriia* 4 (2005), 123–39; Boris Nevezhin, *Zastoliia Iosifa Stalina: Bolshie Kremlevskie priemy, 1930–kh–1940–kh gg* (Moskva: Novyi Khronograf, 2011).
33 Nevezhin, *Zastolia Iosifa Stalina*, 418.
34 Serhiy Zhadan, "The End of Ukrainian Syllabotonic Verse," trans. Wanda Phipps and Virlana Tkacz, in *Modernism in Kyiv: Jubilant Experimentation*, ed. Irena Makaryk and Virlana Tcacz (Toronto: University of Toronto Press, 2010), 517–18.
35 See Mihaly Czikszentmihalyi, *Creativity: Flow and the Psychology of Discovery and Invention* (New York: Harper Collins, 1996); and Pierre Bourdieu, *Distinction: A Social Critique of the Judgment of Taste* (Cambridge, MA: Harvard University Press, 1984).
36 Leszek Kołakowski, "Communism as Cultural Formation," *Survey* 29, no. 2 (1985), 136–48.
37 Iurii Smolych, *Rozpovid' pro nespokii* (Kyiv: Radians'kyi pysmennyk, 1968), and *Rozpovid' pro nespokii tryvae* (Kyiv: Radians'kyi pysmennyk, 1969), and *Rozpovid' pro nespokii nemae kintsia* (Kyiv: Radians'kyi pysmennyk, 1972); Sava Holovanivs'kyi, *Memorial: spohady* (Kyiv: Radians'kyi pysmennyk, 1988), 173. For more on Smolych, see Iryna Tsymbal, "Mozaika Iuriia Smolycha iak zherelo do istorii literaturnoho pobutu," *Spadshchyna: literaturne dzhereloznavstvo* 5 (Kyiv: Stylos, 2010), 228–38, and Iurii Smolych, "Mozaika. Z tykh rokiv (kuriozy)," in *Spadshchyna* 5 (2010), 239–351; letter from Smolych to Paustovskii, TsDAMLM f. 169 op. 2, s. 254, ark. 21-zv.
38 Bohdan Shumylovych, "A Strange Afterlife of Stalinist Musicals in Soviet Ukrainian Television Entertainment of the Late 1960s–early 1970s" (paper presented at the Association of Slavic, East European, and Eurasian Studies-International Association for the Humanities, Lviv, Ukraine, 2016).

Selected Bibliography

Published Primary Sources (document collections, memoirs, literature)

Aleichem, Sholem. *Wandering Stars.* Translated by Aliza Shevrin. New York: Viking, 2009.

Bilots'irkivs'kyi, Lev. *Zapysky suflera.* Kyiv: Mystetstvo, 1962.

Borwicz, Michał. "Ingenierowie dusz." *Zeszyty historyczne* 1962/4.

Bulgakov, Mikhail. *Master i Margarita.* Moskva: Azbuka klassika, 2004.

–. *Sobranie sochinenii v 5 tomakh.* Moskva: Khudozhestvennaia literatura, 1989.

Chekhov, A.P. *Sochinennia v 4-kh tomakh.* Moskva: Pravda, 1984.

Chekhov, Michael. *On The Technique of Acting.* New York: Harper Collins, 1993.

Cherkashyn, Roman, and Iuliia Fomina. *My-Bereziltsi.* Kharkiv: Akta, 2008.

Dąbrowski, Bronisław. *Na deskach świat oznaczających.* 2 volumes. Krakow: Wydawnictwo literackie, 1977.

Deich, Aleksandr. *Golos pamiati.* Moskva: Iskusstvo, 1966.

Dukyna, Natalka. *Na dobryi spomny: povist' pro bat'ka.* Kharkiv: Vydavnytstvo zhurnalu Berezil, 2002.

Glama-Meshcherskaia, Aleksandra. *Vospominaniia.* Leningrad: Iskusstvo, 1937.

Gogol', Nikolai. *Gogol': vospominaniia, dnevniki, pis'ma.* Edited by V. Gippius. Moskva: Agraf, 1999.

Granach, Alexander. *Du mein leibes Stück Heimat: Briefe an Lotte Lieven aus dem Exil.* Edited by Angelika Wittlich and Hilde Recher. Augsburg: Ölbaum, 2008.

–. *There Goes an Actor.* Translated by Willard Trask. Garden City, NY: Doubleday, 1945.

Grzymała-Siedlicki, Adam. *Swiat aktorski moich czasow*. Warszawa: Państwowy instytut wydawniczy, 1973.

Haraszti, Miklos. *The Velvet Prison: Artists under State Socialism*. Translated by Katalin and Stephen Landesmann with Steve Wasserman. New York: Basic Books, 1987.

Hirniak, Iosyp. *Spomyny*. New York: Suchasnist', 1982.

–. "The Birth and Death of the Modern Ukrainian Theater." In *Soviet Theaters 1917–1941*. Edited by Martha Bradshaw, 250–388. New York: Research Program on the USSR, 1954.

Iakir, P.I., ed. *Komandarm Iakir: vospominaniia druzei i soratnikov*. Moskva: Voennoe izdatel'stvo Ministerstva oborony SSSR, 1963.

Iufit, A.Z., ed. *Sovetskii teatr: teatr narodov SSSR 1917–1921: dokumenty i materialy*. Leningrad: Iskusstvo, 1972.

Iureneva, Vera. *Zapiski aktrisy*. Leningrad: Iskusstvo, 1946.

Iura, Hnat. *Zhyttia i stsena*. Kyiv: Mystetstvo, 1965.

Iwaszkiewicz, Jarosław. *Aleja przyjaciół*. Warszawa: Czytelnik, 1984.

–. *Ksiażka moich wspomnien*. Krakow: Wydawnictwo literackie, 1968.

Jelagin, Juri. *Taming of the Arts*. Translated by Nicholas Wreden. New York: E.P. Dutton, 1951.

Kaminska, Ida. *My Life, My Theater*. Translated by Curt Leviant. New York: Macmillan, 1973.

Kaminska, Ruth Turkow. *Mink Coats and Barbed Wire*. London: Collins and Harvill, 1979.

Kapler, Aleksei. *Dolgi nashi*. Moskva: Sovetskaia rossiia, 1973.

Karpenko-Karyi, Ivan. *Dramatychni tvory*. Kyiv: Naukova dumka, 1989.

Khrushchev, N.S. *Vospominaniia: vremia, liudi, vlast'*. Moskva: Moskovskie novosti, 1996.

Khvyl'ovyi, Mykola. *Sanatoriina zona: opovidannia, novely*. Kharkiv: Folio, 2007.

Kołakowski, Leszek. *My Correct Views on Everything*. Edited by Zbigniew Janowski. South Bend, IN: St. Augustine's Press, 2005.

Koonen, Alisa. *Stranitsy zhizni*. Moscow: Kukushka, 2003.

Korniichuk, Oleksandr. *Dramatychni tvory*. Edited by I.O. Dzeverin. Kyiv: Naukova dumka, 1990.

Kostiuk, Hryhorii. *Zustrichi i proshannia: spohady*. 2 volumes. Kyiv: Smoloskyp, 2008.

Kotliarevs'kyi, Ivan. *Poetychni tvory, dramatychni tvory, lysty*. Edited by M.T. Iatsenko. Kyiv: Naukova dumka, 1982.

Kovalenko, Prokhor. *Shliakhy na stsenu*. Kyiv: Mystetstvo, 1964.

Kreczmar, Jan. "Teatr Lwowski w latach 1939–1941: Wspomnienie." *Pamiętnik teatralny* 12, Warsawa, 1963.

Kropyvnyts'kyi, Marko. *Dramatychni tvory.* Kyiv: Naukova dumka, 1990.

–. *Zbirnyk statei, spohadiv i materialiv.* Edited by P. Dolyna. Kyiv: Mystetstvo, 1955.

Krushel'nyts'kyi, Mar'ian. *Mar'ian Krushel'nyts'kyi.* Edited by Les' Taniuk. Kyiv: Mystetstvo, 1969.

Kulish, Mykola. *Tvory v 2-kh tomakh.* Edited by Les' Taniuk. Kyiv: Dnipro, 1990.

Kulish, Volodymyr. *Slovo pro Budynok 'Slovo'.* Toronto: Homin' Ukrainy, 1966.

Kvitka-Osnov'ianenko, Hryhorii. *Povisti ta opovidannia, dramatychni tvory.* Edited by O.I. Honchar. Kyiv: Naukova dumka, 1982.

Labin's'kyi, Mykola, *Les' Kurbas: Filosofiia teatru.* Kyiv: Osnova, 1995.

–, ed. *Molodyi teatr: heneza, zavdannia, shliakhy.* Kyiv: Mystetstvo, 1991.

Labin's'kyi, Mykola, and Les' Taniuk, eds. *Les' Kurbas: Stat'i i vospominaniia o L. Kurbase.* Moscow: Iskusstvo, 1987.

Lavrinenko, Iurii. *Rozstriliane vidrodzennia.* Paris: Institut Literacki, 1959.

Liubchenko, Arkadii. *Shchodennyk Arkadia Liubchenka.* Edited by Iurii Liuts'kyi. L'viv-New York: M.P. Kots', 1999.

Liuts'kyi, Iurii. *Vaplitianskyi zbirnyk.* Edmonton: Canadian Institute of Ukrainian Studies, 1977.

Manizer, Matvei. *Pamiatnik Shevchenko v Khar'kove.* Leningrad: Khudozhnik RFSFR, 1964.

–. *Skul'ptor o svoei rabote.* Leningrad: Iskusstvo, 1940.

Mar'ianenko, Ivan. *Stsena, aktory, roli.* Kyiv: Mystetstvo, 1964.

Markish, Ester. *Stol' dolgoe vozvrashenie: vospominaniia.* Tel Aviv: Izdanie Avtora, 1989.

Miłosz, Czesław. *The Captive Mind.* Translated by Jane Zielonko. New York: Vintage, 1990.

Mykytenko, Ivan. *Tvory.* 4 volumes. Kyiv: Dnipro, 1982.

–. *Teatral'ni mrii.* Kyiv: Mystetstvo, 1968.

Mykytenko, Oleh. *V chervonykh lavakh: z istorii internatsional'nykh zviazkiv ukrains'koi radians'koi literatury 20-kh rokiv.* Kyiv: Dnipro, 1974.

Osterwa, Juliusz. *Reduta i teatr: artikuły, wywiady, wspomnenia 1914–1947.* Edited by Zbigniew Osinski. Wrocław: Wiedza o kulturze, 1991.

Pavlovs'kyi, Vadim. *Shevchenko v pam'iatnykakh.* New York: Ukrains'ka vil'na akademiia nauk v SShA, 1966.

Pylypchuk, R. Ia, ed. *Spohady pro Panasa Saksahans'koho.* Kyiv: Mystetstvo, 1984.

–, ed. *Spohady pro Mykolu Sadovs'koho.* Kyiv: Mystetstvo, 1981.

Revuts'kyi, Valerian, ed. *Les' Kurbas: u teatral'nii diial'nosti, v otsinkakh suchasnykiv—dokumenty.* Toronto: Smoloskyp, 1989.

Revuts'kyi, Valerian, ed. *V orbiti svitovoho teatru.* Kyiv: Vyd. Kots', 1995.

Saksaganskii, Panas [Saksahans'kyi]. *Iz proshlogo ukrainskogo teatra.* Moskva: Isskustvo, 1938.

Sats', Nataliia. *Novelly moei zhizni.* Moskva: Iskusstvo, 1979.

Semenenko, Oleksandr. *Kharkiv, Kharkiv.* New York: Suchasnist', 1976.

Shapoval, Iurii, Serhii Bohunov, and Volodymyr Prystaiko, eds. *Ostannia adresa.* 2 volumes. Kyiv: Sfera, 2003.

Shevel'ov, Iurii. *Vybrani pratsi.* 2 volumes. Kyiv: Kyiv Mohyla Akad, 2008.

Smirnova-Iskander, Aleksandra. *O tekh, kogo pomniu.* Leningrad: Iskusstvo, 1989.

Smolych, Iurii. *Pro teatr.* Kyiv: Mystetstvo, 1977.

–. *Rozpovid' pro nespokii nemae kintsia.* Kyiv: Radians'kyi pysmennyk, 1972.

–. *Ia vybiraiu literaturu.* Kyiv: Radians'kyi pysmennyk, 1970.

–. *Rozpovid' pro nespokii tryvae.* Kyiv: Radians'kyi pysmennyk, 1969.

–. *Rozpovid' pro nespokii.* Kyiv: Radians'kyi pysmennyk, 1968.

Staryts'kyi, Mykhailo. *Poetychni tvory, dramatychni tvory.* Kyiv: Naukova dumka, 1987.

Steshenko, Oksana. *Spohady.* In *Shliaketni ukrainky.* Edited by Iurii Khozhunyi. Kyiv: Vyd. im Oleny Telihy, 2003.

Svidzins'kyi, Volodymyr. *Tvory.* 2 volumes. Kyiv: Krytyka, 2004.

Szyfman, Arnold. *Labirynt teatru.* Warszawa: Wydawnistwo artystyczne i filmowe, 1964.

Teffi, Nadezhda. *Nostalgiia.* Leningrad: Khud Literature, 1989.

Tkacz, Virlana, and Wanda Phipps, eds. and trans. *In a Different Light / V inshomu svitli.* L'viv: Sribne slovo, 2008.

Tobilevych, Sofiia. *Moi stezhky i zustrichi.* Kyiv: Derzhavne vydavnystvo obrazotvorchoho mystetstva i muzyvhnoi literatury, 1962.

Utesov, Leonid. *Spasibo Serdtse!* Moskva: VTO, 1976.

Vasyl'ko, Vasyl', ed. *Mykola Sadovs'kyi i ioho teatr.* Kyiv: Derzhavne vydavnystvo obrazotvorchoho mystetstva i muzychnoi literatury, 1962.

Vasyl'ko, Vasyl'. *Teatru viddane zhyttia.* Kyiv: Mystetstvo, 1984.

–, ed. *Les' Kurbas: Spohady suchasnikiv.* Kyiv: Mystetstvo, 1969.

Velizarii, Mariia. *Put' provintsial'noi aktrisy.* Leningrad: Iskusstvo, 1938.

Vertinskii, Aleksandr. *Dorogoiu dlinnoiu.* Moskva: Pravda, 1991.

Vyshnia, Ostap. *Tvory vchotyr'okh tomakh.* 4 volumes. Kyiv: Dnipro, 1988.

Wat, Aleksander. *My Century: The Odyssey of a Polish Intellectual.* Translated and edited by Richard Lourie. New York: NYRB Books, 2003.

Watters, George Manker, and Arthur Hopkins. *Burlesque.* New York: Samuel French, 1926.

Published Secondary Sources

Agnew, Jean-Christophe. *Worlds Apart: The Market and the Theater in Anglo-American Thought, 1550–1750*. Cambridge: Cambridge University Press, 1986.

Amar, Tarik Cyril. *The Paradox of Ukrainian Lviv: A Borderland City between Stalinists, Nazis, and Nationalists*. Ithaca, NY: Cornell University Press, 2015.

Antipina, Valentina. *Povsednevnaia zhizn' sovetskikh pisatelei 1930–1950e gody*. Moskva: Molodaia gvardia, 2005.

Antonovych, Dmytro. *Trysta rokiv ukrains'koho teatru 1619–1919*. 1928. Reprint, Kyiv: VIP, 2003.

Armstrong, John. *The Soviet Bureaucratic Elite: A Case Study of the Ukrainian Apparatus*. New York: Praeger, 1959.

Babans'ka, Natalia. *Talan: Zhyttia i tvorchist' Marii Zan'kovets'ka*. Kyiv: Mystetstvo, 2004.

Bakhturina, A. Iu. *Okrainy Rossiiskoi imperii: gosudarstvennoe upravlenie i natsional'naia politika v gody pervoi mirovoi voiny*. Moskva: Rosspen, 2004.

Bemporad, Elissa. *Becoming Soviet Jews: The Bolshevik Experiment in Minsk*. Bloomington: Indiana University Press, 2013.

Berkowitz, Joel, ed. *Yiddish Theater: New Approaches*. Oxford: Oxford University Press, 2003.

Bertelsen, Olga. "The House of Writers in Ukraine: Conceived, Lived, Perceived." *Carl Beck Papers in Russian and East European Studies,* No. 2302 (2013), 4–72.

Bhabha, Homi. *The Location of Culture*. London: Routledge, 1994.

Bilenky, Serhiy. *Romantic Nationalism in Eastern Europe: Russian, Polish, and Ukrainian Political Imaginations*. Stanford: Stanford University Press, 2012.

Blium, A.V. *Sovetskaia tsenzura v epokhu total'nogo terrora*. St. Petersburg: Akad proekt, 2000.

Bojanowska, Edyta. *Nikolai Gogol: Between Ukrainian and Russian Nationalism*. Cambridge, MA: Harvard University Press, 2007.

Bon'kovs'ka, Olena. *L'vivs'ke teatr tovarystvo Ukrains'ka Besida, 1915–1924*. L'viv: Litopis, 2003.

Borys, Jurij. *The Sovietization of Ukraine, 1917–1923: The Communist Doctrine and the Practice of National Self-Determination*. Edmonton: Canadian Institute of Ukrainian Studies, 1980.

Braun, Edward. *Meyerhold: A Revolution in Theater*. Iowa City: University of Iowa Press, 1995.

Burke, Peter. *Cultural Hybridity*. Cambridge: Polity, 2009.

Carlson, Marvin. *The Haunted Stage: Theater as Memory Machine.* Ann Arbor: University of Michigan Press, 2003.

Chakrabarty, Dipesh. *Provincializing Europe: Postcolonial Thought and Historical Difference.* Princeton: Princeton University Press, 2007.

Chornyi, Stepan. *Karpenko-Karyi i teatr.* New York: Ukrains'kyi vil'nyi universytet, 1978.

Ciszkewycz, Ihor. "Transformation – A Discovered Form: Berezil Theater, 1922–1934." PhD diss., Southern Illinois University at Carbondale, 1988.

Clark, Katerina. *Moscow, the Fourth Rome: Stalinism, Cosmopolitanism, and the Evolution of Stalinist Culture.* Cambridge, MA: Harvard University Press, 2011.

–. *Petersburg, Crucible of Cultural Revolution.* Cambridge, MA: Harvard University Press, 1995.

–. *The Soviet Novel: History as Ritual.* Chicago: University of Chicago Press, 1984.

Clurman, Harold. *The Fervent Years: The Group Theater and the Thirties.* New York: DaCapo Press, 1983.

Cummings, Milton C., and Richard Katz. *The Patron State: Government and the Arts in Europe, North America and Japan.* New York: Oxford University Press, 1987.

Czikszentmihalyi, Mihaly. *Creativity: Flow and the Psychology of Discovery and Invention.* New York: Harper Collins, 1996.

Danilov, S.S., and S.S. Mokul'skii. *O teatre. Sbornik statei.* Leningrad: Iskusstvo, 1940.

Danilov, S.S., and M.G. Portugalova. *Russkii dramaticheskii teatr XIX-ogo veka.* 2 volumes. Leningrad: Iskusstvo, 1978.

Darnton, Robert. *The Literary Underground of the Old Regime.* Cambridge, MA: Harvard University Press, 1982.

David-Fox, Michael. *Crossing Borders: Modernity, Ideology, and Culture in Russia and the Soviet Union.* Pittsburgh: University of Pittsburgh Press, 2015.

–. *Showcasing the Great Experiment: Cultural Diplomacy and Western Visitors to Soviet Russia, 1921–1941.* New York: Oxford University Press, 2011.

Davis, Tracy G. *The Economics of the British Stage, 1800–1914.* Cambridge: Cambridge University Press, 2000.

Dobrenko, Evgeny. *The Aesthetics of Alienation: Reassessment of Early Soviet Cultural Theories.* Translated by Jesse Savage. Evanston, IL: Northwestern University Press, 2005.

Dunham, Vera. *In Stalin's Time: Middleclass Values in Soviet Fiction.* Durham, NC: Duke University Press, 1990.

Durylin, Sergei. *Mariia Zankovets'kaia.* Kyiv: Mystetstvo, 1955.

Estraikh, Gennady. *In Harness: Jewish Writers' Romance with Communism.* Syracuse: Syracuse University Press, 2005.

Fanger, Donald. *The Creation of Nikolai Gogol.* Cambridge, MA: Harvard University Press, 1979.

Feldman, Walter Zev. "Remembrance of Things Past: Klezmer Musicians of Galicia, 1870–1940." *POLIN* 16 (2003), 29–57.

Finkel, Stuart. *On the Ideological Front: The Russian Intelligentsia and the Making of Soviet Public Sphere.* New Haven: Yale University Press, 2007.

Fitzpatrick, Sheila. *The Cultural Front: Power and Culture in Revolutionary Russia.* Ithaca, NY: Cornell University Press, 1992.

Frame, Murray. *School for Citizens: Theater and Civil Society in Imperial Russia.* New Haven: Yale University Press, 2006.

–. *The St. Petersburg Imperial Theaters: Stage and State in Revolutionary Russia.* Jefferson, NC: McFarland, 2000.

Frey, Bruno. *Arts and Economics: Analysis and Cultural Policy.* 2nd ed. New York: Springer, 2003.

Glaser, Amelia. *Jews and Ukrainians in Russia's Literary Borderlands: From the Shtetl Fair to the St. Petersburg Bookshop.* Evanston, IL: Northwestern University Press, 2012.

Goldstein, Robert Justin, ed. *The Frightful Stage: Political Censorship of the Theater in Nineteenth-Century Europe.* New York: Berghahn Books, 2009.

Greenblatt, Stephen, ed. *Cultural Mobility: A Manifesto.* Cambridge: Cambridge University Press, 2006.

Gross, Jan T. *Revolution from Abroad.* 2nd ed. Princeton: Princeton University Press, 2002.

Groys, Boris. *The Total Art of Stalinism: Avant-Garde, Aesthetic Dictatorsiph, and Beyond.* London: Verso, 2011.

Hamm, Michael. *Kiev: A Portrait 1800–1917.* Princeton: Princeton University Press, 1993.

Hildermeier, Manfred, ed. *Stalinismus vor dem Zweiten Weltkrieg: Neue Wege der Forschung.* Munich: Oldenbourg, 1998.

Hillis, Faith C. *Children of Rus': Right-bank Ukraine and the Invention of a Russian Nation.* Ithaca, NY: Cornell University Press, 2013.

Hirsch, Francine. *Empire of Nations: Ethnographic Knowledge and the Making of the Soviet Union.* Ithaca, NY: Cornell University Press, 2005.

Hoberman, J. *Bridge of Light: Yiddish Film between Two Worlds.* New York: MoMA and Schocken Books, 1991.

Horbachov, Dmytro. *Ukrains'kyi avan-hard, 1910–1930.* Kyiv: Mystetstvo, 1996.

–. *Anatol' Petryts'kyi.* Kyiv: Mystetstvo, 1971.

Horbatowski, Piotr. *W szponach polityki: Polskie życie teatralne w Kijowie 1919–1938.* Warszawa: Oficyna naukowa, 1999.

Hryn, Halyna. "The 'Executed Renaissance' Paradigm Revisited." *Harvard Ukrainian Studies* 27, no. 1 (2004), 67–96.

Huizinga, Johann. *Homo Ludens: A Study of the Play Element in Culture.* Boston: Beacon Press, 1950.

Iakovenko, M.M., ed. *Agnessa: ustnye rasskazy.* Moskva: Zvenia, 1997.

Ielagin, Iurii. *Temnii genii.* New York: Vyd. im. Chekhova, 1955.

Iermakova, Natalia. *Berezil's'ka kul'tura, istoriia, dosvid.* Kyiv: Feniks, 2012.

–. "Allo na khvyli 477: pershe ukrains'ke reviu." *Protsenium* 17 (2007), 7–13.

Igmen, Ali. *Speaking Soviet with an Accent: Culture and Power in Kyrgyzstan.* Pittsburgh: University of Pittsburgh Press, 2012.

Ilnytzkyj, Oleh. *Ukrainian Futurism: A Historical and Critical Study.* Cambridge, MA: Harvard University Press, 1997.

Jackson, Peter. *Making Jazz French: Music and Modern Life in Interwar Paris.* Durham, NC: Duke University Press, 2003.

Kappeler, Andreas, and Mark von Hagen, eds. *Culture, Nation and Identity.* Edmonton: Canadian University Scholars Press, 2003.

Kasianov, Georgiy, and Philipp Ther. *Laboratory of Transnational History: Ukraine and Recent Ukrainian Historiography.* Budapest: Central European University Press, 2009.

Kazovskii, Hillel. "The Art Section of the Kulture Lige." *Jews in Eastern Europe* (1993), 5–23.

Khalid, Adeeb. *Making Uzbekistan: Nation, Empire, and Revolution in the Early USSR.* Ithaca, NY: Cornell University Press, 2015.

–. *The Politics of Muslim Cultural Reform.* Berkeley: University of California Press, 1998.

Kiaer, Christina. *Imagine No Possessions: The Socialist Objects of Russian Constructivism.* Cambridge, MA: Harvard University Press, 2005.

Korniienko, Nelli. *Les' Kurbas: Repetytsiia maibutn'ioho.* Kyiv: Fakt, 1998.

Korzeniowski, Mariusz. *Za Złotą Bramą: działałność społeczno-kulturalna Polaków w Kijowie w latach 1905–1920.* Lublin: UMCS Wydawnictwo Uniwersytetu Marii-Curie Skłodowskiej, 2009.

Kotkin, Stephen. "The State – Is It Us? Memoirs, Archives, and Kremlinologists." *Russian Review* 61 (2002), 35–51.

–. "Modern Times: The Soviet Union and the Interwar Conjuncture." *Kritika: Explorations in Russian and Eurasian History* 2, no. 1 (2001), 111–64.

–. *Magnetic Mountain: Stalinism as Civilization.* Berkeley: University of California Press, 1995.

Kozak, Bohdan, ed, *Zhyttia i tvorchist' Lesia Kurbasa.* L'viv: Litopys, 2012.

Kryzhitskii, Grigorii. *Dorogi teatral'nye.* Moskva: Iskusstvo, 1976.

Kuligowska-Korzeniwska, ed. *Teatr żydowski w Polsce.* Łódź: Wydawnictwo uniwersytetskiego, 1998.

Kuziakina, Natalia. *Theater in the Solovki Prison Camp.* Translated by Boris Meerovich. Newark: Harwood, 1995.

Leach, Robert, and Victor Borovsky, eds. *A History of Russian Theater.* Cambridge: Cambridge University Press, 1999.

LeMahieu, Dan. *A Culture for Democracy: Mass Communication and the Cultivated Mind in Britain between the Wars.* Oxford: Clarendon, 1988.

Leonenko, Ruslan. "Pershi ukrains'ki derzhavni teatry 1917–1919 roky." *Zapysky naukovoho tovarystva im. Shevchenko* (L'viv) (1999), 134–67.

Lewin, Paulina. *Ukrainian Drama and Theatre in the Seventeenth and Eighteenth Centuries.* Edmonton: Canadian Institute of Ukrainian Studies, 2008.

Liber, George. *Total Wars and the Making of Modern Ukraine, 1914–1954.* Toronto: University of Toronto Press, 2016.

–. *Alexander Dovzhenko: A Life in Soviet Film.* London: British Film Institute, 2002.

–. *Soviet Nationality Policy, Urban Growth, and Identity Change in the Ukrainian SSR.* Cambridge: Cambridge University Press, 2001.

Luckyj, George. *Literary Politics in the Soviet Ukraine, 1917–1934.* 2nd ed. Durham, NC: Duke University Press, 1990.

MacFayden, David. *Songs for Fat People: Affect, Emotion, and Celebrity in the Russian Popular Song, 1900–1955.* Montreal: McGill-Queen's University Press, 2002.

Makaryk, Irena. *Shakespeare in the Undiscovered Bourn: Les Kurbas, Ukrainian Modernism, and Early Soviet Cultural Politics.* Toronto: University of Toronto Press, 2004.

Makaryk, Irena, and Virlana Tkacz, eds. *Modernism in Kyiv: Jubilant Experimentation.* Toronto: University of Toronto Press, 2010.

Makaryk, Irena, and Joseph Price, eds. *Shakespeare in the Worlds of Communism and Socialism.* Toronto: University of Toronto Press, 2006.

Maksimenkov, Leonid. *Sumbur vmesto muzyki: Stalinskaia kulturnaia revoliutsiia, 1936–1938.* Moskva: Iuridicheskaia kniga, 1997.

Mally, Lynn. *Revolutionary Acts: Amateur Theatre and the Soviet State, 1917–1938.* Ithaca, NY: Cornell University Press, 2000.

Martin, Terry. *The Affirmative Action Empire: Nations and Nationalism in the Making of the Soviet Union.* Ithaca, NY: Cornell University Press, 2001.

McReynolds, Louise, and Joan Neuberger, eds. *Imitations of Life: Two Centuries of Melodrama in Russia.* Durham, NC: Duke University Press, 2002.

Meir, Natan. "Jews, Ukrainians and Russians in Kiev: Intergroup Relations in Late Imperial Associational Life." *Slavic Review* 65, no. 3 (2006), 475–501.

Miller, Aleksei. "Between Local and Inter-Imperial: Russian Imperial History in Search of Scope and Paradigm." *Kritika: Explorations in Russian and Eastern European History* 5, no. 1 (2004), 7–26.

–. *The Ukrainian Question.* Budapest: Central European University Press, 2003.

–. "Shaping Russian and Ukrainian Identities in the Russian Empire during the Nineteenth Century: Some Methodological Remarks." *Jahrbücher für Geschichte Osteuropas* 49 (2001), 257–63.

Mordinson, G.Z. *Istoriia teatral'nogo dela v Rossii: osnovanie i razvitie gosudarstvennogo teatra v Rossii XVI–XVIII veka.* 2 volumes. St. Petersburg: Sil'van, 1994.

Morozov, Iurii, and Tatiana Derevianko. *Evreiskie kinematografisty v Ukraine, 1910–1945.* Kyiv: Dukh i litera, 2004.

Morrison, Simon. *The People's Artist: Prokofiev's Soviet Years.* Oxford: Oxford University Press, 2009.

Moss, Kenneth. *Jewish Renaissance in the Russian Revolution.* Cambridge, MA: Harvard University Press, 2009.

Mudrak, Myroslava. *The New Generation and Artistic Modernism in the Ukraine.* Ann Arbor: UMI Research Press, 1986.

–. "Vadym Meller, Les' Kurbas, and the Ukrainian Theatrical Avant-garde." *Russian History/Histoire Russe* 8 (1981), 199–218.

Nevezhin, V.A. *Zastoliia Iosifa Stalina.* Moscow: Novyi khronograf, 2011.

O'Keeffe, Brigid. *New Soviet Gypsies: Nationality, Performance, and Selfhood in the Early Soviet Union.* Toronto: University of Toronto Press, 2013.

Pauly, Matthew. *Breaking the Tongue: Language, Education and Power in Soviet Ukraine, 1923–1934.* Toronto: University of Toronto Press, 2014.

Petrovskaia, Ira. *Teatr i zritel' provintsial'noi Rossii.* Leningrad: Iskusstvo, 1979.

Petrovskii, Miron. *Gorodu i miru.* Kyiv: Dukh i litera, 2008.

Petrovsky-Shtern, Yohanan. *The Anti-Imperial Choice: The Making of the Ukrainian Jew.* New Haven: Yale University Press, 2009.

Plamper, Jan. *The Stalin Cult: A Study in the Alchemy of Power.* New Haven: Yale University Press, 2012.

–. "Abolishing Ambiguity: Soviet Censorship Practices in the 1930s." *Russian Review* 60, no. 4 (2001), 526–44.

Plokhy, Serhy. *The Last Empire: Final Days of the Soviet Union.* New York: Basic Books, 2015.

–. *The Cossack Myth: History and Nationhood in an Age of Empires.* London: Cambridge University Press, 2012.

–. *Unmaking Imperial Russia: Mykhailo Hrushevsky and the Writing of Ukrainian History.* Toronto: University of Toronto Press, 2005.

Postlewait, Thomas, and Bruce McConachie. *Interpreting the Theatrical Past: Essays in Theatre Historiography.* Iowa City: University of Iowa Press, 1989.

Potichnyi, Peter, ed. *Ukrainian-Jewish Relations in Historical Perspective.* Edmonton: Canadian Institute of Ukrainian Studies, 1988.

Radziejowski, Janusz. *The Communist Party of Western Ukraine, 1919–1929.* Translated by Alan Rutkowski. Edmonton: Canadian Institute of Ukrainian Studies, 1983.

Ram, Harsha. "The Sonnet and the Mukhambazi: Genre Wars on the Russian Periphery." *PMLA* 122, no. 5 (2007), 1548–70.

–. "Modernism on the Periphery: Literary Life in Post-revolutionary Tbilisi." *Kritika: Explorations in Russian and Eurasian History* 5, no. 2 (2004), 367–82.

Ravel, Jeffrey. *The Contested Parterre: Public Theater and French Political Culture, 1680–1791.* Ithaca, NY: Cornell University Press, 1999.

Reid, Susan E. "Socialist Realism in the Stalinist Terror: The Industry of Socialism Art Exhibition, 1935–1941." *Russian Review* 60, no. 2 (2001), 153–84.

Rév, István. *Retroactive Justice: A Prehistory of Post-Communism.* Stanford: Stanford University Press, 2005.

Richardson, Tanya. *Kaleidoscopic Odessa: History and Place in Contemporary Ukraine.* Toronto: University of Toronto Press, 2008.

Robin, Régine. *Socialist Realism: An Impossible Aesthetic.* Stanford: Stanford University Press, 1992.

Ruban, V.V., ed. *Anatol' Petryts'kyi: portrety suchasnikiv.* Kyiv: Mystetstvo, 1991.

Rubin, Mark, trans. and ed. *Old Jewish Folk Music: The Collections and Writings of Moshe Beregovski.* Philadelphia: University of Pennsylvania Press, 1982.

Rudnitskii, Konstantin, ed. *Real'nost' i obraznost': Problemy sovetskoi rezhissuri 30–40-kh godov.* Moskva: Nauka, 1984.

Scott, Erik. *Familiar Strangers: The Georgian Diaspora and the Evolution of Soviet Empire.* Cambridge: Cambridge University Press, 2016.

Shapoval, Iurii. *Ukraina XX stolittia: osoby ta podii v konteksti vazhkoi istorii.* Kyiv: Heneza, 2001.

–. *Ukraina 20–50-kh rokiv: storinky nenapisanoi istorii.* Kyiv: Naukova dumka, 1993.

Shapoval, Iurii, Volodymyr Prystaiko, and Vadim Zolotar'ov. *ChK-GPU-NKVD v Ukraini: osoby, fakty, dokumenty.* Kyiv: Abris, 1997.

Shkandrij, Myroslav. *Ukrainian Nationalism: Politics, Ideology, and Literature, 1929–1956.* New Haven: Yale University Press, 2015.

–. *Jews in Ukrainian Literature: Identity and Representation.* New Haven: Yale University Press, 2009.

–. *Russia and Ukraine: Literature and the Discourse of Empire from Napoleonic to Post-Colonial Times.* Montreal: McGill-Queen's University Press, 2001.

–. *Modernists, Marxists and the Nation: The Ukrainian Literary Discussion of the 1920s.* Edmonton: Canadian Institute of Ukrainian Studies, 1992.

Shore, Marci. *Caviar and Ashes: A Warsaw Generation's Life and Death in Marxism, 1918–1968*. New Haven: Yale University Press, 2006.

Sintalinskii, Vitalii. *KGB's Literary Archive*. Translated by John Crowfoot. London: Harvill, 1995.

Slezkine, Yuri. *The Jewish Century*. Princeton: Princeton University Press, 2004.

–. "The USSR as a Communal Apartment, or How a Socialist State Promoted Ethnic Particularism." *Slavic Review* 53, no. 2 (1994), 414–52.

Slobin, Mark, Robert Rothstein, and Michael Alpert, eds. *Jewish Instrumental Folk Music: The Collections and Writings of Moshe Beregovski*. Syracuse: Syracuse University Press, 2001.

Smeliansky, Anatoly. *Is Comrade Bulgakov Dead? Mikhail Bulgakov and the Moscow Art Theater*. Translated by Arch Tait. New York: Routledge, 1993.

Snyder, Timothy. *Sketches from a Secret War: A Polish Artist's Mission to Liberate Soviet Ukraine*. New Haven: Yale University Press, 2005.

–. *Reconstruction of Nations: Poland, Ukraine, Lithuania, Belarus, 1569–1999*. New Haven: Yale University Press, 2003.

Starr, Frederick. *Red and Hot: The Fate of Jazz in the Soviet Union*. New York: Oxford University Press, 1983.

Stepanchykova, Tetiana. *Istoriia evreis'koho teatru u L'vovi: kriz' terny do zirok*. L'viv: Liga, 2005.

Stites, Richard. *Serfdom, Society and the Arts in Imperial Russia: the Pleasure and the Power*. New Haven: Yale University Press, 2006.

Swift, E. Anthony. *Popular Theater and Society in Tsarist Russia*. Berkeley: University of California Press, 2002.

–. "Fighting the Germs of Disorder: The Censorship of Russian Popular Theater, 1888–1917." *Russian History/Histoire Russe* 18, no. 1 (1991), 1–49.

Szydłowska, Maria. *Cenzura teatralna w Galicji w dobie autonomycznej, 1860–1918*. Kraków: Universitas, 1995.

Taylor, Richard, and Ian Christie, eds. *Inside the Film Factory: New Approaches to Russian and Soviet Cinema*. London: Routledge, 1991.

Thorpe, Richard G. "The Management of Culture in Revolutionary Russia: The Imperial Theaters and the State, 1897–1925." PhD diss., Princeton University, 1990.

Thurston, Gary. *The Popular Theater Movement in Russia 1862–1919*. Evanston, IL: Northwestern University Press, 1998.

Tkacz, Virlana. "Les Kurbas' Use of Film Language in his Stage Productions of *Jimmie Higgins* and *Macbeth*." *Canadian Slavonic Papers* 32, no. 1 (1990), 59–76.

–. "Les Kurbas and the Actors of the Berezil Artistic Association in Kiev." *Theatre History Studies* 8 (1988), 137–55.

–. "The Birth of a Director: The Early Development of Les Kurbas and his First Season with the Young Theatre." *Journal of Ukrainian Studies* 12, no. 1 (1987), 22–54.

Tomoff, Kiril. *Creative Union: The Professional Union of Soviet Composers*. Ithaca, NY: Cornell University Press, 2006.

Tsymbal, Iaryna. "Istoriia VAPLITE u 3D, " *Spadshchyna* 7 (2012), 128–44.

Tyrowicz, Marian. *Wspomnienia o życiu kulturalnym i obyczajowym we Lwowie, 1918–1939*. Lwów: Ossolineum.

Uvarova, E. *Russkaia sovetskaia estrada: ocherki istorii*. Moskva: Iskusstvo, 1976.

Vasylyshyn, Ol'ha. *Memorial'nyi muzei-sadyba Lesia Kurbasa: Narys-putivnyk*. Ternopil': Ukrprint Zakhid, 2007.

Veidlinger, Jeffrey. *The Moscow State Yiddish Theater: Jewish culture on the Soviet Stage*. Bloomington: Indiana University Press, 2000.

–. "Klezmer and the Kremlin: Soviet Yiddish Folk Songs of the 1930s." *East European Jewish Affairs* 1 (2000), 5–40.

–. *Jewish Public Culture in the Late Russian Empire*. Bloomington: Indiana University Press, 2009.

Veselovs'ka, Hanna. *Teatral'ni perekhrestia Kyieva*. Kyiv: Tsentr imeni Lesia Kurbasa, 2006.

Volyts'ka, Iryna. *Teatral'na iunist' Lesia Kurbasa*. Lviv: Instytut Narodoznavstva NAN Ukrainy, 1995.

Von Hagen, Mark. "The Great War and Mobilization of Ethnicity." In *Post-Soviet Political Order: Conflict and State-Building*, 34–57. Edited by Barnett Rubin and Jack Snyder. London: Routledge, 1998.

–. *Soldiers in the Proletarian Dictatorship: The Red Army and the Soviet Socialist State, 1917–1930*. Ithaca, NY: Cornell University Press, 1990.

Vushko, Iryna. *The Politics of Cultural Retreat: Imperial Bureaucracy in Austrian Galicia*. New Haven: Yale University Press, 2015.

Warnke, Nina. "Going East: The Impact of American Yiddish Plays and Players on the Yiddish Stage in Tsarist Russia, 1890–1917." *American Jewish History* 92, no. 1 (2005), 1–29.

Weeks, Theodore. *Nation and State in Late Imperial Russia: Nationalism and Russification on Russia's Western Frontier, 1863–1914*. DeKalb: Northern Illinois University Press, 1994.

Westerman, Frank. *Engineers of the Soul: In the Footsteps of Stalin's Writers*. London: Harvill Secker, 2010.

Wilmer, S.E. *National Theaters in a Changing Europe*. New York: Palgrave Macmillan, 2008.

Wirtschafter, Elise. *The Play of Ideas in Russian Enlightenment Theater*. DeKalb: Illinois University Press, 2003.

Worrall, Nick. *The Moscow Art Theater*. London: Routledge, 1996.

Yates, W.E. *Theater in Vienna*. Cambridge: Cambridge University Press, 1996.

Yekelchyk, Serhy. *Ukraine: Birth of a Modern Nation*. Oxford: Oxford University Press, 2007.

–. *Stalin's Empire of Memory: Russian Ukrainian Relations in the Soviet Historical Imagination*. Toronto: University of Toronto Press, 2004.

Zaets', Ivan Iakymovych. *Ivan Mykytenko—dramaturh*. Kyiv: Radians'kyi pysmennyk, 1987.

–. *Ivan Mykytenko—Literaturnyi portret*. Kyiv: Dnipro, 1970.

Zhidkov, V.S. *Teatr i vlast': ot svobody do oznachennoi neobkhodimosti*. Moscow: Aleteia, 2003.

Zub, Ivan Vasyl'ovych. *Ostap Vyshnia*. Kyiv: Naukova dumka, 1991.

Index